CW00692657

THE POLITICS OF THE EXCLUDED, *c*.1500–1850

Themes in Focus
Published titles

Jonathan Barry and Christopher Brooks
THE MIDDLING SORT OF PEOPLE: Culture, Society
and Politics in England, 1550–1800

Patrick Collinson and John Craig
THE REFORMATION IN ENGLISH TOWNS, 1500–1640

Moira Donald and Tim Rees
REINTERPRETING REVOLUTION IN TWENTIETH-
CENTURY EUROPE

Christopher Durston and Jacqueline Eales
THE CULTURE OF ENGLISH PURITANISM, 1560–1700

Paul Griffiths, Adam Fox and Steve Hindle
THE EXPERIENCE OF AUTHORITY IN EARLY
MODERN ENGLAND

Tim Harris
THE POLITICS OF THE EXCLUDED, *c*.1500–1850

POPULAR CULTURE IN ENGLAND, *c*.1500–1850

Roy Porter and Marie Mulvey Roberts
PLEASURE IN THE EIGHTEENTH CENTURY

Daniel Power and Naomi Standen
FRONTIERS IN QUESTION: EURASIAN BORDERLANDS,
700–1700

R. W. Scribner and Trevor Johnson
POPULAR RELIGION IN GERMANY AND
CENTRAL EUROPE, 1400–1800

Themes in Focus Series

Series Standing Order

ISBN 0–333–71707–4 hardcover
ISBN 0–333–69353–1 paperback
(*outside North America only*)

You can receive future titles in this series as they are published by placing a standing
order. Please contact your bookseller or, in case of difficulty, write to us at the address
below with your name and address, the title of the series and the ISBN quoted above.

Customer Services Department, Macmillan Distribution Ltd
Houndmills, Basingstoke, Hampshire RG21 6XS, England

THE POLITICS OF THE EXCLUDED, *c*.1500–1850

Edited by

Tim Harris

palgrave

First published 2001 by
PALGRAVE
Houndmills, Basingstoke, Hampshire RG21 6XS and
175 Fifth Avenue, New York, N.Y. 10010
Companies and representatives throughout the world

PALGRAVE is the new global academic imprint of
St. Martin's Press LLC Scholarly and Reference Division and
Palgrave Publishers Ltd (formerly Macmillan Press Ltd).

ISBN 0–333–72223–X hardback
ISBN 0–333–72224–8 paperback

This book is printed on paper suitable for recycling and made from fully managed and sustained forest sources.

A catalogue record for this book is available from the British Library.

Library of Congress Cataloging-in-Publication Data

The politics of the excluded, c.1500–1850 / edited by Tim Harris.
    p.   cm. — (Themes in focus)
    Includes bibliographical references (p.) and index.
    ISBN 0–333–72223–X (hbk)
      1. Great Britian—Politics and government—1485– 2. Political participation—Great Britian. I. Harris, Tim, 1958– II. Series.

JN175 .P65 2000
941—dc21   00–062592

10   9   8   7   6   5   4   3   2   1
10 09 08 07 06 05 04 03 02 01

Printed in China

CONTENTS

ABBREVIATIONS

Add. MSS	Additional Manuscripts
AgHR	*Agricultural History Review*
BL	British Library
Bodl.	Bodleian Library, Oxford
CLRO	Corporation of London Record Office
CSPD	*Calendar of State Papers Domestic*
CSPVen	*Calendar of State Papers Venetian*
DNB	*Dictionary of National Biography*
EcHR	*Economic History Review*
EHR	*English Historical Review*
ERO	Essex Record Office
EYAS	East Yorkshire Archives Service, Kingston upon Hull
HJ	*Historical Journal*
HMC	*Historical Manuscripts Commission*
JBS	*Journal of British Studies*
JMH	*Journal of Modern History*
LMA	London Metropolitan Archives
LP	*Letters and Papers, Foreign and Domestic, of the Reigns of Henry VIII, 1509–47*, ed. J. S. Brewer et al., 21 vols and 2 vols addenda (London, 1862–1932)
NRO	Norfolk Record Office
NS	New Series
OED	*Oxford English Dictionary*
P&P	*Past and Present*
PRO	Public Record Office
RO	Record Office
RSTC	*Revised Short Title Catalogue*
TRHS	*Transactions of the Royal Historical Society*
VCH	*Victoria County History*

NOTES ON CONTRIBUTORS

Alastair Bellany was educated at Oxford and Princeton and is currently Assistant Professor of History at Rutgers University. His study of Jacobean news culture and the political meanings of the Overbury murder affair will be published by Cambridge University Press as *The Politics of Court Scandal in Early Stuart England*. He is also working on a book about the assassination of the Duke of Buckingham.

Mark Goldie is Lecturer in History at the University of Cambridge, and a Fellow of Churchill College, Cambridge. He has published many articles on politics, religion and ideas in seventeenth- and eighteenth-century Britain. He is editor of *John Locke: Two Treatises of Government* (1993), *John Locke: Political Essays* (1997), *The Reception of Locke's Politics* (1999), and *John Locke: Selected Correspondence* (forthcoming). He is currently co-editor of *The Historical Journal*.

Tim Harris is Professor of History at Brown University. He is author of *London Crowds in the Reign of Charles II* (1987) and *Politics under the Later Stuarts* (1993), and editor of *Popular Culture in England, c.1500–1850* (1995), and (with Paul Seaward and Mark Goldie) *The Politics of Religion in Restoration England* (1990). He is currently writing a book on the British Revolutions of the late-seventeenth century.

Steve Hindle is Warwick Research Fellow in the Department of History at the University of Warwick. He received his PhD from Cambridge University, where he was Junior Research Fellow at Girton College. He is the author of *The State and Social Change in Early Modern England, c.1550–1640* (2000) and of numerous articles on rural social relations in seventeenth-century England, and co-editor of *The Experience of Authority in Early Modern England* (1996). He is currently working on the local politics of poor relief in early modern England.

Nicholas Rogers is Professor of History at York University, Toronto. He is the author of *Whigs and Cities: Popular Politics in the Age of Walpole and Pitt* (1989) and *Crowds, Culture and Politics in Georgian Britain* (1998), and co-author with Douglas Hay of *Eighteenth-Century English Society: Shuttles and Swords* (1997). He is currently working on a project concerning naval impressment in the eighteenth century. He is the European editor of *Histoire Sociale/Social History* and co-editor of the *Journal of British Studies*.

Patty Seleski is Professor of History at California State University, San Marcos. Her published work focuses on women in domestic service, particularly on the mistress/servant relationship in eighteenth- and early nineteenth-century London. Her book about domestic servants, *Women of the Labouring Poor*, is forthcoming. She is currently at work on a biography on the late Irish jurist and human rights activist, Sean MacBride.

Ethan H. Shagan is Assistant Professor of History at Northwestern University. He received his PhD from Princeton University and was a Junior Fellow at the Harvard University Society of Fellows. He has published several articles on Tudor and Stuart religion and politics and is co-editing a volume entitled *Catholics and the 'Protestant Nation': Religious Politics in Early Modern England*. He is currently preparing for publication his doctoral thesis entitled 'Popular Politics and the English Reformation, *c*.1525–1553'.

Andy Wood is a Lecturer in History at the University of East Anglia. He is the author of *The Politics of Social Conflict: The Peak Country, 1520–1770* (1999), *Riot, Rebellion and Popular Politics in Early Modern England* (forthcoming), and a number of articles dealing with custom, law, social conflict, and plebeian identities in early modern England. He is currently writing a study of rebel ideology in 1549.

1

INTRODUCTION

Tim Harris

The title of this book needs explaining. This collection of essays is intended to shed light on the politics of those who are often thought of as being excluded from the 'political nation'. If by 'political nation' we mean 'the members of both houses of parliament, the governors of counties and towns, and the enfranchised classes in the constituencies',[1] then the 'excluded' might be said to constitute those who were neither actively involved in the process of governing nor had any say in choosing those who would rule over them – the bulk of the population in early modern England.[2] In many respects this is a book about 'popular politics', although this is a term with its own intellectual baggage,[3] whilst the notion of 'the excluded' potentially embraces those whom we might not readily regard as members of the popular classes. However, the essays in this collection seek to show that these people were not, in fact, excluded from politics. Not only did the mass of the population possess political opinions which they were capable of articulating – often powerfully – in a public forum, but they could also be active participants in the political process themselves. Many of those we think of as being excluded were actually included, either in a formal, institutionalized way, or in an extra-institutional sense.

Until recently, such claims would have been extremely controversial. When I began work on what was to become my first book, at the start of the 1980s, and proudly announced to interested enquirers that I was working on the politics of the London crowd in Restoration England, I frequently encountered sceptical responses, such as 'did the London crowd have any politics worth talking about?'; or, 'wasn't the mob basically unpolitical?' The view that politics was the preserve of the political elite, the top 3 per cent of the population, and that ordinary people were

1

not only excluded from politics but did not have any politics (in a mean-ingful sense) that we could study, was still widespread. Indeed, there remained question marks, at this time, about the political sophistication of the provincial gentry, who were thought to be 'surprisingly ill-informed' about 'wider political issues' even on the eve of the English civil war.[4] If such were the case for the landed elite, how could it make sense to ascribe political awareness to those below them?

Scepticism about the potential for political awareness amongst those below the level of the elite was so fundamental that it can be detected even in the works of those historians who were trying to broaden our conception of politics to allow some space for the excluded. Eric Hobsbawm, one of the pioneers in the study of what we now call 'history from below', writing in the late 1950s, claimed that the pre-industrial mob should be seen as a 'pre-political phenomenon', 'the urban equival-ent to social banditry'. Although he conceded it would be wrong to say the mob had no ideas at all about politics, the urban poor who engaged in mob activity, he affirmed, were 'not committed to any king, ruler or system at all' and 'had no positive programme except the hatred of the rich and a certain sub-anarchist egalitarianism'.[5] J. R. Jones, discussing the crowd disturbances that broke out in London at the time of the Glorious Revolution of 1688 in a book that appeared in 1972, suggested that 'the London masses were not capable of independent and sustained political action' themselves, but that 'radicals' might be able to mobilize 'popular support' when 'there was a good deal of dislocation to trade, resulting in a shortage of employment and high prices for food and fuel'.[6] Buchanan Sharp argued in 1980 that those who engaged in anti-enclosure riots in the west country during the civil war period (mainly propertyless wage-earners) manifested a 'positive political indifference'; 'the issues raised by the conflict between King and Parliament were of little or no concern to many ordinary people when weighed in the balance against such pressing local issues as disafforestation and enclosure'.[7] Similarly, Keith Lindley, in his scholarly examination of the fenland dis-turbances of the period from the 1620s through to the 1650s, which was published in 1982, concluded that the fenland rioters 'did not give expression to political feelings', that 'there is no real evidence that the generality of the fenmen' were 'politically educated by their experiences', and that 'the behaviour of the fenland commoners during the Civil War lends further strength to the view that the bulk of the common people were indifferent to the great issues raised at Westminster'.[8] As recently as 1988, Roger Manning, in his study of social protest and popular disturbances in England between 1509 and 1640, found that the riots and insurrections of this period, not just in the countryside but even in the metropolis, evinced the same basic pattern of 'sub-political behaviour'.[9]

Such scepticism, it is true, had never been universal. Indeed, the arguments cited above were often developed in response to the work of those who were thought to have been too uncritical in according a degree of political awareness to the unenfranchised classes. Students of English history had long shown an interest in forms of mass protest or political agitation out-of-doors, normally in the form of riots and demonstrations or political insurrection at the time of revolutionary upheaval. The study of political crowds or crowd politics in early modern England really began to pick up, however, from the 1950s and 1960s, thanks to the work of scholars such as George Rudé, Edward Thompson and Brian Manning. Both Rudé's pioneering work on the crowd in eighteenth-century Paris and London and Brian Manning's investigation of political demonstrations and riots during the English Revolution focused on forms of collective agitation that were ostensibly 'political' in the narrow sense of the term; Thompson went further, and showed that even rural forms of protest, such as the eighteenth-century food riot, were both ideological and political in nature.[10]

The problem that arose from focusing so heavily on riots and protest to gain insight into the politics of those otherwise excluded from the political nation, however, was that it gave us an episodic history of popular politics.[11] What about when the people were not rioting? If there were no disturbances over a given 20-year period, say, did that mean that the people were not politically aware at that time, or that they had slipped into a lengthy phase of political indifference? Or what about the people who did not join in those political riots that did occur? Were these people unpolitical, or did they just not share the political views of those who rioted? And how do we trace change over time? When I first began my work on the politics of the London crowd it appeared from the existing historiography that the London crowd was pro-parliamentarian in the early 1640s, Presbyterian-royalist in 1647–8, anti-republican and pro-Charles II in 1659–60, anti-Charles II and pro-Whig in 1679–81, anti-James and pro-William in 1688, but pro-Tory and pro-Jacobite by the second decade of the eighteenth century. How do we explain this? Was the crowd fickle in its political allegiance? If so, did that not force us to question the political sophistication or awareness of those who comprised the crowd?

Interest in looking at politics out-of-doors, at exploring the political views, assumptions and activities of the mass of the population below the level of the governing elite, has grown considerably over the last couple of decades. As a result, our understanding of the nature and significance of the politics of the people has become more sophisticated and the ways in which we seek to recapture this politics have grown more refined. It was thought, therefore, that there might be some value in putting together a collection of essays to illustrate some of the latest trends, as a way both of highlighting where we have got to, as well as of raising questions about where we need to go from here.

The intent of this collection is not to present a comprehensive survey of popular politics in England from the early sixteenth to the early nineteenth century. Moreover, there is so much interesting and important work currently being done that it is impossible, even, to offer a complete sampling of the types of approaches currently being pursued in the space available. All that a volume of this nature can hope to do is illustrate some of the recent trends, and if certain empirical themes or analytical paradigms that are currently in vogue do not find expression here, one can only rejoice that this is a reflection of the current healthy state of scholarly enquiry. There is a rationale behind how the volume was put together, however, which it is worth making explicit here. The focus is on the early modern period – the three hundred or so years between the Reformation and the Industrial Revolution – which is broad enough to allow for considerations of change over time whilst at the same time presenting a logical and coherent unit for study. We felt that there needed to be chapters that dealt with rural as well as urban environments, institutional as well as extra-institutional forms of political activity, and which looked not just at the political concerns of the people but also at how the political elite responded to those concerns and whether they thought the people needed to be taken seriously. On top of this, we wanted the various chapters between them to reflect as wide a range of approaches to the study of the politics of excluded, and as wide a variety of repertoires of and forums for popular political expression, as might be possible for a book of this size: hence why some of the chapters focus on crowds, but others focus on rumours, libels or seditious words. Beyond that, as editor I simply invited people doing interesting and cutting-edge research to write on whatever they thought most appropriate. There has been no attempt to impose an editorial line, or to ask contributors to write to a particular brief.

Rather than simply summarize the various arguments put forth by the different contributors, this introduction will seek to establish an appropriate context for what is to follow by addressing four broad interpretative questions. It will begin with a consideration of the extent to which the unenfranchised masses could have been politically aware, and if they were, how they achieved their political education. It will then examine whether these people really were excluded from politics and the ways in which they might have been included (or managed to include themselves) in the political process – and if so, with what impact: that is, did these people's politics matter? A third section will look at women, and consider the question of whether or not they remained excluded from politics. A final section will address the theme of change over time.

I

Before we embark, however, we should discuss terminology, and ask what we should understand by the term 'politics'. For an earlier generation of scholars who taught in (and often had a hand in setting up) politics departments in universities, politics tended to be rather narrowly defined, as something that took place in a particular arena and was participated in by those who worked in that arena. Thus politics was essentially about government, the arena was the institutions of government, and those who served in them were politicians. Such a view still retains much favour. John Horton, for example, has written that 'Politics is paradigmatically concerned with government and legislation; the deliberating, deciding and implementing of the rules by which a state conducts its affairs'.[12] Many political scientists nowadays, however, would regard such a definition as too restrictive. Thus Adrian Leftwich has stated that 'politics comprises all the activities of co-operation and conflict, within and between societies, whereby the human species goes about organizing the use, production and distribution of human, natural and other resources in the course of the production and reproduction of its biological and social life'. What this means is that politics is everywhere and in everything. As Leftwich continues: 'politics is at the heart of *all* collective social activity, formal and informal, public and private, in *all* human groups, institutions and societies, not just some of them, and . . . it always has been and always will be'. Politics is even to be found in informal or temporary groupings of people, and these informal groups might include 'bus queues, football crowds, people meeting for the first time on a camp site'; indeed, we might even find politics 'among children inventing and playing games', or 'among residents of a housing estate'.[13]

The broader definition has much to recommend it. Keith Wrightson has shown how 'a great deal of the social history of early modern England written in the last twenty years has been quite centrally concerned with politics', 'if we did but realise it', not just 'in the sense of "micro-politics" or "local level politics", but in its broader concern . . . with the political dimension of everyday life'.[14] There is undoubtedly much to be gained from asking questions, say, about the politics of the household, or of the family, or the politics of gender. Such a broad definition is not particularly helpful for our purposes, however. To claim that there clearly was a politics of the excluded, because politics is (and always has been) everywhere, would not get us very far. The intent of this collection is to demonstrate that there was a politics of the excluded in the more narrow meaning of the term politics. It seeks to show that ordinary men and women did have opinions about how duly constituted authority was supposed to be exercised, and how those who governed – not just at the local but also the central level – were supposed to rule; that they often engaged in activity that was designed to influence how the political elite ruled over them; and that the ruling elite frequently found that they could not afford to ignore the political opinions and acts of the people they governed.

Our first task, then, must be to consider how those people not usually thought of as being part of the political nation came to be politicized. There is a widely held assumption that mass politicization is linked to the rise of the popular press, and is thus also dependent upon mass literacy. Because literacy rates were low in early modern England, the potential for mass politicization, it might be thought, was limited. David Cressy, in his analysis of subscriptions to the Protestation Oath, the Vow and Covenant, and the Solemn League and Covenant of 1641–4, found that at this time some 70 per cent of the adult male population was illiterate, as measured by the ability to sign one's name – though it should be stressed that his sample was biased towards rural communities. An average for the nation as a whole, however, is not particularly meaningful, since there were marked regional and occupational variations to the literacy profile. Townspeople tended to be more literate than country dwellers, with literacy rates being highest, earliest, in London; only 22 per cent of Londoners were illiterate (as measured by the signature test) in 1641–4. The middling sorts tended to be more literate than the lower orders; tradesmen, craftsmen and apprentices were much more likely to be able sign their names than husbandmen, servants and labourers. Marriage register evidence, which becomes available after 1754, suggests that in the second half of the eighteenth century just under 40 per cent of the adult male population remained illiterate. Moreover, women were beginning to catch up with men. Thus, whereas Cressy calculated that a mere 10 per cent of women were literate in the middle of the seventeenth century, by the end of the eighteenth century this figure had risen to 40 per cent (at a time when the corresponding figure for men was just over 60 per cent). Again, however, the marriage register evidence shows that illiteracy rates remained highest, longest, in rural areas, and declined most rapidly in market towns, with the middling sorts engaged in commerce being much more likely to achieve basic literacy than unskilled, manual labourers.[15] It might therefore seem logical that mass politics should arise first in the metropolis, where people were literate enough to read the pamphlets, broadsides and periodicals that streamed from the London presses first in the early 1640s and then again in the late 1670s and early 1680s, and then spread outwards to provincial towns, with the rise of provincial newspapers in the eighteenth century. Hence also why public opinion, when it first supposedly came into being some time towards the latter end of the early modern period, has tended to be seen as a middle-class or bourgeois phenomenon.

On the surface, there seems considerable evidence to support this scenario. Existing studies of seventeenth-century popular politics have tended to place a heavy emphasis on London. Keith Lindley has written that the year May 1640 to May 1641 'witnessed the rise of mass politics' in London, and this was the time, of course, which saw the breakdown of pre-publication censorship and concomitant flowering of the metropolitan press as politically committed writers and polemicists attempted to appeal to opinion out-of-doors.[16] My own work on London crowds documented the heightened degree of political awareness amongst Londoners at the time of the Exclusion Crisis towards the end of Charles II's reign, and explored the ways in which the opinions of ordinary Londoners were informed and shaped by the press.[17] Work by eighteenth-century historians has shown popular politics flourishing in the provinces, though the studies we have tend to focus on provincial towns and emphasize the importance of the press. Thus Kathleen Wilson, whose study of popular politics in England between 1715 and 1785 takes the towns of Norwich and Newcastle as its two case studies, has described the press as 'that preeminent instrument of politicization in the eighteenth century'. John Brewer's investigation of politics and opinion in the 1760s also sought to link the emergence of what he termed 'an alternative structure of politics' to 'the political education of those "out-of-doors"' provided by the press. To judge from his account, it was particularly 'those out-of-doors' who lived in towns who received this political education. Thus he states that we find 'the same indigenous political culture, centred upon a few taverns or coffee houses' in 'the large provincial towns' as we do in London, and concludes that as a result 'the difference between the political sophistication of London and that of a provincial town was considerably diminished'.[18] On the theoretical level, this scenario seems to receive added endorsement from the work of the German sociologist Jürgen Habermas on the transformation of the public sphere, which, despite having been first published as long ago as 1965, has become extremely fashionable of late following its translation into English in 1989. Thus Habermas dated the rise of public opinion in England to the early eighteenth century, and linked it to the rise of a bourgeois reading public who would gather in coffee-houses to read and discuss political news.[19]

It was simply not the case, however, that only urban literate types in early modern England were informed about politics; if there had ever been any doubts about this matter, they should have been dispelled by David Underdown's ground-breaking study of popular politics in early Stuart England published in 1985, which takes as its focus rural Somerset, Dorset and Wiltshire.[20] We need to rid ourselves of the notion that popular political awareness was intrinsically linked to the existence of the popular political press and thus also dependent upon literacy. To say this is not to deny the importance of the press as an instrument of politicization; it clearly was an influential factor once it had come into being. Rather, it is merely to recognize that there were other ways whereby people could become politicized. Acknowledging this enables us to appreciate the potential for popular political awareness at much earlier times and amongst those people who would not have been able to read.

The pre-eminent instrument of politicization, one might suggest – perhaps in any time period and any society – is the government and what it is doing to people.[21] People in early modern England, as several chapters in this volume bear out, had views about what those responsible for ruling the state were doing because they experienced it first hand. The fiscal policies of the state, its religious policies, foreign policy, economic policy, the way it administered justice, regulated the grain market, or policed society – all could have a direct impact on broad cross-sections of the population. When a government is compelling people to hand over some of their income in the form of taxation, or instructing them how to worship (and severely punishing those who fail to conform), or requiring them to be ready to lay down their lives for their sovereign by serving in the armed forces, for example, it is difficult for such people to remain oblivious to and unconcerned about what the government is up to. With the rise of the political press, people who could read could learn about what the government was doing (or planning to do, or what it was doing in other parts of the country) from pamphlets, broadsides or newspapers. And those who could not read could gather around someone who could and hear political news read aloud. In this way, people could develop opinions about policies that they did not directly experience themselves. But the same was true before the rise of the political press, it was just that then alternative media were used for the spreading of political information. One of the most important was the sermon; the clergy would frequently convey information about matters of state from the pulpit, either because they were requested to do so by the government itself or because they had taken it upon themselves to raise awareness in the community they served about government policy. Political news could also spread through more informal channels, such as manuscript news-letters, libels, word of mouth, rumour, gossip or hearsay, which could serve equally well to inform people about what the government was allegedly up to in other parts of the country or might be intending to do in their locality, as the printed press did at a later date.[22] It was possible, in this manner, for ordinary people in the localities to become informed about, and engage in a debate over the merits of, national policy. One might object that rumour and gossip frequently misrepresented or distorted the truth or spread inaccurate information, but one would also be naïve to think that this was not also the case with the popular political press once it had come into being.[23]

II

If we recognize that there was a potential for ordinary people, in town and countryside alike, to become politicized, how do we measure it? How did the politics of the excluded manifest itself? One answer is through collective agitation – riots, demonstrations, petitions, and even open rebellions. Two chapters in this volume – those by Nicholas Rogers and myself – deal with crowd politics, in the sense of demonstrations either for or against a particular political cause, my own focusing on the Stuart century, and Rogers's on the Georgian period. Moreover, as Andy Wood reminds us in his chapter, what might seem to us to be more purely economic forms of protest, such as anti-enclosure riots (one could add food riots and trade disputes) were often intrinsically political in nature, since the rioters were engaged in making public statements about how they thought those in positions of authority were supposed to

rule and typically chose to pursue all available political avenues of seeking a redress of their grievances – by petitioning local and central
authorities – before having recourse to violence.[24]

Yet there were also other means whereby ordinary people could give
voice to their political opinions. Ethan Shagan looks at rumours in the
1530s, both at how they were transmitted and how they were received.
He shows how 'the protean character of rumours allowed individuals to
express their opinions about Church and state by either changing a
rumour's wording or surrounding the core content of a rumour with
their own gloss', and thus that 'every person in the chain of a rumour's
transmission . . . participated to some degree in the creation of a popular
political discourse' (p. 31). By looking also at the reactions rumours provoked, which ranged the gamut from apathy to revulsion, we can catch a
glimpse of what was indeed a vibrant but also contested popular political
culture in England at the time of the Henrician Reformation. Andy
Wood looks not just at the rituals of popular unrest, or the theatricality
of public encounters between the rulers and ruled, but also at plebeian
speech in the sixteenth and early seventeenth century – at seditious
words, at the various languages of deference and defiance employed by
the poor (including body language), and in more general terms at what
we might label the politics of speech. He makes the telling point that the
government's very desire to scrutinize and censor plebeian speech gives
the lie to those contemporary commentators (and, one might add, latter-
day historians) who refused to acknowledge the existence of popular
politics; the government clearly acknowledged its existence and took it
very seriously indeed. Alastair Bellany focuses on libels, which afforded
one type of space whereby 'dissident, marginal and oppositional voices
. . . could speak without serious risk of intervention', and thus 'made
room for a "politics of the excluded"' (p. 101). Bellany concludes that
'early Stuart politics took on a greater variety of forms and occurred in
a greater variety of sites' than is usually acknowledged, and that 'we
should look for politics in symbols and in ceremonies; on hearses and on
corpses; at the end of ropes and on the points of knives; in churches and
on church doors; in words and in images; on walls and on paper; in print
and in script; indoors and outdoors; among the elites and among the
plebs; among the powerful and among the excluded, the marginal, and
the dissident' (p. 117).

Such insights free us from an episodic approach to the politics of
the excluded. We need not jump from one crowd to the next, or from
one petitioning campaign to another. Political opinions could be made

manifest through other forums, and the process of politicization was going on all the time. There might be periods of heightened activity and of relative quiescence, certain times when there was more political agitation out-of-doors than others, or when the populace appeared more concerned about what the government was doing to them (and willing to vent that concern publicly) than it had in the past; but there was a continuous process of political education going on all the time over the whole of the time period covered by this study. Recognizing this also frees us from seeing popular politics as essentially reactive, and therefore as intrinsically conservative – suppositions which have often led historians to conclude that the people really had no politics of their own. As Shagan argues in his chapter, apparent popular conservatism could at the same time be disturbingly radical. Or, as Wood makes clear, using deferential language or making compliant gestures could be a tactical ploy designed to help the plebs achieve their ultimate ends (though Wood is also at pains to stress the importance of regional variation and change over time). In other words, the common people often had their own agendas which they sought to pursue. They would usually do so in ways that were perceived to stand the greatest chance of eliciting the desired response from their social and political superiors, even to the point of acting out the subordinate role in the hierarchical ordering of society that the elite had ascribed to them, but this did not necessarily make them deferential, or accepting of their lot, or mean that they were essentially without a political vision of their own; indeed, it could often mean the opposite, and reveal how shrewd they were as political operators in this particular culture.

It was not just that ordinary people might seek to intrude themselves into the political process; they were frequently invited to intrude by the ruling classes. Far from being the excluded, they were often included in very explicit ways. The fact that early modern England was not a democratic state should not lead us to conclude that it was non-participatory, as Mark Goldie shows in his chapter. Because early modern England lacked a large, professional bureaucracy, effective government at the local level depended upon the cooperation of unpaid members of the local community – not just from those members of the county and urban elite who served as deputy lieutenants, JPs, town magistrates, sheriffs and grand jurors, but also from middling and even more humble types who might for varying periods of time serve as constables, beadles, tithingmen, nightwatchmen, vestrymen, overseers of the poor, trial or petty jurors, or even perform a stint in the militia or trained bands.

Many of these positions were short-term, with parishioners serving for a period of one or two years by a system of rotation, which meant that over an adult male's lifetime the chances of holding some form of local office could be extremely high. Assuming that each parish in England and Wales had one constable, two churchwardens and two overseers, Goldie computes, this would mean that 'around the year 1700, about one twentieth of adult males were governing in any year' (in some localities, the figure was actually much higher); or, to extrapolate over time, 'in principle, that might mean one half were governing in any decade' (p. 161).

The social profile of those who served in such positions is a complex issue. One was supposed to be a householder of independent means to qualify for office, and the more prestigious offices tended to be dominated by the more prosperous parishioners. This was particularly true of the position of vestryman, as Steve Hindle shows in his chapter in this volume. Hindle warns that in emphasizing the role of popular participation in local government we should not fall into the trap of thinking that participation was unrestricted. The tendency of gentlemen to be absent from the communities in which they were supposed to reside might have opened up a social and political space for those below them to exercise authority, but it was a space that tended to be occupied by the chief inhabitants of the village, or the more prosperous middling sort. Hindle also confirms the trend towards oligarchy in parish government in the later-sixteenth and seventeenth centuries which other historians have noted. He is acutely aware, however, of the importance of regional variation. Rural parishes were more likely to become oligarchic than their urban equivalents because they lacked the multiplicity of minor offices which could provide for a broader base of popular participation.[25] There were also crucial differences between pastoral and arable communities. Moreover, the pattern of local and social relations was never simply one of binary opposition between the middling sort and the poor; there was a three-tier field of force comprising magistrates, vestrymen and the poor, and the poor might often appeal over the heads of the vestrymen to the JPs in order to protect what they believed to be their rights. His account paints a picture of 'popular – though nonetheless circumscribed – political participation' (p. 147) – one which allowed for contestation and negotiation, which shows how political 'out-of-doors' operated at the parish level (and why it needs to be treated so seriously), and which even suggests the existence of a parochial public sphere.

Not all local offices, however, carried the same prestige and power as that of vestryman. Others could be an irritating burden – one thinks, in particular, of the positions of constable, beadle, nightwatchman, or militiaman – and more prosperous types might seek to avoid having to undertake such responsibilities themselves, either by conspiring to have such positions foisted on those who were in no position to object or else by paying for hired substitutes to serve in their stead. Goldie, whilst both acknowledging a drift towards oligarchy over time and accepting that the 'weightier' householders tended to matter more within their communities, nevertheless finds that parish officeholding in early modern England was 'remarkably socially extensive', embracing 'an array of people from minor gentry to cottagers' (p. 163). Rural constables were not infrequently illiterate, and neither having a criminal record nor being a religious nonconformist proved to be a bar to office. In consequence, those responsible for policing the transgressions of the local community might often differ little in social make-up or moral proclivity from those who were being policed. The government was also dependent on local cooperation in a more informal sense to ensure that law and order was maintained and good governance enforced. In the absence of a full-time, professional police force, there was an onus placed on local residents to help in the detection of crime or in the apprehension of criminals, either by coming forward as informers, helping constables make arrests, or rushing to the aid of victims of crime who raised the hue and cry.[26]

Furthermore, both central and local authorities frequently called on the people to occupy public space in order to endorse their acts and to confirm the legitimacy of their rule. Crowds would be invited to celebrate the accession of a new monarch, royal coronations, political anniversaries, hear royal proclamations, witness royal entries or civic inaugurations, watch public executions, and even participate in imposing justice on convicted criminals (this was the logic behind the pillory, of course).[27] We might suggest several reasons why the ruling elite would want to draw the people into the political arena in these ways. Within the prevailing ideological assumptions of the age, it was accepted that government was supposed to be for the common good. In Stuart England, for example, even the staunchest champions of divine-right, absolute monarchy, who insisted that ordinary people should accept their inferior place in the divinely ordained social and political hierarchy and let their sovereign get on with the job of ruling, would have agreed that Providence had lodged such power 'in the Supreme Governor, for the Good of the Community'.[28] Public rallies in support of the government – even if they were carefully orchestrated (or at least sponsored) from above – nevertheless served to offer confirmation that those in power were fulfilling their divinely ordained task. Encouraging crowd celebrations could be a form of propaganda, in other words, a way of announcing to the nation at large that the government had public opinion on its side, even when it perhaps did not. Promoting public spectacles and celebrations could be a means of trying to keep the people content, of distracting them from their everyday woes or their underlying grievances against those in power by throwing a party, thereby helping to prevent potential unrest.[29] Certain rituals, such as royal coronations and processions, or public executions, might serve to awe the public, to remind people of their lowly position in the divinely ordained hierarchy, to promote the splendour of majesty, or (in the case of executions) to advertise the power of state and show people what it could do to them if they chose to step out of line.

The inclusion of ordinary people in the various ways described above, however, also gave them the potential for subversion, opening up a space for them to exercise their own political power. If they did not like certain government legislation, they could choose not to enforce it. There are numerous examples in Restoration England, for example, of constables simply refusing to enforce the laws against nonconformist conventicles, because they sympathized with the plight of their nonconformist neighbours or because they felt that the laws against Protestant dissenters were wrong-headed or inherently unjust. Similarly, local constables and militiamen might refuse to suppress crowd disturbances if they felt that those who were rioting had legitimate grievances.[30] Crowds invited to endorse acts of state power might instead choose to challenge them. Rather than abuse those sentenced to stand in the pillory, they might fête them. They could appropriate political anniversaries for subversive ends; thus during the reigns of Charles I and Charles II, to give one example, the anniversaries of both the Gunpowder Plot (5 November) and Queen Elizabeth's accession (17 November) came to be celebrated by opposition groups who were fearful of the popish leanings of the royal court.[31] Or else they could celebrate alternative anniversaries – the Pretender's birthday on 10 June, for example, rather than the accession of George II, on 11 June – to show disapproval of the current regime. If things got truly out of hand, the government could be brought to its knees. Charles I fled London in early 1642, in the face of widespread alienation amongst the local agents of law enforcement who refused to act against the crowds protesting against the policies of his regime.[32] Rumour, seditious words, anti-government rallies, might, in certain circumstances, even translate into open rebellion, as it did on several occasions during the period covered by this book, from the Amicable Grant of 1525 or the Pilgrimage of Grace of 1536, to the Jacobite risings of 1715 and 1745.[33]

For this reason, those who governed could not afford to ignore the voices of those over whom they ruled. They often found it necessary to cultivate public opinion, solicit support out-of-doors, or at least devise appropriate strategies for managing popular political sentiment, keeping the masses happy, and containing the potential for subversive criticism that might threaten the security of the regime. Social historians have long since noted that the mere threat of disorder could serve to prompt local elites to adjust their policies or grant concessions in order to avoid civil unrest.[34] If riots did break out, they frequently served to recall the elite to the proper performance of their duties; the ringleaders themselves might be punished, but the grievances that provoked the riot in the first place might nevertheless be redressed.[35] The same could be true at the national level. Henry VIII abandoned his Amicable Grant in the face of widespread opposition in 1525, and also made adjustments to royal policy in response to the Pilgrimage of Grace of 1536.[36] Those rulers who showed themselves insensitive to opinion out-of-doors or who failed to pay sufficient attention to the voice of people could run into serious trouble. Charles I is arguably a case in point. The Catholic James II most certainly is. When he found himself faced with extensive anti-Catholic rioting in 1686, in both his English and Scottish capitals and in many provincial towns, in protest against his encouragement of open Catholic worship, instead of reaching the conclusion that his policy might need rethinking since he could not carry his people with him, he chose to push on regardless with his efforts to help his co-religionists, with disastrous consequences for the political stability of his own regime.[37]

One must be careful not to present too simplistic a view of the power dynamics between the governing elite and the bulk of the population. How effective the voice of the people could be in politics and whether it needed to be listened to at any given time would depend upon a myriad of factors: the repressive powers available to the state; the extent of disaffection amongst crucial power brokers in the intermediary levels of central government; how those with political power bases in the localities chose to align themselves; the extent of disaffection amongst the masses and the ability of these people to express their discontent in such a way as to appear to be in need of being taken seriously by those in authority, and so on. Only carefully contextualized studies can allow us to make confident statements about the significance and impact of popular political agitation in any given locality during any particular time period. Having said this, it is worth noting that early modern governments frequently engaged in propaganda initiatives designed to combat popular disaffection and win back public sympathy, a clear testimony to the fact that the governing elite did, indeed, take the voice of the people seriously. Sharon Jansen has shown that in the later 1530s, in response to all the prophecies that were circulating expressing discontent with the policies of the crown, the central government, in addition to trying to silence these prophets, embarked on its own campaign of counter-prophecy, in order to represent itself in a more favourable light.[38] Ethan Shagan has noted that Protector Somerset's method of dealing with the rebels of 1549 'involved an elaborate courting of public opinion and a stunning willingness to commit the regime to fundamental changes in policy at the initiation of the commons'.[39] My own chapter in this volume examines why Charles II's government, in the late 1670s and early 1680s, found it necessary to court public opinion, to the point not only of producing propaganda designed to appeal to the 'vulgar' but also of encouraging public manifestations of support for its regime in the form of addresses and demonstrations. Nicholas Rogers, in his chapter, explores the various strategies pursued by the government over the course of the long eighteenth century to mobilize crowds and render them more domesticated and docile. Their efforts again testify to the extent to which they took the voice of those who comprised the crowd seriously. Yet although their strategies were, over the long run, successful, this just meant that 'plebeian subjects developed new forms of popular politics' through which their concerns and aspirations could find expression (p. 234).

We have found it useful, on a number of occasions thus far, to invoke the term 'public opinion', but it is a term that needs to be treated with care. If we use it in a loose sense to mean the views and opinions of the general public, or those out-of-doors, then we surely can talk about the existence of public opinion in the sixteenth and seventeenth centuries (and even earlier). Yet there also exists a more formal notion of public opinion as being the general sense of the people, which was articulated through public media of expression (particularly the newspaper and periodical press), and as such was recognized as a force in politics that had to be taken into consideration. We could debate whether public opinion in this reified sense existed in Tudor and Stuart times (the evidence presented so far might suggest that it did), but the concept itself was an eighteenth-century one,[40] and only truly came into its own in the early decades of the nineteenth century, as Patty Seleski reminds us in her chapter in this volume. Public opinion, in this sense of the term, was, of course, a construct, something that had to be created and then in turn mobilized on behalf of a particular cause, typically by the press. Seleski examines how this was done with regard to the case of Eliza Fenning, a young servant woman who in 1815 was convicted, on extremely flimsy evidence, of trying to kill the family she worked for and sent to the gallows. The reformist and radical press sought to invoke and manage public opinion on Fenning's behalf, appealing to popular constitutional-ist sentiments by representing the manifest abuses in Fenning's trial as another example of the abuse of state power to oppress the weak, thereby hoping to further the cause of reform at a time when there was increased apprehension about the reactionary politics of the government. There were competing narratives, however, in the construction of Eliza Fenning as a *cause célèbre*. Fenning's supporters tended to target a middle-class readership, predominantly male, using the conventions of melodrama to appeal to respectable, manly public opinion to protect a helpless female victim. There was an alternative reading of the case, however, propagated in part by Fenning herself, which represented Fenning not as a helpless victim but as independent and aggressive in her own defence, the implications of which were more radical. This opened up a space for a counter-offensive by the conservative press, who sought to exploit fears about the insubordination of servants to defend the treatment of Fenning; indeed, Fenning's cleverness and independ-ence could be taken as proof of her guilt! Seleski's chapter raises import-ant questions both about the elusiveness of public opinion (and how it could or could not be harnessed) and also about the class-bound and gendered nature of reformist politics at this time that limited its poten-tial for success.

III

Seleski's emphasis on gender invites us to consider the broader question of where women fit into any discussion of the politics of the excluded in early modern England. It is a theme that is explored by many of the con-tributors to this volume. Even if we accept that the notion of the political nation should be expanded to embrace a much broader proportion of the population than we once thought, was politics nevertheless still predominantly a male preserve? Did women, in other words, remain excluded? Certainly, women's structural relationship to institutional politics was different from men's. Despite the fact that women were not legally prevented from voting in parliamentary elections until the Great Reform Act of 1832, and that if they met the franchise qualification in particular constituencies they technically did have the right to vote, a combination of convention and prejudice dictated that they seldom exercised this right. Women could vote in vestry elections, but again they rarely did so.[41] Even where they were entitled to serve as church-wardens or overseers of the poor, we find that for the most part, as Hindle and Goldie show here, their offices were performed by male deputies. The myriad of local offices might have opened up the potential for more humble types to participate in some of the processes of govern-ment at the local level, but this was not, it seems, an opportunity afforded to women. Furthermore, studies of crowd unrest have noted that women are far less visible in political riots than men, though their presence was often noted in disputes which related to the economic interests of the domestic household, such anti-enclosure riots, food riots, and even riots against the introduction of mechanization into manufac-turing industries which threatened to put the male wage-earner out of work and destroy his ability to support his family. This has led some historians to conclude that women were far more likely to be involved in bread-and-butter disputes than straightforward political ones, even if these bread-and-butter disputes might have had political implications in the broader sense of the term.[42] It is true that we do find women engaging in forms of collective action (demonstrations and petitioning campaigns) that were more overtly political during the years of the civil war and interregnum in the middle of the seventeenth century, but this, it must be acknowledged, was a rather exceptional period. Besides, even here we find a tendency for such women to be preoccupied with issues related (broadly speaking) to the economic health of the domestic household: thus we see women demonstrating or petitioning for peace, against the decay of trade, against imprisonment for debt, or for the release of their husbands imprisoned for a political crime.[43] It might seem logical to suppose that women were less politically aware or engaged than men, because female literacy rates were much lower than they were for their male counterparts. Surely, one might suggest, only elite women exercised any true political agency, and even this was only in the form of illicit behind-the-scenes activity, as courtesans exercising an undue influence on the monarch, or as electoral patrons using their economic muscle to sway elections.[44] Women's entry into the political arena in a more legitimate sense is often taken to be an early nineteenth-century development, something that occurred in the aftermath of the

Napoleonic Wars with the advent of political organizations of female radicals.[45]

It would be wrong, however, to conclude that women were excluded from politics in the early modern period. The rationale for assuming they were can be shown to have been based on false premises. For example, although female literacy rates were lower than those of men, when measured by the criterion of the ability to sign one's name, we have now come to recognize that women were much more likely to be able to read than write. Women who could not sign their names, because they did not attend school long enough to receive instruction in writing, nevertheless might have been just as capable as their male counterparts from the same social class and geographical area of reading cheap printed works.[46] In any case, we have already observed that access to a political education was not dependent upon the ability to read the popular political press. Furthermore, the apparent absence of women from political riots and demonstrations seems to be an optical illusion produced by the sources. Crowds tended to be described in gender-neutral terms – such as 'the rabble', 'the multitude', or 'the mob'; only when contemporary observers sought to highlight the female presence would the gender of the participants be noted. Contemporaries were more likely to do this, it seems, if they wanted to belittle the importance of the protest (for example, by saying that the crowd was composed of women and boys), or else if they recognized that the protest embraced grievances that were regarded (by those doing the describing) as legitimate concerns for women (such as bread-and-butter disputes). It certainly was the case that women were more likely to push themselves to the front of the crowd in bread-and-butter disputes, in order to make an ideological statement about the effect certain policies were having on their ability to feed and nurture their families. Yet if they were not at the forefront of political riots and demonstrations, this does not mean they were not there. They tended not to be arrested for involvement in political protest, but that was because the resources available to the local agents of law enforcement with regard to crowd control were limited, and so authorities tended to go after the more obvious ringleaders and those members of the crowd who seemed to offer the most serious threat to law and order. Hence they picked on men, in part because they were more likely to be the ringleaders in political protests, in part because contemporaries assumed that they were most likely the ones responsible for orchestrating such protests (especially if they became violent), and also because the law assumed that if men and women were acting in concert the men were responsible for what the women did.

In fact, there is little reason to suspect that women were likely to be less politically aware or engaged than their male counterparts. They certainly were involved in political protests, as we discover when the policing agencies decided to cast their net beyond the male ringleaders and the captains of the mob and endeavoured to make mass arrests. For example, 80 women were prosecuted for involvement in the Gordon riots of 1780, 24 were convicted of felony and seven were hanged.[47] They were involved in electoral politics, as spectators at the hustings, participants in the crowds that gathered to cheer or jeer rival candidates, or as street vendors dispersing political propaganda; at times they might campaign actively on behalf of certain candidates themselves. At the Coventry election of 1705, the crowd not only contained a sizeable female contingent, but was addressed in a speech from the hustings by one Captain Kate, who, slapping one of the Tory candidates on the back, proclaimed, 'Now, Boys, or Never, for the Church'.[48] We can find them celebrating political anniversaries, royal coronations or the birthday of the Pretender. They were often invited to enter public space at political processionals, both civic and royal, albeit to represent a stereotypically female virtue. And we can frequently find women giving voice to their political views through the speaking of seditious words.[49] Shagan, in his chapter, notes how women could find a political voice through spreading and manipulating rumours. They could also make their opposition to the political views expressed in rumours, prophecies and seditious words by coming forward as informers. Jansen has found that women of all classes were actively involved in resistance to the Henrician reforms of the 1530s, making their opinions known through prophecy, speech or direct action.[50] We can find women talking about politics in alehouses.[51] We can also find them doing the same in coffee-houses, once thought to be a peculiarly male public space.[52] And we can find them involved in conspiratorial activity against the state. Thus, according to Richard Ashcraft, it was mostly women who were responsible for carrying intelligence reports back and forth between dissidents in Holland and England on the eve of the Monmouth rebellion of 1685.[53] We certainly have to be alert to the fact that the ways in which women participated in politics out-of-doors might have been subtly different from men, and this is a topic that needs further research. We are increasingly coming to realize, however, that those public political spaces once thought to be exclusively male preserves were also inhabited by women.

IV

Finally, let us turn to a consideration of change over time. The differing empirical and topical foci pursued by the various contributors to this volume perhaps make it difficult to formulate any clear generalizations, though their findings do at least point to questions that need to be asked and suggest certain types of conclusions that might be made. The essays, when taken together, seem to posit a warning against invoking notions of 'the rise of' or 'emergence of' when talking about popular politics, mass political activism or public opinion in the time period covered by this book. Those who might have believed that crowd activity and other forms of collective protest prior to the Industrial Revolution were essentially pre-political clearly need to think again. The idea that public opinion first came into being in the late seventeenth or early eighteenth century, or the notion that the masses first became actively engaged in politics during the 1640s as a result of the upheavals of the civil war, also appear to be in need of re-examination. This collection shows that there was a vibrant popular political culture in England in the 1520s and 1530s. Indeed, we could go back earlier. Isobel Harvey has recently made a compelling case for the existence of popular politics in the fifteenth century, with the common voice making itself heard in politics by various means, such as mob activity, petitioning campaigns, the uttering of seditious speeches, or the discussion of political issues in the home or the alehouse. This popular political culture was informed by political verse, which circulated widely among the general public; by royal proclamations, which were read aloud in English in public places, or handbills posted on doors, windows or town crosses; by sermons, processions, gossip and rumour. 'By the middle of the century', Harvey has written, 'popular opinion' had become 'so important that it began to be wooed'.[54] Some might go back even earlier. Do we not see a popular politics at the time of the Peasants' Revolt in 1381?[55]

Yet it is noticeable that whenever scholars, working on various aspects of popular political culture or public opinion formation, seek to revise accepted wisdom about the origins of the phenomena they are investigating, they nevertheless invariably seem to emphasize that there was something new and innovative going on in the time period that they have made the focus of their research. For example, Steven Pincus, criticizing Habermas's notion that the public sphere first came into existence in England at the turn of the eighteenth century, has made a convincing case for the existence of a vibrant and engaged public sphere, centring around the coffee-houses, during the reign of Charles II. But for Pincus, it was then that the public sphere first emerged; as a consequence, he believes, English political culture in the later seventeenth century was significantly different from what it had been in the early Stuart period.[56] Likewise Shagan, in his discussion of Somerset's response to the rebellions of 1549, has argued that 'we can see in Somerset's policy a novel mode of popularity-politics in the process of invention'.[57] Harvey believes that 'popular politics not only existed but grew in importance in the fifteenth century'; in fact, her account suggests that it was distinctively fifteenth-century social, economic, cultural and political developments that enabled a popular politics to come into being at this time.[58]

One might retort that this simply illustrates that professional historians are always engaged in trying to show that the period they are studying is more important than anyone else's – they have to, in order to advance their careers. Less cynically, one might suggest that the demands of modern-day research are such that it is impossible to possess a specialized knowledge of anything more than a relatively narrow time-frame, so that the resultant loss of historical perspective leads us unwittingly to exaggerate the significance or novelty of our own research findings. Yet there is surely more to it than this. I would suggest that the historians cited above actually have identified new trends and developments. This does not mean that we should claim that popular politics 'first emerged' at 'this time' rather than 'that'. What it does mean is that there were significant differences, with respect to popular politics, between the world of the later fifteenth century, say, and that of the period of the Peasants' Revolt; that Protector Somerset found himself in a different situation and facing different types of problems than Henry VIII and therefore found it necessary to have recourse to different strategies of legitimation to sustain his authority in time of crisis; and that the context in which public political debate operated was significantly different by the later seventeenth century, in the aftermath of the civil war and republican experiments in government and with the advent of the coffee-houses as locales for the acquisition, dissemination and discussion of political news, compared to what it had been earlier.

The way forward, I would suggest, is to abandon metaphors associated with rising or emerging (and certainly those which imply coming into existence for the first time), and instead to employ an analytical paradigm that thinks in terms of density. Here I follow a lead suggested by Nicholas Rogers, who has written of the 'denser political space of the early nineteenth century'; denser, he says, in his particular context, 'because the decades after 1790 saw a rapid expansion of the popular press, a deep penetration of political ideologies, both radical and loyalist, the advent of the first popular political societies, and a growing visibility of women as the objects of social and political discourse'.[59] We can easily see how the notion of density might assist our attempts to analyse change over time during the early modern period. The means whereby people could gain access to political information were unquestionably denser towards the end of this period than they were at the beginning. It might have been possible for people to become informed about political developments or the activities of the state prior to the existence of a popular political press, but the flooding of the market – first in the early 1640s, again in the late 1670s and early 1680s, and more permanently after the lapsing of the Licensing Act in 1695 – with cheap printed materials (pamphlets, broadsides and periodicals) deliberately targeted at the masses undoubtedly increased the density of sources from which the masses could gain political information. Although people who could not read could gain a political education – either through their direct experience of what the government was doing to them, or from listening to tracts read aloud, or from hearing word-of-mouth reports and political gossip – denser literacy profiles (in the sense of higher rates of literacy amongst the lower echelons of society) certainly opened up further access to political information. Even if significant proportions of the male and female populations towards the lower end of the social hierarchy might still not have been able to read towards the end of the eighteenth century, their chances of knowing someone who could (and who could therefore convey to them political information gained from reading pamphlets and periodicals) was certainly much greater than it would have been in the early sixteenth century. Then we have to consider the density of communications networks. John Brewer is surely right to point to improvements in communications (he mentions in particular turnpikes and the postal service) as facilitating the dissemination of political news under the Hanoverians and helping to make the popular political culture of the 1760s something different from what it had been earlier, say back in the Exclusion Crisis of 1679–81.[60]

Considerations of density can be important in other contexts. Population density clearly conditioned both the potential for mass mobilization and its degree of menace. Hence why the London crowd appeared so threatening, of course, and why there was increasing concern about potential civic unrest in the capital as the population of the metropolis grew so dramatically over the course of the early modern period.

Population density would also explain why urban politics out-of-doors took on differing hues and significance from that in more sparsely populated rural areas, as well as why popular politics in the mid-fifteenth century needs to be seen in a different structural context from that of the mid-seventeenth century or the late eighteenth century. Related to the issue of population density is that of the density of government. As the population grew, more markedly in some areas than others, and as new problems of managing the increased size of the local population developed (such as maintaining people in employment, caring for the poor, or more generally maintaining law and order), so the institutions of local government needed to adjust in order to accommodate these changes. Such developments are part of the reason behind the trend towards increased oligarchy in some branches of local government in the late sixteenth and early seventeenth centuries, and the dominance of certain local offices by a smaller group of urban or village notables, which in turn helped reconfigure the contours of institutional politics and redefine the politics of exclusion. Then we have the issue of the density of political ideologies; again there are clear differences here that need to be traced between the 1450s, say, and the 1530s, 1640s, 1680s, 1760s or the early nineteenth century. Framing our discussion in terms of an analysis of the density of political space can also help us understand why the containment strategies adopted by the ruling elite for dealing with the political activities of those out-of-doors changed over time.

Finally, approaching our subject in this manner also helps free us from Whiggish notions of an ineluctable progress towards some higher plain, or of a rising crescendo, where popular politics eventually reaches its most sophisticated or intense point after years of development and growth. Some of the factors we need to consider in our discussion of popular politics obviously tended to grow denser over the long term: population, the media, channels of communication, to name the most obvious candidates. But others might not have done, or at least might not have done in the short term. The density of political ideologies or domestic contention might have been at a lower level at some later period of time than they had been earlier. For example, the intensity of political controversy and engagement out-of-doors was arguably greater in the 1640s than it was to be for some time – at least, perhaps, until the Exclusion Crisis. The 1760s was another peak: the density of political ideologies or domestic contention in this decade may or may not have exceeded that of the 1640s or even the Exclusion era, but it was certainly greater than it had been for much of the early Hanoverian period.

Exactly how much mileage there might be to employing the metaphor of density is perhaps best left to readers of this book and future researchers to decide. What is certain is that we should not see the politics of the excluded that happened earlier in the English past as in some ways an inferior creature to that which happened later. What we need is an explanatory model that can accommodate change over time without belittling the political experiences, activities and concerns of the lower orders in whatever period of time we are looking at. This volume, we hope, shows why these need to be taken seriously by historians, and not only suggests ways in which the politics of the excluded may be recreated historically, but also why we should not regard these types as having been excluded from politics in the first place.

NOTES

1. Adam Fox, 'Rumour, News and Popular Political Opinion in Elizabethan and Early Stuart England', *HJ*, XL (1997), 597.
2. The term 'excluded' has been invoked in this way by a number of historians interested in recapturing the political culture of those below the level of the ruling elite. Nicholas Rogers, *Crowds, Culture and Politics in Georgian Britain* (Oxford, 1998), p. 256, embraces the term 'the politically excluded' in his discussion of the Queen Caroline crowds of 1820. John Brewer, *Party Ideology and Popular Politics at the Accession of George III* (Cambridge, 1976), pp. 141, 160, writing of the 1760s, challenges the notion that the 'political nation' should 'be limited to the parliamentary classes', but suggests it should be 'extended to include those of much humbler origin who were either literate or politically interested' but who were 'frequently excluded from the processes of institutional politics'.
3. Tim Harris, *London Crowds in the Reign of Charles II: Propaganda and Politics from the Restoration until the Exclusion Crisis* (Cambridge, 1987), pp. 15–22; Tim Harris, 'The Problem of "Popular Political Culture" in Seventeenth-Century London', *History of European Ideas*, X (1989), 43–58.
4. John Morrill, *The Revolt of the Provinces: Conservatives and Radicals in the English Civil War, 1630–1650* (Harlow, 1980), p. 22.
5. E. J. Hobsbawm, *Primitive Rebels* (London, 1959), pp. 7, 110, 121.
6. J. R. Jones, *The Revolution of 1688 in England* (London, 1972), p. 306.
7. Buchanan Sharp, *In Contempt of all Authority: Rural Artisans and Riot in the West of England, 1586–1660* (London, 1980), p. 8.
8. Keith Lindley, *Fenland Riots and the English Revolution* (London, 1982), pp. 65, 139, 257–8. For criticism of Lindley's conclusions, see C. Holmes, 'Drainers and Fenmen: the Problem of Popular Political Consciousness in the Seventeenth Century', in Anthony Fletcher and John Stevenson (eds), *Order and Disorder in Early Modern England* (Cambridge, 1995), pp. 166–95.
9. Roger B. Manning, *Village Revolts: Social Protest and Popular Disturbances in England, 1509–1640* (Oxford, 1988), p. 3.

10. See especially George Rudé, *The Crowd in History: A Study of Popular Disturbances in France and England, 1730–1848* (New York, 1964); George Rudé, *Paris and London in the Eighteenth Century: Studies in Popular Protest* (London, 1970); E. P. Thompson, 'The Moral Economy of the English Crowd in the Eighteenth Century', in his *Customs in Common* (New York, 1991), pp. 185–258; Brian S. Manning, *The English People and the English Revolution* (London, 1976, 2nd edn, 1991).

11. As exemplified by Wayne Te Brake, *Shaping History: Ordinary People in European Politics, 1500–1700* (Berkeley, 1998).

12. John Horton, 'Political Philosophy and Politics', in Adrian Leftwich (ed.), *What is Politics? The Activity and its Study* (Oxford, 1984), p. 112.

13. Adrian Leftwich, 'Politics: People, Resources and Power', in Leftwich (ed.), *What is Politics?*, pp. 63, 64–5. Emphases in original.

14. Keith Wrightson, 'The Politics of the Parish in Early Modern England', in Paul Griffiths, Adam Fox and Steve Hindle (eds), *The Experience of Authority in Early Modern England* (Basingstoke, 1996), pp. 10–46 (quote on p. 11).

15. David Cressy, *Literacy and the Social Order: Reading and Writing in Tudor and Stuart England* (Cambridge, 1980), figs on pp. 72–3; R. S. Schofield, 'Dimensions of Illiteracy, 1750–1850', *Explorations in Economic History*, X (1972–3), 437–54 (esp. pp. 445–6, 449–50).

16. Keith Lindley, *Popular Politics and Religion in Civil War London* (Aldershot, 1997), p. 4; Dagmar Freist, *Governed by Opinion: Politics, Religion and the Dynamics of Communication in Stuart London, 1637–1645* (London, 1997).

17. Harris, *London Crowds*, chs 5–7.

18. Kathleen Wilson, *The Sense of the People: Politics, Culture and Imperialism in England, 1715–1785* (Cambridge, 1995), p. 29; Brewer, *Party Ideology*, pp. 140, 150, 160. It is not that the historians mentioned in this section would themselves hold to the view that popular politics arose first in the metropolis, and then only later spread to the provinces, as the people who could read were taught their politics by pamphlets and newspapers. Rather, I merely mean to suggest their work might seem to lend support to those who are inclined to believe that this was, indeed, the way the process worked.

19. Jürgen Habermas, *The Structural Transformation of the Public Sphere: An Enquiry into a Category of Bourgeois Society*, trans. Thomas Burger with the assistance of Frederick Lawrence (Cambridge, Mass., 1989).

20. David Underdown, *Revel, Riot and Rebellion: Popular Politics and Culture in England, 1603–1660* (Oxford, 1985).

21. This is a point I argue at greater length in my 'Understanding Popular Politics in Restoration Britain', in Alan Houston and Steven C. A. Pincus (eds), *A Nation Transformed?* (Cambridge, forthcoming). See also Anthony Fletcher and Diarmaid MacCulloch, *Tudor Rebellions* (4th edn, London, 1997), p. 118; Andy Wood, 'The Place of Custom in Plebeian Political Culture: England, 1550–1800', *Social History*, XXII (1997), 46–60.

22. In addition to the chapters by Ethan Shagan and Alastair Bellany in this volume, see: Fox, 'Rumour and Popular Political Opinion'; Thomas Cogswell, 'Underground Verse and the Transformation of Early Stuart Political Culture', in Susan Amussen and Mark A. Kishlansky (eds), *Political Culture and Cultural Politics in Early Modern England* (Manchester, 1995), pp. 277–300; Thomas Cogswell, 'The Politics of Propaganda: Charles I and the People in the 1620s', *JBS*,

XXIX (1990), 187–215; Richard Cust, 'News and Politics in Early Seventeenth-Century England', *P & P*, CXII (1986), 60–90.

23. Cf. John Walter, *Understanding Popular Violence in the English Revolution: The Colchester Plunderers* (Cambridge, 1999), pp. 21–2.

24. See also: Thompson, 'Moral Economy'; John Walter and Keith Wrightson, 'Dearth and the Social Order in Early Modern England', in Paul Slack (ed.), *Rebellion, Popular Protest and the Social Order in Early Modern England* (Cambridge, 1984), pp. 108–28; Harris, *London Crowds*, ch. 7; Wood, 'Place of Custom'; John Bohstedt, *Riots and Community Politics in England and Wales, 1790–1810* (Cambridge, Mass., 1983), esp. ch. 1; Charles Tilly, 'Collective Violence in European Perspective', in Hugh Davis Graham and Ted Robert Gurr (eds), *The History of Violence in America: Historical and Comparative Perspectives* (New York, 1969), p. 10.

25. Nevertheless, Robert Tittler, *The Reformation and the Towns in England: Politics and Political Culture, c.1540–1640* (Oxford, 1998) detects a trend towards oligarchy in towns of middling size during this time period.

26. Keith Wrightson, 'Two Concepts of Order: Justices, Constables and Jurymen in Seventeenth-Century England', in John Brewer and John Styles (eds), *An Ungovernable People: The English and their Law in the Seventeenth and Eighteenth Centuries* (London, 1980), esp. pp. 26–7; Harris, *London Crowds*, pp. 19–21; James Sharpe, 'The People and the Law', in Barry Reay (ed.), *Popular Culture in Seventeenth-Century England* (London, 1985), pp. 244–70.

27. Rogers, *Crowds, Culture and Politics*, p. 13; Colin Lucas, 'The Crowd and Politics between Ancien Régime and Revolution in France', *JMH*, LX (1988), 432–9.

28. Roger L'Estrange, *The Observator in Dialogue*, 3 vols (London, 1684–7), III, no. 5, 19 Feb. 1685.

29. Rosari Villari, 'The Rebel', in Rosari Villari (ed.), *Baroque Personae*, trans. Lydia G. Cochrane (Chicago, 1995), p. 102; Hans Speier, 'The Rise of Public Opinion', in Harold D. Lasswell, Daniel Lerner and Hans Speier (eds), *Propaganda and Communication in World History*, vol. II: *Emergence of Public Opinion in the West* (Honolulu, 1980), pp. 158–9.

30. Harris, *London Crowds*, pp. 70–2, 194; K. J. Lindley, 'Riot Prevention and Control in Early Stuart London', *TRHS*, 5th series, 33 (1983), 118–19, 123–4.

31. David Cressy, *Bonfires and Bells: National Memory and the Protestant Calendar in Elizabethan and Stuart England* (London, 1989), pp. 134–8, 152–5, 175–84; David Cressy, 'The Protestant Calendar and the Vocabulary of Celebration in Early Modern England', *JBS*, XXIX (1990), 43–7; Harris, *London Crowds*, pp. 93, 103–6, 120–1, 123–4, 157, 159, 163, 180, 186–7.

32. Lindley, 'Riot Prevention', p. 124.

33. For useful introductions to the first two, see Fletcher and MacCulloch, *Tudor Rebellions*, pp. 17–49. For Jacobitism, see in particular Paul Kléber Monod, *Jacobitism and the English People, 1688–1788* (Cambridge, 1989).

34. Walter and Wrightson, 'Dearth and the Social Order'.

35. John Walter, 'Grain Riots and Popular Attitudes to the Law: Maldon and the Crisis of 1629', in Brewer and Styles (eds), *Ungovernable People*, pp. 47–84; Thompson, 'Moral Economy'.

36. Fletcher and MacCulloch, *Tudor Rebellions*, pp. 121–2, 125.

37. See my forthcoming *British Revolutions*, to be published by Penguin.

38. Sharon L. Jansen, *Political Protest and Prophecy under Henry VIII* (Wood-bridge, 1991), pp. 57–71, 153–4.
39. Ethan Shagan, 'Protector Somerset and the 1549 Rebellions: New Sources and New Perspectives', *EHR*, CXIV (1999), 47.
40. J. A. W. Gunn, *Beyond Liberty and Property: The Process of Self-Recognition in Eighteenth-Century Thought* (Kingston, Ontario, 1983), p. 260. The earliest usage of the term 'public opinion' cited in the *OED* is by Viscount Boling-broke in 1735. The concept of public opinion is much earlier, however, though it went by a different name; according to the *OED*, the term 'common opinion' dates back to the fifteenth century.
41. Derek Hirst, *The Representative of the People? Voters and Voting in England under the Early Stuarts* (Cambridge, 1975), pp. 18–19; Rogers, *Crowds, Culture and Politics*, pp. 216–17; James Vernon, *Politics and the People: A Study in English Political Culture, c.1815–1867* (Cambridge, 1993), p. 17.
42. Robert B. Shoemaker, 'The London "Mob" in the Early Eighteenth Century', *JBS*, XXVI (1987), 285; Robert B. Shoemaker, *Gender in English Society, 1650–1850: The Emergence of Separate Spheres?* (London, 1998), pp. 233–7. For female involvement in the London weavers' riots of 1675, see Harris, *London Crowds*, pp. 193, 196. For female involvement in food riots and anti-enclosure riots, see: Thompson, 'Moral Economy', pp. 233–6; E. P. Thompson, 'The Moral Economy Reviewed', in his *Customs in Common*, pp. 259–351 (esp. pp. 305–36); Walter, 'Grain Riots'; R. A. Houlbrooke, 'Women's Social Life and Common Action in England from the Fifteenth Century to the Eve of the Civil War', *Continuity and Change*, I (1986), 171–89; John Bohstedt, 'Gender, Household and Community Politics: Women in English Riots, 1790–1810', *P&P*, CXX (1988), 88–122.
43. Antonia Fraser, *The Weaker Vessel* (New York, 1985), pp. 235–43; Patricia Higgins, 'The Reactions of Women, with Special Reference to Women Peti-tioners', in Brian Manning (ed.), *Politics, Religion and the English Civil War* (London, 1973), pp. 179–222.
44. Alan Marshall, *The Age of Faction: Court Politics, 1660–1702* (Manchester, 1999), pp. 49–54; Anne Stott, ' "Female Patriotism": Georgiana, Duchess of Devonshire, and the Westminster Election of 1784', *Eighteenth-Century Life*, XVII (November, 1993), 60–84.
45. A historiographical tendency noted by Rogers, *Crowds, Culture and Politics*, p. 216, though one which Rogers himself seeks to challenge.
46. Keith Thomas, 'The Meaning of Literacy in Early Modern England', in Gerd Baumann (ed.), *The Written Word: Literacy in Transition* (Oxford, 1986), pp. 100–3; Barry Reay, 'The Context and Meaning of Popular Literacy: Some Evidence from Nineteenth-Century Rural England', *P&P*, CXXXI (1991), 113–15.
47. Rogers, *Crowd, Culture and Politics*, p. 226.
48. Tim Harris, *Politics under the Later Stuarts: Party Conflict in a Divided Society, 1660–1715* (London, 1993), p. 191.
49. Wood, below (Chapter 3 in this volume), pp. 81, 84; Harris, *London Crowds*, p. 193, n. 24; Rogers, *Crowds, Culture and Politics*, pp. 215–23.
50. Sharon L. Jansen, *Dangerous Talk and Strange Behavior: Women and Popular Resistance to the Reforms of Henry VIII* (New York, 1996).
51. Harris, *London Crowds*, p. 51.

52. Steven C. A. Pincus, ' "Coffee Politicians Does Create": Coffeehouses and Restoration Political Culture', *JMH*, LXVII (1995), 807–34.

53. Richard Ashcraft, *Revolutionary Politics and Locke's 'Two Treatises of Government'* (Princeton, 1986), p. 468.

54. I. M. W. Harvey, 'Was there Popular Politics in Fifteenth-Century England?', in R. H. Britnell and A. J. Pollard (eds), *The McFarlane Legacy: Studies in Late Medieval Politics and Society* (New York, 1995), pp. 155–74 (quote on p. 169). See also her *Jack Cade's Rebellion of 1450* (Oxford, 1991).

55. See especially Steven Justice, *Writing and Rebellion: England in 1381* (Berkeley, 1994).

56. Pincus, 'Coffeehouses and Restoration Political Culture'.

57. Shagan, 'Somerset', p. 47.

58. Harvey, 'Was There Popular Politics?', quote on p. 156.

59. Rogers, *Crowds, Culture and Politics*, p. 234.

60. Brewer, *Party Ideology*, pp. 158–9.

2

RUMOURS AND POPULAR POLITICS IN THE REIGN OF HENRY VIII*

Ethan H. Shagan

To the people of Norfolk who flirted with heresy in 1530 upon rumours 'that the king's pleasure is that the New Testament in English should go forth',[1] or to the Yorkshire commons who rebelled in 1536 upon rumours that their 'churches should be pulled down',[2] the term 'popular politics' would have made little sense. They had different idioms with which to describe their activities, idioms peppered with the vocabulary of sanctification and the common weal. Politics and rumour, moreover, were starkly separated in contemporary minds, or at least in the minds of the educated elite. Politics was the process by which the nation's 'natural' rulers maintained the social order and good government; rumour was 'the infamy and slander of the common people', spread by those whom 'God hateth and hath banished . . . [from] his most glorious sight'.[3]

Yet something that we would call popular politics was everywhere in the early Reformation, and rumours were the stuff of popular politics. In every village and town, the decrees of the government and the responses of Romanists and reformers were received and interpreted through the filters of oral communication. Through rumour, prophecy, ballad, street theatre and a variety of other genres, England's non-elites evolved their own languages for describing contemporary events. These were necessarily oblique languages whose political significance could *in extremis* be denied; only occasionally did metaphors fall away to reveal naked opinion, and the purveyors of such opinion risked execution if they misjudged the political winds. Yet this obliqueness should not prevent us from appreciating the power of rumours as mechanisms through which ordinary people could comment upon their political circumstances. Rumours could spur people to take up arms or to hide their heads; they could show solidarity between neighbours or exacerbate bitter local conflicts. Regardless of people's individual beliefs, rumours were a medium through which communities monitored their own vital signs, canvassing beliefs and reactions and testing the boundaries of the sayable.[4]

This chapter is a preliminary attempt to foreground popular politics in our understanding of the Henrician Reformation, taking as our subject the myriad political rumours of the 1530s. The content of many of these rumours is familiar: the pulling down of churches, the imposition of new taxes, the death of the king. They have been seen, in so far as they have been noticed, as evidence for a massive undercurrent of antipathy towards government innovations. And indeed, there is no question that the upheavals of the 1530s produced a prodigious quantity of rhetoric highly critical of the regime. But if we analyse rumours not just for their content but also with an eye to the intricacies of their transmission, we can move past this rather simple-mindedly 'revisionist' understanding of popular politics and see something of the public debate that raged over the meaning of Henry VIII's many-faceted revolution.

Since rumours were first and foremost a medium through which ideas were moulded and transmitted, the first part of this chapter will explore the functioning of that medium and the ways in which it could express highly sophisticated political ideas, allowing for the circulation of those ideas on a regional or even national level. By exploring two rumours in depth, analysing first the lines of a rumour's transmission and then the variety of political connotations that a rumour could assume, we will consider the level to which ordinary English subjects could participate in public debate. As will be seen, the protean character of rumours allowed individuals to express their opinions about Church and state by either changing a rumour's wording or surrounding the core content of a rumour with their own gloss; every person in the chain of a rumour's transmission thus participated to some degree in the creation of a popular political discourse. Such evidence belies the claims of historians who have seen early modern English people as essentially 'pre-political', lacking the communications to develop political understanding at anything higher than the local level.[5]

The second part of this chapter will build upon these ideas by exploring how anti-government rumours were received by those who heard them, and thus how they fitted into a wider popular-political framework. Rumours, it will be argued, were not a closed system whose significance can be unambiguously reconstructed from their content alone. Rather, the purveyors of rumours were in constant dialogue with their consumers, a dialogue which at times turned those consumers into rumour-pedlars themselves but at other times produced reactions ranging from apathy to revulsion. If we study not merely the rumours themselves but the reactions they produced, we can begin to glimpse a more vibrant and contested popular political culture than that which revisionist historians of the Reformation, with their emphasis on 'popular conservatism' and 'popular resistance', would have us understand.[6] The uttering of rumours against the king and his policies was, at least in some sense, a 'conservative' act as the revisionists use the term. But it was also in a very real sense as subversive as the policies it opposed, and the debate between these different readings of 'conservatism' was at the heart of the process by which English people negotiated the changes of the 1530s. Elucidating these processes can both demonstrate the complexity of popular politics and suggest that we need to reconsider the historiographical commonplace that has equated conservatism, Catholicism and resistance.

I

To begin with, it is necessary to lay popular beliefs aside and simply focus on the ways in which rumours spread. This is an essential prerequisite to a more complex analysis of their political significance, since for rumours the medium itself was, if not 'the message', then at least the factor that enabled their political viability. What made rumours so important was that they were *unofficial*, spreading and changing along channels that were not only independent of the royal government but were uncontrolled and uncontrollable. It was exactly this freedom of movement that made rumours 'political', since every person spreading them was implicated in the creation of their meaning. Rumour-mongers might, when caught, claim only to have repeated what they had heard, and this plausible deniability was an important factor in keeping rumours afloat. But it was also a sham. People heard a great many unconfirmed reports on highways and in alehouses but chose carefully which stories they repeated and the manner in which they repeated them.[7]

The best way to approach these issues is through the detailed analysis of a single example: the rumour in 1536–7, which helped ignite the Pilgrimage of Grace, that the government would plunder and tear down parish churches. The standard version of this rumour's outbreak, described in detail by Margaret Bowker, is as follows. Between 23 and 26 September 1536, an official of the archdeaconry of Lincoln called

John Pryn, and his registrar Peter Effard, were proving wills and carrying out other routine activities in and around the Lincolnshire towns of Caistor and Louth. However, with other commissioners due to arrive in a few days' time and tensions running high after Bishop Longland's rapid implementation of the king's radical new injunctions, the visit became anything but routine. According to William Morland, a monk of Louth Park recalling events after the Pilgrimage of Grace, it was Peter Effard who first brought the horrifying word that the government was about to confiscate chalices from parish churches and that there should be only one parish church within every six or seven miles. Since he was a former mayor of Lincoln and an experienced diocesan official, his story was widely believed and a panic was created. By 1 October, the eve of the expected arrival of the subsidy and suppression commissioners, the vicar of Louth preached a fiery sermon warning the people to beware of the crown's predations, and the people of Louth instituted a twenty-four-hour guard around their church. The next day the Lincolnshire rebellion exploded, and the large number of priests who had gathered at Caistor and Louth to receive the episcopal visitors took the rumours back with them to their own towns and villages.[8] In this version of the rumour, then, 'popular politics' is very hard to find; the rumour was planted by a member of the county elite and led to such universal accept-ance and rapid and unified action that the people spreading the rumour after Effard seem to have exercised little more agency than telegraph wires.

This narrative, however, immediately begs certain questions. Most importantly, why was Peter Effard, who certainly should have known better, telling this rumour during his tour of Lincolnshire? Did he simply make it up to start a panic? Did he construct it logically out of facts at his disposal and believe it to be true? In this case, there turns out to be a trick answer: Effard did not really invent the rumour at all, nor even introduce it to Louth. It is true that, in one of his depositions, William Morland said that the rumour 'came of a word that one Peter, scribe to Doctor Prynne . . . did say at Louth at the commissaries' court there, this examinate hearing the same'.[9] However, in another deposition taken some days earlier, the same William Morland had told a subtly but crucially differ-ent version of the story: 'He sayth that during this time of his being at Kedington and thereabouts *upon a 3 weeks before Michaelmas* a great rumour was busily spoken of, *specially* after the commissaries' visitation kept at Louth church . . . by one Master Peter . . . that the chalices of parish churches should be taken away, and there should be but one parish church within 6 or 7 miles.'[10] Here, then, Effard was not inventing a story but merely repeating commonly available rumours. Three weeks before Michaelmas, moreover, was 8 September, or more than three weeks before the outbreak of the rebellion.

Once this initial confusion is resolved, other manuscript evidence for the earlier circulation of the rumour is quickly forthcoming. The most ambitious claim for the rumour's antiquity came from a man called Bernard Fletcher, who reported that 'about 8 weeks afore the insurrection or thereabouts he heard it bruited that the chalices and other jewels of the church should be taken away and in the lieu of them they should have chalices of tin'.[11] This claim of eight weeks is exceptional, but claims of the rumour circulating a month before the outbreak of violence are commonplace. Nicholas Leche, parson of Belchford, said that the rumours were well known 'upon a month before the insurrection'.[12] George Haddyswell of Horkstow heard the rumour 'a month before the insurrection or thereabouts', and also heard it commonly reported that 'all the gold coined and uncoined should be brought to the tower to be touched' and that no children would be christened without tribute to the king.[13] 'A fortnight before the insurrection' Bryan Stanes of Miningsby heard both about the chalices and that 'the king's officers would take away all their corn and cattle'.[14] Philip Trotter of Horncastle gave perhaps the most vivid description of the rumour's early circulation:

> He sayth that it was commonly bruited in every place a month before the insurrection that there was no remedy for the redress of the causes above expressed, that is to say for taking away the church goods and other things, but only by insurrection and to beat them down to the ground that would attempt any of the same causes. And this respondent being demanded where he heard this thing bruited, he sayth he being a mercer travelled from market to market, and there he heard this bruit.[15]

This last comment, that the rumour was heard at market and transmitted by local merchants, is crucial since it implies that even this extraordinary rumour circulated in quite ordinary ways. Much other evidence bears out this inference. The monk William Morland, for instance, reported that on Michaelmas he had dined at the town of Grimsby with 'a very tall man, having a tall woman to his wife'. Later in the evening more people arrived in the house, including a sailor from Hull, who was asked the inevitable question: 'What news with you?' He responded: 'We hear at Hull that ye should have a visitation here shortly and therefore we have taken all our church plate and jewels and sold them, and paved our town withal.'[16] Such transmission of the rumours through ordinary social channels, whether between strangers or between friends, was typical. Henry Thornbek, cellarer of Barlings Abbey, heard the rumours 'noised by diverse men' on Michaelmas Day 'at a fair kept at Swaton beside Sleaford'; fairs were a natural place for overtly political rumours to mix with the usual gossip and tall tales.[17] And the vicar of Louth reported first hearing the rumour from, among others, one William Man 'that singeth the bass in the choir at Louth'. We can only assume that casual conversation between these two men was not unusual.[18]

Here, then, we have a very different narrative of the rumour's outbreak from the one presented by Margaret Bowker. Rather than being planted by a single individual, it emerged gradually out of a morass of commonly circulating ideas about the king, his injunctions and the state of the Church. Rather than remaining unified, many different versions and glosses of the rumour circulated simultaneously, some fixated on chalices, others on the tearing down of churches, still others on the government's attacks on more secular wealth. The rumours are significant not in their origins but in their movement and repetition, allowing individuals to express their fears, measure responses, and, in extreme cases like that of Philip Trotter, even suggest solutions. Peter Effard quickly becomes a marginal figure in this story, but the point is that he would have been marginal even if he had really invented the rumours. Inventing a rumour is the most insignificant of acts. Most rumours fail to spread, however, because they are not integrated into a community's discourse. Such integration is only possible when a rumour is constructed out of elements already present, allowing people a new and legitimized way of saying things already in their minds.

Over the next four months, as rebellion ebbed and flowed across the north of England, stories of the tearing down of churches and the plunder of their wealth spread quickly over vast distances. Roughly similar stories can be found exciting the rebels throughout Yorkshire, Northumberland, Cumberland, Lancashire and other places as well.[19] One can imagine that at least in some cases the rumours spread much as they had in Lincolnshire, through merchants travelling the roads and people greeting each other with the query: 'What news?' However, as the rebellion took hold a number of more coherent and systematic mechanisms were also created for conveying the same basic information. A friar called Robert Esch, for instance, was given the job of composing, copying and circulating manuscript bills, many of which specifically referred to the government's plan to pull down churches.[20] These bills were both delivered to individuals and nailed up in public places for general perusal. Messengers were also employed by the rebels: two canons from Lincolnshire travelled to Yorkshire as *agents provocateurs*, announcing at the Tabard Inn in Beverley that Lincolnshire had risen for 'the wealth of holy church'.[21] In the visual media, at least one version of the rebellion's banner contained a picture of a chalice, which according to Philip Trotter of Horncastle was intended to remind people 'that the chalices, crosses and jewels of the church should be taken away'.[22]

A fundamentally different process was at work here than in the more organic transmission of the rumours before the rebellion's outbreak, a difference created by the 'official' nature of the information being transmitted. Organized efforts to spread news had pretensions to respectability: the king himself used circular letters, banners and proclamations, and by co-opting these media the rebellion attempted to turn free-flowing rumour into something much more precise and controllable. This was especially true of nailing up bills in public places, a practice which both evoked the power of the written word and mimicked the government's own method of spreading information; the potential effectiveness of such mimicry can be seen from a 1539 incident at Aylesford, Kent, where seditious bills were nailed to posts before dawn and the townsfolk mistook them for 'the king's grace's proclamations'.[23] There was a world of difference between hearing information from a local acquaintance or a travelling merchant in an alehouse and hearing that same information from a representative of 'the commons' or in a bill from the 'captain' of an ongoing rebellion. The latter scenario, while no less 'political', removed agency from the consumers of information by limiting their opportunity to recreate that information in their own image. This, then, is the difference between rumour and news, and our example well reflects that difference as it is currently understood by sociologists.[24] Rumour is unofficial or improvised news, whose claim to legitimacy depends more upon the resonance of its content than upon the reliability of its source. Of course, the same information can constitute both news and rumour at different times, as rumours are 'confirmed' by official agencies. Such confirmation does not necessarily make the information any more true, but it certainly changes its meaning. The story of the assault on the churches, then, became something very different when manipulated by the Pilgrimage's leaders.

Yet such manipulations were neither perfectly precise nor necessarily long-lived, and news circulating through the rebellion's 'official' channels was quickly transmuted into rumour again as it seeped outward beyond the limits of the rebellion itself. For instance, around Whitsuntide 1537 in the Oxfordshire town of Thame, the rumour was circulating that 'the king will have the crosses and jewels of our church'. Far from coming out of official sources, this rumour spread much as had the initial rumours in Lincolnshire. A man called John Strebilhill, for instance, first heard it spoken by one Robert Jons as they walked home from evensong; Jons suggested that '4 or 5 of the best [men] of the town' should get together to 'sell the best part of our jewels' before they could be taken away.[25] Similarly, at Shrewsbury in March a prominent newcomer to the community called Nicholas Holte heard the rumours as he was pub-crawling; at both 'the sign of the lion' and 'a tavern...called [the] sceptre' he heard aspects of the rumour 'that the king's grace would have but one church where now be 2...[and] in every parish church but one chalice'.[26]

In East Anglia the rumours seem to have been particularly rife. In Ipswich in March 1537, the two town bailiffs investigated a chantry priest called James Crawford who cut down over 500 young trees growing on chantry lands. When told that he might be deprived of his living for making such waste, he responded that he would rather sell the land than the king should have it.[27] In Norfolk in the spring of 1537 there were 'common false tales and sayings...that they must put away all their church and guild lands by the first day of May or else that the king's high-ness would seize them to his grace's own use forever'.[28] In the town of Aylsham accusations focused not only on the king but on parliament as well, with rumours that 'there was an act of parliament that if their church lands were not sold before Mayday the king would have it'.[29] Clearly the rumour's content was again free to evolve with local circumstances.

It is in Buckingham, however, that we can most clearly see the almost feverish movement of the rumour. The tale had first reached the town around Christmas 1536, but its dissemination gradually increased until by February it was in the mouths of 'a great multitude of people by reason of the fair, where this matter was hotly talked of'. The aggregate term 'multitude' can be analysed more closely in this case, since the gen-tlemen who investigated the rumour traced several lines of transmission. One such line concerned a 'barber's boy of Aylesbury' who reported to Mr Ralph Lane that 'the jewels of Aylesbury church should be fetched away'. The barber's boy admitted under questioning that he had heard the rumour from 'his dame', who in turn admitted hearing it 'at the common bakehouse'. She claimed not to have believed it, however, because the wife of the parish clerk had also been at the bakehouse and had denied that the rumour was true.[30]

More dramatic, however, was the information discovered by the authorities when they traced the rumour back to the bakehouse itself. Henry Robyns, servant to the Buckingham baker Edward Bylyng, gave the following description of the rumour's spread:

> The said deponent sayeth that he daily carryeth bread from Buckingham to Padbury and three towns more adjoining to Buckingham, and so from town to town to the number of thirteen towns of any side of Buckingham. And now of late ... many persons of the inhabitants of the said towns where he carried bread demanded of him at sundry comings whether Buckingham church was put down or not. To whence he answered nay, and sayeth further that like tales went upon Padbury church, that the lead thereof should also be conveyed to Aylesbury.

Here is more evidence of extraordinary communications along entirely ordinary local routes. Most astonishing, however, was one particular embroidery from a baker's servant called John Thornton, who said that 'if anybody went to put down the churches, that Mr. Thomas Gyfford of Twyford would send to Robert Gally of Buckingham ... that he should raise the country eight miles about Buckingham, to the intent to come to Buckingham with an hour's warning to take part with Buckingham to resist the pulling down of the church'. The transformation of a rumour from bald information to complex political posturing was but a simple step.[31]

When taken together, all of these details present a very clear picture. Political rumours, even when not presented in quasi-official forms, could and did circulate on a massive scale. Not only did these particular rumours spread through the entire north in association with the Pilgrimage of Grace, but they also circulated in at least six different midland counties without any apparent coaxing.[32] They circulated, moreover, in a form that was intrinsically and essentially free from government control, or indeed from any control at all; every person who channelled the rumour was free to manipulate its content and meaning, with the viability of their interpretation dependent only upon the resonance of that interpretation to the next person in the chain. Rumours were truly a medium of and by the people. And while we have avoided thus far discussing their political contents and meanings, it was exactly such political connotations that determined a rumour's viability. It is thus to the politics of rumours that we now turn.

II

The rumours of the plunder of churches are simply too big to permit a thorough study of their political content, not only because of their intrinsic complexity but because the 1536 rebellion warped their meaning, twisting them into uneasy alignment with a variety of only semi-related positions concerning agrarian policy, taxation and heresy. To analyse how rumours conveyed political meaning, we need instead a rumour that circulated on a comparable scale and was of comparable importance but that remained more or less constrained by its own subject matter. Just such a rumour circulated in the winter of 1537–8, bringing the electrifying report that Henry VIII was dead.

The rumour's chronology is worth recounting in some detail. The earliest probable account comes from a manuscript dated merely 'September', almost certainly September 1537, in which one Symond Wylkynson from Donnington, Lincolnshire, was accused of having told 'diverse persons' that the king was dead; several other people from the same village were already in the stocks for having spread the story.[33] The next reference to the rumour comes from a letter which John Babyngton, gentleman of Nottinghamshire, wrote to Thomas Cromwell on 18 October 1537: 'this day, the vigil of Saint Luke, I have heard tidings which I trust in God be untrue . . . which is here spoken, as God forbid, the king's highness Henry VIII to be departed from this present life.'[34] Then in late November, a variety of people in Leicestershire, including a harper and a chaplain, told the rumour to a visiting husbandman from Northamptonshire. The rumour was apparently ubiquitous in Leicestershire; when the visitor expressed scepticism and said that there was no such news where he came from, the harper replied: 'a great deal of wheat will not stop these mouths that say so here'.[35]

By December 1537, the rumour exploded into view all over England. In Berkshire, a dizzying array of husbandmen, tailors, weavers and servants were interrogated for having spread the rumour in and around the household of Sir John Norris.[36] In Oxford, a groom of the king's chamber and a goldsmith accused a servant of saying that 'the king's grace is dead'.[37] In Bedfordshire, a monk of Woburn Abbey reported that around Christmas 'one Dan Lawrence Bloneham raised conversation among them and said that the king's grace was departed this world'.[38] In Sussex, three friars at Lewes claimed to have heard the rumour from an alehouse keeper, while in Horsham the king's death was reported by 'a very simple person' called Peter ap Rythe.[39] In Kent, the wife of John Robyns told two local labourers that 'the king's grace was dead'.[40]

By January 1538 the rumour had also spread to the west country, where it was heard in Gloucestershire and Dorset.[41] On 12 February, a woman named Agnes Davy spread the rumour in Carleforth, Suffolk.[42] In March, a variation on the tale was spread in Warwickshire.[43] As late as June, even after the rumour appears to have died out in most places, it could still be found circulating in the Yorkshire parish of Kirkby Moorside.[44] In all, the rumour appeared in at least 15 different English counties between September 1537 and June 1538, including locations as far west as Gloucestershire, as far east as Suffolk, as far south as Sussex and Kent, and as far north as Yorkshire.

There is also voluminous evidence that this rumour circulated freely along its own channels rather than through conscious manipulation. In Kent, for instance, a fisherman called Thomas Graunte heard the rumour from a merchant travelling along the roads; being a practitioner of a semi-itinerant profession himself, Graunte contributed to the rumour's spread by telling it door-to-door as he sold his daily catch.[45] In Leicestershire, the rumour was heard by two travellers from Northamptonshire who were visiting to consult with a 'wise man' about some property that had been stolen from them; they later took the rumour back with them to Northamptonshire, where one of the traveller's wives told the story to another traveller visiting from Huntingdonshire.[46] In Warwickshire, a woman called Phelypps heard the rumour 'of another woman as she came from the market, whom she had not seen before'.[47] Although the rumour itself may have been extraordinary, its paths of circulation were not.

Where, then, did such a rumour come from, and what did it mean? One possible explanation is that there may have been a 'kernel of truth' within it: Queen Jane did in fact die in the autumn of 1537 from complications arising from the delivery of Prince Edward. For Madeleine and Ruth Dodds, two of the most thorough historians of the period, there was no doubt that this was the source of the rumour: 'On the death of Queen Jane rumours had been blown abroad that both the king and the prince were dead as well.'[48] Yet in fact this chronology makes no sense. Jane died on 24 October, by which time the rumour was already circulating in Nottinghamshire and probably in Lincolnshire. Again, the genesis of popular rumours cannot be traced to discrete persons or events.

Rather, as the sociologist Jean-Noël Kapferer has written, they arise 'from a constructive process' in which members of a community 'put their intellectual resources together to arrive at a satisfying definition of reality'.[49] In this case, the particular 'intellectual resources' being energized were the ubiquitous discourses of magic and prophecy through which early modern English people constructed so much of their mental world.

In the years before the outbreak of the rumour, and indeed for some time afterwards, a flurry of prophecies predicted that the king would die.[50] For instance, one prophecy called the 'Prophecy of the Six Kings' or the 'Mouldwarp Prophecy', already at least a century old by the 1530s, was often used as a commentary on Henry VIII's reign. In this prophecy each of the six kings after King John was signified by an animal, ending with the 'mouldwarp' (a synonym for mole), a creature 'accursed of God's own mouth' and a 'great wretch'. The prophecy foretold that this mole would be forcibly driven from England by a dragon, a wolf and a lion (conventionally seen as three foreign monarchs), after which the nation would be divided into three parts. The mole, thus proved cowardly, would pass the rest of his life in sorrow on an island in the sea and would die by drowning.[51]

Problems of chronology notwithstanding, this prophecy was resurrected in the 1530s with Henry VIII in the starring role. As early as 1533, the prophetess Mistress Adamas was accused of saying 'that the king's grace is called in her book of prophecies the mouldwarp, and is cursed with God's own mouth'.[52] Two years later, the vicar of Isleworth was accused of using almost exactly the same language, saying that 'the king was molywarpe that Merlin prophesied that turned all up, and that the king was accursed of God's own mouth'.[53] In May 1537, Richard Bishop of Bungay, Suffolk, was accused of saying that 'he knew where was a certain prophecy ... and, if so be as the prophecy sayth, there shall be a rising of the people, this year or never. And that the prophecy sayth the king's grace was signified by a mole, and that the mole should be subdued and put down'.[54] In November 1536, a prisoner in an Exeter jail told a fellow inmate that he would be freed shortly by 'the general pardon given at the change of a head', for the king would either 'be killed or else driven forth of the land, and ... the saying is that he shall be driven of the land ... and then he shall be set in a place by the water and suddenly he shall be drowned'.[55]

Other prophecies also predicted Henry VIII's downfall and death. The prophecies of 'Rymour, Beid, and Marlyng', for instance, predicted the coming of a mysterious 'child with a chaplet' who would conquer

England, winning a horrific battle to claim the crown which was 'his right'. In this case, the prophecy presented the conqueror/child in an explicitly Catholic context, showing him travelling to Rome to be honored by the Pope.[56] Another prophecy came from the monks of Furness Abbey in Lancashire, many of whom openly supported the Pilgrimage of Grace, who predicted that 'in England shall be slain the decorate rose in his mother's belly' or, in an alternate version, 'the red rose should die in his mother's womb'.[57] This was interpreted to mean that the king, with his heraldic emblem of the red rose, would die by the hands of priests, since the church was the mother of the crown. Lay people could also use magic and prophecy against the regime. In January 1538, for instance, a woman called Mabel Brigge of Holderness, Yorkshire, was accused of holding a magical fast to bring about the death of the king. She called it a 'charitable fast', noting that she had fasted that way once before and the object of the fast had broken his neck. She hoped the same fate would befall '[those] that hath wrought all this business in this world, and that was the king and this false duke [of Norfolk]'. Mabel Brigge was executed in April 1538.[58]

There is strong evidence that the rumours of the king's death were moulded within this magical or prophetic rhetoric. Agnes Davy of Suffolk, for instance, was indicted for announcing 'that the king our sovereign lord was dead and that my lord prince was sick and almost dead and that the king of Scots would enter the north parts of the realm and the French king the south parts'.[59] This is clearly a version of the belief, common to the mouldwarp prophecy and several others, that England would be divided into several parts following the king's defeat. For Agnes Davy at least, news of the king's death indicated that prophecies were being fulfilled. In late December, a London woman told of the king's death as she had heard it from an old servant called Clerk: 'as the king sat upon his horse, h[e saw] God's marks upon his hand and kissed them, and said *Laudes Deo*, and aft[er he lay] 24 hours in a trance and departed . . . and [Clerk] said further, now we shall have a merry world.'[60] This language matches no extant prophecies but is clearly linked to a previous understanding of the king's death as some sort of fulfilment. And most significantly, when the rumour finally got to Yorkshire in June 1538, it was explicitly understood as the result of Mabel Brigge's fast. The parish priest of Kirkby Moorside told the parish clerk, 'I can tell you other news: the woman's prayer that was put to death at York hath light of one of them that we were talking upon the last week, for the king is dead.'[61]

We cannot know exactly how these prophetic influences were interpreted, and blaming the rumours on pre-existing prophecies does little
more than defer the unanswerable question of the rumours' origins.
The close relationship between rumour and prophecy, however, points
to a larger conclusion: the meanings of rumours cannot be judged by
their gross message, but rather depended upon subtle variations in both
content and context. When most people passed along the rumour that
the king was dead, they did so not merely in neutral or arbitrary form,
but rather interpreted the king's death for their listeners, either through
the words of the rumour itself or through their subsequent discussion of
its significance. In many depositions this language is preserved and
shows something of the way in which complex political ideas could be
vocalized through the use of rumour.

The most common gloss on the rumour of the king's death was that
a change in monarchs would mean an end to the oppressive taxation
that had characterized Henry VIII's reign. This spin on the rumour was
not an example of popular fantasy, but rather shows a complex understanding of the English constitution. Early modern lawyers held that the
government flowed directly from the person of the sovereign, so that
without a monarch the government ceased to function.[62] In particular,
taxes enacted by parliament were granted only for the use of a given
monarch and became void when that monarch died. A great many English people seem to have been aware of this fact in the winter of 1537–8.

For instance, Thomas Skey of Thornbury, Gloucestershire, first heard
the rumour of the king's death from a man named John Blake in January 1538. When Skey asked for more details, Blake replied that he had
heard the news at Dorchester but that it 'might not be yet known', that is
to say, the king's death was being kept a secret. When asked why, Blake
responded, 'They would gather the king's money first.' In this version of
the rumour, in other words, it was being bruited about that the king's
death was being kept secret until all outstanding taxes could be collected.[63] Similar language had been used in Lincolnshire three months
earlier when Symond Wylkynson of the town of Donnington 'said to
diverse persons that the king should be dead and that it must be in secret
kept till such time as my lord privy seal had levied the tax'.[64]

Several examples of this economic understanding of the king's death
can also be found in and around Kent. In December 1537, for instance, a
London woman travelling in Kent heard the rumour of the king's death
with a unique appendix: 'Now we shall have a merry world . . . [and] we
have had many payments for I have paid 2s of late.'[65] In this case, the

critical factor was not that the king's death was being hushed up, but that it would mean a reprieve from taxation for oppressed English subjects. Similar ideas appear in depositions from Higham, Kent, where the wife of a man named John Robyns said that 'about a fortnight before Christmas last past she heard [that]...the king's grace was dead and there should no more money be gathered'.[66] In Canterbury in late December, we again see an attempt to delay the payment of taxes until the news of the king's death was made official; the rumour was so rife that people were being told openly not to be 'hasty to pay your money, for the king is d[ead]'.[67]

Taxation also crept into the rhetoric of the king's death in the case of Thomas Graunte, a fisherman from Wingham, Kent, who first heard the news from a travelling merchant on the road from Dover. The merchant asked him, 'What tidings of the king's money?' and Graunte answered that in his locality the 'king's money', that is taxes, had all been paid. At this point, as if to tease the poor fisherman, the merchant let slip the news he had obviously been eager to tell: 'The king was dead.' The merchant's intent was apparently to play games with a poor yokel who had paid his money when he did not legally have to. In Graunte's hands, however, the rumour took on very different economic implications. He told his customers that they 'should have their money again, for I hear say that the king's grace should be dead, as God forbid it should'.[68] Again, as in Higham, the news was transmuted into a belief that good order would return to the kingdom and that people's wealth would be restored.

Reasons why economic policies were central to popular interpretations of the king's death are not hard to find. According to Michael Bush, the taxes of the 1530s were not only oppressive in their weight, but also seemed to many English people to be contrary to traditional practice and the ancient constitution. In particular, the simultaneous imposition of both subsidies and fifteenths, in a period of peace when the king was supposed to live off ordinary rather than extraordinary revenues, was highly irregular.[69] While some fiscal innovations of the period were curtailed in response to the Pilgrimage of Grace, many others were not, and the many real taxes levied by the government were augmented by a whole series of imaginary taxes rumoured to be imminent; in Yorkshire in early 1538, for instance, rumours of new 'plough nobles and poll groats' led at least some people to speak of a new rising.[70] Moreover, the subsidy grant of 1534 was still being collected in 1537, and clerical taxation remained at extraordinary levels.[71]

What is most important here, however, is not the evident opposition to taxation but the belief among some English people that Henry VIII was personally responsible for oppressive economic policies and that his death would alter them. In the Pilgrimage of Grace, the rebels went to great lengths to construct their grievances against 'evil counsellors' rather than the king himself. Lists of enemies of the commons often included Cromwell, Cranmer and Latimer, but only very rarely and obliquely was Henry VIII himself accused. Even the rumoured plundering of churches could be constructed against evil counsellors; when one man in Dent (Lancashire) called Henry VIII a thief, the rest of the crowd told him that it was 'not the king's deed but the d[eed] of Crumwell, and if we had him here we would crum him'.[72] Almost any rhetoric against royal policy left room for the claim that the king was a friend of the commons who had merely been seduced by evil advisers. Rumours of the king's death, however, permitted no such loophole. By the winter of 1537–8, perhaps as a result of the king's personal betrayal and repression of the northern rebels, it is apparent that something had changed. The heat of rhetoric had significantly increased, and at least within the comparatively deniable medium of rumour, some people were openly allowing themselves to consider the possible economic benefits of a new monarch.

But who would this monarch be? Besides economic interpretations, another complex of connotations and meanings that was immediately attached to the king's death related to the royal succession. Most significantly, there are several cases in which the rumour was expanded to include not only Henry himself but his son Edward as well. Early on, of course, this was not the case; Edward was not born until 12 October 1537, by which time rumours of the king's death were almost certainly spreading in Lincolnshire and Nottinghamshire. Within two months, however, a new dynamic had developed. At the end of November 1537, for example, the Northamptonshire husbandman John Petyfer travelled with a friend through Leicestershire, stopping in the town of Lutterworth with a local wheelwright named Pryst. In Pryst's house they met a harper named Harrison, who asked: 'What news hear you, John Petyfer, in your country?' When Petyfer answered that he had no news, Harrison responded: 'It is rumoured in this country that the king and the prince be both dead'. Petyfer did not immediately believe the tale, but when he heard an identical rumour at the next town on his itinerary he became convinced. Petyfer thus arrived home in Northamptonshire with the story that 'the king and the prince were departed', and this was the version that subsequently circulated in both Northamptonshire and Huntingdonshire.[73]

Similarly, Agnes Davy was indicted in Suffolk in February 1538 for spreading a version of the rumour that included both Henry and his son. As already noted, she said: 'that the king our sovereign lord was dead, and that my lord prince was sick and almost dead, and that the king of Scots would enter the north parts of the realm and the French king the south parts'.[74] By March 1538, furthermore, the death of the prince had replaced the death of the king completely in some accounts. In Warwickshire, for instance, a man named Phelypps announced that 'he had heard that the prince's grace . . . should be departed' without mentioning the king at all.[75]

Another incident regarding Edward's death, which may or may not have contributed directly to the rumours but was certainly part of the same political discourse, concerned a magical rite that took place in London. On 3 January 1538, a man called Fulk Vaughan observed a suspicious event in a churchyard near his house:

> He saw a number of people gazing upon a thing in the churchyard . . . and being desirous to know whereupon they looked, went unto them and then heard them say that it should be a child buried. And afterward this deponent sayth that the clerk of the church took out a piece of cloth knit like a winding sheet, and ripped it and found therein an image of wax made to the form of a young child, and 2 pins thrust in to it.

Vaughan, disturbed by this magic but unsure of its exact meaning, went to an expert named Pole and asked what it meant to bury the mutilated likeness of a child. Pole replied that it was 'made to waste one', and when pressed by Vaughan whether it was really possible to kill a person in such a way, Pole answered, 'That may be done well enough.'[76] Although it is not said explicitly in Vaughan's deposition, there can be no doubt that the wax image was made to represent Prince Edward. The investigation into the incident was led by the powerful trio of Thomas Wriothesley, Alderman Paul Withipol and Thomas Starkey, an indication that very large stakes were involved indeed.[77] Furthermore, an undated manuscript from Oxford contains a confession concerning what is undoubtedly the same event, describing 'an image of wax found in London way the which had a knife sticking through his eyes or his heart, representing the prince's person, and as that did consume so likewise should the prince'.[78]

It is clear, then, that the death of the prince was very much a hot topic in the winter of 1537–8. The significance of the inclusion of Edward within a discourse originally about the king alone is not hard to decipher. The birth of Edward in October 1537 was a crushing blow to Romanists who were counting on a Marian succession and who regarded the failure of Henry's second and third wives to provide him with sons as divine retribution for the divorce and the schism from Rome. Thus for religious conservatives, the meaning of a rumour of Henry's death changed dramatically after Edward's birth, no longer representing a delivery from danger but instead putting an infant on the throne with the possibility of a radical regency. In order for the news of the king's death to carry the same weight, Edward had to be included as well. Certain English people thus applied their own views of government and its proper functioning to the meaning of a popular rumour, using the medium itself as a way to present their own spin on political events to their fellow subjects.

A similar phenomenon can be found in another version of the rumour that indicated that the Marquis of Exeter, rather than Prince Edward, had died along with the king. This spin on the rumour first appeared in mid-December 1537, when the abbot of Reading wrote to Cromwell to report 'the most lamentablest and heaviest tidings that ever was heard to any one now living, that our most gracious king should be dead and the lord marquis of Exeter'.[79] When the matter was investigated by royal commissioners, they discovered that throughout the vicinity the rumour included the death of the marquis. Such news was reported by, among other people, John Sowthen (butler to Sir John Norris), Nicholas Wylkynson (servant to the abbot of Reading), Thomas Hynde (servant to Sir John Norris), John Mylche (a smith) and Thomas Barnes (whose identity is not known, but who told the rumour to two servants and a tailor).[80]

Why, nevertheless, would the Marquis of Exeter, of all people, have been included in the rumour? Henry Courtney, Marquis of Exeter and Earl of Devon, was Henry VIII's first cousin, grandson of Edward IV through princess Catherine, and is best known for his alleged involvement in a 1538 conspiracy to have himself named as Henry VIII's heir. Given his history, it is very odd that he would be included in a political rumour whose meaning, in the final analysis, involved a return to union with Rome that Exeter supported. However, at the end of 1537 the Exeter Conspiracy was still nearly a year away, and as with so many 'conservatives' in the 1530s, Courtney had associated himself closely with the regime. He subscribed to the articles against Wolsey in 1529, signed the letter to Pope Clement VII demanding the royal divorce in 1531, and acted as commissioner for the deposition of Catherine of Aragon in 1533. He was second in command to the Duke of Norfolk in the suppression of the Pilgrimage of Grace in Yorkshire, and in May 1537 he acted as Lord High Steward at the trial of one of the noble collaborators with the Pilgrimage, Lord Darcy. Regardless of his ties to conservatives at court, therefore, Exeter's public persona was clearly as a Henrician insider, one of the king's henchmen in securing the divorce and the break from Rome. Moreover, he was a semi-legitimate claimant to the crown who could have presented a female heir like Mary with a considerable challenge. The inclusion of Exeter in the rumour of the king's death, therefore, was probably similar to the inclusion of Edward: in order for the king's death to mean what certain elements in the country wanted it to mean, not only Henry but his entire radical regime had to be eliminated.[81]

In a variety of ways, therefore, the rumours of the king's death formed part of a popular political discourse concerning the future of the English crown. Certainly this discourse was much wider than the rumours alone, and English people found other ways of discussing the succession. The Kentishman Richard Oversole told a palemaker in 1538, for instance, that if anything happened to the king one of the Percies 'would be next to the crown'.[82] The parish priest of Brabourne, also in Kent, expressed his fear of a succession battle by saying that since Queen Jane 'was not crowned . . . there is like to be business in time to come'.[83] Yet such talk courted death, and it could not be forgotten that the highest peer in the realm, the Duke of Buckingham, had within living memory been summarily tried and executed for merely listening to a prophecy that he would inherit the throne. Rumours were a comparatively safe way for people to express their hopes and fears, since their inherent deniability allowed even quite radical views of the succession to be canvassed.

And it must be remembered how radical these views were. Anyone who considered excluding Prince Edward from the succession by imagining his death was going far beyond the pale of ordinary political discourse. Not only was Edward the legitimate heir by almost any standard, since his mother had married Henry VIII after both Catherine of Aragon and Anne Boleyn were dead, but the mere idea of imagining the death of an infant heir to the throne ran counter to every instinct in the early modern political imagination. The healthy birth of a male heir was what every subject prayed for and what every kingdom required to prevent the horrors of internecine war. A rumour of the prince's death only weeks after his birth struck at the very heart of the monarchy and shows the extent to which rumours could function as the rhetorical basis for the most violently anti-government political beliefs.

With its explicit comments on the crown's economic policies and the royal succession, the rumour of the king's death thus served as a vehicle through which a variety of complex political views could be expressed. Moreover, it is virtually impossible to imagine a politically innocent transmission of this rumour, since its mere uttering was certainly seditious and quite possibly treasonous. Yet in our discussion of the rumour we have thus far discussed only the beliefs and attitudes of the people who spoke it aloud, not the beliefs and attitudes of those to whom it was spoken. If it was seditious or treasonous to tell such a rumour, what was it to hear it told? With the rumour of the king's death, as with other political rumours in the 1530s, the full picture can only be seen when we expand our perspective and examine not merely the purveyors of rumours but their consumers as well. With the political complexity of the rumours now established, we can attempt to put them back into context and examine how they functioned within the political debates of ordinary English people.

III

The two rumours we have examined thus far are only a tiny fraction of the political rumours known to have circulated between 1535 and 1540. Other rumours included, but were not limited to: rumours of war, invasion or rebellion; rumours of new taxes on bread, pig, goose and capon; rumours of a ten per cent property tax on all goods; rumours of a duty on the export of cloth; rumours of a tribute to be paid to the king at every christening, marriage and burial; rumours that the king had gone on pilgrimage to St Michael's Mount; rumours that Cromwell had been named Henry VIII's heir; and rumours that Cromwell had fled the country or been killed. Having shown the extent to which such rumours can and should be viewed as explicitly political, these rumours would seem to provide excellent evidence for the 'revisionist' view of the Reformation, the idea that the Henrician Reformation was fundamentally 'unpopular' and that the nation's entrenched conservatism prevented Henry VIII and his heirs from altering the religious views of most English people. Yet when we look more closely, we find that the rumours actually provide evidence for a very different process at work. Certainly many people did oppose royal policy, and that was why the rumours spread. But 'conservatism' could cut in many ways, and it was by no means clear to everyone that certain types of political action – for instance, imagining the death of God's anointed representative on Earth – were particularly 'conservative' ways to behave.

If we begin our analysis where we left off, with the rumour of the king's death, it quickly becomes clear that the purveyors of the rumour did not meet with a uniformly positive response. Even when the rumour was not spoken with a particularly virulent gloss, it sometimes received a virulent response. The fisherman Thomas Graunte, for instance, seems to have been ambivalent about the rumour, happy to spread the uncon-firmed report yet at the same time saying 'God forbid' it should be true. Some of his neighbours, however, were outraged; two witnesses confirm that when Graunte told the news to Agnes King of Wingham, Kent, she replied: 'Take heed what you say, I will advise you, for if it were so all the realm should repent it.'[84] Similarly, when a stranger announced the king's death to Walter Byrdley and Symon Bettyrton in Dorchester, the two men responded quite differently. Byrdley went out to spread the rumour himself, but Bettyrton responded with anger, railing against the unfortunate stranger: 'Thou naughty knave, why sayest thou so? And if thou were in some places, thou wouldst be set by the heels.'[85] It is clear from the evidence that such words were really spoken rather than invented after the fact, since they were reported not by Bettyrton but by Byrdley. Already in these two cases, then, we can see a spectrum of local opinions. Some people spread the rumours enthusiastically, some spread them reluctantly, and some were horrified that they were spread at all.

Another example is the case of Maude Kebery of Lincolnshire. According to a report written by investigating officials, Kebery refused to admit spreading the rumour until her own mother confronted her in front of local magistrates and forced her to confess:

> There was also now Maude Kebery, who they said first did report the said words, then denied the same before us, that she neither said them nor no other, saving that she said, 'God save his grace'. [Then] her mother before her face said that she said she heard say he was dead, and then the said Maude confessed that she heard it spoken in the street, and of whom she would not confess.

This case may not involve 'politics' at anything higher than the family level, but it certainly shows how the complexity of local disputes could shatter the consistency of any anti-royal rhetoric.[86]

In cases where the local political connotations of the rumour are more obvious, we can see clearly how the arrival of the rumour could divide

communities. At Higham, for instance, the wife of John Robyns reported
that two weeks before Christmas 1537 she had heard a man named
William Thurston say that 'the king's grace was dead and there should
no more money be gathered'. This was clearly a spin on the rumour that
was highly radical in its willingness to blame the king himself rather than
his counsellors for economic mismanagement. Other people, however,
managed to twist their reading of the rumour into a much less seditious
form without losing its basic economic flavour. John Robyns, for
instance, claimed only that Thurston had said 'that the king's grace had
remit and forgiven the fifteenth', while the version recalled by the
labourer Richard Hall was that 'the king's grace's will was that no more
money should be gathered, and that money the which was gathered
already should be restored again amongst the poor people'. Here all
notion of the king's death has disappeared, and we witness the apotheosis of the king into a popular hero for returning previously gathered
taxes to the people. Significantly, no one suggests that their taxes were
not too high; everyone here is in some sense conservative. But a reading
is available that permits strong pro-Henrician sentiment in the locality.[87]

The most colourful case of local dispute surrounding this particular
rumour comes from the parish of Kirkby Moorside in Yorkshire. Early
in the morning of Whitmonday 1538, a young man named William
Wood arrived in chapel before matins and overheard a shockingly seditious conversation. The parish clerk, Robert Lyon, informed the parish
priest, Sir Robert Keriby, that the king was dead. The priest responded
with venom, saying (apparently in reference to the suppression of the
Pilgrimage of Grace): 'Vengeance must needs light upon him because he
hath put so many men wrongfully to death.' The clerk answered in kind,
saying: 'If Crumwell were dead also it would not half a penny lose, for ye
shall hear much mischief among them therefor.' The priest then
concluded in grand fashion, responding: 'If any of the great men had
had a switch at the king's neck a twelvemonth since, before this business
began, he should have had small peril for it.'[88]

William Wood, horrified by what he had overheard, revealed himself
to the priest and the clerk and told them: 'Your communication is
naught for to be heard, for there is many more in the south parts hath
been put to death for less saying than this.' He then grabbed another
man who was in the chapel at the time and asked him to bear witness
with him to what the two traitors had said. Having thus secured a second
witness, Wood made clear his intentions to inform the authorities.[89]
The priest and the clerk, realizing that their lives were now in serious

jeopardy, tried a variety of tactics to keep Wood's mouth shut. The priest first tried threatening him, saying: 'Know that [if] thou go out of this dale to show anything that we have said either to knight or justice, I shall have of thee either a leg or an arm.'[90] The clerk tried the opposite tactic, trying to make friends with Wood by asking him to 'tarry and drink' before he left.[91] Most interestingly, the priest tried playing to localist solidarity to prevent Wood, who was apparently a drifter recently returned from London, from informing on them. The priest pulled aside Wood's uncle, complained that the young William was a 'vagabond' and said: 'it was better that he, the said William Wood, had a mischief rather then he should hurt any neighbour for ought that we have said'.[92] It is certainly possible that Wood made up this entire story; the justices apparently mistrusted him and investigated his rather seedy background thoroughly.[93] Yet regardless of the details, it seems clear at least that Wood took advantage of the rumour's existence to destroy his local enemies, and at most that he acted as a conscientious subject in the face of grave sedition.

If we cast our nets wider, examining local responses to other anti-government rumours of the period, we begin to see in a more general sense how the rumours themselves were only one part of a vibrant popular political debate. One example concerns rumours in the aftermath of the Pilgrimage of Grace that there would be renewed rebellion. In May 1537, a man called Robert Seymon met a stranger called Richard Bishop while walking in Tyndale Wood. They exchanged pleasantries, which encouraged Bishop to begin talking politics. He said to Seymon, 'Ye seem to be an honest man and such a one as a [man] might open his mind unto.' Seymon replied that he was 'a plain man, [and] ye may say to me what ye will'. Bishop, thus reassured, began a fierce tirade calling for armed rebellion:

> We are used under such fashion nowadays as it hath not been seen, for if 3 or 4 of us be coming together, the constables will examine what communications and stock us if we will not tell them. Good fellows would not be so used long, if one would be true to another ... If 2 or 3 [hundred] men would rise and one to be assured of another, [they] should have company enough to subdue the gentlemen.[94]

Having stated his opinions, Bishop proceeded to spread seditious rumours. He claimed that 'the earl of Derby is up with a number of men, and is proclaimed traitor in the parts where he dwelleth', and that 'my lord of Norfolk's grace is in the north and is so set about that he cannot come away when he would . . . and also Mr. Bayly and Mr. Whyt is left at home for no other cause but to keep down poor people for rising'. Robert Seymon, however, would have none of this. He told Bishop, 'God speed you well, for I will not meddle with you', and then went straight to tell the authorities. Even to the end, though, Bishop did not understand that his new friend was not really a co-conspirator; he called to Seymon as he walked away, 'Fare well, my friend, and know me another day if ye can.'[95]

In a similar example two Yorkshiremen, Richard Mallome and John Boys, walked home from Malton market one Saturday in the company of a man named Brian Wodcok. Wodcok raised the issue of taxation, saying that he had heard a rumour 'that my lord of Westmorland had promised to the king's highness that he should gather plough nobles and poll groats in all his lands and lordships for the king'. Moreover, Wodcok gave his opinion of the likely result of such an action: 'If it were so . . . there will be more business and rising than ever there was, for whereas there rose but one before, there would rise three now for this matter.' His listeners, however, were unimpressed. They asked him pointedly where he had heard such words, and Wodcok, sensing danger, answered evasively: 'If I could not tell where I heard them, I were a fool to speak therein.' Mallome answered him by saying, 'I advise thee to speak no more of such matters', and Wodcok replied, 'Why then let it rest where it is.' However, given that the depositions of Mallome and Boys are the only evidence surrounding the case, it is clear that they decided to inform the authorities of what they had heard.[96]

In one case the whole drama of a rumour's arrival in a locality, transmission and subsequent denunciation can be seen occurring in a single afternoon in a single alehouse. A woman called Agnes Filer was working at an inn in Otley, Somerset, in March 1539 when one Edward Loxton entered, asked for 'a pot with ale', and 'tarried drinking the space of an hour'. When she asked him, 'What news?', he responded with serious tidings indeed: 'He answered and said, "we shall have war", and further he said that he heard say that my Lord Crumwell was gone away.' Loxton soon departed, and two hours later another man took his place at the alebench, this time one John Brady, servant to the local gentleman Henry Capell. Brady also called for a 'pot with ale', and as he sat drinking Filer 'rehearsed to him what news she had heard of the said Edward Loxton'. According to the unfortunate barmaid, however, Brady would have none of this talk:

[He] answered and said that that news was false and untrue, and that the said Edward Loxton was a naughty and false knave so to bruit abroad any such things. And . . . the said Brady said to her further that he was glad that she had rehearsed it to him, for he would bring her before his master for it. And so the said Brady brought this deponent before his master the foresaid Henry Capell, before whom she hath deposed.[97]

The rumour-mongers of Otley discovered what some of their neighbours considered the boundaries of acceptable discourse within the space of only a few hours.

In a case from the Isle of Wight, conflicting accounts make the truth of the matter impossible to discern, but the contours of local dispute are plainly visible. According to one account, a large group of men were drinking in the 'church house' at Freshwater on 8 July 1536 when a pedlar entered and announced that 'he heard at London that Queen Anne was put to death and boiled in lead'. This rumour allegedly met with vigorous approval from the town's parson, Sir Nicholas Porter, who responded: 'While the king and his Council were busy to put down abbeys and pull away the right of Holy Church, he was made cuckold at home.' Porter evidently misjudged his audience; while they were willing to put up with nasty tales about the queen, seditious words about the king were another matter entirely, and not just one but four witnesses took their story to the authorities. The story grows more complex, however, because several other witnesses denied categorically that the parson had spoken such words and claimed that the parson's accusers had gone around town attempting to convince people to perjure themselves against him. In this case we can never know the truth, but it is clear that differences of opinion over acceptable responses to royal policy led to a major community dispute.[98]

Some of the most interesting cases of local dispute come from the rumours of the assault on the churches in 1536–7. John Parke of Newton, Northamptonshire, for instance, reported that around midsummer 1537 he overheard a dangerous conversation at matins. He said that a man called John Hewet reported that he had 'heard say that the leads of Buckingham church were valued', which induced Sir John Harbrowne, parson of Newton, to report 'that he heard say at Higham upon the Saturday before that Buckingham church was down'. This produced a muted prayer from a man called John Newman: 'God forbid that we should have any more churches down.' At this point, however,

John Parke stood up and, according to his own testimony, lambasted the rumour-mongers: 'John Parke said to the same John Newman, "be contented, for the king is supreme head of the church and we must be ruled as it shall please the king to have us." And [he] said to the same John Newman, "beware what thou speakest, for a little word is treason." '[99] Parke's words sound suspiciously like royal propaganda, and there is no corroborating evidence that he ever said them; nonetheless, his willingness to embrace royal rhetoric so completely as a tool against his neighbours is surely proof of significant political tensions.

In Ipswich, where the chantry priest James Crawford cut down more than 500 saplings to prevent the king from taking possession of them, there are no such doubts about what was said and done. Having heard reports of the alleged waste that Crawford had made on chantry lands, one of the town's two bailiffs and three other men of the parish investigated the felled trees and 'made a tally thereof'. They then called Crawford before a gathering of community leaders and explained to him that under the terms of his lease, he could be deprived of his living for having cut the trees down. It is not surprising, of course, that local parishioners would have been angry at Crawford's actions, and such anger in itself does not show political disagreement. The language of their confrontation, however, is informative. When Crawford answered his neighbours by saying, 'I had rather sell than the king should have it', they responded with a declaration of loyalty: 'Then the said bailiff and others of the parish answered, "we had rather spare the wood for the king's grace than ye should sell it."' Here, then, other members of the community were well aware of the rumours but preferred to let the crown take control than to let a local priest create such disorder. Crawford was indeed deprived of his chantry.[100]

In the Norfolk town of Aylsham, however, we see this sort of local debate at its most feverish. The town was evidently riddled with religious conflict; one man, for instance, was arrested for saying that 'he should honor God as well with a fork full of muck as with a wax candle', while another was arrested for erecting a cross 'whereupon was made the image of the pope with his 3 crowns gilded'. When the rumour arrived in town that 'there was an act of parliament made that if their church lands were not sold before May Day the king would have it', a whole host of local and national issues thus came into play as the people of Aylsham tried to manoeuvre within this dangerous situation. In particular, a number of men of the town sold the church's lands 'to defeat the king thereof'. However, it was suggested that these men, rather than acting in the town's best interests, had 'converted the money coming of the sale thereof to their own use'. Thus when these same men attempted to obtain the keys to the church's coffers, which apparently contained jewels and plate worth nearly £500, the churchwardens baulked. Not only did they act to protect church property from these conservatives-cum-profiteers, but they did so using language that savoured of loyalty to the regime:

> When they [several men of the town] heard that the king's visitors should come to town, they said they would sell their best cross and other jewels before their coming thither, and commanded the church-wardens to deliver to them the keys of the chest where the cross and the jewels did lie. Which to do the said churchwardens denied and refused, saying that if it were the king's pleasure to have it he was most worthy.[101]

In none of these cases are the disputes over religious ideology per se; there are no evangelicals visible here.[102] Rather, the disputes are about something which historians, with deceptive simplicity, have called 'conservatism'. Conservatism in this period is usually associated with those who opposed Henry VIII's innovative policies, and it is such conservatism that has recently been credited by some historians with preventing the successful implementation of the Henrician Reformation. Yet in these cases it is clear that substantial elements of the English nation were not nearly so sure of what constituted conservatism as many historians seem to be. Certainly nearly everyone believed in certain core notions such as the rule of law and the divine foundation of authority. But if the king, who was God's anointed representative, ordered the dismantling of churches, what was the appropriate response? Indeed, in a society steeped in the theology of hierarchy and obedience, could any 'response' be entirely conservative without threatening to tear apart the very notion of conservatism? In the perverse circumstances of the Reformation, with king and Church arrayed against one another, new ideas of popular conservatism would have to be evolved.

The political rumours of the 1530s were one step in that evolution. For all the sincerely conservative beliefs that lay behind them, they struck many members of the community as disturbingly radical.[103] Indeed, that was part of why they circulated in the first place: they were an eminently deniable and curiously refracted way of saying things that were not ordinarily sayable. But the existence of such 'radically conservative' rumours should not fool us into thinking that the majority of the population supported them. The content of rumours shows not the 'pulse of the nation', but rather the kinds of issues that were *contested* within that nation.[104] And in the 1530s, one issue at the heart of popular politics was the quest for a safe path through the casuistical minefield created by the Reformation. Allegiance to the Church and allegiance to the king, from time out of mind not merely compatible but interdependent, were suddenly and violently torn apart. At the same time the king implemented, with a host of scriptural, historical and practical validations, a variety of controversial policies ranging from increased taxation to the dissolution of the monasteries. Some people responded to these developments unequivocally, manipulating rumours in such a way as to oppose the crown in quite explicit fashion. Yet to many others this cure seemed worse than the disease, and various types of accommodation were attempted. When confronted with 'radically conservative' rhetoric, the kind that called not for obedience or even compromise but for popular resistance and the death of the king, many 'conservatives' baulked. They answered the rumours with harsh words and frequent denunciations to the authorities, making it clear that while they were not necessarily happy with everything the government did, there were certain places they would not go. Through the process of telling, repeating and rejecting rumours that interpreted the relationship between crown, Church and community, the English nation struggled to find stability within the chaos.

IV

English historians have long argued over whether the activities of the lower classes in the early modern period can legitimately be called 'political'. Eric Hobsbawm, in his classic discussion of *Primitive Rebels*, argued that 'traditional forms of peasant discontent . . . [were] virtually devoid of any explicit ideology, organization, or programme'. He thus called such forms 'pre-political', defining pre-political people as those 'who have not yet found, or only begun to find, a specific language in which to express their aspirations about the world'.[105] Hobsbawm's Marxist leanings put a unique spin on the terms 'ideology' and 'organization', but his ideas have nonetheless had an enormous impact on historians of early modern England.[106]

This chapter has gone some way towards banishing such a limiting model from English historiography. Whether there were ever 'pre-political' people is a matter for others to debate, but the people of early modern England cannot be placed under that heading. As the evidence from rumours has shown, such topics as taxation, the royal succession, ecclesiastical policy and the very nature of the relationship between crown and Church were the subject of heated debate in the early modern English countryside. Lacking the mass medium of print, such debates followed different paths from what we would perhaps expect, following the lines of least resistance made available by word-of-mouth communication along England's well travelled roads and trade networks. From Yorkshire to Kent, and perhaps in the wilds of the far north as well, English people had access to similar news and information and took part in overlapping debates, facilitated by the astonishing speed with which rumours raced across the country.

Admittedly, these rumours did not provide political 'organization' in a modern sense. But they provided a forum for the dissemination and interpretation of ideas, and it was these ideas that made such organization possible. Recent work on the Pilgrimage of Grace has shown the extent to which the commons were able to use the existing machinery of militia musters to organize a viable fighting force.[107] Likewise, research on Kett's rebellion of 1549 has shown the ability of people below the level of the gentry to operate an oppositional pseudo-government on a vast scale and to claim a direct role in the creation of government policy.[108] The ability of early modern people to organize politically is rapidly becoming clear.

Yet if the political nature of popular revolts is now largely accepted, we also need to accept that the decision *not to revolt* could be a politically complex one. Acceptance of royal policies cannot be seen as simple capitulation, a mere failure to rebel. As we have seen, the people who most vigorously and publicly opposed the crown in the 1530s faced not only prosecution from the authorities but also the bitter anger of many of their neighbours, even those whom they expected to be sympathetic to their cause. These neighbours were not, for the most part, evangelicals, but rather people who had internalized much of the rhetoric of the royal supremacy. Whether for ideological reasons or not, many people seem to have been more troubled by treasonous words than by the idea of enhanced royal power. These people still objected to oppressive taxation, but they strongly resisted blaming the crown for their troubles, and the idea of outright opposition horrified them. The rumour of the assault on churches could in one setting spark rebellion, but in other settings it could produce flurries of loyalist rhetoric and statements that if it would prevent local disorder, the king was more than welcome to the wealth of the Church. Many people evidently found ways to negotiate the casuistical dilemmas of the early Reformation without in any way diminishing their allegiance to the crown.[109]

The relationship between these beliefs and the later growth of English Protestantism is beyond the scope of this essay, although the evidence presented here clearly begs the question. What this essay has shown, however, is that revisionist notions of popular resistance and popular conservatism are themselves in need of revision. If 'resisters' in the 1530s met with such vigorous resistance themselves, and if 'conservatives' could be denounced by their neighbours as dangerously radical, then where exactly did 'traditionalism' lie? The revisionists have assumed that since nearly everyone in this society was conservative in their religious beliefs, opposition to royal policies must have been normal, and the most vocal opponents of the crown must have been merely the visible tip of a very large iceberg. When we examine the situation more closely, however, we find that these vocal opponents of the regime cannot be taken as proxies for 'conservatism' as a whole, but rather were the extreme end of a large 'conservative' spectrum. While people at different points on this spectrum may have shared many religious beliefs, they differed dramatically in their views of the relationship between crown and Church, as well as in their views of their own relationship to those institutions. The most 'radical' conservatives, those who spoke violently seditious words against the crown, make attractive objects of study, and we are naturally drawn to them in our attempts to create simple and easily digestible historical narratives. But in reality, the same qualities that make them attractive to us made them terrifying to their contemporaries, and we must not take their behaviour as normative. If we want to understand the English Reformation, we must instead examine the long, contentious and inherently *political* process through which the majority of English people negotiated conflicting pressures from both Romanists and evangelicals and slowly evolved their own beliefs.

NOTES

*I would like to thank Peter Lake, Tim Harris, Ann Hughes, Peter Marshall, Diarmaid MacCulloch and Sarah Paul for reading various drafts of this chapter. Earlier versions were presented at the 1997 Northeast Conference on British Studies and at the 1996 Princeton University Graduate History Association Colloquium, and I would like to thank all the participants for their helpful advice and criticism.

1. BL, Cotton MS Cleopatra E.V., fols 389r–v.
2. PRO, SP 1/118, fol. 267r. This manuscript is calendared in *LP*, XII, i, 1018 (I have wherever possible included *LP*, calendar references in square brackets beside manuscript references, showing volume numbers in large Roman numerals, part numbers in small Roman numerals, and entry numbers in Arabic numerals).
3. BL, Add. MSS 48,047, fols 63v–64r. This quote is from a 1538 charge to inferior courts, discussed in G. R. Elton, *Policy and Police: The Enforcement of the Reformation in the Age of Thomas Cromwell* (Cambridge, 1972), pp. 46, 336–8.
4. The best scholarly treatment of popular political rumours in early modern England, which appeared while this chapter was being revised for publication, is A. Fox, 'Rumour, News and Popular Political Opinion in Elizabethan and Early Stuart England', *HJ*, XL (1997), 597–620. Fox's argument is complementary, though by no means identical, to my own, and the two pieces can be read together to show the evolution of popular politics in an age of increasing participation in the apparatus of government. Other accounts of popular political rumours in England include Elton, *Policy and Police*, ch. 2; R. B. Manning, 'Violence and Social Conflict in Mid-Tudor Rebellions', *JBS*, XVI (1977), 18–40; C. Ross, 'Rumour, Propaganda, and Popular Opinion during the Wars of the Roses', in R. A. Griffiths (ed.), *Patronage, the Crown, and the Provinces in Later Medieval England* (Gloucester, 1981); D. Freist, *Governed by Opinion: Politics, Religion and the Dynamics of Communication in Stuart London, 1637–1645* (London, 1997), ch. 5. Important historical treatments of rumours outside England include G. Lefebvre, *The Great Fear of 1789: Rural Panic in Revolutionary France*, trans. Joan White (New York, 1973); A. Farge and J. Revel, *The Vanishing Children of Paris: Rumor and Politics Before the French Revolution*, trans. C. Mieville (Cambridge, Mass., 1991); J.-M. Matz, 'Rumeur publique et diffusion d'un nouveau culte à la fin du moyen age: les miracles de Jean Michel, Évêque d'Angers (1439–1447)', *Revue d'histoire de l'église de France*, LXXVII (Jan.–June, 1991), 83–99; R. Guha, *Elementary Aspects of Peasant Insurgency in Colonial India* (Delhi, 1983), ch. 6; A. A. Yang, 'A Conversation of Rumors: The Language of Popular *Mentalités* in Late Nineteenth-Century Colonial India', *Journal of Social History*, XX (1987), 485–505; L. Viola, 'The Peasant Nightmare: Visions of Apocalypse in the Soviet Countryside', *JMH*, LXII (1990), 747–70; E. Bradlow, 'The "Great Fear" at the Cape of Good Hope, 1851–52', *International Journal of African Historical Studies*, XXII (1989), 401–21; L. White, 'Between Gluckman and Foucault: Historicizing Rumor and Gossip', *Social Dynamics*, XX (1994), 75–92.

5. See E. J. Hobsbawm, *Primitive Rebels: Studies in Archaic Forms of Social Movement in the 19th and 20th Centuries* (New York, 1965). The idea that rumours were 'pre-political' in the early modern period is made explicit in Manning, 'Violence and Social Conflict in Mid-Tudor Rebellions', p. 18. A similar but currently more trendy mode of de-politicizing sixteenth-century popular culture is implicit in the explosion of recent scholarship which sees the rise of a so-called 'public sphere' of political discourse in the seventeenth or eighteenth century; the *locus classicus* of this theory is J. Habermas, *The Structural Transformation of the Public Sphere: An Inquiry into a Category of Bourgeois Society*, trans. T. Burger with F. Lawrence (Cambridge, Mass., 1991).

6. The most succinct outline of the revisionist position is C. Haigh, *English Reformations* (Oxford, 1993). Other, sometimes quite different, versions of revisionism are in E. Duffy, *The Stripping of the Altars: Traditional Religion in England, c.1400–1580* (New Haven, 1992); J. J. Scarisbrick, *The Reformation and the English People* (Oxford, 1984); C. Haigh (ed.), *The English Reformation Revised* (Cambridge, 1987); C. Haigh, *Reformation and Resistance in Tudor Lancashire* (Cambridge, 1975).

7. The social scientific literature on rumours is vast. The classic treatment is G. W. Allport and L. Postman, *The Psychology of Rumor* (New York, 1947). This work has been surpassed by, among other studies, M. L. De Fleur, 'Mass Communication and the Study of Rumor', *Sociological Inquiry*, XXXII (Winter 1962), 51–70; T. Shibutani, *Improvised News: A Sociological Study of Rumor* (Indianapolis, 1966). By far the most sophisticated and useful study is J.-N. Kapferer, *Rumors: Uses, Interpretations, and Images*, trans. B. Fink (New Brunswick, 1990).

8. M. Bowker, 'Lincolnshire 1536: Heresy, Schism or Religious Discontent?' *Studies in Church History*, IX (1972), 198. On the Lincolnshire rising, see also M. E. James, 'Obedience and Dissent in Henrician England: The Lincolnshire Rebellion, 1536', *P&P*, XLVIII (1970), 3–70; S. J. Gunn, 'Peers, Commons and Gentry in the Lincolnshire Revolt of 1536', *P&P*, CXXIII (1989), 52–79.

9. PRO, E 36/119, fol. 72r [*LP*, XII, i, 481].

10. PRO, E 36/119, fols 48v–49r [*LP*, XII, i, 380]; my italics. Oddly, Bowker cites *this* reference to the *Letters and Papers* calendar, while reciting a narrative that clearly refers to the deposition on fols 72–3. Since she does not cite the manuscript directly, however, it is impossible to pinpoint the source of her error.

11. PRO, E 36/119, fol. 9v [*LP*, XII, i, 70].

12. PRO, E 36/119, fol. 15r [*LP*, XII, i, 70].

13. PRO, E 36/119, fol. 7v [*LP*, XII, i, 70].

14. PRO, E 36/119, fol. 11v [*LP*, XII, i, 70].

15. PRO, E 36/119, fol. 15r [*LP*, XII, i, 70]. C. S. L. Davies recognized that 'several witnesses' said that the rumours had begun 'about a month or six weeks before the outbreak of the rebellion', yet almost in the same breath said that the diffusion of the rumour was due to the rumour-mongering of Peter Effard. The explanation for this contradiction is unclear: C. S. L. Davies, 'Popular Religion and the Pilgrimage of Grace', in A. Fletcher and J. Stevenson (eds), *Order and Disorder in Early Modern England* (Cambridge, 1985), p. 67.

16. PRO, E 36/119, fol. 72v [*LP*, XII, i, 481].
17. PRO, SP 1/109, fol. 8v [*LP*, XI, 828].
18. PRO, E 36/119, fol. 2r [*LP*, XII, i, 70].
19. The government's keen interest in the Pilgrimage of Grace and subsequent interrogation of many participants naturally affects our source-base for these rumours, both providing more evidence than would usually be available and emphasizing the extent to which rumours were subversive. Nonetheless, there is no reason to discount this evidence as atypical. In the late sixteenth and early seventeenth centuries, when assize records become available and State Papers are more complete, it is clear that political rumours were ubiquitous; for the early period, we must rely upon bouts of (perhaps not unreasonable) government paranoia to provide us with evidence (see Fox, 'Rumour and Popular Political Opinion').
20. M. L. Bush, *The Pilgrimage of Grace: A Study of the Rebel Armies of October 1536* (Manchester, 1996), pp. 60–1.
21. PRO, SP 1/109, fol. 39r [*LP*, XI, 841].
22. PRO, E 36/119, fol. 19r [*LP*, XII, i, 70].
23. PRO, SP 1/130, fol. 144r [*LP*, XIII, i, 607]. On the authority of writing in this period, see A. Fox, 'Custom, Memory and the Authority of Writing', in P. Griffiths, A. Fox and S. Hindle (eds), *The Experience of Authority in Early Modern England* (London, 1996).
24. See especially Kapferer, *Rumors*; Shibutani, *Improvised News*.
25. PRO, SP 1/123, fol. 121r [*LP*, XII, ii, 357].
26. PRO, E 36/120, fol. 105r [*LP*, XII, i, 808].
27. PRO, SP 1/130, fol. 10v [*LP*, XIII, i, 477].
28. PRO, SP 1/91, fol. 216r [*LP*, VIII, 518]. As Geoffrey Elton noticed, the *LP* date of this manuscript is off by two years: Elton, *Policy and Police*, p. 70.
29. PRO, SP 1/120, fol. 247v [*LP*, XII, i, 1316].
30. PRO, SP 1/116, fols 75r–76v [*LP*, XII, i, 456].
31. PRO, SP 1/116, fols 75r–76v [*LP*, XII, i, 456].
32. This is a conservative figure. There are several examples of what appear to be this same rumour elsewhere, but these may have been referring to the dissolution of monasteries rather than parish churches (for example, PRO, SP 1/120, fols 87r–91v [*LP*, XII, i, 1202]).
33. PRO, SP 1/106, fol. 142r [*LP*, XI, 417]. Geoffrey Elton believed that this manuscript was actually from 1536, on the grounds that 'the tone of the denunciation suggests that it should be placed before the Lincolnshire rising in October 1536': Elton, *Policy and Police*, p. 73, fn.1. Having read the manuscript, I do not understand his reasoning, and the existence of a single example of the rumour exactly a year before its more general outbreak seems farfetched.
34. PRO, SP 1/125, fols 237r [*LP*, XII, ii, 935].
35. PRO, E 36/120, fols 57r–v [*LP*, XII, ii, 1208].
36. PRO, SP 1/127, fols 123r–135r [*LP*, XII, ii, 1256].
37. PRO, SP 1/127. fol. 81 [*LP*, XII, ii, 1220].
38. PRO, SP 1/132, fol. 97r [*LP*, XIII, i, 981].
39. PRO, SP 1/127, fol. 38r [*LP*, XII, ii, 1185]; PRO, SP 1/127, fol. 161r [*LP*, XII, ii, 1282].

40. PRO, E 36/120, fol. 176r.
41. PRO, SP 1/128, fol. 86r [*LP*, XIII, i, 76]; SP 1/128, fol. 61r [*LP*, XIII, i, 57].
42. PRO, KB 9/545, fols 85r–86r.
43. PRO, SP 1/130, fols 81v–82v [*LP*, XIII, i, 543].
44. PRO, SP 1/133, fol. 241r [*LP*, XIII, i, 1282]; E 36/120, fols 152r–v [*LP*, XIII, i, 1350].
45. BL, Cotton MS App. L, fols 73r–74r [*LP*, XIII, i, 76].
46. PRO, SP 1/127, fol. 59r and PRO, E 36/120, fols 57r–v [*LP*, XII, ii, 1208].
47. PRO, SP 1/130, fol. 82r [*LP*, XIII, i, 543].
48. M. H. Dodds and R. Dodds, *The Pilgrimage of Grace, 1536–1537, and the Exeter Conspiracy, 1538*, 2 vols (Cambridge, 1915), II, 297.
49. Kapferer, *Rumors*, p. 139.
50. For political prophecies circulating in the 1530s, see S. L. Jansen, *Political Protest and Prophecy under Henry VIII* (Woodbridge, 1991); S. L. Jansen Jaech, 'The "Prophisies of Rymour, Beid, Marlyng": Henry VIII and a Sixteenth-Century Political Prophecy', *The Sixteenth Century Journal*, XVI (Fall 1985), 291–9; A. Fox, 'Prophecies and Politics in the Reign of Henry VIII', in A. Fox and J. Guy (eds), *Reassessing the Henrician Age: Humanism, Politics and Reform, 1500–1550* (Oxford, 1986); K. Thomas, *Religion and the Decline of Magic* (New York, 1971); R. Taylor, *The Political Prophecy in England* (New York, 1911); M. H. Dodds, 'Political Prophecies in the Reign of Henry VIII', *Modern Language Review*, XI (1916), 276–84; T. M. Smallwood, 'The Prophecy of the Six Kings', *Speculum*, LX (1985), 571–92; G. Williams, 'Prophecy, Poetry, and Politics in Medieval and Tudor Wales', in H. Hearder and H. R. Lyon, (eds), *British Government and Administration: Studies Presented to S. B. Chrimes* (Cardiff, 1974).
51. For a transcription of one extant copy of the Mouldwarp Prophecy, see J. Hall (ed.), *The Poems of Laurence Minot* (Oxford, 1887), pp. 97–105.
52. BL, Cotton MS Cleopatra E.IV, fol. 99r [*LP*, VI, 923].
53. Jansen, *Political Protest and Prophecy*, p. 37.
54. F. Palgrave, 'The Confessions of Richard Bishop and Robert Seyman', *Norfolk Archaeology*, I (1847), 217–19.
55. PRO, E 36/122, fol. 34r [*LP*, XII, i, 685].
56. Jaech, 'Prophisies of Rymour', especially pp. 293–5. See also Fox, 'Prophecies and Politics'; Thomas, *Religion and the Decline of Magic*, p. 402.
57. PRO, SP 1/118, fol. 4r [*LP*, XII, i, 841].
58. PRO, SP 1/130, fols 24r–v [*LP*, XIII, i, 487].
59. PRO, KB 9/545, fol. 86r.
60. BL, Cotton MS App. L, fol. 61r [*LP*, XIII, i, 6].
61. PRO, SP 1/133, fol. 241r [*LP*, XIII, i, 1282].
62. For an example of this phenomenon upon Henry VIII's actual death in 1547, see PRO, STAC 3/6/54. In this case, a man called Robert Davyes claimed that according to 'diverse men learned in the laws of this realm' the suit pending against him in ecclesiastical court was only a legal proceeding by licence of Henry VIII 'during his pleasure' and was thus 'by the death of our said late king clearly determined and void'. It appears from the case that such reasoning was successful.
63. PRO, SP 1/128, fol. 63r [*LP*, XIII, i, 58].

64. PRO, SP 1/106, fol. 142r [*LP*, XI, 417].
65. BL, Cotton MS App. L, fol. 61r [*LP*, XIII, i, 6].
66. PRO, E 36/120, fol. 176r.
67. BL, Cotton MS App. L, fol. 73v.
68. BL, Cotton MS App. L, fol. 73r.
69. M. L. Bush, '"Enhancements and Importunate Charges": An Analysis of the Tax Complaints of October 1536', *Albion*, XXII (1990), 403–19; M. L. Bush, '"Up for the Commonweal": The Significance of Tax Grievances in the English Rebellions of 1536', *EHR*, CVI (1991), 299–318; M. L. Bush, 'Tax Reform and Rebellion in Early Tudor England', *History*, LXXVI (1991), 379–400.
70. PRO, SP 1/128, fol. 126r [*LP*, XIII, i, 107].
71. R. Hoyle, 'War and Public Finance', in D. MacCulloch (ed.), *The Reign of Henry VIII: Politics, Policy and Piety* (New York, 1995).
72. PRO, SP 1/109, fol. 37v [*LP*, XI, 841].
73. PRO, E 36/120, fol. 57r; PRO, SP 1/127, fol. 59r [*LP*, XII, ii, 1208].
74. PRO, KB 9/545, fols 85r–86r.
75. PRO, SP 1/130, fol. 81v [*LP*, XIII, i, 543].
76. PRO, E 36/120, fol. 71r [*LP*, XIII, i, 41].
77. Elton, *Policy and Police*, p. 49.
78. PRO, SP 1/141, fol. 67r [*LP*, XIII, ii, 1200].
79. PRO, SP 1/127, fol. 57r [*LP*, XII, ii, 1205].
80. PRO, SP 1/127, fols 123r–134r [*LP*, XII, ii, 1256]. While I am focusing here on national issues, local issues could also be crucial in shaping political rumours. In the Berkshire outbreak, for instance, it was bruited that the king had been poisoned by a priest, apparently because he had been in love with the daughter of the local gentleman John Norris. For a detailed account of chains of transmission in the Berkshire outbreak, see Elton, *Policy and Police*, pp. 75–7.
81. On Exeter, see *DNB*; Dodds and Dodds, *The Pilgrimage of Grace*, II, 193. A number of sources demonstrate that Exeter was being imagined outside court circles as a possible heir; see for instance *LP*, XIV, ii, 818 and *Archaelogia*, XXII (1829), 25. Many other religious conservatives such as Stephen Gardiner, John Longland, Thomas Howard and John London also received their share of hatred from Catholics in the countryside for collaborating with the regime. From the commons' point of view, perceived attacks by these men on local assets and local values were apparently of more pressing concern than their private religious convictions. I owe thanks to Peter Marshall for discussing these ideas with me.
82. PRO, SP 1/140, fol. 33r [*LP*, XII, ii, 996].
83. BL, Cotton MS App. L, fol. 74r.
84. BL, Cotton MS, App. L., fol. 73r [*LP*, XIII, i, 76].
85. PRO, SP 1/128, fol. 63v [*LP*, XIII, i, 58].
86. PRO, SP 1/106, fol. 142r [*LP*, XI, 417].
87. PRO, E 36/120, fol. 176r.
88. PRO, SP 1/133, fol. 241r [*LP*, XIII, i, 1282]. Another deposition of William Wood, with small variations, is in PRO, E 36/120, fol. 152r [*LP*, XIII, i, 1350].
89. PRO, SP 1/133, fol. 241r [*LP*, XIII, i, 1282].

90. PRO, SP 1/133, fols 241r–v [*LP*, XIII, i, 1282].
91. PRO, E 36/120, fol. 152v [*LP*, XIII, i, 1350(2)].
92. PRO, SP 1/133, fol. 241v [*LP*, XIII, i, 1282]; PRO, E 36/120, fols 152r–v [*LP*, XIII, i, 1350(2)].
93. PRO, E 36/120, fols 153r–154v [*LP*, XIII, i, 1350(2)].
94. PRO, SP 1/120, fols 100r–104v [*LP*, XII, i, 1212].
95. PRO, SP 1/120, fol. 104v [*LP*, XII, i, 1212].
96. PRO, SP 1/128, fol. 126r [*LP*, XIII, i, 107(2)].
97. PRO, E 36/120, fol. 55r [*LP*, XIV, i, 557].
98. PRO, SP 1/130, fols 34r–36v [*LP*, XIII, i, 493].
99. PRO, SP 1/126, fol. 107r [*LP*, XII, ii, 1068].
100. PRO, SP 1/130, fols 10v–11r [*LP*, XIII, i, 477].
101. PRO, SP 1/120, fols 247r–v [*LP*, XIII, i, 1316].
102. There are other cases, of course, in which religious differences and nascent Protestantism did lead to disagreement over political rumours. In York-shire, for example, the reform-minded chaplain William Senes was called a 'whoreson knave' for opposing another priest, 'Mr. Drapper', who argued that he had the right to resist if the king tried to take away his chalice: see A. G. Dickens, *Lollards and Protestants in the Diocese of York* (London, 1982), p. 39. Other examples of similar phenomena are in PRO, SP 1/123, fols 120r–122v and PRO, SP 1/132, fol. 97r.
103. This issue of 'when a conservative is not a conservative' has been much discussed by historians. For early modern Europe, the most important treatment is C. Condren, 'Radicals, Conservatives and Moderates in Early Modern Political Thought: A Case of Sandwich Islands Syndrome?', *History of Political Thought*, X (1989), 525–42. Another fascinating discussion of the issue in a very different context is D. Field, *Rebels in the Name of the Tsar* (Boston, Mass., 1976).
104. Indeed, in periods the government itself swung to the conservative end of the spectrum a series of 'reformist' rumours can be seen: in 1530 that the king had endorsed the vernacular bible (BL, Cotton MS Cleopatra E. V., fols 389r–v), in 1543 that priests were dangerous and that their weapons should be confiscated (for example PRO, SP 1/206, fols 90r–94r [*LP*, XX, ii, 186]), and in 1554 that the King of Spain would invade (A. Fletcher and D. MacCulloch, *Tudor Rebellions*, 4th edn (London, 1997), p. 82).
105. Hobsbawm, *Primitive Rebels*, pp. 2, 96.
106. Hobsbawm's formulation has been adopted explicitly in Manning, 'Violence and Social Conflict in Mid-Tudor Rebellions'. Another elitist approach to early modern politics, although quite distinct from Hobsbawm's, is Elton's belief that 'politics are the activities of men in political society, and though they may be the active concern of the few, their effects spare none': G. R. Elton, 'Politics and the Pilgrimage of Grace', in his *Studies in Tudor and Stuart Politics and Government*, 4 vols (Cambridge, 1974–92), III, 183–4.
107. See Bush, *The Pilgrimage of Grace*.
108. D. MacCulloch, 'Kett's Rebellion in Context', *P&P*, LXXXIV (1979), 36–59; E. H. Shagan, 'Protector Somerset and the 1549 Rebellions: New Sources and New Perspectives', *EHR*, CXIV (1999), 34–63.

109. These ideas have some similarities to those expressed in Robert Whiting, *The Blind Devotion of the People: Popular Religion and the English Reformation* (Cambridge, 1989), although I would disagree with Whiting in distinguishing so sharply between 'spiritual' and 'non-spiritual' motivations for accepting the Henrician Reformation.

3

'POORE MEN WOLL SPEKE ONE DAYE': PLEBEIAN LANGUAGES OF DEFERENCE AND DEFIANCE IN ENGLAND, C.1520–1640

Andy Wood[1]

Subaltern groups are always subject to the activity of ruling groups, even when they rebel and rise up. . . . Every trace of independent initiative on the part of subaltern groups should therefore be of incalculable value for the integral historian.

A. Gramsci, *Selections from the Prison Notebooks*

(Eng. trans., London, 1971), p. 55

I

In May 1525, the Suffolk town of Lavenham became the site of a remarkable encounter between noble authority and plebeian resistance. Over the spring of that year, Cardinal Wolsey's demands for an 'Amicable Grant' intended to finance Henry VIII's foreign adventures had faced growing hostility across East Anglia and southern England.[2] Opposition was most public in the textile region of southern Suffolk and northern Essex. Here, negotiations between the wealthy clothiers and the Duke of Suffolk had highlighted the government's weakness after the Duke had suggested that the clothiers disregard the formal assessments made of their wealth and instead pay what suited them.[3] News of the negotiations leaked out and by 9 May a crowd of some thousands, composed of weavers, farmers and labourers, had gathered at Lavenham. According to the later narrative compiled from gentry eyewitnesses by the courtier

67

Ellis Griffith, the 'folk of...Lavenham...had...agreed, in common with the men of the towns of Kent, Essex, Suffolk and Norfolk, to rise at the sounding of bells.'[4]

Hearing of the Lavenham gathering, the Dukes of Norfolk and Suffolk raised 'their tenants and serving-men to form an army'. Events moved too swiftly for them: 'before the Dukes had mustered their people, over 10,000 "fighters" had mustered in Lavenham'. Proceeding with a mounted force to the town, Suffolk intended to mount a pre-emptive attack, but was dissuaded by Norfolk, who was concerned as to the loyalties of their newly levied force. As the Dukes discussed the matter, a delegation from Lavenham was sent to talk to them.

> A long conference ensued, and the lords agreed to hear the people's grievances. Thereupon a large number of them came to meet the lords, and began, with the characteristic indiscretion of the ignorant, to speak all at the same time like a flock of geese in corn.

The Dukes imposed noble order upon popular chaos, ordering the rebels to

> consider whether they would maintain their foolish purpose against the king and his council...or would submit to the king's grace for violating the law. If the latter, they should appoint one of their number to plead their cause.[5]

At this point in Griffith's account, incipient rebellion transformed into a demonstration of popular faith in the nobility. Returning to Lavenham, the commons decided to sue for mercy.

> In order to show their obedience to the king and their repentance... they sent sixty of their number in their night-shirts to meet the lords, whom they found ready to listen civilly to their plaints, and to become their keepers and protectors against the king's ire.[6]

The negotiations were protracted by the representatives' need to seek advice from their 'comrades in the town'. Finally, the commons chose to accord 'with the will of the lords and such gentlefolk of the district as were there on horseback'. Delegates returned to the Dukes, 'in their [night]shirts, bareheaded, and kneeling down'. To further emphasize their submission, some wore halters around their neck.[7] Faced with their subordinates' penitence, the Dukes inquired as to their grievances. John Grene, a weaver, 'a little man, wizened and ill-formed', spoke for the others, explaining that they had intended to march on London to present their grievances to the king. Grene was an articulate man, who so impressed one attorney present at Lavenham that he informed Griffith that 'no four of the ablest lawyers in the kingdom, even after a week's consultation, could make an answer so meet as did the weaver within less than two hours' space'. Yet Grene's eloquence was not wholly original. In his speech, Grene drew upon the stock of allegory and metaphors by which early modern plebeians understood power and justified rebellion. Asked who was their captain, Grene replied 'for soth his name is Povertie, for he and his cosyn Necessitie, hath brought us to this dooyng'.[8]

The Dukes did their duty. Order was returned to the region: 'everything was smoothed among the people in that part of the kingdom'. Grene and 13 others were carried to gaol in London, to await appearance before the court of Star Chamber. And the Dukes represented the grievances of their suffering people to the crown. In Hall's account,

> the kyng was sore moved, that his subjectes were thus stirred and . . . saied, I will no more of this trouble: Let letters be sent to all shires, that this matter maie no more be spoken of, I will pardon all theim that have denied the demaunde, openly or secretly: Then all the lordes kneled downe, and hartely thanked the kyng.[9]

The Amicable Grant was 'quietly dropped'.[10] Following John Grene's appeal 'on his bended knees' and Wolsey's admonition, the Lavenham men were released with the Cardinal's gift of silver. Some 525 people were later indicted for riot at the Court of King's Bench; but the Dukes of Norfolk and Suffolk had deflected the more serious treason prosecutions at Star Chamber.

On the surface, the events at Lavenham seem to confirm that historiography which has seen early modern society as ideologically homogeneous and rebellion as a functional mechanism for the presentation of limited, defensive grievances.[11] In this interpretation, both gentry and plebeians perceived of their social world as divided into hierarchical 'orders'. The proper object of government was to maintain that social balance. Where the status quo was threatened by government (as in the 1536 Pilgrimage of Grace), or by the gentry (as in the 1549 East Anglian and southern rebellions), the commons rose in order to recall their betters to their appropriate roles. Popular revolt was therefore reactive,

and popular politics conservative. This explanation of early modern
rebellion determines our understanding of the larger pattern of social
relations: if labourers, artisans and farmers remained deferential even
when in rebellion, then their everyday relations with their rulers must
also have been built upon such norms.

Yet the events of 1525 will bear an alternative reading. If we look
beyond the stylized exchange between the Dukes and the rebel representatives to focus upon events within Lavenham, the defining features of
the confrontation become fear and hatred rather than deference and
subordination. Some members of the crowd allegedly 'railed openly on
the Duke of Suffolke . . . and threatened [him] with death'. The negotiations were watched from the town: 'should the lords be observed to raise
an alarm', the plan was 'to set the bells in motion'.[12] It will be recalled
that the crowd had gathered after hearing the great bells of Lavenham.
Medieval and early modern rebellion was so often spread by the sound
of bells that to 'ring awake' became an established euphemism for revolt.
The association was spelt out most lyrically in one of the secret letters by
which the rebels of 1381 had communicated their plans: 'Jon Balle
gretyth yow wele & doth yowe to understande he hath rungen youre
belle'.[13] In 1525, a fresh peal of the Lavenham bells was to be taken by
the commons as a sign that the Dukes had proved traitors, and that the
people of the neighbouring villages should gather to oppose them.
Upon the safe return of their representatives, the rebels 'began to babble
and shout, every man with his plan'. Some wished to accept the Dukes'
offer of representation. Others

> protested their preference to die like men in their quarrel with such as
> were daily despoiling them of whatever God sent them for the labour
> of their hands . . . After a prolonged talk the majority chose the worse
> part, and sent . . . companions . . . to sound an alarum.

Outright rebellion was prevented by the foresight of one of the wealthy
clothiers of the town, who had removed the clappers from the bells in
advance. Without any sound from Lavenham, the nearby villagers,
'noticing that their comrades in the town did not come forth and that the
bells did not sound, began to lose courage and to fear in their hearts that
they were betrayed'.[14] The second round of negotiations therefore
resulted from the loss of the rebels' capacity to organize a larger force.

The Lavenham encounter justifies the circumspection with which
early modern social historians have approached the history of relations

between ruler and ruled.[15] Recognizing that early modern society was based upon neither publicly recognized class conflict nor unambiguous hierarchy, social historians have tried to balance evidence for riotous 'class conflict' with proof of popular deference. In consequence, social relations have often been seen in transitional terms, possessed of both a nascent class consciousness and the remnants of medieval hierarchy. Yet this more nuanced appreciation remains full of difficulties. For while there is too much evidence to the contrary to maintain that plebeians saw their world in terms of a hierarchically graded 'society of orders', neither does it seem appropriate to conceive of two centuries of social relations as constituting but a lintel within the great arch of English class formation.[16]

Rather than seeing deference and class at opposite ends of a long historical process, we ought rather to perceive of them as in constant, trans-historical friction. Unequal societies routinely produce social conflicts over resources, power and space. A large part of such struggles will involve subordinates in an attempt to develop a public voice within which complaints can be voiced and (possibly) alternatives to the dominant order created. Similarly, elites will seek to prevent subordinates from acquiring such a collective voice. This is likely to be true to a greater or lesser extent in any given society. But in societies such as that of sixteenth- and early seventeenth-century England, in which literacy (while growing in its significance) remained relatively limited, in which public speech formed an important part of political culture, and in which the ruling elite expected a large amount of visible deference, then subalterns' public words should be likely to constitute an especially contested terrain. If we are to develop a richer appreciation of early modern social relations, the politics of speech ought therefore to lie at the heart of our enterprise.

Unequal societies breed conflict not only over the use and distribution of resources, but also over the concepts by which social inequality is justified. In particular, elites seek to legitimize their rule by persuading subordinates to adopt demeaning views of themselves and of their own class. Subalterns are less likely to be persuaded to participate actively in their own subordination than they are to limit their collective political ambitions. Hence, successfully dominant ideologies will often function negatively, by proscribing the limits of the possible. The terminology of governance and order therefore become central to both the hegemonic pretensions of elites and to any popular resistance. In the past century, the language of democracy has constituted one such very obvious conceptual battleground. In the sixteenth and seventeenth centuries, the languages of law, custom and religion constituted another. Hence, early modern labourers facing the enclosure of their commons often represented that loss as an immoral and unchristian act of theft by 'rich men', as much as they spoke of its debilitating material effects.[17] Rather than giving simple expression to conflicts occurring within the 'objective' realm of economics, the terminology of social confrontation and accommodation therefore enjoyed a life of its own.

All of the above constitutes a set of obvious, trans-historical truisms.[18] This set of sociological abstractions only becomes of historical interest when located within time and place; for while domination, exploitation and resistance might well possess cross-cultural similarities, their forms and outcomes are more often historically specific. This chapter will seek to identify some defining features of early modern English social relations, through accessing the reported speech, actions and writings of the lower orders. It proceeds from a consideration of how elite political discourses coloured plebeian understandings of order, conflict and collectivity. We shall see how both popular and elite definitions of social conflict could flagrantly ignore local subtleties of social structure and power relations to define instead a confrontation between 'rich' and 'poor'. In that confrontation, 'great men' were felt to hold the advantage, for popular speech was often subject to outside scrutiny. The records upon which our investigation of popular speech will proceed were far from neutral; rather, accounts of seditious speech were implicated within the conflicts they describe, as the authorities sought simultaneously to investigate, codify and crush popular politics. Silence, then, could be as important in social relations as speech and action. For in the most extreme of contexts, where 'poore men' (and poor women) spoke, they laid themselves open to allegations of sedition or rebellion. But in other contexts, plebeians could be more autonomous. An important part of our story therefore focuses upon regional variation in popular politics. In some areas and at some times, relatively inclusive common cultures were developed within which labourers, artisans and smallholders were freer to speak and act than elsewhere. Hence, the speech of poor women and men in some places could be more muted, more resentful and more vicious, than elsewhere. Finally, although this piece is concerned with the identification of broad, generic similarities in plebeian speech between the Reformation and the English Revolution, important discontinuities occurred in the context and content of that speech. In particular, the last decades of the sixteenth century saw 'the poor' identifying a wider range of opponents as wealthy farmers and merchants were placed alongside the gentry and nobility into a broadened category of 'the rich'.

II

Contemporary elite discussions of the sociopolitical structure of Tudor and early Stuart England placed a heavy emphasis upon order and hierarchy. At either ends of our period, Sir Robert Filmer and Sir Thomas Elyot found a cosmic truth within the ordering of human affairs: 'everything is order, and without order may be nothing stable or permanent'.[19] Such writers shut their eyes to the flux of social and economic change which moved about them. Similarly, they disregarded the complexity of the relationship between the gentry and what Elyot called 'the *plebs*'; the significance of cultural and social divisions amongst the *plebs*; and the dynamic interplay between elite and popular politics. More sophisticated commentators also found it difficult to break out of the hierarchical paradigm. Sir Thomas Smith's jumbled account of the sociopolitics of Elizabethan England both restated and undermined the conventions of patriarchalism. Emphasizing over and again the submission which inferiors owed to their governors, Smith nonetheless saw what Elyot and Filmer could not: that power was diffuse within early modern society, and that social relations were multifaceted.[20] Exempting yeomen from 'the lowest and rascall sort of people' due to their role in local government, he went on to write of how even the 'fourth sort of men which doe not rule . . . be commonly made Churchwardens, alecunner and manie times Constables'.[21] If anything, exchange between village and court politics deepened over the course of Smith's life. The increasing literacy of the wealthier yeomen farmers of the midlands and south helped to demarcate them from their poorer neighbours, as did their growing institutional engagement with the central state. Steve Hindle writes in this volume of how the new authority of the 'better sort of people' could simultaneously broaden the basis of governance and narrow the meaning of community.[22]

Yet Elyot's and Filmer's simple patriarchal certainties held a greater force within elite culture than did Smith's ambivalences. Sir Thomas Elyot wrote all too easily of how 'the potter and tinker . . . shall little do in the ministration of justice . . . a weaver or fuller should be an unmeet captain of an army'.[23] For as we have already seen, John Grene the weaver was more than capable of leading his neighbours against the Dukes of Norfolk and Suffolk. Elite social theorists were therefore left with a problem: how to reconcile the evidence of popular politics with the supposed domination of patriarchalism. In the case of Ellis Griffith's account of the Lavenham encounter, the tension is highlighted rather than resolved: the reader is left to contrast the formulaic reference to the 'characteristic indiscretion of the ignorant' with the later eloquence of John Grene. Sir Thomas Elyot simply ignored the problem: to him, gentility implied a simple superiority, while popular politics, if it existed at all, was necessarily chaotic and communistic.

In recent years, social historians have protested that the simplistic polarities defined by Elyot bore little relation to the complexities of early modern social structures. Historians now believe that an informal 'language of sorts' provided a truer reflection of the distribution of wealth and power than did the status-based terminology of a hierarchical society of 'orders' and 'estates'.[24] Of special importance here was the development of the term 'middling' or 'better' sort to describe that growing middle stratum of local society upon which parochial, hundredal and borough government depended. It is certainly the case that plebeians (that is, those of non-gentle status) rarely made use of the language of orders, but rather represented local society in more gritty terms. Direct conflict with the gentry was defined in terms of disparities of power: in 1518, for instance, Richard Walkerdyne of Youlgreave (Derbyshire) drew a clear distinction between himself ('a pore man') and his gentle opponent Robert Bradbury ('a man of great power & substance'). In other contexts, distinctions between 'the gentlemen' and 'the commons' seemed less important than internal divisions amongst the latter. Established but scarcely wealthy villagers of the seventeenth-century Peak Country of Derbyshire, for instance, felt a clear difference between themselves ('the inhabitants'; 'the poorer sorte of freehoulders'; 'the tenants'; 'the neighbours') and those at the bottom of the micro-society of the village ('very poore people'; 'the poorer sort of people'; 'beggers & lived upon the almes of the Towne & Parishe'; 'hirelings').[25] Such evidence has led to a healthy scepticism as to 'the validity of thinking in terms of a basic social polarity' in the period, and in drawing a 'dichotomy between rulers and ruled'.[26]

Yet this critique misses both the continuing willingness of contemporaries to conceive of a simple division between 'rich' and 'poor' and the enduring authority of patriarchal categories. Like other dominant ideologies, patriarchalism spoke more to the needs of the gentry and nobility than it persuaded labourers or yeomen to accept their place. Representing one reflex response of lords, magistrates and monarchs, patriarchalism helped to unify elite opinion around a set of important assumptions. Hierarchical categories simultaneously distinguished the gentry and nobility from 'the *plebs*', and validated that distinction. The gentry believed themselves to be discriminated by their honour, civility, rationality and culture because they knew 'the commons' or 'the *plebs*' (Elyot used the terms interchangeably) to be collectively devoid of those qualities. In its most extreme manifestations, patriarchalism led gentlemen to attribute animalistic qualities to those beneath them, especially when in rebellion. At its least extreme, it encouraged a set of paternal images: the gentleman as a kindly father; tenants and labourers as occasionally unruly children. This polarized vision of society was laden with grandiose anxiety. Gentle complainants to the Jacobean court of Star Chamber combined hauteur and fear in their descriptions of rioters: 'a multitude of the common people'; 'the vulgar and common sorte of people'; 'the rude and ignorant multitude'; 'the basest and unrulye people'; the 'vulgar sort'. Such 'pore and simple people' when in rebellion comprised an 'uprore and Tumulte of a multitude of people'. Occasions of disorder, perceived as leading to a levelling anarchy, demonstrated the lower orders' need for the bridle of authority.[27] As a cliché, this was simultaneously fantastic, internally coherent and enduring: even Oliver Cromwell, who ought to have known better, occasionally spoke in the tongue.

In proscribing the roles of superior and inferior, patriarchalism established public norms by which social relations could be practised. But while appearing to silence popular politics, patriarchalism provided terminology and images which plebeians could exploit. The cornerstone of patriarchalism lay in its linkage of social, political and domestic authority. Just as the adult man ruled over the women, children, apprentices and servants of his household, so the lord ruled his tenants, the magistrate ruled the people, and the monarch ruled the realm. Hence, for men to rebel against social or political authority was to undermine their own domestic authority: 'Take away all kings, princes, rulers, magistrates, judges and such states of God's order . . . [and] no man shall sleep in his own house or bed unkilled, no man shall keep his wife, children and possessions in quietness; all things shall be in common', as the Homily on Obedience had it in 1547.[28] But if men owed their authority to the monarch, then they could also make legitimate claims in that capacity. The tenants of Begbrooke (Oxfordshire) found within the language of male responsibility a discourse around which they could organize their complaints against an enclosing, rack-renting lord. As they explained to the Court of Requests in 1604, their lord had caused 'great oppressions' to the 'pore tenants' such that their 'poore wives and familie are like to be utterlie undone and perish'. The threat of eviction was represented not only as an attack upon community and custom, but as an invasion of domestic space. Some of the inhabitants had dwelt within the village for 50 or 60 years, 'uppon poore cottages', but were 'now threatened to be putt out wives and poore children'. The fear of dispossession was a common one. A manuscript circulating amongst the tenants of the northern border counties in 1619 warned that should their lords' attempt to dissolve the custom of tenant right prove successful, their rents would be raised, their cottages lost and the landlords 'wold turne them theire wifes and theire children a begginge lyke Rogues and vagabonds over the face of the earth'.[29] We should not see such statements as mere hyperbole. The tenant or labourer had good grounds for fearing dispossession in the later sixteenth and early seventeenth centuries, when the decline of 'gentylnes' amongst lords seemed to be proved by the numbers of vagrants on the roads.

The language of patriarchalism enabled the textile workers of Suffolk and Essex to criticize the clothiers who employed them in 1525, who 'give us so little wages for our workmanship, that scarcely we be able to live, and thus in penurie we passe the tyme, we our wifes and children'. It allowed the men of Kent to develop their denunciation of the Amicable Grant, 'rekonyng theymselves, theyr childrene and wyfes, as desperates, and not greatly caring what they doo, or what become of thayme'. The weaver John Grene based his appeal to Cardinal Wolsey upon his manly duties, worrying before Star Chamber that 'when we return to our homes we shall have no means of providing meat, drink and clothing for ourselves, our wives and kin'. And the crowd gathered at Lavenham on 9 May 1525 ordered itself according to the gender of its members: 'Then began women to wepe and young folkes to crie, and men that had no woorke began to rage, and assemble theimselfes in compaignies'.[30] Susan Amussen's claim that economic dependence was felt to weaken plebeian men's claims to full masculinity allows us to make fuller sense of another of the clichés of popular protest: the threat to 'die like men in the quarrel'. For collective resistance allowed men simultaneously to assert themselves against their social betters and thereby to reassert their masculinity.[31]

Not all plebeian women stood by weeping while their menfolk marched to confront 'great men'. In fact, the Lavenham women's reported behaviour of 1525 seems to have been the exception to the rule. That women frequently took a large part in early modern crowd action is now well known. In some regions, such as in the fenlands or in the Yorkshire valley of Nidderdale, collective traditions of women's autonomous action were well established by the early seventeenth century. In 1602, 'Captain' Dorothy Dawson led her female neighbours onto the contested Thorpe moor, where the enclosing landlord's labourers were building walls across the commons. Cheered on by the men of their villages, the women broke down enclosures and attacked the workmen. Similar events took place in the fens. Yet when questioned by the Star Chamber as to their actions, both the Nidderdale and the fenland women denied any leading role in the organization of the riot. Only a few, such as Captain Dorothy, were prepared to speak publicly of their role.[32] Like plebeian men, the rest concealed their thoughts and actions behind a veil of silence and the assumption of female incompetence made by jurists and magistrates.

Plebeian women were just as capable of manipulating patriarchal categories as were men, justifying attacks upon officers come to distrain their goods as the defence of their homes and thereby of their honour.[33] Placed in the difficult context of the courtroom, women found domestic justifications for their public defence of common land, which they identified as protecting their household economies. Where fending off accusations of enclosure riot, women did well to suppress any wider claims to property or rights. Hence, most of the women of Shepshed (Leicestershire) argued that they had only broken down enclosing fences upon their commons in order 'to thenent they might enjoy their husbands right of comon'. But Alice Mitchell let the cat out of the bag: she explained that Joan Perkins had come and asked her if 'she wold not gow wth her & the rest of her neighbours to throwe downe the said ditches'. Without making any reference to their cover story – that they were asserting their husbands' rights there – Alice slipped into a more open account of their motives: the women had broken the fences in order to maintain '*their* Rights of comon'.[34] Like their menfolk, plebeian women therefore took advantage of their rulers' blindspots: in this case, exploiting the elite male inability to think of women as effective political actors in their own right.[35]

III

The periodic theatricality of public encounters between ruler and ruled could be advantageous to both sides. We have seen how at Lavenham in 1525 the representatives of 'the people' appeared to the Dukes of

Norfolk and Suffolk as penitents, wearing nightshirts and halters as if prepared for their own execution. We have also seen how John Grene appealed to Cardinal Wolsey 'on his bended knees' in the Star Chamber. The Lavenham commons were not the only plebeians to shift so easily between rebellion and self-abasement. Save only for the remarkable Captain Dorothy, the women enclosure rioters of Nidderdale went upon their knees in 1602 to beg their landlord Sir Stephen Proctor not to enclose their commons. A few years later, Sir William Killigrew distrained cattle from men who had destroyed his fenland enclosures. They subsequently came in 'submission and tears' to ask for the return of their livestock. The body language of deference crept into written petitions: unemployed weavers of Wiltshire wrote as suppliants to the Privy Council 'most humbly even upon our knees' to

> begge and intreat of your Lordships thoroughly to weigh and consider this our most lamentable condicion that if it be possible a remedy may be found that wee as forlorne wretches perrish not in the same.[36]

Visible subordination helped to gloss over the awkward facts of plebeian assertion and rebellion: privy councillors reading the Wiltshire weavers' grovelling address would not forget the weavers' riotous reputation. Compliant or recalcitrant postures helped plebeians to achieve their immediate aims: the removal of unjust taxes, the return of common land, the creation of employment. The gentry played their part too, representing as gracious grants what were really hard-won popular gains. And both sides colluded in concealing the negotiation, confrontation, threat and brokerage which went on behind the veil of deference and paternalism.

Social hierarchy was reproduced in theatrical performance and the social organization of emotional expression. Everyday power relations demanded of plebeians that they disguise their feelings. Deference to a lord or employer could secure work, land, credit, gifts, charity or patronage. And the converse was equally true: misplaced truculence, a willingness to speak out of turn, a refusal to follow the public behaviour expected of subordinates, could all lead to trouble. The records of court archives are replete with cases of labourers whose reputation as idlers or trouble-causers had lost them the patronage of their lord or richer neighbours. The Norfolk labourer Barnard Shippabotham, for example, found himself denounced by the rulers of his village in 1606 as a 'comon alehouse hauntor', a blasphemer, 'a comon defamer and detractor of the neyghbours where he dwelleth', a 'rayler', and 'a verie foule mouthed person'. As such, he had clearly set a bad example to others within the village. But perhaps Barnard's greatest sin was his failure to accept the economic priorities of the local employing class: most damningly, 'he refuseth to work on harvest, and at other tymes, except he have unreasonable wages'.[37] In such villages, individual defiance was unwise. Rather, labourers did better to keep their mouths shut; to avoid alehouses when in sight of their betters; and to request higher wages in words which their superiors found unthreatening. Barnard's poor neighbours, then, might have been such women and men of whom the radical Roger Crab wrote in 1655:

> when the all-seeing eye looks into every Ale-house of this Nation, and seeth of which sort are most there . . . they will appear to be labouring poor men which in times of scarcity pine and murmure for want of bread, cursing the rich behinde his back, and before his face, cap and knee and [assume] a whining countenance.[38]

Commons and gentry alike were born into a system of social relations which operated within a sequence of overlapping dualities: between speech and silence; respect and hatred; conformity and rebellion; public and private; deference and defiance. Those dualities were coded within the semiotics of authority and subordination. When the rebel representatives gathered to negotiate with the Dukes of Norfolk and Suffolk outside Lavenham in 1525, they obscured the confrontation by dressing in their nightshirts and placing halters about their necks. In so doing, they identified themselves as penitents and as proper subjects for royal punishment. On other occasions, plebeians had come before authority dressed in a similar fashion: in the aftermath of the 'Evil May Day' riots of 1517, some 411 condemned rioters were paraded before Henry VIII and Queen Catherine 'with halters around their necks'. In another highly theatrical scene, Henry pardoned the prisoners because 'our most serene and most compassionate queen, with tears in her eyes and on her bended knees, obtained their pardon from His Majesty, the act of grace being performed with great ceremony'.[39]

The halter, then, was accepted as a sign of submission. But halters could have other meanings too. In 1549, the people of Lavenham again rose in rebellion. In circumstances which remain obscure, representatives of the Privy Council met with the Suffolk rebel leaders to consider their demands. In the course of the negotiations, the Suffolk commons were persuaded to disband, clearing passage for royal forces to confront Robert Kett's rebels at Norwich.[40] Twenty years later, a Lavenham man named James Fuller admitted to plotting a new rising against the 'riche churles' and 'heardemen' of the area with John Porter, a weaver of the same town.[41] Porter and Fuller's plot grew from their reading of the events of 1549:

> we wyll not be deceyved as we were at the laste rysinge, for then we were promised ynoughe and more than ynoughe. But the more was an hawlter.

The halter called forth a vivid image of social subordination, laced with betrayal: halters were worn by beasts of burden, pulling ploughs in the field. In the collective memory of the commons of Lavenham, they had been promised much by the 'rich churles' in the negotiations of 1549. But thereafter they had only been placed more firmly under the halter. There was a further meaning to the word. The suppression of rebellion in 1549 had been attended by hangings: in Norwich and Norfolk; in Oxfordshire and Buckinghamshire; in the West Country; and in Suffolk.[42] The halters which in 1525 had signified ritual submission were remembered after 1549 as nooses.[43] Fuller dwelt morbidly upon images of public execution in the revenge fantasy which he reconstructed in his admission of guilt:

> But nowe *we* wyll appoynte them that shall take the riche churles and sett *them* on *theyre* horsebackes under a tree, whereuppon *we* wyll hange a wythe and putte it aboute *theire* neckes and then dryve *theire* horses from under *them* and so lett *them* hange.   [My emphasis]

Fuller's plan might be read as a euchronic reworking of the executions of 1549, but on this occasion with roles reversed. The rich churles are set on *theyre* horses (the horse itself a sign of authority), and hanged with their own halters. Fuller's fantastic inversion of the symbols of class authority and his intended targets spoke within a larger idiom and ideology of popular rebellion.

The simplest syllables of that idiom were spoken in the undeveloped, outright rejection of authority. William Cratchman's harsh opinion of the Justice of the Peace Sir William Warde that 'the divell shatt justices when he was made one' landed him in trouble in 1609. The labourer Jeremy Vanhill was not much taken in by the grandeur of Gloriana.

In 1585 he was sentenced to be hanged for his opinion of Elizabeth I: 'Shyte uppon your Queene; I woulde to god shee were dead that I might shytt on her face'. Mary Bunton was equally blunt: in 1599, she was alleged to have stated that 'I care not a turde for the Queene nor hir precepts'.[44] There was a simple logic about such statements, founded as they were upon an appreciation of the care which the gentry, nobility, clergy and monarchy took about the display of their honour. Such things have been said of those in authority in a great many societies. But in Tudor and early Stuart England, in particular, they were regarded with a special gravity.

The alleged words of Mary Bunton, Jeremy Vanhill and the others survive within the historical record by virtue of governmental attempts to restrict popular political expression. After 1534, successive Acts of Parliament extended medieval treason law to cover speech and writing deemed 'seditious': either against the policies, personnel or social basis of the state.[45] In attempting to regulate speech, writing and print, pre-civil war government sought to monopolize the flow of political information and thereby to reshape the public sphere. Although this ambitiously hegemonic project lay beyond the capacities of the early modern state, it succeeded in modulating the tone and volume of plebeian criticism and in undermining the capacity of private complaint to develop into public rebellion. After all, we only know that James Fuller and John Porter of Lavenham had intended to lead a rising of the commons because Fuller had subsequently betrayed Porter. Every case of seditious words lodged within the archives of the criminal courts or the Privy Council therefore speaks not only of some plebeians' capacity to formulate a social critique, but also of the willingness of others to inform against them.

One unintended consequence of the Tudor treason and sedition legislation was to create a body of information detailing popular opinion. A harsh irony underlies historians' current use of such material: documents now used in exploration of popular politics were first created in an attempt to silence it.[46] Traces of plebeian social critique remain in sources other than the records of investigations into seditious speech: very rarely, for instance, an anonymous threatening letter or libel might survive, mixed up amongst the estate papers of a noble house, or attached as evidence in complaint to a legal forum.[47] These sources are not without their difficulties. The deliberate anonymity of letters and libels makes their provenance difficult to establish. The surviving records of sedition prosecutions or of the Privy Council's investigations into planned risings are equally problematic. Many of those accused of seditious speech understandably denied the alleged words. Witnesses might have to be bribed or coerced, suborned or coached. Finally, the documentation upon which sedition prosecutions were based does not simply reflect early modern social relations; rather, it helped to constitute them. Between the speech of the witness or accused, the transcribing clerk and the interrogating magistrate, lay the charged, distorting electrics of early modern power relations. Nonetheless, there are good reasons for deploying such sources in description of plebeian attitudes to their rulers.

First, given the nature of our quarry, we need not be driven by the historian's obsessive search for the true, objective source. Rather, the biases, absences, repetitions and contradictions within the record can be as revealing as any more straightforward statement. Secondly, a surprising number of those accused of giving voice to seditious opinions admitted to some or all of the offending words, and in a small minority of cases expanded upon them before the authorities. Finally, even where seditious speech was denied by the accused, the terminology of the alleged social critique was often quite predictable, revealing generic qualities which are frequently identical to the terminology of anonymous threatening letters or openly acknowledged speech. From the accumulation of such material, we can start to chart the outlines of a partially submerged plebeian language of class.

IV

Early modern English women and men were prone to perceive of the world in terms of duality and conflict. Stuart Clark has written that this willingness 'to see things in terms of a binary opposition was a distinctive aspect of the prevailing mentality', and has drawn attention to 'the extraordinary pervasiveness of the language of "contrariety", the most extreme of the relations of opposition'. Godly puritans saw the forces of Christ and Antichrist arrayed about them. The rather less godly were often just as willing to believe stories of how papists conspired to burn towns and slaughter Protestants. And witchcraft seemed to be a means by which the impotent poor could invert their powerlessness, overturning both moral and social hierarchies within the community.[48] If this was true of religious and magical beliefs, it was equally true of social relations. Plebeian definitions of social conflict worked within a dualistic perception of society in which large, abstract social categories confronted one another over access to material resources and moral authority. Those opposing blocs were identified by a series of overlapping terms. On one side stood 'the gentlemen'; the 'rich men'; the 'rich churles' who were also 'traitors'. On the other were 'the trewe comons', 'the people', 'the neighbours', 'the poor'.

Like hierarchical definitions of society, this polarized, conflictual language tottered at the edge of yawning contradiction. Precisely who constituted 'the commons' or 'the rich' could vary greatly. Thus, relatively wealthy, office-holding villagers of the sixteenth century could identify themselves as a part of 'the poor' or the 'trewe comons' when in rebellion against noble authority, but in more day-to-day contexts distinguish themselves from the labourer.[49] Local social divisions seeming fixed within the records of parochial administration might dissolve before the definition of a conflict between 'the commons' and 'the rich'. This language was conceptually and historically mutable. Crudely stated, the moral and social opposition imagined between a 'trewe comons' and their 'traitorous' gentle and noble opponents held most meaning before the late sixteenth century. Thereafter, although that conceptual arrangement continued to influence popular definitions of social opposition, its authority was gradually undermined in the face of the increasing involvement of richer villagers and townspeople in the 'oppression' of 'the poor'. Within southern, agrarian regions most of all, the 'rich' had broadened as a category of plebeian social critique to include those of non-gentle, but still wealthy, status. Early modern popular appreciations of social conflict therefore possessed strongly regional flavours.[50]

Prior to the English Revolution the miners, cottagers and poor tenants of the Derbyshire Peak Country rarely identified fundamental differences between themselves and the few richer farmers and minor merchants of the region. Rather, their enemies were the 'great and powerful men' who came exclusively from the established gentry and nobility of the region.[51] In contrast, the recorded speech of the poor of late sixteenth-century East Anglia and the south-east defined 'the rich' as a much larger category, encompassing 'rich farmers', 'cornmongers' and 'merchants' as well as the gentry, the nobility and the 'traitors' of the Privy Council.[52] My over-simplified comparison between regional cultures relates partly to differences in economies and social structures. In contrast to the early seventeenth-century Peak Country, within the wealthier, more urbanized, and more structurally complex economies of arable East Anglia and the south-east, local 'middling sorts' were both more numerous and politically prominent. But the comparison also highlights regional distinctions in the quality of social conflict and social relations.

Social conflict in the late Tudor and early Stuart Peak Country was prominent and open, casting the major gentry families of the region against the numerous miners and poor tenants. The broad basis of local authority in Peak villages, combined with quasi-democratic institutions such as the free miners' barmote courts, enabled plebeian opposition to be built upon public, communal organization.[53] In contrast, in East Anglia beyond the fens by the late sixteenth century, 'the poor' rarely rioted in defence of customary rights or common land.[54] Knowledge and institutional control of local custom was more the property of established, richer farmers, and based more heavily upon written documentation.[55] Greater access to literacy, sometimes coupled with an attraction to godly religion, divided richer villagers from their poorer neighbours.[56] Facing a larger, more stable local elite, and with less access to the legitimizing institutions and discourse of custom, the poor of East Anglia were less able to mount effective, public opposition to their rulers than was the case in the Peak Country. One result was that the form of plebeian social critique in East Anglia beyond the fens was more covert, less effective and much more vicious.

In some cases, such as that of poor Jeremy Vanhill, misplaced public speech could lead to the gallows. In many others, the sentence was less extreme. Alice Richardson, for instance, was condemned by the Mayor's Court of Norwich to be 'whipped at Brydewell for [unspecified] sedicious words' in 1596. Forty-five years earlier, William Harrison of the same city was led around the market on horseback with a paper upon his head denouncing the words he had spoken in support of Robert Kett's recent rising. The previous year had seen some repeated critics of the city's magistracy having their ears nailed to the pillory in the marketplace.[57] The immediate purpose of such punishment was to humiliate the lower-class critic. The broader objective was to sow suspicion amongst dissidents. The critically minded labourer had therefore to be wary before whom she or he spoke, and where. Walking down a country road in 1597, James Smith and Robert Drewe fell to conversation concerning the failings of the nobility and the crown, the corruption of the merchants and the high price of corn. Their talk ended up before the Privy Council, after it was reported by a servant of Sir Nicholas Woodhouse who was hiding beneath a hedge as they passed.[58] Hearing the rich criticized within the seemingly secure preserve of the alehouse, an audience felt a set of conflicting responses: should they betray the speaker to the authorities, and so risk ostracism? Or would it be better instead to risk accusation of complicity, and put one's trust in group solidarity? Where alehouse talk was reported to the authorities, it is notable that suspects often fell over one another to deny or modify their purported words, and to shift blame for the beginnings of the conversation, or for the most inflammatory terminology, onto someone else.[59] The routine, trans-historical tendency of class societies to modify or silence the public speech of subordinates was therefore given a hard legal twist in early modern England.

The result was that the act of speech as much as its content became a source of suspicion, both between subordinates and rulers and amongst subordinates. In May 1537, the Privy Council heard how Richard Bishop of Bungay (Suffolk) had asked of Robert Seymon 'what tythyngs here you'. Seymon responded with a mixture of social commentary and current affairs. Perceiving that Bishop did not dissent from his opening statement that 'this is an hard world for pore men', Seymon grew more confident. Telling Bishop that he seemed 'to be an honest man and such on[e] as a man myght open hys mynde unto', Seymon spoke of the recent conspiracy in Walsingham (Norfolk) to 'put down the gentilmen', and of a prophecy that there should one day be a great gathering at Mousehold Heath 'and the prowdest Pr[i]nce in Chrystendome shulde be there subduyt [i.e., subdued]'. He added a revealing assessment of the surveillance of popular opinion: 'Wee ar so used nowe a days at Bungay as was nev[er] sene affore this; for if ii or iii gud felows be walkyng togedr, the constables come to theyme and wolle knowe what communy-cacon they have or ellys they shalbe stokkyd'. From this, Seymon concluded that 'if ii men were to gether on[e] myght say to another what he wold as long as the iii.rd. was not ther'.[60]

Both sides understood the individual and collective self-regulation produced by the treason and sedition legislation. One commentator on the 1555 Act concerning seditious slander stated unequivocally that under its edicts 'we are forebidden to thincke evill, and muche more to speake evill'. But in its practical operation, government had necessarily to be more attuned to the censored speech of the lower orders. Perhaps more than anything else, this concern to scrutinize and record plebeian opinion gives the lie to Sir Thomas Elyot's refusal to acknowledge a pop-ular politics. Prior to the confrontation at Lavenham, the Privy Council knew that trouble was afoot, noting how 'the people sore grudgethe and murmereth, and spekith cursidly among theymselves *as far as they dare*'.[61] Similarly, the Kentish husbandman Edward Ewer did his best to adjust his feelings to political circumstances, remarking of Elizabeth I that 'yt would never be a merrye worlde till her majestie was dead or killed; and that her majestie was ruled by her lordes at ther pleasure, *but we must not saye soe*'.[62] Where dissidents were uncovered, their public repentance was often felt to be more conducive to the maintenance of order than their physical punishment. It was the practice of the court of Star Chamber to reduce sentences upon those it found guilty upon their 'humble submission'.[63] The same principle operated in other contexts: in the spring of 1606, Richard Clarke of Walpole (Norfolk) was denounced by his fellow labourers to the justices for his seditious conversation. Clarke had imagined Walpole's village green becoming the site of a rising of the poor: 'tush, tush, yt would be a better world if ther were two or three hundred of us together by the eares here in this grene'. But the bench allowed Clarke to accept his culpability in return for denying the validity of his opinion. Clarke took the offer: 'he did speake the same, but he did speake yt unadvisedlye, and is sorrye for it'.[64] The mercy which flowed from the bench was intended to confirm the gentry and nobility in their authority.[65] It was all the more infuriating, therefore, that some plebeians spat the opportunity of repentance back in the face of their governors.

Robert Burnam of Norwich had been one of Kett's rebels in the summer of 1549. He had little regard for the county's gentry, or for the city's magistracy, and was prepared to give public voice to his opinions at the most dangerous of times.[66] With Robert Kett's body still hanging from the walls of the city's castle, Burnam frightened his fellow watchmen in June 1550 with his belief that 'the gentylmen might have the higher hande styll [and] the poore commons shulde be trodden under Foote; and destroye the Realme'. The others warned Burnam that his words were charged with danger for them all: 'He was requyred to leave suche talke. But he wolde not'. Burnam had already offended the mayor with words spoken less than a month after the suppression of the rebellion, at which time he was lodged in the city's gaol. Their exchange was captured by the clerk of the Mayor's Court. Burnam told the mayor:

> Mr Mayor ye do me wrong to kepe me here without any cause where unto Mr Mayor answered and sayed noo Burnam I kepe the[e] not here, and he sayed yes, ye scribes and pharisees ye seke innocent bloude, But if I cannot have Justice here, I shall have it of bettermen and I ask no favour at your hands.

The churchwardens of his parish had come to him after that confrontation, 'and did advyse him to turne his harte and become a newe man'. Burnam had then replied that he had given no offence, and so was reminded of his reputation: that it was well known that one gentleman captured by the rebels during the summer had said that 'he was not affrayd of his lief of no man but of the saide Burnam'. At Burnam's angry response that 'There are to many gentylmen in Englande by five hundred', the churchwardens warned him that he faced prison. By the following March, Burnam's neighbours had come to see him as something of a liability: John Petyver felt that 'a good worde were as soone spoken as an evill and that Burnam were a foole.' Petyver's opinion seemed confirmed when in July 1550 Burnam's ears were cut off at the pillory.

Robert Burnam lost his ears in exchange for a few moments of verbal freedom. The bargain was a hard one, but he was not the only plebeian to strike it. While the legally enforced logic of deference ensured that some working people kept their mouths shut, it pressured others into giving voice to their resentments. One Norwich apprentice was so angered by the City's supervision of his mates' drinking games that when dragged into gaol in February 1551 he exploded with a statement of suppressed religious and social grievances:

> we cannot playe for a halpenny worth of ale at the cardes but we are sente hither to prysone for it. But their are a sorte of chorles that have the church goodes in their handes, that the poore can have noon. And I wolbe one of them that shall pluk it from them one Whitson Sondaye.

There was something liberating about those moments when poor men and women spoke publicly against authority. For the resentful labourers and artisans of post-rebellion Norwich, knowing how closely their actions and words were monitored, to speak of politics became a moment of transgressive freedom. 'By the masse he durst be bolde to speke it', announced William White in June 1550 of the wonderful but inaccurate rumour that the Earl of Warwick had been overthrown.[67] A couple of years later, 'Collerd the cobler' met with Mr Davey the Alderman in Norwich market. Following his refusal to pay the bizarre tax then demanded upon facial hair, Collerd had earlier been ordered to remove his beard. According to the subsequent record of the City's court, Davey told Collerd that 'Mr Mayor commaunded the[e] to have of thy bearde, I p[er]ceyve well thow hast it not of yet'. The hirsute rebel recalled that 'I was ones shaven and I made an othe I wold never have of my berde agayn I was so evell shaven', before spitting out as forceful a statement of verbal repression as might be imagined: 'this is noo moore but to pycke quarrells against poore men. But poore men woll speke one daye'.[68]

V

Collerd the cobbler was not representative of his class. When in immediate contact with the gentry, the labourer was wise to couch complaint within acceptable terminology. Alternatively, the threatening letter or burlesque libel might guarantee anonymity, as could disguise or (in riots) the protection afforded by numbers.[69] That elite opinion found social disorder synonymous with cacophonous, collective speech reveals much about the politics of language in the period. Readership of chronicles taught the Tudor and Stuart gentleman that the lower orders were not only stupid, barbarous and levelling, but were also prone to revolt. Elite histories recalled the events of 1381 or 1450 in auditory terms as 'The Noise: *rumor, rumor magna, rumor pessima*'.[70] Accounts of the events of 1536 and 1549 merely perpetuated the genre: hence, commotion meant rebellion, and rumour implied sedition.[71] The simultaneous anonymity and ubiquity of popular complaint preceding rebellion rendered plebeian opinion inscrutable. Rebellion in Westmorland in 1536 was inspired by a 'great murmer' amongst the congregation at Kirkby Stephen church. Rebel policy in that year seemed not to originate with 'any council', but rather drew from 'a common bruit that went among the commons'. Common speech enabled discussion and organization to be mounted behind a screen of noise: the 'Evil May Day' of 1517 appeared to elite opinion to have been spread by 'a common secret rumour, and no man could tell how it began, than on May Day next the City would rebel and slay all aliens'. The contradictory formulation betrayed official anxieties: that while such speech was common to the masses, it remained secret to the authorities.[72]

In rearticulating individual speech within the 'common voice', plebeians evaded the atomizing repression of the treason and sedition legislation and helped to foster local political cultures apart from their rulers. In late Tudor Kirkbyshire and Nidderdale (Yorkshire), Sir Stephen Proctor knew that he had plumbed the depths of the commons' hatred, for he had witnessed their riots against his enclosures and heard their muffled speech against his Protestant religion. When he awoke one morning to find a pair of gallows erected outside his new mansion house, Proctor knew why they had been left there; but not exactly by whom. Representing popular speech and action in terms of collectivity and anonymity, Proctor's submissions to the court of Star Chamber betrayed his anxieties: to him, the commons of Kirkbyshire and Nidderdale formed a 'great shuffling'; 'a greate uprore of people'. Collectively, they comprised the 'Comon voice of the Countrye'. Popular 'murmeringe' produced a consensus: that Proctor's enclosures would be 'the undoinge of the whole Contry . . . some sayinge that they had rather ther lives were taken awaye then their livings'.[73] The collectivization of speech protected leaders and organization from scrutiny, while validating criticism within a larger body of public opinion. In 1629, the magistrates of Maldon (Essex) arrested Dorothy Berry for her part in two food riots. Asked 'whoe p[ro]cured her' to riot, Dorothy answered 'the Crie of the Country and hir owne want'.[74] It was the legitimizing country's voice that cried against high prices in Maldon, just as it spoke against Proctor in Nidderdale.

Anonymity gave plebeians the delightful opportunity to taunt their betters. In 1631, a letter placed within the porch of Dr Richman, 'a grave p[rea]cher' of Wye (Kent) warned of the hunger of the poor before concluding:

> will you knowe my name you
> must be wise in the same[75]

For magistrates and gentry to be 'wise' of their plebeian critics, they needed to gain access to popular speech. In some contexts, this was relatively easy. In the immediate aftermath of the defeat of Kett's rebellion, the traumatized and terrified labouring poor of Norwich, having witnessed the Earl of Warwick's repression within the city, spoke often to the authorities of one another's seditious words. But the surprise with which that rebellion had initially been greeted by East Anglia's gentry suggests that popular speech could avoid surveillance.[76] The struggles over tenant right in the Jacobean northern border counties constitutes an important contrast to that of post-rebellion Norwich.[77] Here, lords knew that their attempts to abolish the custom of tenant right were stirring up trouble, for they were aware of the collective murmer that the tenants intended to 'first deale by law' in the defence of their customs, 'and then if they could not prevaile that way they wold fight for it'.

In the course of this threatened 'insurrection', the border tenantry intended to have their landlords for breakfast, and would be led by a 'Captain' who 'wold be the first to help to cutt theire Landslords throats'.[78] The gentry were understandably anxious to identify this frightening person. Yet the historical record does not speak only of gentle fears. Plebeian deponents to the Star Chamber confirmed in 1619 and 1620 that their neighbours were indeed giving voice to such opinions.[79] Various candidates were canvassed for the position of 'Captain'. Rumour around Kendal had it that one Thomas Johnson, a yeoman who had made himself prominent in the legal defence of tenant right, held that secret office. This local hero was known by 'common report' to have remarked in public to Sir Francis Duckett 'That the landlords were but a breakfast for theire tenants, and rather then the tenants wold loose theire lyveings they wold all joyne together and loose theire lyves'.[80] But Sir Francis remembered those words as having been spoken to him by Samuel Tomlinson, and recalled Tomlinson's words as follows: 'That they, meanynge the tenants, had but a life to be loose and they wold loose it before they lost theire lyveings'. One Richard Mawson had then added that 'they to witt the tenants wold deale first by law, & if that wold not serve then they wold fight for it'. Sir Francis concluded that Mawson's assertion must have been the result of drink, and dropped the matter. The following morning, the gentleman encountered the tenant once more, and asked 'if he were in the same mynd or noe'. Mawson bluntly 'answeared he was the same man as before'.[81]

Certainty in the legitimacy of their 'ancient laudable customs', combined with a strong sense of solidarity and long experience of public organization, gave the Jacobean border tenants confidence to speak in forthright language. Samuel Knipe, another one of the leaders of the tenants' resistance, was taken before the justices of Westmorland and examined as to his role in the troubles. Asked if he 'was the begainer of theise troubles and suites in the cuntrie, he answered . . . no: it was not hee but some of the Landslords'. Twelve years earlier, Timothy Lloyd had found his involvement in the Midland Rising against enclosures similarly empowering. Confronted by the Lord Lieutenant of Warwickshire, he had 'verie insolentlie' said that 'he had bene authorised by Captayne Powche' to knock down enclosures, '& that the said Captayne Powche had authoritie to cutt downe all enclosures betweene . . . Northampton and the cytie of Yorke'.[82] In such instances, the act of open rebellion, even (as here) in its suppression, could excite plebeians into deliberate, conscious statements of opposition.

Again, then, we are reminded of the importance of regional variation in the political capacities of early modern plebeian cultures. In the

Jacobean border counties as in the Peak Country at the same time, labourers, tenants, miners and cottagers organized openly against their social superiors, and spoke with clarity and force about social antagonisms. In contrast, this chapter has stressed the very different pattern in East Anglia beyond the fens. This variation in plebeian politics, and hence in social relations, was not simply a product of local social structure. It had rather to do with the active maintenance or otherwise of political traditions and social alliances amongst the 'commons'. Social historians have long been wary of identifying clear moments of discontinuity, preferring instead to emphasize long-term changes and continuities. Nonetheless, something very significant happened in East Anglia after 1549. Prior to Kett's rebellion, seditious mutterings against 'rich men' were often to be heard within the alehouses of Norfolk, Suffolk and Essex – and in much the same idiom as that of the later sixteenth century. But such murmuring added itself to the public clamour of organized, assertive resistance. We have seen how the inhabitants of Lavenham and its surrounding villages turned out in their thousands to defeat the Amicable Grant. In the early sixteenth century, if we can trust the record of Star Chamber litigation, East Anglian villagers took their place in forthright resistance to enclosure.[83] After 1549, resistance to enclosure became much more muted.

If a discontinuity had occurred in the form and social basis of popular resistance, then East Anglian labourers and artisans of the late sixteenth century at least spoke in the same terminology as the men and women who followed Robert Kett to Mousehold Heath. Miners and villagers of the later Tudor and early Stuart Peak Country tended to see 'great men' and 'rich and powerful men' as intending the destruction of their customs and spoke publicly and with confidence to equity courts in such terms.[84] The fears and revenge fantasies of East Anglian labourers and artisans, by comparison, were less public and more extreme. Sitting in their alehouses, they spoke of how 'rich men' starved the poor and imagined bloody day-dreams of 'knocking down' the 'rich churles'.[85] Speaking at some time around 1537, John Walter of Griston (Norfolk) gave clear expression to such dark thoughts.[86] He intended to gather 'iii or iiii good Felowes', who would ride through the night with bells and assemble a host at the market town of Swaffham. One 'bold felowe' should then

stande forth & sey: ye knowe howe lyttyll faver [the gentlemen]...
bere to us pore men. Let us therfore nowe go hence to ther howssys,

& ther shall we have harnesse substaunce & get vytayle. And so many
as wyll nott turn to us let us kylle them ye evyn ther chylderne in the
cradells. For yt were a good turne yf ther were as many genytlmen in
Norff[olk] as ther be whyte bulls.[87]

What is remarkable about such vicious talk is that it was so rarely
fulfilled.[88] Conceivably, this had something to do with the morality of
popular rebellion. When East Anglian plebeians recalled the events
of Kett's rebellion, they remembered it as a confrontation between the
'rich men' and the 'commons'. In 1549, 'Charitie', 'neighbourliness' and
'gentylnes' had seemed to confront 'treachery' and 'oppression'.[89] The
memory was a bitter one, and its articulation could provoke sanguine
fantasies in which old wrongs were righted and gentle blood spilt. But
the image of blood spilt spoke of liberation and sacrifice as much as it did
of revenge. Kett's rebels had argued that by virtue of the 'precious
blood' shed by Christ, 'bondmen' had been made free. In making the
claim, they refreshed the old connection between divinity and poverty.
Perhaps in failing to enact their oft-stated revenge fantasies upon the
bodies of their 'oppressors' in 1549, the 'trewe commons' doomed
themselves as a social class; for their opponents were not so restrained.
But that restraint itself spoke to the moral values for which the rebels
claimed to stand, and which their opponents seemed in that year to so
obviously lack.

NOTES

1. I am very grateful to Tim Harris, Steve Hindle, Mark Knights, Simon
   Middleton and Keith Wrightson for their comments on an earlier draft of
   this essay.
2. G. W. Bernard, *War, Taxation and Rebellion in Early Tudor England:
   Henry VIII, Wolsey and the Amicable Grant of 1525* (Hassocks, 1986).
3. For recent accounts of the East Anglian disturbances of 1525, see ibid., ch. 6;
   D. MacCulloch, *Suffolk and the Tudors: Politics and Religion in an English
   County, 1500–1600* (Oxford, 1986), pp. 289–99. The social composition
   of the crowd gathered at Lavenham is discussed in MacCulloch, *Suffolk*,
   pp. 294–7; R. L. Woods, 'Individuals in the Rioting Crowd: A New
   Approach', *Journal of Interdisciplinary History*, XIV (1983), 1–24.
4. What follows is based upon Griffith's account: see *HMC, Welsh MSS*, I, ii–v,
   supplemented by E. Hall, *Chronicle of the History of England during the Reign of
   Henry IV and the Succeeding Monarchs, to the End of the Reign of Henry VIII*
   (London, 1809), pp. 696–702; R. Holinshed, *Chronicles: England, Scotland
   and Ireland*, 6 vols (London, 1807–8), III, 709–10.

5. *HMC, Welsh MSS*, I, iii.
6. Ibid., iii.
7. Ibid., iii–iv; Hall, otherwise in agreement with Griffith's account, says the halters were worn by penitent rebels at Bury St Edmunds: *Chronicle*, p. 700.
8. Hall, *Chronicle*, p. 700. Griffith gives Grene's response as follows: 'they knew no captain other than Poverty, which caused them to rise and do that which was not lawful for them to do': *HMC, Welsh MSS*, I, iv. On the meaning of the 'Captain Poverty' allusion, see M. L. Bush, 'Captain Poverty and the Pilgrimage of Grace', *Historical Research*, CLVI (1992), 17, 27, 36. For the sanction of rebellion by Necessity, see, for instance, *HMC, Salisbury*, XIII, 168–9; B. Sharp, *In Contempt of all Authority: Rural Artisans and Riot in the West of England, 1586–1660* (Berkeley, 1980), p. 34; *The Moderate*, 31 Jul.–7 Aug. 1649, BL, [T]homason [T]racts, E. 568 (9). For the legal acceptance of arguments from necessity, see S. Hindle, *The State and Social Change in Early Modern England* (Basingstoke, 2000), ch. 5.
9. Hall, *Chronicle*, p. 701.
10. MacCulloch's phrase: *Suffolk*, p. 293.
11. For the alleged political conservatism of early modern revolts, see P. Zagorin, *Rebels and Rulers, 1500–1660*, vol. 1: *Society, States and Early Modern Revolution: Agrarian and Urban Rebellions* (Cambridge, 1982), pp. 61–86. For the Pilgrimage of Grace as a restitution of a 'society of orders', see M. L. Bush, *Pilgrimage of Grace: A Study of the Rebel Armies of October 1536* (Manchester, 1996), pp. 14, 21, 32, 37, 59, 64, 83, 93, 99, 177, 179, 180, 184, 210. M. E. James has seen revolt as a means of renewing social hierarchy: 'Obedience and dissent in Henrician England: the Lincolnshire Rising, 1536', *P&P*, XLVIII (1970), 1–78.
12. Hall, *Chronicle*, p. 699; *HMC, Welsh MSS*, I, iii.
13. S. Justice, *Writing and Rebellion: England in 1381* (Berkeley, 1994), p. 191.
14. *HMC, Welsh MSS*, I, iv.
15. See especially K. E. Wrightson, *English Society, 1580–1680* (London, 1982), esp. chs 1 and 6; K. E. Wrightson, 'The Social Order of Early Modern England: Three Approaches', in L. Bonfield, R. M. Smith and K. E. Wrightson (eds), *The World We have Gained: Histories of Population and Social Structure* (Oxford, 1986), pp. 177–202; J. A. Sharpe, *Early Modern England: A Social History, 1550–1760* (London, 1987), ch. 4; D. Underdown, *Revel, Riot and Rebellion: Popular Politics and Culture in England, 1603–1660* (Oxford, 1985), pp. 168–74.
16. For a fuller critique, see A. Wood, *The Politics of Social Conflict: The Peak Country, 1520–1770* (Cambridge, 1999), ch. 1.
17. For more on this, see A. Wood, 'The Place of Custom in Plebeian Political Culture: England, 1550–1800', *Social History*, XXII (1997), 46–60.
18. I base the preceding comments upon my reading of A. Leftwich, *Redefining Politics: People, Resources and Power* (London, 1983), esp. ch. 1; J. C. Scott, *Domination and the Arts of Resistance: Hidden Transcripts* (New Haven, 1990), esp. chs 3–5; R. Sennett and J. Cobb, *The Hidden Injuries of Class* (New York, 1972); E. P. Thompson, *Customs in Common* (London, 1991), ch. 2; H. Newby, *The Deferential Worker: A Study of Farm Workers in East Anglia* (London, 1977); A. Gramsci, *Selections from the Prison Notebooks* (Eng. trans., London, 1971).

19. R. Filmer, *Patriarcha and Other Writings*, ed. J. P. Somerville (Cambridge, 1991), pp. 1–68; T. Elyot, *The Book Named the Governor* (London, 1907), quotation at p. 3.

20. For a stimulating discussion of Smith, see P. Collinson, *Elizabethan Essays* (London, 1994), pp. 14–21.

21. T. Smith, *De Republica Anglorum* (Cambridge, 1982), pp. 74–7.

22. Steve Hindle, below (Chapter 5 of this volume), pp. 125–47.

23. Elyot, *Book Named the Governor*, p. 5.

24. See especially the two highly influential pieces by K. E. Wrightson: 'Estates, Degrees and Sorts: Changing Perceptions of Society in Tudor and Stuart England', in P. Corfield (ed.), *Language, History and Class* (Oxford, 1991), pp. 30–52; K. E. Wrightson, 'Sorts of People in Tudor and Stuart England', in J. Barry (ed.), *The Middling Sort of People: Culture, Society and Politics in England, 1550–1800* (Basingstoke, 1994), pp. 28–51.

25. Quotes from: PRO, REQ2/3/301; PRO, DL4/119/1; PRO, DL4/67/64; PRO, DL4/121/1681/6; PRO, C21/C11/10; PRO, E101/280/18.

26. T. Harris, 'Problematising Popular Culture', in T. Harris (ed.), *Popular Culture in England, c.1500–1850* (Basingstoke, 1995), p. 16.

27. PRO, STAC8/27/8. 2; PRO, STAC8/18/19. 14; PRO, STAC8/5/21. 17; PRO, STAC8/145/20; PRO, STAC8/203/30; PRO, STAC8/189/9. 2; PRO, STAC 8/10/18; PRO, STAC8/303/7.

28. G. R. Elton, *The Tudor Constitution: Documents and Commentary* (Cambridge, 1960), p. 15.

29. PRO, STAC8/142/16. 9; PRO, STAC8/34/4. 45. For another example, see PRO, STAC8/161/16. 2.

30. Bernard, *War, Taxation and Rebellion*, p. 111; *HMC, Welsh MSS*, I, v; Hall, *Chronicle*, pp. 699–700.

31. S. D. Amussen, '"The Part of a Christian man": The Cultural Politics of Manhood in Early Modern England', in S. D. Amussen and M. A. Kishlansky (eds), *Political Culture and Cultural Politics in Early Modern England* (Manchester, 1995), pp. 222–3. *HMC, Welsh MSS*, I, iii. For the promise of some of Kett's rebels to 'like men die in the quarrell', see Holinshed, *Chronicles*, III, 974.

32. On the fens, see PRO, STAC8/5/21. On Nidderdale, see PRO, STAC8/227/3. 4, 8. On the under-researched subject of women's riot, see R. A. Houlbrooke, 'Women's Social Life and Common Action in England from the Fifteenth-Century to the Eve of the Civil War', *Continuity and Change*, I (1986), 171–89.

33. For examples, see PRO, DL1/352, answer of Anthony and Elizabeth Harding and attached depositions; PRO, STAC5/E12/14. On women's representation of violence, see G. M. Walker, 'Crime, Gender and the Social Order in Early Modern Cheshire', University of Liverpool PhD thesis (1994). On household boundaries and women's honour, see L. Gowing, *Domestic Dangers: Women, Words and Sex in Early Modern London* (Oxford, 1996).

34. PRO, STAC8/219/23. 13.

35. After the bodies of executed Cumberland rebels were spirited away by their mothers and wives in May 1536, Henry VIII refused to accept that this conspiracy 'could not have come only of women's heads', and ordered further

investigation: see S. M. Harrison, *The Pilgrimage of Grace in the Lake Counties, 1536–7* (London, 1981), p. 127; PRO, SP1/120, fols 108, 110r–111r.

36. PRO, STAC8/227/3. 8; K. Lindley, *Fenland Riots and the English Revolution* (London, 1982), p. 54; Sharp, *In Contempt*, p. 71. For other examples of collective plebeian supplication, see B. L. Beer, *Rebellion and Riot. Popular Disorder in England during the Reign of Edward VI* (Kent State University Press, 1982), p. 99; PRO, DL4/109/8; PRO, E134/13ChasI/East14.

37. NRO, N[orfolk] Q[uarter] S[essions] C/S3/15, articles against Barnard Shippabotham.

38. R. Crab, *The English Hermite and Dagons Downfall* (1655 and 1657; repr., London, 1990), p. 19.

39. Quoted in S. L. Jansen, *Dangerous Talk and Strange Behaviour: Women and Popular Resistance to the Reforms of Henry VIII* (Basingstoke, 1996), p. 107.

40. The fullest accounts of the events in Suffolk in 1549 are in MacCulloch, *Suffolk*, pp. 300–9; Beer, *Rebellion and Riot*, pp. 142–3.

41. *Calendar of Patent Rolls, Elizabeth I. Vol. V: 1569–72*, no. 1818.

42. For Norfolk and Norwich, see PRO, SP10/8/55(I); Holinshed, *Chronicles*, III, 982–4. For Oxfordshire and Buckinghamshire, see PRO, SP10/8/32; A. Vere Woodman, 'The Buckinghamshire and Oxfordshire Rising of 1549', *Oxoniensia*, XXII (1957), 78–84. For the West Country, see Beer, *Rebellion and Riot*, pp. 182–4.

43. In Holinshed's account of Kett's defeat at Dussindale, the defeated rebels initially refused the Earl of Warwick's pardon, 'notwithstanding all such faire offers of pardon, they tooke it that there was nothing meant but a subtill practise, to bring them into the hands of their adversaries the gentlemen, that had prepared a barrell of ropes and halters, with which they purposed to trusse them up': *Chronicles*, III, 983.

44. Gowing, *Domestic Dangers*, p. 107. For similar references, see NRO, N[orwich] C[ity] R[ecords], 20A/10, fol. 8v; John Rylands Library, Nicholas MS., 72/8–9; J. S. Cockburn (ed.), *Calendar of Assize Records: Kent Indictments, Elizabeth I* (London, HMSO, 1979), cases 1479, 2709. On the meaning of such humour, see M. D. Bristol, *Carnival and Theatre: Plebeian Culture and the Structure of Authority in Renaissance England* (London, 1985), pp. 134–5.

45. J. Bellamy, *The Tudor Law of Treason: An Introduction* (London, 1979); R. B. Manning, 'The Origin of the Doctrine of Sedition', *Albion*, XII (1980), 99–121; G. R. Elton, *Policy and Police: The Enforcement of the Reformation in the Age of Thomas Cromwell* (Cambridge, 1972).

46. For an early example of the use of such material, see J. Samaha, 'Gleanings from Local Criminal-Court Records: Sedition amongst the "Inarticulate" in Elizabethan Essex', *Journal of Social History*, VIII (1975), 61–79. On its use as a source for popular politics, see most recently A. Fox, 'Rumour, News and Popular Political Opinion in Elizabethan and Early Stuart England', *HJ*, XL (1997), 597–620.

47. For examples, see *HMC, Salisbury*, XIII, 168–9; *HMC, Rutland*, I, 406; J. O. Halliwell (ed.), *The Marriage of Wit and Wisdom: An Ancient Interlude* (London, 1846), pp. 140–1; PRO, STAC8/10/18; PRO, SP16/175/81 (I).

48. C. Hill, *Antichrist in Seventeenth-Century England* (1971; 2nd edn, London, 1990); P. Lake, 'Anti-Popery: The Structure of a Prejudice', in R. Cust and

A. Hughes (eds), *Conflict in Early Stuart England: Studies in Religion and Politics, 1603–1642* (London, 1989), pp. 80–3; S. Clark, 'Inversion, Misrule and the Meaning of Witchcraft', *P&P*, LXXXVII (1980), 105.

49. Bush, *Pilgrimage of Grace*, pp. 310–11, 313.
50. On the changing geography of enclosure rioting, see R. B. Manning, *Village Revolts: Social Protest and Popular Disturbances in England, 1509–1640* (Oxford, 1988), esp. chs 2–4, 10; A. Charlesworth (ed.), *An Atlas of Rural Protest in Britain, 1549–1900* (London, 1983), pp. 8–21, 29–39, 72–80. On intra-regional differences in the west country, see Underdown, *Revel, Riot and Rebellion*, esp. chs 2–5.
51. The ensuing discussion of the Peak Country is based on Wood, *Politics of Social Conflict*, chs 1, 6–7, 9–11.
52. The clearest examples I have found are NRO, NQS C/S3/13A, examination of Roger Wells and William Seaborne, 7 Mar. 1600; ERO, Q/SR 131/34–6; Cockburn (ed.), *Kent Indictments*, case 2589. For other examples, see Cockburn (ed.), *Kent Indictments*, cases 2589, 2802; P. Clark, 'Popular Protest and Disturbance in Kent, 1558–1640', *EcHR*, 2nd Series, XXIX (1976), 367, 369; ERO, Q/SR 136/111; Samaha, 'Gleanings', pp. 72–3; PRO, SP12/263/86 (I); PRO, SP12/262/151 (I); K. S. Martin, *Records of Maidstone: Being Selections from Documents in the Possession of the Corporation* (Maidstone, 1928), pp. 263–5.
53. Other free mining areas bred similarly assertive plebeian cultures, see A. Wood, 'Custom, Identity and Resistance: English Free Miners and their Law, *c*.1550–1800', in P. Griffiths, S. Hindle and A. Fox (eds), *The Experience of Authority in Early Modern England* (Basingstoke, 1995), pp. 249–85.
54. Of the few exceptions to the prevailing pattern within Jacobean East Anglia, most occurred within areas of wood-pasture. For these exceptions, see PRO, STAC8/17/11; PRO, STAC8/73/19; PRO, STAC8/98/7; PRO, STAC8/127/13; PRO, STAC8/193/10. In contrast to East Anglia beyond the fens, organized and articulate public opposition to enclosure still prevailed within the fenlands. See PRO, STAC8/69/16; PRO, STAC8/5/2; PRO, STAC8/7/3; PRO, STAC8/27/8; PRO, STAC8/18/19; PRO, STAC8/5/21; PRO, STAC8/113/11; PRO, STAC8/129/13; PRO, STAC8/43/8; PRO, STAC8/44/11; PRO, STAC8/205/23; PRO, STAC8/203/30; PRO, STAC8/226/24; PRO, STAC8/189/9; PRO, STAC8/15/13; PRO, STAC8/311/3.
55. See A. Wood, 'Custom and the Social Organization of Writing in Early Modern England', *TRHS*, 6th Series, IX (1998), 257–69.
56. See especially K. E. Wrightson and D. Levine, *Poverty and Piety in an English Village: Terling, 1525–1700* (1979; 2nd edn, Oxford, 1995); S. D. Amussen, *An Ordered Society: Gender and Class in Early Modern England* (Oxford, 1988).
57. NRO, NCR, 16A/13, pp. 82–3, 135; NRO, NCR, 16A/6, p. 128. I am very grateful to Carole Rawcliffe and Paul Griffiths for discussions about the Norwich Mayor's Court material.
58. PRO, SP12/263/86 (I).
59. For a very revealing example, see NRO, NCR 12A/1(a), fols 123r–5r.
60. PRO, SP1/120, fols 100r–4v. On the Walsingham conspiracy, see C. E. Moreton, 'The Walsingham Conspiracy of 1537', *Historical Research*, LXIII (1990), 29–43. For the prosecution of other sixteenth-century seditious prophecies, see NRO, NCR 12A/1(a), fol. 5r; NRO, NCR 12A/1(b), 6 March

1554; Cockburn (ed.), *Kent Indictments*, cases 422 and 429; *Acts of the Privy Council, 1558–70*, 299; J. S. Cockburn (ed.), *Calendar of Assize Records: Sussex Indictments, Elizabeth I* (London, HMSO, 1975), case 1574; J. S. Cockburn (ed.), *Calendar of Assize Records: Surrey Indictments, Elizabeth I* (London, HMSO, 1980), case 1509; Samaha, 'Gleanings', 73; PRO, SP12/244/42. Mousehold Heath was, of course, the site of the Kett's rebel camp in 1549.

61. Fox, 'Rumour', p. 599; Bernard, *War, Taxation and Rebellion*, p. 117.
62. Cockburn (ed.), *Kent Indictments*, case 2442.
63. *HMC, 13th Report*, App. IV, 255.
64. NRO, NQS C/S3/15, information of Richard Braye. For similar repentance, see NRO, NCR, 16A/6, p. 107.
65. This is Douglas Hay's reading of the subject: see his 'Property, Authority and the Criminal Law', in D. Hay et al. (eds), *Albion's Fatal Tree: Crime and Society in Eighteenth-Century England* (London, 1975), pp. 40–9.
66. For Burnam, see NRO, NCR, 12A/1(a), fols 8r–9r; NRO, NCR, 16A/6, pp. 1–2, 52, 82. For a similar case, see the seditious career of Jerome Quasshe: NRO, NCR, 16A/3, pp. 9–10; NRO, NCR, 16A/6, pp. 54–5; NRO, NCR, 20A/2, fol. 40r.
67. NRO, NCR 12A/1(a), fol. 5v.
68. NRO, NCR 12A/1(a), fol. 29r; NRO, NCR, 16A/6, p. 373.
69. For important insights into anonymity and rebellion, see E. P. Thompson, 'The Crime of Anonymity', in Hay et al. (eds), *Albion's Fatal Tree*, pp. 255–344; A. Howkins and L. Merricks, '"Wee be Black as Hell": Ritual, Disguise and Rebellion', *Rural History*, IV (1993), 41–53.
70. Justice, *Writing and Rebellion*, p. 208.
71. The subject awaits its historian, but for the time being see C. Hill, 'The Many-Headed Monster', in his *Change and Continuity in Seventeenth-Century England* (1974; 2nd edn, New Haven, 1991), pp. 181–204. For the representation of Kett's rebellion, see especially Holinshed, *Chronicles*, pp. 963–1011; B. Beer, 'The Commosyon in Norfolk, 1549', *Journal of Medieval and Renaissance Studies*, VI (1976), 73–99; W. Gordon Zeeveld, 'Social Equalitarianism in a Tudor Crisis', *Journal of the History of Ideas*, VII (1946), 35–55.
72. Sharp, *In Contempt*, p. 34; Bush, *Pilgrimage of Grace*, pp. 42, 46, 209, 292; Jansen, *Dangerous Talk*, p. 106.
73. PRO, STAC8/4/3. 18 & 3; PRO, STAC8/184/33; PRO, STAC8/227/4. I hope to write about Proctor's troubles with the recusant commons and gentry of Nidderdale elsewhere.
74. ERO, D/B3/3/208, no. 14. For the riots, see J. D. Walter, 'Grain Riots and Popular Attitudes to the Law: Maldon and the Crisis of 1629', in J. Brewer and J. Styles (eds), *An Ungovernable People: The English and their Law in the Seventeenth and Eighteenth Centuries* (London, 1980), pp. 47–84.
75. PRO, SP16/175/81 (I).
76. For Warwick's repression, see PRO, SP10/8/55 (I). For the Norfolk gentry's lack of co-ordination in the face of rebellion, see D. MacCulloch, 'Kett's Rebellion in Context', *P&P*, LXXXIV (1979), 38–9.
77. On the tenant right disputes, see A. Appleby, 'Agrarian Capitalism or Seigneurial Reaction? The Northwest of England, 1500–1700', *American Historical Review*, LXXX (1975), 574–94; R. W. Hoyle, 'Lords, Tenants and

Tenant Right in the Sixteenth Century: Four Studies', *Northern History*, XX (1984), 38–63; R. W. Hoyle, 'An Ancient and Laudable Custom: The Definition and Development of Tenant Right in North-Western England in the Sixteenth Century', *P&P*, CXVI (1987), 24–55.

78. PRO, STAC8/34/4. 45.
79. PRO, STAC8/34/4. 28.
80. PRO, STAC8/34/4. 43.
81. PRO, STAC8/34/4. 46.
82. PRO, STAC8/34/4. 45; PRO, STAC8/221/1. 2.
83. Manning shows that while the 12 per cent of the enclosure riot cases heard by the Henrician and Edwardian court of Star Chamber came from Norfolk, Suffolk, Essex and Cambridgeshire, those counties accounted for only 3 per cent of such cases in James I's reign: *Village Revolts*, pp. 323, 327. See also J. A. Guy, *The Cardinal's Court: The Impact of Thomas Wolsey in Star Chamber* (Totawa, NJ, 1977), p. 110.
84. See for instance PRO, DL4/72/31; PRO, DL4/75/10; PRO, E178/611.
85. ERO, Q/SR 136/111, 131/34–6; ERO, microfilm T/A 465/1, Colchester Borough book of examinations and recognisances, unfoliated. 18 February 1623 (i.e., 1624); P. Clark, *English Provincial Society from the Reformation to the Revolution: Religion, Politics and Society in Kent, 1500–1640* (Hassocks, 1977), p. 80; Sharp, *In Contempt*, p. 38; Underdown, *Revel, Riot and Rebellion*, p. 117; NRO, NCR 12A/1(a), fol. 37r; J. S. Cockburn (ed.), *Calendar of Assize Records: Hertfordshire Indictments, Elizabeth I* (London, HMSO, 1975), case 751; Cockburn (ed.), *Kent Indictments*, cases 2228, 2908.
86. Elton, *Policy and Police*, p. 143, dates Walter's statement as June 1540; MacCulloch, *Suffolk*, p. 299, dates it to the autumn of 1536. For similar impulses in 1596, see John Walter's 'A "Rising of the People"? The Oxfordshire Rising of 1596', *P&P*, CVII (1985), 90–143.
87. PRO, SP1/160, fol. 157r.
88. R. B. Manning, 'Violence and Social Conflict in mid-Tudor Rebellions', *JBS*, XVI (1977), 35. For an important exception, which saw the seemingly purposeless slaughter of four gentlemen by Yorkshire rebels in 1549, see A. G. Dickens, 'Some Popular Reactions to the Edwardian Reformation in Yorkshire', *Yorkshire Archaeological Journal*, XXXIV (1939), 151–69. For the lack of interpersonal violence in English food and enclosure riots, see C. S. L. Davies, 'Peasant Revolt in France and England: A Comparison', *AgHR*, XXI (1973), 122–34.
89. For the perceived lack of 'gentylnes' from the gentry, see NRO, NCR, 16A/6, p. 33. For the 'small favour shewyd to the pore neybores', see MacCulloch, 'Kett's Rebellion', p. 47. For immediate recollections of the rebellion, see NRO, NCR 12A/1(a), fols 10v–11r, 31r, 81r; NRO, NCR, 16A/6, p. 3.

4

LIBELS IN ACTION: RITUAL, SUBVERSION AND THE ENGLISH LITERARY UNDERGROUND, 1603–42[1]

Alastair Bellany

In the late summer of 1637, Thomas Wentworth, Charles I's Lord Deputy in Ireland, tried to calm the frayed nerves of his ally William Laud, Archbishop of Canterbury. Laud had been upset by a series of 'libels' posted around London that had bitterly attacked him for his role in the recent pillorying and mutilation of three Puritan critics of his regime. Wentworth drew on his own experience to offer Laud some comforting advice. 'Those infamous and hellish libels', he wrote, 'are the diseases of a loose and remiss government', and 'all great ministers are commonly made the objects of them'. Ignoring them, he suggested, might actually be the best tactic.

> I remember when I was employed at York in rating the fines of knighthood I was libelled all over that part of the kingdom: in one hung up in effigy with Empson and Dudley; in another, my Lord Treasurer that was, and myself, painted upon gibbets, our names underwrit with a great deal of poetry besides. These and other libellous cartels of several sorts were brought me by dozens. I had offer made me, that the authors of some of them should be found out; my answer was thanks for their good intentions towards me, but that I know myself innocent, that I could not wish so much ill to any as to ruin them through the discovery, that I hoped they might in time better understand me and themselves, and then I was sure their own

guilt and shame would be their sufficient punishment. Till then I must possess myself in silence and patience. Thus did I quite spoil their jest, there was no noise of them at all went abroad. And . . . within a month the humour was spent, so as I never heard more of them since.[2]

To Thomas Wentworth, 'infamous and hellish' libels were a normal, if regrettable, part of the political world. Vitriolic verse, slanderous squibs and crude caricatures were, he acknowledged, the price of power. Various legal remedies – up to and including Star Chamber prosecution – were available to punish these assaults on reputation, but Wentworth believed that the cure might exacerbate the disease, that the glare of official attention might actually make a libel more widely known. And thus Wentworth's advice to Laud: ignore libels, and they might wither on the vine.

For many years, historians were content to follow Wentworth's advice. Recently, however, libels have enjoyed some systematic historiographical attention. They have been rediscovered, if not yet fully rehabilitated; slowly but surely, a number of scholars have begun to restore libels and libelling to their appropriate place in early modern political culture.[3] This appropriate place, it now seems, is a very important one. The letters, commonplace books and poetry miscellanies left by the elites – and the rather more fragmentary records left by and about the lower orders – show that libels were frequently composed, widely circulated and assiduously collected in early seventeenth-century England. Judged by volume alone, libels deserve to be treated as an important form of political expression. Historians have read libels as manifestations of political perception, as windows into what contemporaries were thinking and feeling about important individuals, like Robert Cecil or the Duke of Buckingham, or controversial events like the Overbury murder scandal of 1615–16 or the Spanish match crisis of the early 1620s.[4] Libels have also been used to gauge the extent of politicization in early modern England, with data on their production and circulation deployed to rebut claims about both the innate provincialism of the early modern gentry and the apolitical nature of their social inferiors. And by treating libels as forms of political media, historians have begun to read them not only as reflections of perceptions but also as active forces in shaping perceptions – as *agents* in opinion formation.[5] For libels were an important part of a broader, vibrant 'news culture' – a web of practices and media – that spread political information and comment widely, if unevenly, through early seventeenth-century society. This information and comment did not simply reflect opinion. In many cases, it may have helped structure it. Of course, some of the versified political libels that survive in commonplace books and miscellanies were probably produced and circulated within small coteries of poetically-inclined friends for their own, essentially private, use and amusement. But recent research has unearthed evidence that other libels circulated on a much broader scale, becoming, in a meaningful sense, public.[6] Many libels, like some of the hybrid pictures and poetry circulated against Wentworth in Yorkshire, were posted in public places for passers-by to read. Some – particularly short verses, prose squibs and ballads – may have been disseminated orally, and thus consumed by the illiterate as well as the literate. Most of all, libels were spread over a wide geographic sphere, and a somewhat more constrained social one, through the two essential practices of early modern news culture: the widespread sharing and copying of manuscript news within groups of friends, neighbours and colleagues.[7]

The authorities could do little to stop the production and dissemination of libels. Libels were produced anonymously and circulated by means that the authorities had neither the resources nor the sustained will to suppress effectively. A few writers and readers did fall into the clutches of the law, but they were a tiny and unlucky minority.[8] Libellers' ability to evade control by operating beneath the reach of effective censorship suggests we might profitably purloin an evocative label from the historiography of pre-revolutionary France and identify this world as a type of 'literary underground': a cultural space – a group of practices and genres – that existed beneath the censorship.[9] In this space, dissident, marginal and oppositional voices – but not only or necessarily these – could speak without serious risk of official intervention. This space made room for a 'politics of the excluded'.

This essay explores some of the ways libels worked in early seventeenth-century England. I want in particular to focus on the ways in which libels – acting in concert with other 'underground' genres, such as newsletters, manuscript separates and surreptitious print – played a critical, subversive role in shaping public perceptions of political events and personalities. To this end, I want to explore libels-in-action in three early seventeenth-century events. The three events – the 1604 funeral of John Whitgift, Archbishop of Canterbury; the 1628 execution of John Felton, the assassin of the great court favourite, George Villiers, Duke of Buckingham; and the 1637 pillorying, branding and mutilation of three Puritans, Henry Burton, John Bastwick and William Prynne – have a number of things in common. All three occurred during moments of political crisis or controversy, when the event's meaning was of immediate political significance. And all centred on public or semi-public rituals, explicitly designed to express certain very specific meanings. Through standardized, repetitive forms and actions, draped in many layers and various types of symbolism and performed in and through meaningful units of space, all three rituals told stories, argued cases.[10] These rituals were thus forms of political communication. But they were forms of communication that were highly vulnerable to misinterpretation or deliberate reinterpretation. In all three cases, the official meanings of the ritual were bolstered, glossed or fixed, through the circulation of printed material. But in all three cases, libels and other products of the literary underground challenged and subverted the intended meaning of these rituals and their printed glosses. Libels generated these alternative meanings in numbers of ways – through words, of course, but also through the appropriation of ritual forms and ritualized presentation (like the gallows on Wentworth's Yorkshire libels), and through the meaningful positioning of libellous texts in ritual and civic space.[11] Thus our case studies of the roles of ritual and libel in generating and contesting meaning should not only provide an opportunity to explore the politics of the excluded, but should also permit us some provisional thoughts on the ethnography of political communication in the generation before the English Revolution.

I

Archbishop John Whitgift died at Lambeth on the last day of February 1604, and his corpse was removed to the Archiepiscopal Palace in Croydon, Surrey, the following day. The morning after, it was privately buried in St John's Church in Croydon, the final resting place of a number of Whitgift's predecessors.[12] Nearly four weeks later, on 27 March, more elaborate funeral services were staged at St John's. Like most elite funerals of this era, Whitgift's rites were designed to express the honourable station of the deceased. The Archbishop was a royal councillor, and several of his colleagues, including his successor, Richard Bancroft, attended the funeral. Two noblemen, the Earl of Worcester and Lord Zouch, both of whom had been Whitgift's pupils at Cambridge, 'did him the honour in attending the hearse and carrying his banners', the heraldic flags displaying the arms of the see of Canterbury and perhaps those of Whitgift's earlier ecclesiastical and university appointments.[13] The presence of privy councillors and noblemen and the use of heraldic banners were all visible, symbolic indications of Whitgift's status. Though the funeral sermon, preached by Gervase Babbington, Bishop of

Worcester, does not survive, it too was most likely designed not solely to
stir its audience to contemplate mortality and salvation but also to praise
the deceased, adding further symbolic capital to Whitgift's worth.[14]
Whitgift's hearse must also have played its part. Usually decorated with
sumptuous mourning cloths, the elite funeral hearse was a platform for
various marks of status – whether heraldic (in this case, the arms of Whitgift's offices) or poetic (elegies and epitaphs in honour of the deceased).[15]
We do not know what verses, if any, were attached to the hearse in
Whitgift's honour, but they may well have included the Latin epitaphs,
later inscribed on his monument, which celebrated the Archbishop's
long and distinguished academic, ecclesiastical and political career, his
service to the crown and his great charitable works in Croydon itself.[16]

Whitgift's funeral rites were thus symbolic displays of his status: they
did him honour. Their meaning was glossed and fixed by the publication
of at least two laudatory epitaphs. One I.R., apparently an old client of
the late Archbishop, offered an elaborate acrostic epitaph as his last act
of service. The epitaph depicted Whitgift's funeral as an occasion for
mass mourning in the Church and the nation at large:

> Come mournful Muses, and musicians eke,
> Help with your tunes, set dreary doleful like:
> Bring us your sackbuts that will rend the ground,
> Your citars and bandoras, with their silver sound:
> Sweet voiced Cliopae sing to our verse,
> Help us this day about his sable hearse.

The whole Church, from the Archbishops to the choir boys, were to
'keep . . . this funeral both with tongue and pen'. 'Masters of children,
vergers all attend', he added, 'Keep a decorum till the heralds end'.
'Come Canterbury', the poem called,

> let us weep with thee,
> For thou shalt miss White-gift, as well as we.
> Clad all our choir and church with black throughout,
> Let city, walls, and streets be hung about:
> Kent with her wealth, can not give blacks to all,
> That would be mourners at this Fu-ne-ral.[17]

But Whitgift's last rites were vulnerable to reinterpretation. The late
Archbishop was, to say the least, a controversial figure, and his death

came at a crucial juncture in English ecclesiastical politics. In 1604, the direction of English ecclesiastical and religious policy once more seemed open to serious debate.[18] The accession of a new king in 1603 had revived the hopes of those eager to see further Protestant reform of the English Church. To these reformers – the Puritans – Whitgift's passing was an occasion for some joy, for his tenure as Archbishop had seen the Elizabethan Puritan movement and its reformist agenda brought to the verge of political defeat. But any Puritan joy was tempered by the knowledge that Whitgift's successor, Richard Bancroft, was perhaps even less likely to sympathize with renewed Puritan reformism. This Puritan resentment towards Whitgift and his successor was vented in an execrable piece of verse composed for the Archbishop's funeral. Recalling the savage irreverence of the Marprelate anti-episcopal pamphlets a decade and a half earlier, the mock epitaph was proudly titled 'The Lamentation of Dickie for the Death of Jockie' – Dickie being Richard Bancroft, and Jockie, John Whitgift.[19]

The libel's subversive message worked in two ways. The first involved direct participation in the funerary ritual itself. As we have seen, it was customary to place commemorative poetry on the hearse as a kind of last gift in honour of the deceased. The hearse was a platform for marks of the deceased's status, and conventional epitaphs were understood as declarations of honour. But at Whitgift's funeral, someone, whether the libel's author or the owner of a copy, ritually dishonoured Whitgift by pinning upon the hearse 'The Lamentation of Dickie for the Death of Jockie'.[20] This purposeful invasion of symbolic space, positioning the libel within a ritual context, gave the poem an additional, non-textual, subversive charge.

The major work of subversion, however, was performed by the text itself. The libel drew its power from a heady combination of Puritan polemic (against church courts, non-residency, the persecution of the godly) and a carnivalesque literary technique, in this case a series of inversions and reversals that twisted elegy into comedy, honour into dishonour, and order into disorder. The heart of the libel reimagined Whitgift's funeral, transforming the decorous, ordered and hierarchical rites of honour into a rowdy, dirty, dishonourable and even popish event. In the libel's anti-funeral, Whitgift's mourners are no longer men of honour, representations of the late Archbishop's status, but personifications of the vices nurtured by the Archbishop's rule: 'popish Ambition', 'vain Superstition', 'coloured Conformity', 'cankered Envy', 'cunning Hypocrisy', 'feigned Simplicity', 'masked Impiety' and 'servile Flattery'. In the libel's anti-funeral, these vices were to:

dance about his hearse,
And for his dirge chant this verse:
'Our great patron is dead and gone
And Jockie hath left dumb Dickie alone'.

Thus the powerful mourners attending the hearse become outrageous vices dancing around it. The Protestant psalms of the funeral service become a papist 'dirge' reimagined as a mocking rhyme.

The poem then suggests recruiting some of Croydon's famous charcoal burners to make up the numbers of mourners:

If store of mourners yet there lack
Let Croydon colliers be more black
And for a coffin take a sack
Bearing the corpse upon their back.[21]

At the end of the topsy-turvy funeral procession comes Bancroft, the 'chief mourner', 'singing this requiem' (again, a popish funerary custom): 'Jockie is gone / And Dickie hopes to play Jockie alone'. In the libel, Whitgift's funeral thus becomes a ritual of social derogation. Instead of lying in a coffin on a hearse, Whitgift's corpse sits inside a sack carried on the backs of colliers. Instead of mourners dressed in the stately black of mourning clothes, Whitgift is attended by mourners blackened from burning charcoal. Instead of deference and title, we have 'Dickie' and 'Jockie'. And instead of Croydon's people as the objects of Whitgift's great charity, we have Croydon's inhabitants as the agents of the Archbishop's dishonour.[22]

This was literary resistance, but it was resistance nonetheless, and the authorities treated it as such. We do not know how long the libel remained on the hearse, or how many people read it there, but we do know that copies circulated orally and in manuscript, initially among the community of the godly, but eventually finding their way into the collections of gentlemen outside that community.[23] The alleged author of the poem, one Lewis Pickering, a significant Puritan point of contact at the early Jacobean court, was severely punished in Star Chamber, and his case became the central precedent in a newly reformulated seditious libel law under which Englishmen were prosecuted well into the eighteenth century.[24] But Pickering's trial did more than punish a single libeller; it was also a semi-public forum for the reconstitution of Whitgift's damaged honour. The privy councillors sitting in Star Chamber used the occasion not only to lambast the libeller but also to praise Whitgift: the ritual proceedings of the law court were deployed to reverse the damage done by the libel.[25]

II

On 23 August 1628 a disgruntled soldier named John Felton slipped into an inn on Portsmouth High Street and stabbed to death the second most powerful man in England: George Villiers, Duke of Buckingham, beloved favourite of two English kings. The rich archive of contemporary response to Buckingham's assassination provides perhaps the best example in pre-revolutionary England of a public contest between official and unofficial versions to establish the meaning of an event.[26] In essence, the contest pitted two diametrically opposed versions of the assassination against each other: a version that vilified Buckingham as the quintessence of political, moral and religious corruption and celebrated his assassin as the godly avenger of the country's woes; and a version that mourned the Duke as an exemplary friend of kings, a leader of men fallen innocent victim to a diabolical, irreligious assassin in thrall to the forces of popular unrest. John Felton himself played only a limited role in this debate. His deeds in Portsmouth, his words to the onlookers as he was carried to the Tower of London, and two sets of statements he had written before the murder and which had made their way into public circulation – all were seized upon and dissected by contemporaries, sympathetic and hostile, but all were absorbed into a larger debate over which Felton had virtually no control. Felton's significance, and the meaning of his actions, became the property of the authorities who tried him and the legions of poets and news scribblers who wrote about him. Our case study concerns just one corner of this fascinating debate, the contested meanings that clustered around the rituals of Felton's execution and subsequent hanging in chains.

The official version of the assassination was presented to the Caroline public in two forms. At an informal level, a number of poets took it upon themselves to respond to the glut of verse celebrating the murder by circulating poems – counter-libels – of their own. The more formal official response was made through the mechanisms of the law. Felton's trial, for instance, provided the authorities with a public occasion on which to present the assassin as an unpatriotic, atheistical coward motivated by private spleen – a far cry from the libellers' Felton, the brave patriot hero and godly anti-Catholic who killed to release his fellow countrymen from the thrall of the demonic Duke.[27] But the most spectacular vehicles for expressing the official interpretation of the assassination were the rites of execution.

John Felton was hanged at Tyburn on 29 November 1628. The early modern public execution had two components: the punishment itself, designed to inflict the king's (and God's) revenge upon the body of the lawbreaker; and the verbal preliminaries to that punishment, which ideally centred on the open confession and repentance of the criminal. As much as the physical act of execution, the criminal's confession functioned, in principle at least, to reassert the moral, social and political hierarchies that had been breached by the crime.[28]

By the time he reached Tyburn, Felton had been for some weeks under the supervision of specially chosen clerics and, presumably under their guidance, he was ready to make a suitably repentant end. Eyewitness reports agree that he vigorously disavowed his crime to the crowd that had come to see him die.[29] But the audience for Felton's final repentance was not limited to the onlookers. It was massively enlarged by the publication of a cheap printed pamphlet claiming to contain Felton's last speech 'word for word as he spake it'. The printed speech attempted to fix in place the official meaning of the rites of execution. In the pamphlet, Felton played the stereotypical repentant criminal. He beseeched God for forgiveness and thanked Him for His comfort. He thanked Buckingham's widow for forgiving 'that horrid fact that I have committed'. And he thanked the authorities for sparing him the 'crueller death' he richly deserved. According to the pamphlet, Felton repeatedly described his actions as 'foul' and 'horrible', 'vile' and 'bloody'. 'Oh Lord', he cried, 'I have dishonoured Thee, I have brought a scandal upon my Religion, for which fact O Lord, I have deserved ten thousand punishments to be inflicted upon me'. 'Gentlemen', he continued, 'Know that in this bloody and heinous fact . . . I was seduced by the Devil'.[30]

The printed Felton had thus fully internalized the official version of his offence. His repentance – on the scaffold and fixed in print – had restored the moral and political order. It had also, or so it was hoped, undercut the position of his many well-wishers, for the political capital to be made out of Felton's repentance was immense. One poet taunted the assassin's 'friends' that they could never assimilate a repentant Felton to their heroic version of the assassination:

> But let him look that no remorse he show
> Lest you unsaint him; for your discontent
> Will not permit that any such repent.[31]

But the official gloss on Felton's execution and confession was challenged by an alternative, unauthorized version, constructed in the literary underground, which gave the execution a political meaning derived from a very different understanding of Felton's crime. A number of the verse libels circulating at this time reimagined Felton's last moments, transmuting a criminal's execution into a patriot hero's selfless sacrifice. In the literary underground, Tyburn was transformed from a scene of deserved punishment and honest repentance into the stage for an unrepentant and subversive martyrdom.

One of the most accomplished and widely copied poems to reinterpret the meaning of Felton's death was 'To his confined friend Mr. Felton', perhaps written by the Oxford poet Zouch Townley, shortly before the execution.[32] For Townley, Felton's physical suffering in prison – suffering that was rumoured to have included torture – and his inevitable death on the gallows were further testaments to the heroic bravery he had already demonstrated on Portsmouth High Street. Indeed, for Townley, Felton's suffering and death were an appropriately heroic closure to the narrative of his life. A reprieve, Townley wrote, would deprive the assassin's 'great story' of 'something of its miracle and glory'. The threat of torture, which occasioned the poem's composition, was not, for Townley, a physical display of royal power over Felton's body but a manifestation of Felton's power, another opportunity for him to display his bravery: 'I would have posterity to hear, / He that can bravely do, can bravely bear.' 'If every artery were broke', Townley avowed, he was sure that 'Thou would'st find strength for such another stroke.' The poem closed by evoking Felton's death as a last patriotic sacrifice:

> Farewell: undaunted stand, and joy to be
> Of public sorrow the epitome.
> Let the Duke's name solace and crown thy thrall:
> All we by him did suffer, thou for all.
> And I dare boldly write, as thou dar'st die,
> Stout Felton, England's ransom, here doth lie.

Another poet challenged official meanings by composing an alternative last speech for Felton, emphasizing, like Townley's apostrophe, the theme of private suffering for the public good.[33] In this speech, so different from the one he actually gave, Felton described the experience of simultaneous 'sorrow and joy':

> I grieve my friends and country thus to leave;
> I joy I did it of her foe bereave.
> My grief is private, as of flesh and blood;
> My joy is public: 'tis a public good.
> Let none lament my loss: for you shall find
> By loss y' have gained in another kind,
> Since he that caused all your ill is gone.

These libels, and others like them, thus challenged and subverted the official version of Felton's performance on the gallows by reimagining his last words and death as part of a secular martyrdom, a selfless sacrifice of one man for a whole nation's good.

The authorities were not finished with Felton, however. The final act of the punitive drama was the removal of his body from Tyburn to be hung in chains outside Portsmouth. This symbolic gesture was calculated to express the true horror of Felton's crime – and the severity of the king's response – by making the decomposition of the assassin's body a public, visible event. The shameful hanging in chains and the denial of honourable burial in consecrated ground were a form of ritual expulsion, situating the assassin outside normal political and religious society – a message reinforced by locating the gibbet in a liminal, marginal place, just outside Portsmouth.[34] Felton-in-chains was to be a vivid declaration of royal power and of royal love for the slain Duke. But this final expression of royal vengeance was contested as vigorously as the earlier attempts to discipline Felton's body. The intended significance of Felton hanging in chains was subverted by the libellers, the gesture transformed in the literary underground from an act of punitive degradation into an act of glorification.

Three related poems on Felton-in-chains survive, two glorifying and one denigrating him. The most widely copied and most eloquent of the three was a stunning work of apotheosis. Although it hedged its bets on the morality of the assassination, refusing to say whether Felton's 'elegy' written in blood was 'bad or good', its challenge to official intentions and meanings was potent.[35] According to the poet, Felton's hanging in chains did not shame or degrade his body but actually honoured it, laying it to rest in a glorious tomb of natural splendour, in which the elements and the creatures of the air would mourn the assassin, first preserving his body and finally removing it from the corruption of the earthly grave. In the tomb, the poet noted conventionally, the worm devours the corpse of every man equally, even a king. As Felton's intact body, embalmed by the clouds' tears, is carried up to heaven by 'pitying' birds, the punitive ritual intended to degrade Felton is reimagined as the act that allows him to transcend the corrupt mortality of the king himself. Felton is no longer the subject of royal power; he has transcended it.

III

I want to turn, finally, to a different type of execution, a different set of strategies of bodily discipline, and a different set of libellous inversions. In the early summer of 1637, three Puritans, William Prynne, Henry Burton and John Bastwick, were tried in the court of Star Chamber and convicted of the crime of seditious libel.[36] Their principal offence had been the publication and dissemination of a series of pamphlets inveighing against the ecclesiastical policies of William Laud, Archbishop of Canterbury – policies which they, and an increasing number of others, perceived as dangerous Trojan horses in which the alien disease of popery could be smuggled back into Protestant England.[37] The pamphlets surreptitiously authored, printed and distributed by Prynne, Burton, Bastwick and their allies expressed these anxieties in a style so confrontational that it forced the authorities to respond.

The seditious libel trial of Burton, Bastwick and Prynne – the Puritan triumvirate – was thus a kind of show trial that, along with the Star Chamber prosecution of the troublesome Bishop John Williams and the famous Ship Money trial of the same year, would offer the Caroline public an explicit defence of controversial royal policies.[38] The first part of the show, the actual trial in Star Chamber, remained under official control, but after the trial, the authorities chose to continue making their case to a wider public. The first route they chose was punitive. Having refused to make legally admissible answers to the charges, the three men were fined £5000 each and condemned to stand in the pillory and have their ears cut off. Prynne, since he was a recidivist, was to be branded on the cheek with the initials S.L., for Seditious Libeller. After their pillorying, the three were to be confined in 'perpetual imprisonment'. The second method of continuing the royal case was through the press. Archbishop Laud had delivered a lengthy speech in Star Chamber in order, as he put it, 'to satisfy both the court and the auditory that there was no change of religion thought on'.[39] On the advice of his counsellors, the king ordered the speech printed, thus providing the public with an official gloss on the case. As Laud put it in the preface to the text, 'this speech uttered in public, in the Star Chamber, must now come to be more public in print'.[40] Some care was taken that the book be widely distributed. Laud sent copies to Wentworth for circulation among the elite in Ireland, and nearly a year later he offered to send copies to the ambassador in Holland 'if you have any friends there which understand English'.[41] The pamphlet certainly piqued public curiosity. Shortly after its publication, one newsmonger reported that the book was selling so fast it was hard to get a copy.[42] The text itself combined a detailed rebuttal of the Puritan claims of Laudian innovations in the Church with a searing attack on the three accused men. Presenting the king and himself as the epitomes of moderation, Laud depicted the three libellers as dangerous, deluded fiends motivated by private rancour, malevolence and greed whose bitter and false libels against the bishops were also de facto attacks on the 'majesty', 'honour', 'safety' and 'religion' of the king. Their goal, Laud argued, was a 'parity in the Church or Common-wealth', their intent 'to raise a sedition, being as great incendiaries in the state ... as they have ever been in the Church'.[43]

Both the punitive rituals around the pillory and Laud's gloss on the libellers' crime proved dangerously vulnerable to subversive reinter-pretation. The pillory – along with the physical degradation involved in branding the cheek and mutilating the ears – was intended as an engine of ritual humiliation. To stand in the pillory was to be cast in the role of the meanest criminal, and thus to lose all rank and honour. The pil-lory was therefore an especially appropriate punishment for libelling, because it theatrically expressed the commonplace perception of the libeller as a creature of the lower orders, an agent of popular unrest.[44] This social derogation was intended to have an especially punitive edge for the Puritan triumvirate – a lawyer, a cleric and a doctor, gentlemen all. Like many corporal punishments in this period, the mutilations were also meaningful symbolic acts: cutting the ears, for instance, gestured at one of the senses through which the poison of libel was conveyed.

But the three victims, and some vocal members of the audience that gathered to see them pilloried, refused to accept their apportioned roles in the ritual drama.[45] Many in the substantial audience did not behave as they ought. The newsletter writer Rossingham reported that as Bastwick was taken to the pillory in Westminster Palace, 'the light common people strewed herbs and flowers before him', a gesture that a more sympathetic observer interpreted as part of the 'honour' shown the prisoners.[46] When Burton's ears were cut, many in the crowd 'wept and grieved much', 'roaring as if every one of them had at the same instant lost an ear'.[47] Most remarkably, a number of the audience dipped their handkerchiefs in Burton's blood as it dripped down through the scaffold, treating it, like the relics of a Catholic martyr, 'as a thing most precious'.[48]

In words and gestures from the scaffold, the three victims also managed to subvert the official script. Bastwick resisted, in part, by playing the joker. Two well-informed newsmongers reported that the doctor had quipped from the pillory that since there were 'collar days in the King's court', this was his 'collar day in the King's palace', a likely allusion to the royal ceremonial surrounding the Order of the Garter. Bastwick's joke turned the wooden 'collar' of the pillory around his neck into his Garter badge: a mark of shame became a royal mark of honour.[49] Bastwick's wife underlined her husband's unpenitent performance, grabbing a stool so she could climb up and give him a kiss, and then taking his severed ears home with her in a handkerchief. According to one commentator, the crowd shouted 'for joy' at the kiss, admiring its 'tender love, boldness, and cheerfulness'.[50] The same source noted that all three men acknowledged their loyalty and obedience to the king, thus undercutting Laud's claim that they were seditious, but did not repent their attack on the bishops and their policies.[51]

But martyrdom, not wit or politics, was the main order of the day.[52] Through a series of speeches and gestures – appropriated from the pages of John Foxe – all three men publicly refashioned their punishments, shaping the ritual humiliation of the seditious libeller into the glorious martyrdom of the servants of Christ.[53] The blood dripping from their mutilated ears, the pain of the knife's edge and the heat of the branding iron were refashioned into analogies of Christ's wounds, Christ's agony. 'We come here', Bastwick was reported as saying, 'in the strength of our God, who hath mightily supported us, and filled our hearts with greater comfort than our shame or contempt can be'. As the executioner approached him, Prynne avowed 'I shall bear in my body the marks of Lord Jesus'; as he was being cut and branded, he did not flinch 'or so much as changed his countenance', but 'looked up as well as he could towards Heaven, with a smiling countenance'. When some in the crowd warned Burton of the executioner's approach and 'prayed God to strengthen him', he told them he trusted in God's help and would not 'fear to follow my master Christ'.[54] And thus, as Henry Jacie noted, 'having joyfully and triumphantly suffered, despising the (intended) shame', the three were taken back to their cells.[55]

When he was informed of the events in Westminster Palace Yard, Laud was appalled at the mismanagement, lamenting to Wentworth that no 'thorough' government was possible 'where there shall be such slips in business of consequence' such that 'Prynne and his fellows should be suffered to talk what they pleased while they stood in the pillory, and win acclamations from the people'. Laud also noted with dismay that the mismanagement had continued after the pilloryings, when lax security allowed all the prisoners to be cheered and comforted by well-wishers, not only as they were leaving London for their imprisonment in different far-flung corners of the country, but also on various provincial stops *en route*.[56]

The literary underground played a crucial role in reinforcing this subversion of punitive ritual and extending its impact beyond the confines of the live event. As Laud was painfully aware, not only had the Puritans been allowed to talk to the crowd, but they had also had 'notes taken of what they spake, and those notes spread in written copies about the City'.[57] In various unpoliced writings – transcribed notes, newsletters and the like – the Puritan version of events was spread throughout the country and overseas. Before long, a Foxean martyrological account of the trial and pillorying had been surreptitiously printed in the United Provinces. At least three editions were produced in 1637 and 1638 by three different Dutch presses, some of whom had been involved in the production of the pamphlets that had led to the triumvirate's prosecution.[58] Like those earlier works, the account of the trial and pillorying was smuggled into England – perhaps sold individually or in small batches to travellers leaving for home, or imported *en masse*, like the 300 or 400 copies of a 1633 anti-ceremonialist work that was disguised as a shipment of plain paper 'and so never looked into, or let pass by negligence, or falsehood of the [customs] searchers'.[59] Once in England, the pamphlet circulated in both printed and transcribed copies, presumably through the same networks of stationers, apprentices and friends that had circulated earlier anti-Laudian works. Any exact estimate of distribution and readership is impossible, but there was at least a social breadth to the tract's Puritan readership. A copy was found by the authorities in the book collection of one Knowles, a minister, while the London Puritan artisan Nehemiah Wallington transcribed a copy into one of his notebooks.[60] The pamphlet compiled ostensibly eyewitness accounts both of the trial and of the speeches and actions on the pillory, accounts that had presumably already circulated in the manuscript notes taken at the event or in conversation. Produced and circulated in the literary underground, the pamphlet fixed in print a subversive portrait of 'those three renowned soldiers and servants of Jesus Christ, who came with most undaunted and magnanimous courage' to their fates.[61] A more legalistic critique of the proceedings was also circulated in illicit print, this time in the form of two petitions, one lengthy, one brief, on behalf of Prynne's imprisoned servant Nathaniel Wickens.[62]

In July and August 1637, manuscript libels of various types began to circulate.[63] Prynne himself was responsible for the first, a short squib in Latin and English allegedly composed as he was being taken from Westminster Palace back to his prison cell. The verse challenged the official meaning of the initials S. L. branded on his cheek, turning the mark of a dishonoured felon into the testimony of a joyful martyr: 'S. L. Stigmata Laudis' (Laud's Scars): 'Triumphant I return, my face descries, / Laud's scorching scars, / God's grateful sacrifice'.[64] Several other libels – in prose, verse, song and image – were posted in significant public spaces in London. One, pinned to the south door of St Paul's Cathedral – not only a showpiece of Laudian church refurbishment, but also the heart of London's book trade and one of the main meeting places for the exchange of political gossip and news – declaimed that Laud had leased the church from the Devil 'for service' and 'to damn the souls of men'.[65] Another, 'fastened to the north gate of St. Paul's', declared that 'the government of the Church of England is a candle in the snuff, going out in a stench'.[66] A 'short libel' posted on the Cheapside cross mobilized the martyrological discourse of persecution to declare that 'the Arch-Wolf of Cant. had his hand in persecuting the saints and shedding the blood of the martyrs', while another, in part a ballad set to the fictional tune of 'Here's a health to my Lord of Holland', branded Laud the 'captain of the devil's army against the saints'.[67]

Most fascinating of all, however, was a libel discovered hanging upon the Standard in Cheapside – the libel that prompted Wentworth's recollections of the Yorkshire gibbets and verses. Like the Yorkshire libels, the libel on the Standard was a combination of the visual and the verbal. It too was a form of mock execution. According to Laud's anxious description, the libel consisted of a 'narrow board', to one end of which was nailed a printed copy of the Archbishop's speech in the Star Chamber. The pamphlet had been 'singed with fire' and 'the corners cut off instead of the ears'. Sketched upon it was a 'pillory of ink' with, as Laud put it, 'my name to look through it'. Written on the board were at least two explanatory glosses for the viewer: 'The man that put the saints of God into a pillory of wood, stands here in a pillory of ink'; and 'The author deserves to be used thus as well as the book.'[68]

This hybrid of carnivalesque mimetic execution and anti-Laudian critique worked on several levels. The location of the libel gave it an audience, helped make it public: Cheapside was a busy thoroughfare and the square pillar of the Standard a prominent landmark. But the location may also have given the libel meaning. The Standard in Cheapside had been the site of major public executions in the later Middle Ages, and may have been used in the early seventeenth century for Cheap ward's public pillory.[69] Thus the libel may have usurped punitive space from the authorities in order to enact a symbolic punishment of its own. The text of the libel worked by reversing the ritual shaming undergone by Prynne and his friends – now the 'Saints of God' – symbolically replacing them in the pillory with the writings and the person of the Archbishop. Singeing, mutilating and pillorying Laud's speech was both a symbolic degradation of that speech and its interpretation of events, and a symbolic mutilation and pillorying of the Archbishop himself.

The subversion of the punishments of Burton, Bastwick and Prynne drew some official response. In Chester, men who had visited Prynne on his journey northwards were arrested by High Commission and compelled to suffer ritual humiliation in the public spaces of the Cathedral and Common Hall. As Peter Juice, a stationer, stood in the Cathedral, the bishop of Chester's chaplain compared Prynne and his fellows to Corah, Dathan and Abiram, the enemies of Moses and Aaron, who had been swallowed up by the earth while their supporters were struck with plague sent from God.[70] Calvin Bruen suffered a similar shaming ritual, while the pictures of Prynne that Bruen had commissioned from a local scrivener were seized and burned. Even their frames were ordered to be destroyed.[71]

But the libels, the illicit pamphlets, the notes, the newsletters, even those pictures commissioned by Chester's godly, had all done significant work in reinforcing the three men's subversive resistance on the scaffold, creating from their supposed humiliation a redemptive triumph that came back to haunt both Laud and his king. In 1640, amid the ruins of the Caroline personal rule, Prynne and Burton returned to London. The two men – both cropped, one branded – entered the capital city like kings before their coronations, or like Christ entering Jerusalem, cheered by large crowds scattering flowers and herbs before them. A godly Northamptonshire lawyer exclaimed in his diary:

> Oh blessed be the Lord for this day; for this day those holy living martyrs Mr Burton and Mr Prynne came to town, and the Lord's providence brought me out . . . to see them; my heart rejoiceth in the Lord for this day, it's even like the return of the Captivity from

Babylon. There went to meet them about 1500 or 2000 horsemen, and about 100 coaches, and the streets were all thronged with people, and there was very great rejoicing; Lord keep them and be with them and bring confusion . . . upon their cursed and malicious adversaries, let them fall before them even as Haman before Mordecai.[72]

If, as Brian Manning suggests, the ceremonial entry of Burton and Prynne was 'the first instance of popular intervention in the affairs of the Long Parliament', then we might well argue that the pre-revolutionary literary underground had helped educate the London populace for its new and ultimately destabilising political role.

IV

When the martyrs returned to London, the literary underground's war against William Laud was shifting to a new front – the newly liberated printing press. Anti-Laudian cartoons, poems, anagrams and songs began to emerge from the manuscript underground, bursting into cheap print now freed from the restraints of even partially effective censorship. The martyrs themselves soon put their own cases – both legal and religious – to the print-reading public. The political crisis that began in 1640 thus marks a major turning point in the history of libels and the literary underground: during the revolutionary decades, the increased availability of print reproduction diminished, although it did not eliminate, the role of manuscript and oral dissemination of dissident literature. But the world of the Thomason Tracts and the world of the early Stuart literary underground remain inseparable. We cannot explain the sheer generic variety and abundance of the printed political ephemera of the early 1640s without exploring the sheer generic variety, abundance and energy of the early Stuart literary underground that preceded it. Christopher Hill once asked how we got from Marprelate to the Levellers and identified a few, printed, stepping stones across Jacobean and Caroline England. It surely also makes sense to read 'The Lamentation of Dickie for the Death of Jockie' and the pillory of ink on the Standard in Cheapside as two stops on an underground tradition that carried Martin's odd-couple marriage of Puritanism and irreverence from the later sixteenth-century to Richard Overton and the Levellers.[73]

Our brief survey of libels in action suggests a number of further conclusions. Libels and other underground genres clearly provided excluded groups or men with dissident opinions with opportunities for active resistance. Underneath the censorship existed space for public challenges to the authorized versions of policies and events. The effectiveness and social scope of this type of resistance is harder to gauge; we need far more work on the audience and reception of libels. But resistance it was, and resistance capable of restructuring political perceptions in potentially destabilizing ways. 'The Lamentation of Dickie' may have changed few people's opinions of John Whitgift, but the libel may have encouraged Puritan solidarity in the difficult, confusing early years of James I. The case of John Felton was altogether more serious. In 1628 and 1629, verse libels helped create, express and sustain a set of political perceptions that diverged markedly from the perceptions held by the king and the men who would become his closest advisers. This gulf in political perception played a significant role in structuring the establishment of the Personal Rule. It may also have something to teach us about why the Personal Rule ended as it did. And when we explain the end of the Personal Rule, as well as some of the revolutionary events that followed it, we must also acknowledge the role of libels and surreptitious print in expressing, creating and sustaining a subversive martyrological interpretation of the Burton, Bastwick and Prynne case of 1637.

These case studies remind us that early Stuart politics took on a greater variety of forms and occurred in a greater variety of sites than some political historiographies acknowledge. These stories suggest that we should look for politics in symbols and in ceremonies; on hearses and on corpses; at the end of ropes and on the points of knives; in churches and on church doors; in words and in images; on walls and on paper; in print and in script; indoors and outdoors; among the elites and among the plebs; among the powerful and among the excluded, the marginal, and the dissident. One of the great merits of revisionist histories of early Stuart politics was their contention that much of what mattered to political history occurred outside Parliament – whether in the localities or at court.[74] The great challenge for post-revisionism is to continue broadening the subjects of political history by tracking down more and more sites of political activity and meaning, and collecting and decoding the many political languages and processes at work there. Once we become used to interpreting the politics of gibbets crudely drawn on Yorkshire walls, or of 'pillories of ink' drawn on pamphlets hung on London landmarks – in short, once we become ethnographers of early Stuart political culture – then, perhaps, we can offer new solutions to some of our oldest historiographical problems.

NOTES

1. An earlier version of this paper was presented to audiences at Stanford, George Washington and Rutgers Universities and has benefited from their questions and criticisms. Thanks also to Tom Freeman, Brad Gregory, Paul Seaver and Kevin Sharpe for advice on particular issues, and to Deborah Yaffe, editor supreme.

2. City of Sheffield RO, Strafford Papers, Str 7, fol. 55v.

3. See Richard Cust, 'News and Politics in Early Seventeenth-Century England', *P&P*, CXII (1986), 60–90; Pauline Croft, 'The Reputation of Robert Cecil: Libels, Political Opinions and Popular Awareness in the Early Seventeenth Century', *TRHS*, 6th Series, I (1991), 43–69; Pauline Croft, 'Libels, Popular Literacy and Public Opinion in Early Modern England', *Historical Research*, LXVIII (1995), 266–85; Alastair Bellany, ' "Raylinge Rymes and Vaunting Verse": Libellous Politics in Early Stuart England', in Kevin Sharpe and Peter Lake (eds), *Culture and Politics in Early Stuart England* (London, 1994), pp. 285–310; Adam Fox, 'Ballads, Libels and Popular Ridicule in Jacobean England', *P&P*, CXLV (1994), 47–83; Thomas Cogswell, 'Underground Verse and the Transformation of Early Stuart Political Culture', in Susan D. Amussen and Mark A. Kishlansky (eds), *Political Culture and Cultural Politics in Early Modern England* (Manchester, 1995); Andrew McRae, 'The Literary Culture of Early Stuart Libelling', *Modern Philology*, XCVII (2000), 364–92.

4. On Cecil, see Croft, 'The Reputation of Robert Cecil'. On Overbury and Buckingham, see David Underdown, *A Freeborn People: Politics and the Nation in Seventeenth-Century England* (Oxford, 1996); Bellany, 'Raylinge Rymes and Vaunting Verse'; A. Bellany, *The Politics of Court Scandal in Early Modern England: News Culture and the Overbury Affair, 1603–1660* (Cambridge University Press, forthcoming). On the Spanish Match, see Thomas Cogswell, 'England and the Spanish Match', in Richard Cust and Ann Hughes (eds), *Conflict in Early Stuart England: Studies in Religion and Politics, 1603–1642* (London, 1989).

5. For the role of news in constructing perceptions of politics as a conflictual process, see, for example, Cust, 'News and Politics'. On agency, cf. Christian Jouhaud, *Mazarinades: La Fronde des mots* (Paris, 1985), an analysis of the 'Mazarinades', the libel-like texts printed in France during the Fronde.

6. Although it has provided fruitful stimulus for many historians, Jürgen Habermas, *The Structural Transformation of the Public Sphere*, trans. Thomas Burger and Frederick Lawrence (Cambridge, Mass., 1989), offers an altogether too rigid set of definitions of 'public' to be of real use in analysing this material.

7. The essential guide is Harold Love, *Scribal Publication in Seventeenth-Century England* (Oxford, 1993), repub. in paperback as *The Culture and Commerce of Texts: Scribal Publication in Seventeenth-Century England* (Amherst, 1998).

8. On anonymity as effective disguise, see James C. Scott, *Domination and the Arts of Resistance: Hidden Transcripts* (New Haven and London, 1990), pp. 140–52; E. P. Thompson, 'The Crime of Anonymity', in Douglas Hay et al. (eds), *Albion's Fatal Tree: Crime and Society in Eighteenth-Century England* (New York, 1975).

9. Robert Darnton, *The Literary Underground of the Old Regime* (Cambridge, Mass., 1982).

10. Defining what ritual is and does is notoriously difficult. For helpful guidelines, see Edward Muir, *Ritual in Early Modern Europe* (Cambridge, 1997), introduction; David Kertzer, *Ritual, Politics and Power* (New Haven, 1988), whose definition I follow.

11. On the positioning of Italian libels in space, see Peter Burke, 'Insult and Blasphemy in Early Modern Italy', in his *The Historical Anthropology of Early Modern Italy* (Cambridge, 1987), p. 99.

12. An extract from the Croydon Register printed in D. W. Garrow, *The History and Antiquities of Croydon* (Croydon, 1818), p. 289, states that Whitgift was buried before his funeral. This extract is the only evidence I have found for the hasty burial. Historians of death ritual have noted that early modern elite funerals needed time for preparation, but the usual solution to the inevitable effects of delay was to embalm the body or encase it in lead. See David Cressy, *Birth, Marriage and Death: Ritual, Religion, and the Life-Cycle in Tudor and Stuart England* (Oxford, 1997), p. 427. For examples of elite funerals performed without the corpse, see Clare Gittings, *Death, Burial and the Individual in Early Modern England* (London, 1984), pp. 167–8. An interesting comparative case on funerary ritual, honour and dishonour is Craig Koslofsky, 'Honour and Violence in German Lutheran Funerals in the Confessional Age', *Social History*, XX (1995), 315–37.

13. Sir George Paule, *The Life of the Most Reverend and Religious Prelate John Whitgift, Lord Archbishop of Canterbury* (London, 1612), p. 93. Whitgift's memorial included the arms of the See of Canterbury, the See of Worcester and the Deanery of Lincoln and of three Cambridge colleges: *A Short Chronicle Concerning the Parish of Croydon* (Croydon, 1882, reprinted 1970), p. 54; John Corbet Anderson, *Croydon in the Past: Historical, Monumental, and Biographical* (Croydon, 1883), p. 5.

14. On heraldic funerals, see Gittings, *Death, Burial and the Individual*, ch. 8. On funeral sermons, see Ralph Houlbrooke, *Death, Religion, and the Family in England, 1480–1750* (Oxford, 1998), ch. 10. Paule, *Life of Whitgift*, p. 93 notes Babbington's sermon was on 2 Chronicles 24:15–16: 'But Jehoiadah waxed old, and was full of days, and died. An hundred and thirty years old was he when he died. And they buried him in the City of David, with the kings, because he had done good in Israel, and towards God and his house'.

15. On the hearse as symbolic platform, see Gittings, *Death, Burial and the Individual*, p. 171; on the placing of elegies and epitaphs on hearses and monuments, see Houlbrooke, *Death, Religion, and the Family*, p. 328.

16. Inscriptions given in Anderson, *Short Chronicle*, pp. 54–5, and, with translations, by Garrow, *History and Antiquities of Croydon*, pp. 285–8.

17. I. R., *An Epitaph, On the Death of the Late Most Reverend Father in God, Iohn: by his Providence the Arch-Byshop of Canterburie his Grace* (London, 1604), sigs. A2v–A3r. The other surviving printed epitaph is Thomas Churchyard, *Churchyards Good Will: Sad and Heavy Verses, in the Nature of an Epitaph, for the Losse of the Archbishop of Canterbury* (London, 1604).

18. A full consideration of the legal, political and ecclesiastical significance of this case is given in Alastair Bellany, 'A Poem on the Archbishop's Hearse: Puritanism, Libel, and Sedition after the Hampton Court Conference', *JBS*, XXXIV (1995), 137–64.

19. At least three versions of the poem survive. The most complete text is among the papers of Sir Peter Manwood, BL, Add. MSS 38139, fol. 58r and is printed in Bellany, 'Poem on the Archbishop's Hearse', p. 138. The other two extant copies are fragments of the whole. One is in the 2nd Earl of Clare's commonplace book, BL, Harley MS 6863, fol. 71; the other is in John Hawarde's account of the Star Chamber prosecution of the poem's alleged author: see William Paley Baildon (ed.), *Les Reportes Del Cases in Camera Stellata (1593–1609) From the Original MS. of John Hawarde* (London, 1894), p. 223. The poem and case are briefly discussed in Croft, 'Libels, Popular Literacy and Public Opinion', p. 275. On the connections between the culture of libelling and the style of the Marprelate and anti-Marprelate pamphlets, see Patrick Collinson, 'Ecclesiastical Vitriol: Religious Satire in the 1590s and the Invention of Puritanism', in John Guy (ed.), *The Reign of Elizabeth I: Court and Culture in the Last Decade* (Cambridge, 1995).
20. *Les Reportes*, p. 223.
21. The Croydon colliers produced and sold charcoal for the London market and were a frequent butt of literary witticism: see Anderson, *Short Chronicle*, pp. 170–2. The evocation of dirt might also have worked to subvert the legitimate elegists' poetic elaborations on the 'white' in 'White-gift': e.g., I.R.'s evocation of Whitgift as a 'pearl, or sunshine bright, / Virgin-like pillar, and star shining light', in *An Epitaph*, sig. A2r. Mary's Archbishop Bonner had been noted for his Croydon complexion, see Patrick Collinson, *Elizabethan Essays* (London, 1994), p. 175, a reference I owe to Tom Freeman.
22. In addition to the monumental epitaph, both I. R., *An Epitaph*, sig. A3v and Churchyard, *Churchyards Good Will*, sig. B4r, stress Whitgift's close and charitable relations with Croydon.
23. On the libel's circulation, see Bellany, 'Poem on the Archbishop's Hearse', pp. 153–5.
24. Bellany, 'Poem on the Archbishop's Hearse', pp. 151–7.
25. Paule, *Life of Whitgift*, p. 92; *Les Reportes*, pp. 225–8.
26. See my *Death of a Favourite: John Felton, Charles I and the Assassination of the Duke of Buckingham* (Manchester University Press, forthcoming); and 'Raylinge Rymes and Vaunting Verse'. See also James Holstun, ' "God Bless Thee Little David": John Felton and his Allies', *ELH*, LIX (1992), 513–52, and the chapter on Felton in his forthcoming *Ehud's Dagger* (Verso Books).
27. Attorney-General Heath's speech at Felton's trial, PRO, SP 16/121/78.
28. See J. A. Sharpe, ' "Last Dying Speeches": Religion, Ideology and Public Execution in Seventeenth-Century England', *P&P*, CVII (1985), 144–67; Peter Lake, 'Deeds Against Nature: Cheap Print, Protestantism and Murder in Early Seventeenth-Century England', in Sharpe and Lake (eds), *Culture and Politics*, pp. 257–83. Both essays are indebted to Michel Foucault, *Discipline and Punish: The Birth of the Prison*, trans. Alan Sheridan (London, 1977), part 1.
29. E.g. Thomas Barrington to his mother, 30 November 1628, in Arthur Searle (ed.), *Barrington Family Letters, 1628–1632* (Camden Society, Fourth Series, XXVIII, London, 1983), p. 39.
30. *The Prayer and Confession of Mr. Felton, Word for Word as hee Spake it immediately before his Execution. Novemb. 29, 1628* (London, 1628), pp. 1–6.

31. Printed in J. A. Taylor, 'Two Unpublished Poems on the Duke of Buckingham', *Review of English Studies*, XL (1989), 232–40.

32. Printed in F. W. Fairholt (ed.), *Poems and Songs Relating to the Duke of Buckingham* (Percy Society: London, 1850), pp. 74–6. On Townley, see John Pory to Joseph Mead, 14 November 1628, in Thomas Birch, compiler, *The Court and Times of Charles I* (London, 1849), I, 427–8, which includes a copy of the verses. For evidence of circulation, see the copy transcribed by the reformed highwayman John Clavell, printed in J. H. P. Pafford, *John Clavell, 1601–43: Highwayman, Author, Lawyer, Doctor* (Oxford, 1993), pp. 152–3.

33. Printed in Fairholt, *Poems and Songs*, p. 76.

34. On the location, see John Pory to Joseph Mead, 12 December 1628, BL, Harley MS 383, fols 77–8, transcribed in William S. Powell (ed.), *John Pory, 1572–1636: Letters and Other Minor Writings* (Chapel Hill, 1977), microfiche, p. 139. For ritual expulsion, see Michael MacDonald and Terence Murphy, *Sleepless Souls: Suicide in Early Modern England* (Oxford, 1990), pp. 18–20.

35. Poem printed (from BL Sloane MS 826, fol. 197r) in David Norbrook and H. R. Woudhuysen (eds), *The Penguin Book of Renaissance Verse, 1509–1659* (London, 1992), pp. 148–9. The poem is discussed by Gerald Hammond, *Fleeting Things: English Poets and Poems, 1616–1660* (Cambridge, Mass., 1990), pp. 65–6; Holstun, 'God Bless Thee Little David', pp. 541–2; David Norbrook in 'Lucan, Thomas May, and the Creation of a Republican Literary Culture', in Sharpe and Lake (eds), *Culture and Politics*, p. 55, and in David Norbrook, *Writing the English Republic: Poetry, Rhetoric and Politics, 1627–1660* (Cambridge, 1999), p. 55. James Holstun is preparing the case that this poem was written, as one manuscript copy suggests, by John Donne, an identification that Norbrook in *Writing the English Republic*, p. 55, fn.66, finds 'implausible', though not on grounds of poetic skill. Copies of the two other Felton-in-chains verses can be found in BL, Add. MSS 15226, fols 28r–v, and Bodl., MS English Poetry e.14, fol. 76v.

36. For an important account of the case and grudging recognition of the damage it did to the Caroline regime, see Kevin Sharpe, *The Personal Rule of Charles I* (New Haven and London, 1992), pp. 758–65. See, too, Stephen Foster, *Notes From the Caroline Underground: Alexander Leighton, the Puritan Triumvirate, and the Laudian Reaction to Nonconformity* (Hamden, Conn., 1978), ch. 5.

37. There is, of course, a rich and controversial debate about the relation between these perceptions and the reality of Laudianism. For the range of opinion, see Nicholas Tyacke, *Anti-Calvinists: The Rise of English Arminianism, c.1590–1640* (Oxford, 1987); Peter Lake, 'The Laudian Style: Order, Uniformity and the Pursuit of the Beauty of Holiness in the 1630s', in Kenneth Fincham (ed.), *The Early Stuart Church, 1603–1642* (London, 1993); Sharpe, *The Personal Rule of Charles I*, ch. 6.

38. Charles I's relations with the 'public' – his shifting attitude to the task of explaining himself to his subjects – needs further study. For an important case study, see Thomas Cogswell, 'The Politics of Propaganda: Charles I and the People in the 1620s', *JBS*, XXIX (1990), 187–215.

39. Laud to Wentworth, 28 June 1637, in *The Works of the Most Reverend Father in God, William Laud, D.D.* (Oxford, 1847–60), VII, 355–6.

40. William Laud, *A Speech Delivered in the Star-Chamber, on Wednesday, the XIVth of Iune, MDCXXXVII. At the Censure, of Iohn Bastwick, Henry Burton, & William Prinn; Concerning Pretended Innovations in the Church* (London, 1637), sig. A3v.

41. Laud to Wentworth, 28 June 1637, in Laud, *Works*, VII, 355–6; Wentworth to Laud, 28 August 1637, Strafford Papers Str P 7, fol. 41v; Laud to Sir William Boswell, 24 May 1638, in Laud, *Works*, VI, 528. According to M. A. Shaaber's *Check-list of Works of British Authors Printed Abroad, in Languages other than English, to 1641* (New York, 1975), p. 111, a Dutch translation of Laud's speech was published in 1638 as *Een Oratie, die onlangs ghedaen is in de Ster-Camer*.

42. Rossingham newsletter, 29 June 1637, PRO, SP 16/362/76, printed in S. R. Gardiner (ed.), *Documents Relating to the Proceedings Against William Prynne* (Camden Society, NS XVIII, London, 1877), p. 83; W. Hawkins to Robert Sidney, 2nd Earl of Leicester, 29 June/9 July 1637, *HMC, De L'Isle*, VI, 114.

43. Laud, *Speech Delivered in the Star-Chamber*, sigs. A4r–v; a1v–a3r; a3v; p. 5, pp. 16ff; on libel and sedition, see Bellany, 'Poem on the Archbishop's Hearse', p. 156.

44. On social status and libelling, see Bellany, 'Poem on the Archbishop's Hearse', p. 159.

45. For Elizabethan Catholics and their martyrs, see Peter Lake and Michael Questier, 'Agency, Appropriation and Rhetoric under the Gallows: Puritans, Romanists and the State in Early Modern England', *P&P*, CLIII (1996), 64–107. More generally, see, too, Thomas W. Laqueur, 'Crowds, Carnival and the State in English Executions, 1604–1868', in A. L. Beier, David Cannadine and James M. Rosenheim (eds), *The First Modern Society: Essays in English History in Honour of Lawrence Stone* (Cambridge, 1989).

46. Rossingham newsletter, 6 July 1637, PRO SP 16/363/42, printed in Gardiner (ed.), *Documents Relating to William Prynne*, pp. 86–7; *A Briefe Relation of Certaine Speciall and Most Materiall Passages, and Speeches in the Starre-Chamber* (Leiden, 1638) [STC 1570], p. 18.

47. Rossingham newsletter, 6 July 1637, PRO, SP 16/363/42, printed in Gardiner (ed.), *Documents Relating to William Prynne*, pp. 86–7. See, too, Garrard's report to Wentworth, 24 July 1637, Strafford Papers 17 (137): 'The place was full of people, who cried and howled terribly, especially when Burton was cropped'.

48. *A Briefe Relation*, p. 31; a bemused Sir Kenelm Digby, a Catholic, refers to the 'puritans' collecting the 'bloody sponges and handkerchiefs that did the hangman service in the cutting off their ears', in a 27 July 1637 letter to Viscount Conway, PRO, SP 16/364/68. On Protestant 'relic behaviour' more generally, see Brad Gregory, *Salvation at Stake: Christian Martyrdom in Early Modern Europe* (Cambridge, Mass., 1999), pp. 175, 299. For Elizabethan Catholic examples, see Lake and Questier, 'Agency, Appropriation and Rhetoric', p. 33.

49. Rossingham newsletter, 6 July 1637, PRO, SP 16/363/42, printed in Gardiner (ed.), *Documents Relating to William Prynne*, pp. 86–7; Garrard to Wentworth, 24 July 1637, Strafford Papers 17 (137). On the Order of the Garter in Caroline court culture, see Sharpe, *The Personal Rule of Charles I*, pp. 219–22, and Roy Strong, *Van Dyck: Charles I on Horseback* (New York, 1972). For another example of humour as a means of subverting punitive

ritual, see the account of the 1615 hanging of James Franklin, the Overbury murderer, in J. Payne Collier (ed.), *The Egerton Papers* (Camden Society, XII, London, 1840), pp. 474–6.

50. Garrard to Wentworth, 24 July 1637, Strafford Papers 17 (137); *A Briefe Relation*, p. 18.
51. *A Briefe Relation*, pp. 18, 21, 31.
52. John R. Knott, *Discourses of Martyrdom in English Literature, 1563–1694* (Cambridge, 1993), pp. 134–44.
53. Knott, *Discourses of Martyrdom*, p. 140, emphasizes the Foxean origins.
54. *A Briefe Relation*, pp. 18, 23 (mispaginated as p. 21), 31. For greater detail, see Knott, *Discourses of Martyrdom*, pp. 140–2.
55. Henry Jacie to John Winthrop, *Winthrop Papers*, 5 vols (Massachusetts Historical Society, 1929–47), III, 487.
56. Laud to Wentworth, 28 August 1637, in Laud, *Works*, VI, 497–8. See, too, the Attorney-General's examination of John Maynard and James Ingram, 22 September 1637, PRO, SP 16/368/14.
57. Laud to Wentworth, 28 August 1637, in Laud, *Works*, VI, 497–8. Notes taken at executions were an important source for many of the great martyrological accounts of the early modern era. Note-takers, using shorthand and other forms of speed writing, were also common at sermons and at legal events in early seventeenth-century England.
58. The Short Title Catalogue identifies the publishers as Stam of Amsterdam (in 1637) [STC 1569], W. Christiaens of Leiden (in 1638) [STC 1570], and the Richt Right Press of Amsterdam (in 1638) [STC 1570.5]. According to the STC, Christiaens had published earlier works by Bastwick.
59. Sir William Boswell to Secretary John Coke, 20/30 September 1633, in W. W. Greg (ed.), *A Companion to Arber* (Oxford, 1967), p. 291.
60. PRO SP 16/413/77, 'An Inventory of the Books found in Mr Knowles his house', 15 February 1638; Paul Seaver, *Wallington's World: A Puritan Artisan in Seventeenth-Century London* (Stanford, 1985), pp. 159–60; *Historical Notices of Events Occurring Chiefly in the Reign of Charles I by Nehemia Wallington* (London, 1869), I, xxxviii–xlv, 62–63, 71, 73ff. Sharpe uses a manuscript transcription of Bastwick and Burton's speeches reported in the pamphlet: *The Personal Rule of Charles I*, pp. 762–3.
61. *A Briefe Relation*, p. 18.
62. *Woodstreet-Compters-Plea, for its Prisoner. Or The Sixteen Reasons, which Induce mee Nathaniel Wickins . . . To Refuse to Take the Oath Ex Officio* (Richt Right Press: Amsterdam, 1638) [STC 25587]; *To the Kings Most Excellent Majesty. The Humble Petition of Nathaniell Wickens a poore Prisoner in the White-Lyon in Southwark in the County of Surrey* (1639), which is not in the STC. A copy is preserved in PRO, SP 16/424/105.
63. These libels are discussed briefly by Cogswell, 'Underground Verse', p. 277, and Dagmar Freist, *Governed by Opinion: Politics, Religion and the Dynamics of Communication in Stuart London, 1637–1645* (London, 1997), pp. 129–30.
64. The verses, in Latin and English, are reported by Rossingham in his 6 July 1637 newsletter (PRO, SP 16/363/42) and were printed in *A Briefe Relation*, p. 21. See, too, Knott, *Discourses of Martyrdom*, p. 143.

65. Laud to Wentworth, 28 August 1637, ciphered side-letter, in Laud, *Works*, VI, 371–2.

66. Laud's diary entry for 25 August 1637, in Laud, *Works*, III, 229.

67. 'Arch-Wolf' libel, found in early July, noted in Laud's diary entry for 7 July 1637, in Laud, *Works*, III, 228; ballad reported in Laud to Wentworth, 28 August 1637, ciphered side-letter, in Laud, *Works*, VI, 371–2. Laud's diary entry for 29 August refers to 'Another short libel against me, in verse', but does not reveal the content: see *Works*, III, 229.

68. Described in Laud to Wentworth, 28 August 1637, ciphered side-letter, in Laud, *Works*, VI, 371–2; Laud's diary notes that the libel was discovered on 25 August, Laud, *Works*, III, 229.

69. On executions at the Standard, see John Stow, *A Survay of London*, (ed.) Henry Morley (London, 1890), p. 260. There are literary references to pillorying in Cheapside collected in Edward H. Sugden, *A Topographical Dictionary to the Works of Shakespeare and his Fellow Dramatists* (Manchester, 1925), p. 112. See, too, Tim Harris, *London Crowds in the Reign of Charles II: Propaganda and Politics from the Restoration until the Exclusion Crisis* (Cambridge, 1987), pp. 24, 187–8; Ian Archer, *The Pursuit of Stability: Social Relations in Elizabethan London* (Cambridge, 1991), pp. 1, 200, 219, a reference I owe to Paul Seaver.

70. *Petitions of Peter Juice and Calvin Bruen in The Severall Humble Petitions of D. Bastwicke, M. Burton, M. Prynne And of Nath. Wickins, Servant to the said Mr Prynne. To the Honourable house of Parliament* (London, 1640), [BL TT E207(4)], sigs. D2v and E3r ff.

71. Andrew Foster, 'Church Policies of the 1630s', in Cust and Hughes (eds), *Conflict in Early Stuart England*, p. 207; Knott, *Discourses of Martyrdom*, p. 143.

72. Diary of Robert Woodforde, New College, Oxford, MS 9502, entry for 28 November 1640; Prynne and Burton's return is curiously underanalysed, with the notable exception of Brian Manning, *The English People and the English Revolution*, 2nd edn (London, 1991), pp. 51–3. See, too, Conrad Russell, *The Fall of the British Monarchies, 1637–1642* (Oxford, 1991), pp. 221–2.

73. Christopher Hill, 'From Marprelate to the Levellers', reprinted in *The Collected Essays of Christopher Hill*, I (Amherst, 1989). On Overton and the Marprelate tradition in the 1640s, see Nigel Smith, *Literature and Revolution in England, 1640–1660* (New Haven and London, 1994), ch. 9.

74. The *locus classicus* is Conrad Russell, *Parliaments and English Politics, 1621–1629* (Oxford, 1979), ch. 1.

5

THE POLITICAL CULTURE OF THE MIDDLING SORT IN ENGLISH RURAL COMMUNITIES, *c.*1550–1700

Steve Hindle

In *De Republica Anglorum*, published in 1583, Sir Thomas Smith famously described the structure of the English commonwealth in terms of four ranks of men, descending from the gentry at its apex to day-labourers at its base. Simultaneously, however, he noted the more fundamental distinction between 'them that bear office, and them that bear none'. In this way, Smith transformed his own four-class social hierarchy into a binary, indeed adversarial, model of political participation. The threshold of access to the circuits of authority was, nevertheless, relatively low. Smith noted that, next to the gentry, yeomen had 'the greatest charge and doing in the commonwealth' and conceded that in villages even 'such low and base persons' as 'poore husbandmen', 'copiholders' and 'artificers' (among others) 'be commonly made Churchwardens, alecunners, and manie times Constables, which office touch more the commonwealth'.[1] Smith's list of the considerable public responsibilities exercised by the middling sort included 'administration in judgements', 'correction of defaults', 'election of offices', 'appointing and collection of tributes and subsidies' and 'making lawes'. Thus even in the formal tradition of political thought, the widespread participation of men of middling status was recognized as a significant structural characteristic of the English state.

This essay tests Smith's analysis against surviving evidence of the role of the middling sort in governing English rural communities in the

sixteenth and seventeenth centuries. As such it is concerned with the
'bottom line' of early modern government, the interface between legitimate and illegitimate political participation.[2] Its principal focus is the
evolution of the characteristic institutional forum in which popular
political culture found expression: the parish vestry. It will suggest, first,
that the vestry was in some sense the successor of the manorial court,
that 'little commonwealth, whereof the tenants are the members, the
Lord the body, and the law the head'.[3] Vestrymen and manorial jurors
were of broadly similar social status, being mainly drawn from the chief
inhabitants of the local community. Like manorial homages, vestries had
a de facto tendency towards oligarchy: in each case, political participation was relatively circumscribed, and reflected the social and economic
ascendancy of village elites. Secondly, however, it will argue that the
similarities between the two institutions were largely superficial, since
homagers and vestrymen enjoyed entirely different relations both with
their superiors and with their neighbours. The increasing range of
activities for which the parish became responsible in the late sixteenth
century contributed to the transformation of social and political relationships in the countryside, especially by conferring even more discretionary authority on vestrymen, and thereby added even greater depth
and complexity to relations between the 'better' and 'worse' sort in the
local community. Thirdly, it will suggest that the late sixteenth-century
tendency of gentlemen to absent themselves from the communities in
which they were supposed to reside as paragons of hospitality and paternalism created a social and political space in which the village elites came
to exercise authority. Rural governance therefore became increasingly
reliant on men of middling rather than gentle status. It seems likely that
only a minority of rural villages could claim a resident squire even in
the Elizabethan period, ensuring that only the yeomen – the 'plebeian',
'vulgare and common sorte of people' of whom the heraldic purist Sir
John Ferne was so dismissive in 1586; the 'midle people, betweene
Cottagers and gentlemen' of whom George Tooke wrote so approvingly
in 1635 – were present to run their local affairs.[4] Finally, it will tease out
the wider significance of the emergence of the parish vestry for the long-
term development of English political culture. Above all, it will suggest
that the growth of the state narrowed both the meaning and significance
of community in rural society. Those small knots of reliable men to
whom authority was delegated from the turn of the sixteenth century
in turn became agents of social and political transformation in rural
England.

I

The evolution of vestries has been variously associated both with the decline of manorial courts and with the growth of the secular administrative responsibilities of the parish. The historiographical orthodoxy is that the institutionalization of poor relief was a decisive moment in the jurisdictional transition from manor to vestry, since the acts of 1598–1601 effectively transformed each parish into a welfare republic.[5] In practice, however, this process was rather more complicated. In the first place, recent research into manorial jurisdictions has associated the late Elizabethan period not so much with a decline as with a flourishing of the activity of manorial courts leet.[6] Indeed, at the same time as legislation placed new powers in the hands of parish officers, many manors guarded jealously their leet jurisdiction, powers that Tudor parliaments increased rather than diminished.[7] Secondly, the sluggishness with which welfare provision was actually enforced in the countryside meant that vestries remained relatively rare until the civil war: only the harvest crisis of 1647–50 finally provoked the overwhelming majority of parishes to appoint overseers for the collection of poor rates.[8] The widespread inauguration of the vestry was accordingly delayed in many places until the Restoration or even later. Strong manorial structures, moreover, endured as long as did open-field husbandry, that is (in many cases, at least) to the end of the seventeenth century, and perhaps even beyond. Especially where numerous manors fragmented the territory of the parish, it might not be until the eighteenth century that the vestry became a more significant body than the manorial court. Where manor courts were weak, particularly where enclosure had removed the necessity for communal self-regulation or where manorial and parochial jurisdiction were coextensive, the vestry might flourish.[9]

The measurement of the general applicability of these models is complicated by the evidential problem of detecting vestries in action. Vestry decisions are often concealed in churchwardens' or overseers' accounts, buried amidst the arcana of audit and appointment. The fact that the term 'vestry' is not always used to describe those who met in the name of the parish has led to the suggestion that 'leading parishioners' is a more appropriate term than 'vestrymen'.[10] Even where special books were provided specifically for the purpose of keeping vestry minutes, it is misguided to assume that the foundation of the vestry was coincident with the purchase of the book. Nonetheless, some impressionistic evidence of the spread of the vestry emerges from a survey of the earliest

dates from which vestry minute books survive. In the four counties of
Essex, Hertfordshire, Lincolnshire and Norfolk, 106 parishes have vestry
minute books originating from before 1700; of these, only 12 date from
before 1600; 7 from between 1600 and 1619; 21 from between 1620 and
1639; 15 from between 1640 and 1659; 21 from between 1660 and 1679;
and 30 from between 1680 and 1699. Of the 132 ancient parishes in Hertfordshire, only 27 (20 per cent) have vestry minutes predating 1730.

Whatever the precise chronology of the transition from manor to
vestry, the similarity in the composition of the two bodies has often
been noted. The seventeenth-century vestrymen of Whickham (County
Durham), for example, were arguably the direct heirs of the manorial
jury for they were often also the leading copyholders of the local
manor.[11] The relationship between manor and vestry was, however,
rather more complex. The manorial court classically expressed the
medieval 'ascending' concept of political authority, and the activities of
homagers hint at the self-reliance and potential for independence
among peasants who had standing in the village irrespective of the
demands made of them by landlords. The vestry, by contrast, embodied
a 'descending' theory of governance, and the status of vestrymen was
enhanced precisely because they wielded authority on behalf of external
powers over whom they had little influence. Although the vestry is
'sometimes cited as successor to the manor court', in practice it seldom
'enjoyed the democratic structure of its predecessor'.[12]

As detailed work on medieval governance has shown, moreover, parishes themselves had elaborated sophisticated administrative structures
long before the fading of the authority of the manor.[13] Originating in the
mid-sixteenth-century metropolis, Beat Kumin has argued, the trend
towards 'oligarchic parish government' had by the late Tudor period
spread beyond London and provincial capitals.[14] It is nonetheless striking
how frequently the sources refer ambiguously to parish meetings attended,
and officers chosen, by 'the inhabitants' or 'the neighbours'. What, for
example, is one to make of vestry memoranda at Sigglesthorne (East
Yorkshire) of agreements made 'by the neighbours of the parish'? At
Frampton (Lincolnshire), vestry minutes of the 1620s speak both of
the 'nomination' and 'election' of officers, and variously refer to the
constituency as 'the minister and inhabitants', 'the minister and neighbours', or the 'inhabitants and parishioners'. By the 1630s, Frampton
vestry elections were conducted 'according to our ancient custom', itself
a formulation which implies a departure from fully open or democratic
participation.[15] The ambiguity of these formulations should remind us

that even where participation in parish governance was not regulated by a formal constitution, the parish vestry consisted of an inner group of trustees, which was answerable in some often ill-defined sense to a wider body of members or subscribers. As an early eighteenth-century satirist argued, even where the number of vestrymen 'by their own accounts, to about twenty-six amounts', a 'small detachment' of them, 'more sly, more crafty and more rich', tended to 'govern the rest'.[16]

It is equally difficult to specify the chronological development of the 'select' or 'close' vestry: that is, 'a body of one or two persons or occasionally more, serving for life and filling vacancies among themselves by co-option'. Unlike the 'open vestry', the select vestry had 'no organic connection with the inhabitants at large, but acted in all respects in their name and on their behalf', and select vestrymen only 'were intended by the word "inhabitants"'. This, then, was 'a fragment of the parish which conceived itself to be endowed with all the legal powers of the parish as a whole'.[17] For all practical purposes, select vestries justified their jurisdictions in one of two ways: either by prescription (or 'immemorial custom'), or by bishop's faculty. The former variant emerged from the oligarchic structure which had existed even within the open vestry. In those areas where constables and churchwardens were already allowed an important say in the nomination or appointment of their successors, where periodic consultative meetings were attended only by the parish officers, and where the right of a small number of men to speak on behalf of the inhabitants as a whole had been recognized, it was a short step for self-selecting bodies of men to justify their perpetual existence on the basis of a custom 'whereof the memory of man runneth not to the contrary'. This claim might easily be extended to include not only the ancient ecclesiastical functions of the parish, but also the newer obligations imposed by Tudor statutes. Such self-conscious statements of the latent oligarchic principle seem to have become especially common in the counties of Northumberland and Durham during the late sixteenth century. Prescription therefore provided the select vestry with an extra-legal constitution, albeit one which was consonant with both medieval custom and Elizabethan legislation.[18]

The members of 'customary' select vestries, however, were all too conscious that the mere assertion of tradition might not deter an indignant crowd of protesting ratepayers. Incumbents and churchwardens accordingly sought to articulate the prescriptive structure of their vestry in an authoritative document, or bishop's faculty, whereby the oligarchic structure of parish governance might be formally established or confirmed by the ecclesiastical hierarchy. Although their legal status was called into question with the attack on episcopacy in 1641, vestries based on these formal constitutions thrived well into the nineteenth century.[19] The survival rate of bishop's faculties in *parish* archives is negligible, perhaps because by definition they contained evidence of an older customary form of parish management which might be cited against the 'four and twenty' in the future. Faculties might accordingly have been deliberately destroyed by the very oligarchies whose actions they justified. Statements at visitations or in minute books that officers had been chosen 'by the parish', even in the absence of any other formal evidence of their structure, should not be taken to imply that select vestries did not exist.[20] Systematic work on those bishop's faculties which have survived in *episcopal* archives might well confirm the Webbs' assessment that while select vestries by prescription seem to have cropped up, sporadically, over the greater part of England, they appear to have been the common form only in the northern counties; and that (by implication) formally-constituted select vestries were more characteristic of the south and east (and especially of parishes in and around the metropolis). Yet, it is likely to remain the case that close vestries will prove easiest to identify in operational terms, either by their practice of appointing new members by co-option, or by their emphasis on secrecy.

Only very occasionally, however, was the need for secrecy explicitly justified. At Swallowfield (Wiltshire), anything done or said by the vestrymen under the terms of 26 resolutions drawn up in 1596 was to be 'kept secret and not to be revayled further than [the] company' and none of company were to 'use any comunycation or means consernyne the meetyngs'. Although the vestries of neither Finchingfield nor Braintree (Essex) openly passed resolutions to similar effect, their deliberations were almost certainly concealed from the parishioners at large. The sheer number of parish chests with surviving hasps and locks also hints at restrictive procedures and at the importance which was attached to secrecy in town government: at Mildenhall (Suffolk), for example, there was not only a lock on the great chest in the vestry but on the vestry door itself.[21] The chief inhabitants of Swallowfield justified the secrecy of their proceedings on the grounds that publicity may 'tend to or procure the discredett or disgrace of our meetings and good intent, or of owre company'.[22] Co-option, meanwhile, was ubiquitous. In Whickham, where a close vestry of 24 men emerged in the early seventeenth century (and was subsequently supplemented by a sub-committee numbering 16 in the early eighteenth), 'members appear to have served for life, adding to their numbers by co-option when occasion arose'. In practice, this might mean that the numbers serving at any one time were very small indeed. At Bedale (North Yorkshire), the number of vestrymen was sometimes allowed to fall well below the customary level before replacements were admitted: judging by the number of new members admitted together 'to make full and perfect the said number' of 24, there were only 21 serving vestrymen in 1664, 19 in 1661, 17 in 1630, 16 in 1652, and as few as 9 in 1646. Those making the new appointments were described variously as 'the parson and such of the twenty-four as subscribed', and 'the parson and such of the surviving number'. In other parishes, the evidence for co-option is rather more ambiguous. In Cranbrook (Kent), it was the custom of each churchwarden, at the end of his first year of office, to recruit the colleague with whom he would serve for the second year, 'with the consent of parishioners'.[23]

It therefore seems appropriate to concur with the anonymous early eighteenth-century poet who bemoaned that:

> whence these modern Vestries, call'd
> Select, derive the Pow'r they hold,
> Like many others, I'm inclin'd
> To think, is difficult to find.[24]

Where select vestries did exist, they almost certainly both reflected and fostered an increasing self-consciousness among parish notables. Bishop's faculties were most frequently issued in the seventeenth century, almost invariably in response to initiatives by local elites.[25] The vicar-generals' books of the diocese of London contain 42 bishop's faculties either confirming or instituting select vestries over the period 1601–62. Thirty of these documents date from the period 1611–37, and a further 11 from the period 1660–62.[26] Although faculties stipulated rules and regulations specific to each vestry, it is clear that as early as the 1610s a generic formula had been adopted to justify the circumscription of participation in parish affairs. While the number and quorum of vestrymen might therefore vary from parish to parish, the impulse behind the select vestry was general. The rhetoric of these documents is very revealing of the attitudes of the middling sort both to one another, and to their poorer neighbours. In Ealing (Middlesex), for instance, parish meetings had allegedly been characterized by 'much disorder', both in 'taxing men indiscretely by the consent of the inferior sort of people' and 'in disorderly placing of many in the church contrary to their rank and degree'. At Isleworth (Middlesex), audits had apparently been under-mined by the dissent of the 'evil disposed and others of the inferior and meaner sorte of the parishioners'. At Twickenham (Surrey), such dissent had been all the more significant because 'the meaner and inferior sort of the multitude were so far the greater in number'. At Enfield (Middle-sex), the formula referred to 'the great confusion and disorder at the church meetings by reason of the ignorance and weakness in judgement of matters of that nature by some of the parishioners that resort thither'. The result was 'great disquietness and hindrance to the good proceedings which they desire should be in their parish'. At Chigwell (Essex), the admitting of 'the parishioners of all sorts' to their church meetings had created confusion and disorder since so many of them were 'ignorant or weak in judgement and others were not so readie to yield to that which the better sort of the parishioners would determine and agree upon as they should be'. Business could not therefore be dispatched without much 'difficulty and trouble'. At Hanwell (Essex) and at Acton (Middlesex), it was claimed, the multitude was simply uninterested in proceeding 'for the benefit of the church by counsel or otherwise'. By the 1620s, faculties uniformly referred to the need for church business to be 'dispatched and done peaceably with discretion and in good order'. At St Mary Islington (Middlesex), parish business had customarily been determined 'by the parishioners and the better sort of inhabitants without contradiction' until 'of late certain refractorie and contentious persons of mean condi-tion had endeavoured to resist and hinder the good determinations and proceedings' at vestry meetings.[27]

The wave of faculties issued at the Restoration are particularly interesting for the light they throw on parish government during the revolution. The 'late unhappy wilfulness and disorder in this kingdom' had, it was alleged, provoked 'irregularity in the management and dis-patch of affairs relating to the good of the parish', specifically 'remissness and neglect in things necessary', 'heate and violence in other things less requisite', and 'faction in all [others] by the meaner sort of people who have least interest and little judgement'. Despite the good intentions of those who were of 'far better rank and condition', business 'had been carried tumultuously rather by number than by worth'. In 'the late times of distraction', it seems, all 'claimed a liberty' to attend parish meetings, and 'the multitudes that soe mett were often so disorderly and tumul-tuous that nothing could be quietly and peaceably determined but with so much confusion and disorder' as 'tended to the obstruction of the business in hand and even to the breach of the peace'.[28]

In all these cases, both before 1637 and after 1660, successive chancel-
lors of the diocese granted permission for the canons of the Church of
England to be breached. The 'ancient custom' of the Church had been
that anybody 'rated toward the poor in the parish had from time to time
a voice in the election of the church officers and hath been admitted to
the church meetings'.[29] But where the good governance of the parish
was being undermined by tumult and faction, the right to attend was
restricted. The numbers of chosen vestrymen varied according to the
size of the parish: at Ealing, 21 men in addition to the vicar; at Isleworth,
20 besides the vicar and churchwardens; at Twickenham, 12 plus the
vicar and parish officers. Although the size of the quorum fluctuated
accordingly, it invariably included the vicar and almost always at least
one churchwarden. The character and condition of the vestrymen was
stipulated with increasing precision over time: in the 1610s, they should
'be grave and honest men fit for the place' who had no reputation for
'drunkenness whoredom or other evil life'; by the 1620s, they were to
be 'men of the ancienter and better sort of the parish' who 'for the most
parte have born the office of constable or other office of respect'. In
short, they were to be those who would 'seeke the good of the parish and
the well governing thereof'.[30] By the early 1660s, two other issues had come
to the fore: vestrymen should be those most likely to reduce and encourage the parish 'to a fitt conformity to the order and government established
both in church and state' who would also incite the parishioners 'to do
some good works of charity towards the relief of the poor'.[31]

Select vestrymen were accordingly granted important powers of
initiative and control: at Twickenham, the churchwardens were 'not to
engage in any parish cause at an annual charge of more than 20s without
the consent of the vestry'; at Ealing, although public notice was to be
given before all meetings, the vestrymen were given leave to appeal to
the bishop for permission to summon a meeting even if the vicar refused.
Furthermore, the chancellor refused to countenance the maintenance
of other customary procedures: proposals precluding the vestrymen
from taxing the parish without public warning 'to the end that none
should be charged further than is fit' and from choosing a parish clerk
'without the presence and consent of the vicar' were simply struck through
in the order book.[32] Nonetheless, bishop's faculties did significantly limit
the jurisdiction of the select vestry. Five regulations were usual: vestrymen were forbidden from summoning any minister before them; from
interfering with churchwardens' bills of presentment; from questioning
the churchwardens about the making of presentments; from examining

the presented parties before them; or in any other way from intermeddling with the cognizance of the ecclesiastical courts. As far as the church hierarchy was concerned, the provision of effective parish governance was one thing, the shorting of the circuits of ecclesiastical justice entirely another. So long as vestries did not develop into consistories on the Genevan model, therefore, the bishops were prepared to countenance the consolidation of authority into the hands of the parochial elite.[33]

So just how 'elite' were these men? The ideal vestryman, thought an anonymous early eighteenth-century poet, was:

> not so *Rich* to be [a] danger, he would not be *Just*;
> Nor so *Poor* you need fear any breach of his *Trust*.[34]

Detailed measurement of the social and economic status of vestrymen is possible only where attendance lists can be correlated with tax records, wills and legal papers. The evidence available, however, concurs with the rhetoric of bishop's faculties in suggesting that vestrymen were the 'better sort' of the parish as contemporaries understood the term. The vestry of Terling (Essex) was overwhelmingly drawn from the most prosperous ranks of the community: 87 per cent of those who served in the period 1670–99 were either yeomen or gentlemen. In Restoration Frampton, 28 of the 33 vestrymen who can be traced in hearth tax records were assessed on two or more hearths, and 26 contributed to the free and voluntary gift of September 1661, their demonstration of loyalty collectively amounting to £910s., or 70 per cent of the parish contribution.[35] Less systematic work confirms this picture: thus, 13 out of 20 churchwardens in mid-seventeenth-century Solihull (Warwickshire) lived in houses with two or more hearths. In country parishes generally, the yeomen in parish office 'so far outnumber those of any other class as to make it appear almost a status obligation'. In this respect, vestries were little different from manor courts: thus the leet jurors of Prescott in the late 1650s had an average of four hearths, and almost two-thirds of them enjoyed the status of yeoman at the very least.[36]

Perhaps unsurprisingly, vestries and town meetings were relatively exclusive not only in terms of social status but also in terms of gender. Although some of those few female churchwardens who were appointed – including those at Morebath (Devon), Tynemouth (Northumberland) and St Applegrove (Somerset) – actually served their turn, it was far more common for the office to be exercised by male deputies, especially after the Restoration. Thus although the rota system for parish office in

Highley (Shropshire) was based on houses rather than individuals, and therefore included women, females do not appear to have served in practice. All six of the women entitled to serve as overseer of the poor in Ribchester (Lancashire) in the period after 1660 actually served by deputies. The rationale for such decisions, as a Gray's Inn lecturer argued in 1622, was that women's incapacity 'for the most part' to learn the law rendered them incapable of exercising discretion. The comparative rarity of any formal female participation in parish governance is only thrown into greater relief by fragmentary evidence that elected women officers were a characteristic of festivals or other inversion rituals: thus in the Elizabethan celebrations of their Hocktide feast, the 'best inhabitants both men and women' of the Hertfordshire parish of Hexton used to 'elect two officers called the hockers, a man and woman, whose office it was to provide the hock ale and to govern and order the feast for that year'.[37]

Whether or not vestries were formally 'select', therefore, it seems that active participation in their business was relatively circumscribed.[38] In the period 1607–82, the records of 64 meetings of the vestry of Frampton survive, with an average attendance of between eight and nine members. Only 164 vestrymen served in these years, 33 of them (20 per cent) serving more than five times. Indeed, three men performed more than 20 years' service. If anything, participation grew even more concentrated over time: the 58 vestries for which records survive in the period 1693–1750 comprised 139 individuals, between 10 and 11 of whom served at any one time. Of these, 43 (31 per cent) served more than five times. On the single occasion where wider participation is indicated, in 1716, the signatures of six frequently-attending vestrymen are subscribed with the terse reference to 'near twenty more men that ran away to the alehouse before the work was half done'.[39]

A similar concentration of authority in the hands of the middling sort is evident elsewhere. In Elizabethan and early Stuart Cranbrook, the wealthy clothiers and parish gentry dominated the vestry, and formed a self-defining and self-perpetuating oligarchy. In Solihull, 'a relatively small group of landed families tended to keep the key offices in their own hands'. The close vestry of Whickham was oligarchic almost by definition. In Highley, a wide range of powers and responsibilities became concentrated into the hands of a group of men which for most of this period comprised only 20 per cent or so of all heads of household in the community. Even within these oligarchies, it seems, smaller groups of influential men might dominate parish affairs: thus while nine of the

13 vestrymen of Shelton (Norfolk) who approved a local rate in 1629 had served as constable, 16 of the 18 members of the vestry of Bushey (Hertfordshire) who approved assessments in 1632 had done so. The creation of sub-committees to police certain social problems also reflects the concentration of power in fewer and fewer hands: in 1654, the Frampton vestry nominated *six* officers to police in-migration on its behalf. Each of those appointed had served both as overseer and as churchwarden in the years preceding this decision. In Braintree in 1627, the leading vestrymen, those who occupied the 'fower fore stooles of the Companye', were delegated to 'conferre of and conclude concerninge orders for the house of correction'.[40]

Rural parishes were more likely than their urban or metropolitan equivalents to become oligarchic because they lacked the multiplicity of minor offices which might broaden the base of participation and lessen the gradient of social and political hierarchy.[41] This trend towards the contraction of participation in parochial governance was, moreover, almost certainly enhanced by mid- to late-sixteenth-century religious innovation. The Devon parish of Morebath is the most revealing example of these developments. Before the Reformation, perhaps a quarter of the households exercised some kind of responsibility on behalf of the community and were held accountable to it annually. By the mid-1580s, only one householder was being elected to office in the parish church. In the words of Eamon Duffy, this symbolized 'the permanent collapse of a parochial structure which had involved much of the adult population in a continuous round of consultation, decision-making, fund-raising and accounting, a scale of involvement which makes the communal life of this remote moorland village look as participatory and self-conscious as the most sophisticated of European medieval cities'.[42] As we shall see, however, it was not merely the Reformation which restructured the nature of parish politics. The transformation of the parish from a religious body with some secular functions to an organ of secular government with some religious responsibilities was also the product of social, economic and (above all) political change.

II

The parish, no less than the county commission of the peace, was subject to the growing pretensions of the Elizabethan state.[43] This increase of governance obviously depended on supervision and coordination by magistrates, but even the legislators themselves recognized that the parish was the one organization with sufficient local presence and administrative machinery to deal with collective responsibilities. Thus a unit which had been developed to deal with the agricultural problems of the local peasantry became appropriated for a much wider series of purposes. Having to a very large extent functioned outside the state system, the parish now changed its character, becoming to an unprecedented extent a local expression of state authority. The laws for which parish officers now assumed responsibility are well known: the appointment of surveyors to coordinate the repair of local roads by an act of 1555; the collective provision and maintenance of weapons under the militia statute of 1557; and, most significantly, the matrix of discretionary powers for the relief and regulation of the poor under a series of acts codified in 1598 and 1601.[44] These legislative initiatives were, however, only the beginning of the governmental process, and were reinforced by a continuous stream of orders in council. Parish officers regularly received exhaustive sets of articles, some issued directly by the itinerant justices of assize, others on the initiative of magistrates.[45] By the early seventeenth century, therefore, the relatively autonomous medieval parish had become incorporated within a national system of provincial governance. This trend seems to have reached its apogee during the 1630s when petty sessions meetings were apparently attended by 'all [the] officers and chief inhabitants' of all parishes.[46]

Service in parish office therefore came both to reflect and to amplify a constitutional sense of obligation. Participation was 'inspired not merely by obedience but by the acknowledgement of a shared public duty', a duty articulated with a kind of 'rhetorical patriotism' which find both national and intensely localized expression.[47] Thus, in criticizing the nefarious activities of the vestrymen of neighbouring parishes in 1636, Alexander Strange, rector of Layston (Hertfordshire), satirically envisaged 'some good patriote or other in the parish of Kingstone' contemplating the ruthless eviction of those families which might become a burden to ratepayers.[48] Furthermore, the officers of the civil parish increasingly exercised their prerogatives to remould the contours of community in accordance with their own preoccupations. This was most obviously true with respect to their responsibilities for classifying the poor into the categories of deserving and undeserving, and in turn of rating the local inhabitants on the basis of their wealth. At Layston, for example, regulations for making the parish rates were redrafted in the 1620s 'with the consent of the best sort of the inhabitants'. At Long Newton (County Durham) in the 1660s, the vestrymen minuted their tripartite classification of the poor: those in receipt of regular relief; those who presently maintained themselves but, 'imployment being taken away by the enclosure', were 'like to be burdensome to the towne'; and those 'with diverse children and nothing to maintaine them but the poore mans hand labour'.[49] These classifications almost certainly exerted an influence on the language of social description used in the countryside. But it is no accident that just as vestries came to regulate relationships among the parishioners as a whole, they also turned their attention to protocol within their own meetings.

The surviving evidence of vestry procedure is fragmentary. From July 1617, the Bedale vestrymen took an oath to take 'indifferent orders for all things appertaining to the church'; to make 'levys and casts throughe the whole parishe without favour or feare of any man'; to bestowe revenue 'to the most proffitt and need of the church'; and to 'faithfully and truly dispose and distribute' all donations for the poor of the parish or to charitable endowments 'according to the minde and direction' of the benefactors. The oath was to be sworn 'by God and by the contents of this [the vestry] book'. The affirmation at Constantine (Cornwall) was rather more terse, being simply 'to oblige [themselves] to give attendance at all public meetings for the use of [their] parish'.[50] From 1597, every meeting of the Bedale vestry began with the reading not only of the names of the members 'so that notice may be taken of them that be absent', but also of the ordinances previously agreed upon so that the 24 'shall proceed in their determinations accordingly'. At Braintree from 1632 meetings began with the reading over 'of what was agreed upon the last meeting'.[51] Whether there was a formal address at such meetings remains unclear. At Layston, the surviving text of an 'advice to the parishioners' suggests that a charge resembling that given to manorial or quarter sessions juries may well have been delivered.[52] There are other indications of the possibility of formal oratory, for even in the satirical attacks on vestries, each member is described as rising to his feet in turn.[53] At Braintree, 'the four and twenty' took their seats round the council table in strict order of seniority as they 'were placed in the church', and were forbidden to move or leave until business was completed. Fines for early departure were also levied at Constantine. At Braintree, each gave counsel in his turn as he sat, the youngest first. Votes 'for the determyninge of differences which maye arise among the companye' were taken secretly by the putting of buttons into a box.[54] At Constantine, simple majority voting was employed from 1578, so that any order made with the assent of 7 of the 12 'law-makers' would be binding on the vestry as a whole. By the late 1620s, the vestrymen could cite this practice as 'an ancient custom', and by 1650 it had hardened into a doctrine of collective responsibility: any 'difference or matter of quarrell' was to be decided 'by the major part of the voices of the twelve men and so to stand as if they have all agreed'. Most formal of all, however, were the proceedings at Swallowfield: it was agreed 'that no man shall do anything one agaynst another nor agaynst any man, by worde nor deede upon affection, or mallece, in our meetynge nor be discontented one with an other'; that 'every man shalbe hard at our meeting quyetly one after an other'; that 'non shall interrupte an other in his speeche'; and that 'every man shal speake as he is fyrste in accompt, and so in order that thereby the depthe of every mans Judgment with reason may be considered'. Furthermore, no man was to 'skorne an others speeche', and counter-arguments were to be presented only on completion of the proposition in order that 'all that shall be spoken may be quietly taken and heard of all, be it against any man or with him'.[55]

The formal language in which debates, resolutions and elections were recorded was evidently calculated to reflect the communal ethic. The preservation of at least an image of unanimity was especially important where the parish was involved in the defence or prosecution of legal actions. At Bedale it was ordered that when the churchwardens sued parishioners for arrears they 'shall for the ease of the charge of the parish join in one common name'. While the Swallowfield vestrymen similarly promised to join together in 'purse, travell and credit' in defence of any suit prosecuted against any one of them, the 'companye' of Braintree vowed to unite with the overseers should they be sued about the making of rates.[56] In assuming a corporate identity at law in this way, vestries pooled their resources in a manner which might well have rendered their subordinates vulnerable to prosecution for conspiracy. More generally, however, the very use of the terms 'the parish' or 'the inhabitants' was a ploy whereby the decisions of *parochiani meliores et antiquiores* could be made to seem rather more representative and consensual than they actually were. The rhetorical self-descriptions employed by parish elites found their counterpoint in the language used by parish officers to disdain those 'lewd', 'idle', 'thriftless' malefactors – backbiters, sowers of sedition and discord, talebearers, brawlers, chiders – who threatened good order in their communities.[57] Add to these the binary oppositions so characteristic of the language of dissociation employed in rural England, and one begins to sense the role of the middling sort in the social construction of a world view in which the better ordering of the parish was the specific responsibility of its 'principall members'. Although, therefore, consent and agreement resonate through vestry minutes, they may well be symptomatic of the deliberate misuse of the language of consensus politics. The atmosphere of the vestry was, after all, bureaucratic: there were motions to be debated, petitions to be heard and accounts to be received.[58]

Business was only closed at Bedale when the vestrymen either notified their colleagues of their intention to attend the next meeting or indicated a means 'of sending their voices by some of their neighbours'. At Braintree, some form of commensality followed the meeting, either at the house of one of the members, each taking their turn, or at one of the two principal inns, each man bearing the cost of his own meal. At Cranbrook, the vestrymen always dined together at The George, while at Layston they apparently conducted business over dinner in an inn of the same name. Such exclusive sociability inevitably led to criticism that vestrymen made secret assessments 'not onely in private houses but sometimes in alehouses'; devised rates which provoked 'oftentimes great contentions'; and failed to account to the whole body of parishioners 'how their money is bestowed'.[59] Here lie the sources of that stream of public complaint in which the select vestry had 'the worst possible reputation for secrecy', and was 'associated in the public mind with exclusiveness, jobbery and corruption'.[60]

Parish officers were also responsible for regulating the status relationships throughout the wider community. This was most obviously true in their setting of the coordinates of those local 'social maps' of community and entitlement, the church seating plan and the poor rate assessment.[61] Concern over pew placement at a time of increasing social mobility and social differentiation frequently led to vestry regulation of seating arrangements, and especially to the arbitration of those which proved controversial. Thus, in the late 1620s, the vestry of Sherborne (Dorset) ordered the churchwardens to place 'the most ancient onlie of the towne' in the main body of the church, and not to 'place boyes before auncient men'. Similar concerns were revealed at Sigglesthorne, where in 1634 the vestry made 'an order for the seats in the church for each man and his wife and servants'; and again in 1712 when the building of a new loft occasioned controversy about entitlement to pews between ancient residents and newcomers. At Constantine, the 'twelve men' agreed in 1650 to meet annually 'to order seats in the church according to their discretion and to take to their assistance the churchwardens and the minister'. At Braintree, each of 'the four and twenty' was allocated a specific pew or 'stoole' in the parish church, while at Frodsham (Cheshire), the parish officers were almost invariably drawn from the men owning seats in the more prestigious two centre ranks of pews.[62] The 'social map of community' was not, however, only carved in box pews; it was also chiselled in funeral monuments. At Cranbrook, it seems, burial within the church was itself a symbol of vestry status. The vestry's introduction of a system of fines for the unauthorized reopening of vaults in the chancel of the parish church of Boxford (Suffolk) in 1608 similarly reflects the desire to regulate the use of symbolic social space at a time when honour, status and reputation found expression not only on this side of the grave.[63]

Even more time-consuming than the spatial ordering of the parish church, however, was the regulation of the condition and conduct of the parish community, and especially of its poorest members. The central task was the assessment, collection and distribution of poor rates under the terms of the Elizabethan statutes. Although the analysis of the social meaning of the poor rate in seventeenth-century England remains at a relatively preliminary stage, the activities of parish officers seem to have drawn upon 'a common fund of ideas' about riches, idleness and poverty which approached the status of moral orthodoxy.[64] A provisional audit of this fund discloses the terms of the calculus drawn up by parish officers: that the relief of the poor was an inescapable duty; that man's relationship to property was one of temporary stewardship rather than absolute ownership; that almsgiving must be discriminating in order that resources be bestowed on the deserving poor; that charity began at home and moved outward to kindred and neighbourhood; that idleness was dangerous; that the poor should behave with forbearance and patience even in the face of oppression; and that the covetousness of the propertied was corrosive of social harmony and social order. The policies adopted by vestries suggest that these ideas were in fact taken seriously rather than taken for granted.[65] The Swallowfield vestry even ventured forth a statement of the principle of charity to the poor: 'that all shall do their best to helpe the honest poore, the blynd, the syck, the lame and diseased persons'. This bald statement of the charitable imperative nevertheless found its counterpoint in the explicit injunction that the poor should know their place, and should be condemned as 'comon disturbers of peace and quyetnes' if they inappropriately compared themselves with their betters and 'set them at nought'. The Swallowfield vestry evidently decided who 'belonged' in the parish, and unhesitatingly excluded 'pilferers Backbyters hedge breakers, & myscheveous persons, & all suche as be prowde, dissentious & arrogant persons' from the moral community.[66]

More constructive schemes were forthcoming elsewhere. The employment of the labouring poor was attempted at Frampton from 1622 and at Braintree from 1628. The Bedale vestry delayed the raising of a stock for the setting of the poor on work until 1649, when their hands were forced by 'the great necessity and want of relief'.[67] Elsewhere, it seems, vestries preferred the coordinate of pauper apprenticeships to the provision of paid employment. One of the most sophisticated of these schemes was developed at Constantine as early as 1596. Some 60 poor boys and girls were placed out among 50 of their neighbours, where they were to remain until reaching the age of 24. Householders were to provide each parish child with board and clothing, unless their age prevented them from maintaining themselves, in which case the parish officers would provide apparel. Any inhabitant who refused to maintain a poor child was to pay a shilling a week to the parish fund. The policy was elaborated further in 1650, when all those inhabitants who had children beyond their means were ordered by the vestry to bind them apprentices. All single mothers were forced into service if they were 'able and the children weaned'. Such was the concern about these issues in North Nibley (Gloucestershire) that in 1604 the vestry ordered censuses not only of those children 'who are fit to be bound apprentice to other men, and that now live pilfering and stealing in every corner', but also of 'those bastards there are in the parish that either receive relief from the parish or from their reputed fathers, and who such reputed fathers are'.[68]

The administration of the act of 1601 was supplemented by the responsibility for the administration of endowed charities, which seems to have fallen to vestrymen in many parishes. At both Solihull and Yardley (Warwickshire) the trustees of the charity estates consisted exclusively of 'wealthy and substantial inhabitants'. Elsewhere, it seems, the vestrymen administered parish charities directly. By the 1630s, the Bedale vestry regularly gave public notice after morning prayer that it would meet that afternoon to appoint new brothers of Christ's Hospital. The vestrymen of Braughing (Hertfordshire) distributed 20s. yearly under the terms of a bequest intended to subsidize the weddings of the poor maids of the parish. In the years 1626–43, the vestrymen bestowed gifts on 41 brides, although on at least one occasion the award was made conditional on the woman not bearing a child within nine months of the wedding ceremony. This hint of discrimination is bolstered by the fact that the late Caroline allocations went exclusively to Braughing women who married endogamously.[69] The axiom that charity began at home inevitably implied exclusions, as the rules of entitlement to seventeenth-century endowments reveal, perhaps most vividly at Geddington (Northamptonshire) from 1636.[70]

Exclusion could also take more direct forms, especially where poor migrants threatened to become a drain on parochial resources. In 1598, the Constantine vestry compelled landlords who admitted strangers to maintain lodgers and their prospective families at their own expense. By 1650, they had changed tack and insisted that irresponsible landlords should be rated for the poor 'not according to their ability', but 'according to the damage and charge' which they 'bring the parish unto by their folly'. A census of unauthorized inmates was taken at a parish meeting in North Nibley in 1604. The vestry of Boxford agreed in 1608 that the taking of any lodgers would be permitted only after the prior consent of six of the chief inhabitants and with bonds of indemnity, an order repeated with stiffer penalties in 1625. At Hexham (Northumberland) in the 1630s, the vestry insisted on the expulsion of inmates to prevent 'prejudice and damage' to the town should this 'beggarly brood fall into poverty'.[71] The orders of 1630 for the good government of the parish of Aughton (Lancashire) prohibited parishioners from accepting single pregnant women as lodgers. In some parishes, such as Lytham (Lancashire) in 1627, the prohibition even extended to parents who offered house-room to their unmarried pregnant daughters.[72]

Such regulations represent the unwelcoming, not to say the unwelcome, face of community, a countenance which frowned most severely on the 'imprudent' sexual and marital practices of the migrant poor. Although the inhibition of pauper marriages was strictly illegal, it seems to have been widespread in the period before the 1662 settlement laws clarified the ambiguities of entitlement to parish relief among young married couples. It was achieved either by the raising of objections at the calling of the banns, viva voce in the chancel of the parish church, thus leaving little or no imprint in the historical record; or by having a quiet word with the minister beforehand, discouraging him from calling the banns in the first place. Whatever the real identity of those who made objections, they were almost always cloaked in the language of community: those objecting are described as 'the parishioners'; 'the inhabitants'; or the 'parish'.[73]

So much for the responsibilities and obligations of parish officers. What of the rights of those over whom they exercised authority, and on whose behalf they theoretically spoke? The most important of those rights was that of attending the annual audit of the parish accounts, but as we have seen, the tendency towards oligarchy, whether confirmed by bishop's faculty or not, may have restricted participation even here. The importance of public accounting for protecting the rights of the inhabitants is nicely encapsulated in the nostalgic call

> for revivification
> Of honest old Vestrys, that long were disus'd,
> Which was the true cause why the Plebs were abus'd.
> For Justice from thence was always to be had,
> T'Encourage the Good and to Punish the Bad.[74]

The oligarchic impulse therefore implied that 'ordinary folk had duties but few rights in the vestry'.[75] There were, however, further complexities, for at the local level, the pattern of social and political relations was less a matter of binary opposition between vestrymen and poor parishioners, than a matter of tertiary mediation which also involved magistrates. In years of dearth or exceptional hardship in particular, appeals to the justices were often made over the heads of vestrymen by the poor themselves, who had gradually come to regard outdoor relief as a customary right. In this sense, the vestry itself was the arena in which the very nature of social responsibilities between the poor and their betters would perforce be renegotiated, a process which enabled the propertied to pass off as a gift what had previously been perceived as a right, and to stigmatize the recipients.[76]

The governance of rural parishes did not, therefore, inhere in one class or another but arose in conjunction with the tension between different groups both within and beyond the social field of the local community. It is overwhelmingly clear that pastoral and arable regions were characterized by significantly different degrees of participation in the process of governance. The political geography of pastoral areas was relatively independent of gentry influence, and the associational life of the community was dominated by men of more humble status. In some cases, at least, this might permit the appropriation by the middling sort of the vestry – an arena which, after all, was potentially gentry-controlled – as a body within which a sophisticated political culture of rights might develop. In the arable areas, by contrast, participation was moulded, if not directly controlled, by landholding gentry who asserted their private interests through patronage and through the authority of such public institutions as quarter sessions. This had very substantial significance for the meaning of the rule of law in the two types of community: in the pastoral regions, vestries might exercise their responsibilities to guarantee the rights not only of their members but also of their subordinates. In the arable regions, parish governance was much more likely to be a matter of social control by local elites, acting in the interests of their gentry patrons. Such an analysis is obviously predicated upon the 'ideal types' of community which have become familiar as conceptual tools in early modern historiography. But there were obviously more subtle complexities at play in the process by which ten thousand parishes became integrated into a single political society.

III

The significance of popular participation in early modern English governance is gradually gaining the status of historiographical orthodoxy. The political nation is increasingly perceived to have had a depth and extent which an earlier generation of scholars would have found surprising, even alarming. But in emphasizing the role of popular participation in the agencies of the state, there is a danger that historians might become deaf to the cadences of community. Formal participation in parish governance was by no means unrestricted, and 'chief inhabitants' seem to have been particularly aware of their own status. Indeed, the very fact that political participation was relatively circumscribed was arguably constitutive of the increasing self-consciousness of elites: thus the vestrymen of Layston regarded themselves as 'the principal members' of their community, and those of Constantine as the 'law-makers of the parish'. The chief inhabitants of Swallowfield went even further, expressing the wish to be 'estemed to be men of discretion, good Credett, honest Myndes & Christian lyke behaveour'. In doing so, they both recognized the significance of, and sought to endow themselves with, the charisma of office. But in adding the rider 'one towards another', they emphasized the exclusive nature of their self-perception.[77]

   This self-perception might, of course, be contested. Vestry authority might not only be resented, but actually overthrown, as both the bishop's faculties of the Restoration and the 'confused and disorderly' chorus of 'noe four and twenty, noe foure and twenty' in the vestry *coup* at Braintree in 1713 suggests.[78] But in finding a language not only to describe themselves, but also to describe the conduct, character and status they found so offensive in others, the middling sort created, and were themselves in turn created by, a new political idiom.[79] The language of sorts gave expression to the publicly negotiated meanings of parish politics, collective meanings which became inscribed in the quintessential texts of political practice themselves. Vestry minute books and bishop's faculties therefore provide a cultural grammar of the parish, albeit an all-too-frequently laconic one. The political culture they reveal is in some ways covert, consisting rather of unstated premises than of measurable attitudes (it is, after all, often those premises and categories which are seldom put into words whose influence is greatest).[80] Nevertheless, the very fact that there could be at least semi-public debate and disagreement over the key issues of parish politics – the allocation of resources, the entitlement to charity or other customary perquisites, the right to belong – suggests that in some sense the vestry had become a 'parochial public sphere'. Vestrymen, like jurymen, expressed 'a collective politico-religious consciousness that can be described only as a sort of embryonic public opinion'.[81] The processes of election and association, debate and decision making, however attenuated they may have been in practice, only seem to have strengthened the political idiom of the middling sort and the social identities to which it gave expression, to the extent that politics 'out-of-doors' had to be taken very seriously indeed by the mid-seventeenth century.[82]

The medieval village community had never, of course, been independent of 'that amalgam of royal, parliamentary, judicial, and administrative economic and religious agencies plus personal contacts through which *de facto* England was governed'.[83] The emergence of the parish vestry, the culmination of a long-term tendency towards oligarchy in parish governance, and especially the spread of its select or close variant, nevertheless represents a distinctive phase in the formation of the English state. The reshaping of the forms and processes of governance in the late Elizabethan period had both central and local implications, and the planes of the communities of realm and parish intersected and overlapped in the vestry.[84] Whereas manor courts did not meet in parish churches (even though they were almost certainly the only buildings large enough for the purpose), vestries almost invariably tended to do so. The simple fact of this relocation rendered the presence of the state all the more palpable in the local community, for if Elizabethan vestries met in parish churches they did so in the presence of the royal arms, the 'dragon and the dog' having replaced Christ crucified as *the* central symbol in parochial political culture in the mid-sixteenth century. The royal arms both appropriated to the crown the paschal symbolism of resurrection and eternal life and symbolized the Tudor conjunction of Church and state.[85] Furthermore, the very fact that the chief inhabitants of seventeenth-century parishes held sway not in their capacity as manorial jurors but by virtue of their role in the administration of the civil parish is indicative of the incorporative nature of state formation in the early modern context.[86] Popular – though nonetheless circumscribed – political participation of the kind suggested here was commonplace throughout the sixteenth and seventeenth centuries, and villages across Europe doubtless had their ruling elites. The most striking cultural characteristic of the English polity was, however, the extent to which the interests of local oligarchies intersected with the centralized policies of Church and state.

NOTES

1. Thomas Smith, *De Republica Anglorum*, ed. and trans. Mary Dewar (Cambridge, 1982), pp. 65, 74, 76–7.
2. Patrick Collinson, '*De Republica Anglorum*: Or History with the Politics Put Back', in his *Elizabethan Essays* (London, 1994), p. 25.
3. John Norden, *The Surveyor's Dialogue* (London, 1618 [*RSTC* 1864]), p. 27.
4. Anthony Fletcher and Diarmaid MacCulloch, *Tudor Rebellions*, 4th edn (London, 1997), p. 117; Sir John Ferne, *The Blazon of Gentrie, Comprehending Discourses of Armes and of Gentry* (1586) [*RSTC* 10824], p. 6; George Tooke, *The Legend of Brita-Mart* (London, 1635) [*RSTC* 24116], sig. c3v. For Ferne, see J. P. Cooper, 'Ideas of Gentility in Early Modern England', in his *Land Men and Beliefs: Studies in Early Modern History* (London, 1983), pp. 65–72; Felicity Heal and Clive Holmes, *The Gentry in England and Wales, 1500–1700* (London and New York, 1994), pp. 9–10, 29–31, 39, 97. For Tooke, see Markku Peltonen, *Classical Humanism and Republicanism in English Political Thought, 1570–1640* (Cambridge, 1995), pp. 293–6.
5. F. G. Emmison, *Elizabethan Life: Home, Work and the Land* (Chelmsford, 1976), p. 198.
6. Most particularly by Walter J. King, 'Leet Jurors and the Search for Law and Order in Seventeenth-Century England: "Galling Prosecution" or Reasonable Justice', *Histoire Sociale/Social History*, XIII (1980), 305–23; Walter J. King, 'Untapped Sources for Social Historians: Court Leet Records', *Journal of Social History*, XIV (1982), 699–705; and Walter J. King, 'Early Stuart Courts Leet: Still Needful and Useful', *Histoire Sociale/Social History*, XXIII (1990), 271–99. For other studies emphasizing the thriving manorial courts of Elizabethan England, see Matthew Griffiths, 'Kirtlington Manor Court, 1500–1650', *Oxoniensia*, XLV (1980), 260–83; Marjorie K. McIntosh, 'Social Change and Tudor Manorial Leets', in J. A. Guy and H. G. Beale (eds), *Law and Social Change in British History* (London, 1984), pp. 73–85; and Christopher Harrison, 'Manor Courts and the Governance of Tudor England', in C. W. Brooks and Michael Lobban (eds), *Communities and Courts in Britain, 1150–1900* (London, 1997), pp. 43–59.

7. Griffiths, 'Kirtlington Manor Court', p. 281.
8. Tim Wales, 'Poverty, Poor Relief and the Life-Cycle: Some Evidence From Seventeenth-Century Norfolk', in R. M. Smith (ed.), *Land, Kinship and Life-Cycle* (Cambridge, 1984), pp. 357, 359; John Morrill and John Walter, 'Order and Disorder in the English Revolution', in A. J. Fletcher and John Stevenson (eds), *Order and Disorder in Early Modern England* (Cambridge, 1985), p. 156; Anthony Fletcher, *Reform in the Provinces: The Government of Stuart England* (New Haven, 1986), p. 187.
9. Harrison, 'Manor Courts', p. 51; Griffiths, 'Kirtlington Manor Court', p. 281.
10. Judith Maltby, *Prayer Book and People in Elizabethan and Early Stuart England* (Cambridge, 1998), p. 193.
11. David Levine and Keith Wrightson, *The Making of an Industrial Society: Whickham, 1560–1765* (Oxford, 1991), pp. 344–5, n. 148. The personnel of the homage and of the manor court in Braintree (Essex), notes Dr Emmison, were somewhat similar, despite the lack of overlap in functions between the two bodies. F. G. Emmison (ed.), *Early Essex Town Meetings: Braintree, 1619–1636; Finchingfield, 1626–34* (London and Chichester, 1970), p. xv.
12. Christopher Dyer, 'The English Medieval Village Community and its Decline', *JBS*, XXXIII (1994), 413–14; Harrison, 'Manor Courts', p. 45, n. 9. For the ascending/descending distinction, see Walter Ullmann, *A History of Political Thought: The Middle Ages* (Harmondsworth, 1965), pp. 12–13.
13. On oligarchy within the manorial court in particular and in the medieval village community more generally, see Dyer, 'English Medieval Village Community', pp. 418–24.
14. Beat Kumin, *The Shaping of a Community: The Rise and Reformation of the English Parish, c.1400–1560* (Aldershot, 1996), p. 253.
15. EYAS, PE 144/23, Sigglesthorne Parish Church Book, 1629–1766, unfol; Steve Hindle, 'Power, Poor Relief and Social Relations in Holland Fen, *c*.1600–1800', *HJ*, XLI (1998), 78. Cf. A. W. Ashby, 'One Hundred Years of Poor Law Administration in a Warwickshire Village', *Oxford Studies in Social and Legal History*, III (1912), 43. The complexities of the meanings of 'inhabitants' and 'parishioners' in this context are explored in Sidney Webb and Beatrice Webb, *English Local Government from the Revolution to the Municipal Reform Act: The Parish and the County* (London, 1926), pp. 173–5.
16. Jonathan Barry, 'Bourgeois Collectivism? Urban Association and the Middling Sort', in Jonathan Barry and Christopher Brooks (eds), *The Middling Sort of People: Culture, Society and Politics in England, 1550–1800* (Basingstoke, 1994) p. 100; Anon., *The Parish Gutt'lers: or, The Humours of a Select Vestry* (London, 1722), p. 10.
17. Webb and Webb, *The Parish and the County*, p. 173.
18. For this and the succeeding paragraph, see Webb and Webb, *The Parish and the County*, pp. 175–97.
19. Henry Spelman, *De Sepultura*, in his *English Works* (London, 1641) [*Wing* S4924], p. 184.
20. Eric Carlson, 'The Origins, Function and Status of Churchwardens, With Particular Reference to the Diocese of Ely', in Margaret Spufford (ed.), *The World of Rural Dissenters, 1520–1725* (Cambridge, 1995), pp. 183–6.

21. Steve Hindle, 'Hierarchy and Community in the Elizabethan Parish: The Swallowfield Articles of 1596', *HJ*, XLII (1999), 851; Emmison (ed.), *Early Essex Town Meetings, passim*; Craig, 'Co-operation and Initiatives', p. 377. Cf. Paul Griffiths, 'Secrecy and Authority in Late Sixteenth- and Early Seventeenth-Century London', *HJ*, XL (1997), 925–51.

22. Hindle, 'Hierarchy and Community', p. 801.

23. Levine and Wrightson, *The Making of an Industrial Society*, pp. 344–5; North Yorkshire RO, PR/BED 2/1, Bedale Churchwardens Accounts *c*.1576–1675, unfol. (resolutions of 13 June 1630, 5 April 1646, 6 June 1652, 17 November 1661, 9 September 1663, 28 August 1664); Patrick Collinson, 'Cranbrook and the Fletchers: Popular and Unpopular Religion in the Kentish Weald', in his *Godly People: Essays in English Protestantism and Puritanism* (London, 1983), p. 401.

24. Anon., *The Parish Gutt'lers*, p. 4.

25. Kumin, *Shaping of a Community*, p. 252.

26. LMA, DL/C/338–344.

27. LMA, DL/C/340, fols 47v–49, 129, 130v–31, 184v–85; DL/C/341, fols 149v–50, 162–63, 163–63v; DL/C/343, fols 86–86v.

28. LMA, DL/C/344, fols 128–29v, 205, 207v–09v, 210–11v, 213v–14, 214v–16.

29. LMA, DL/C/343, fol 106.

30. LMA, DL/C/340, fols 47v–49, 96v–98, 115v–16, 129, 130v–31.

31. LMA, DL/C/344, fols 128–29v.

32. LMA, DL/C/340, fols 96v–98.

33. LMA, DL/C/340, fols 48v–49.

34. Anon., *The Vestry: A Poem* (London, 1701), p. 6.

35. Keith Wrightson and David Levine, *Poverty and Piety in an English Village, 1525–1700*, 2nd edn (Oxford, 1995), p. 104 and table 4.7; Hindle, 'Power, Poor Relief and Social Relations', p. 79.

36. V. H. T. Skipp, *Crisis and Development: An Ecological Case Study of the Forest of Arden, 1570–1674* (Cambridge, 1978), p. 82; Mildred Campbell, *The English Yeoman under Elizabeth and the Early Stuarts* (New Haven, 1942), p. 318; King, 'Leet Jurors', p. 310.

37. Gwyneth Nair, *Highley: The Development of a Community, 1550–1880* (Oxford, 1988), p. 129; Sara Mendelson and Patricia Crawford, *Women in Early Modern England, 1550–1720* (Oxford, 1998), pp. 50, 56–7; BL, Add. MSS 6223, fols 11v–12v.

38. Hindle, 'Power, Poor Relief and Social Relations', p. 79.

39. Lincoln Archives Office, Frampton PAR 10/2, unfol. (3 April 1716).

40. Collinson, 'Cranbrook and the Fletchers', p. 401; Skipp, *Crisis and Development*, p. 82; Levine and Wrightson, *The Making of an Industrial Society*, p. 354; Nair, *Highley*, p. 131; Joan Kent, *The English Village Constable: A Social and Administrative Study, 1580–1642* (Oxford, 1986), pp. 145–6; Hindle, 'Power, Poor Relief and Social Relations', pp. 89–90; Emmison (ed.), *Early Essex Town Meetings*, p. 47.

41. Nick Alldridge, 'Loyalty and Identity in Chester Parishes, 1540–1640', in S. J. Wright (ed.), *Parish, Church and People: Local Studies in Lay Religion, 1350–1750* (London, 1988), pp. 108–9.

42. Eamon Duffy, 'Morebath, 1520–1570: A Rural Parish in the Reformation', in J. Devlin and R. Fawning (eds), *Religion and Rebellion* (Dublin, 1997), pp. 36–7.
43. Fletcher, *Reform in the Provinces*, p. 372.
44. 2 and 3 Philip and Mary, c. 8 (1555); 4 and 5 Philip and Mary, c. 2 (1557); 39 Elizabeth I, c. 3 (1598); 43 Elizabeth I, c. 1 (1601).
45. Steve Hindle, *The State and Social Change in Early Modern England, c.1550–1640* (Basingstoke, 2000), chs 1 and 6.
46. PRO, SP16/182/40, 185/27, certificates of the magistrates of Edwinstree and Odsey hundreds, Hertfordshire, 11 January 1631, 18 February 1631. In March 1631, Bedfordshire JPs described their petty sessions as meetings of 'all high constables and principal inhabitants', PRO, SP16/186/92–I.
47. Patrick Collinson, 'The Elizabethan Exclusion Crisis and the Elizabethan Polity', *Proceedings of the British Academy*, LXXXIV (1994), 74–75.
48. Steve Hindle, 'Exclusion Crises: Poverty, Migration and Parochial Responsibility in English Rural Communities, c.1560–1660', *Rural History*, VII (1996), 135.
49. Hindle, 'Exclusion Crises', p. 136; Peter Rushton, 'The Poor Law, the Parish and the Community in North-East England, 1600–1800', *Northern History*, XXV (1989), 145.
50. North Yorkshire RO, PR/BED 2/1, unfol., copy of a letter from Bishop Thomas Moreton of Chester, 24 June 1617; Cornwall RO, DD P39/8/1, unfol., resolutions of the 1720s.
51. North Yorkshire RO, PR/BED 2/1, unfol., resolution of 20 February 1597; Emmison (ed.), *Early Essex Town Meetings*, p. 84.
52. Hertfordshire RO, D/P 65/3/3, pp. 326–38.
53. Thus Richard Stole stood before addressing the Kingstone vestry in Alexander Strange's address. Hertfordshire RO, D/P 65/3/3, pp. 326–38. Various participants (including the minister) rose to their feet in the vestry meeting depicted in a satire of 1701. Anon., *The Vestry*, pp. 6, 7, 10.
54. Emmison (ed.), *Early Essex Town Meetings*, pp. 90, 103.
55. Cornwall RO, DD P39/8/1, unfol., resolutions of Easter 1578, Easter 1590, 6 June 1629, 20 October 1650; Hindle, 'Hierarchy and Community', pp. 848–9.
56. North Yorkshire RO, PR/BED 2/1, unfol., resolution of 12 December 1595; Hindle, 'Hierarchy and Community', pp. 849–50. Emmison (ed.), *Early Essex Town Meetings*, p. 44.
57. See Marjorie McIntosh, 'Finding Language for Misconduct: Jurors in Fifteenth-Century Local Courts', in Barbara A. Hanawalt and David Wallace (eds), *Bodies and Disciplines: Intersections of Literature and History in Fifteenth Century England* (Minneapolis, 1996), pp. 103, 119, n. 67.
58. Alldridge, 'Loyalty and Identity in Chester Parishes', pp. 110–11. Cf. Paul Slack, *Poverty and Policy in Tudor and Stuart England* (London, 1988), pp. 190–1.
59. North Yorkshire RO, PR/BED 2/1, unfol., resolution of 20 February 1597; Emmison (ed.), *Early Essex Town Meetings, passim*; Webb and Webb, *The Parish and the County*, p. 222; Collinson, 'Cranbrook and the Fletchers', p. 375; Hindle, 'Exclusion Crises', p. 136; Hertfordshire RO, D/P 65/3/3, p. 105; *Vox Ruris Reverberating Vox Civitas Complaining This Year 1636 Without Cause*

Against the Country Taken From Her Owne Common Report and Written by Notarius Rusticus (1636) [*RSTC* 18698], p. 6.

60. Webb and Webb, *The Parish and the County*, pp. 157, 161.

61. David Underdown, *Revel, Riot and Rebellion: Popular Politics and Culture in England, 1603–1660* (Oxford, 1985), p. 32.

62. Dorset RO, PE/SH-VE1, Sherborne Parish Book of Church Orders, fols 32 (July 1628), 33 (March 1630); EYAS PE 144/23, unfol; Cornwall RO, DD P39/8/1, unfol., resolutions of 20 October 1650; Emmison (ed.), *Early Essex Town Meetings, passim*; Maltby, *Prayer Book and People*, p. 210.

63. Collinson, 'Cranbrook and the Fletchers', p. 175; Suffolk RO, FB77/E2/3, unfol., resolutions of 28 March 1608.

64. Ian Breward, 'The Direction of Conscience', in Ian Breward (ed.), *The Work of William Perkins* (Abingdon, 1970), p. 75. The following analysis owes much not only to Breward, but also to Patrick Collinson, 'Christian Socialism in Elizabethan Suffolk: Thomas Carew and His *Caveat for Clothiers*', in Carol Rawcliffe, Roger Virgoe and Richard Wilson (eds), *Counties and Communities: Essays on East Anglian History* (Norwich, 1996), pp. 161–79; Patrick Collinson, 'Puritanism and the Poor', in Sarah Rees Jones and Rosemary Horrox (eds), *Utopias, Ideals and Institutions, 1200–1630* (Cambridge, forthcoming); and Andrew McRae, *God Speed the Plough: The Representation of Rural England, 1500–1640* (Cambridge, 1996), pp. 58–79. Cf. the more selective reading of Puritan attitudes to the distribution of wealth in Christopher Hill, 'William Perkins and the Poor', in his *Puritanism and Revolution: Studies in the English Revolution of the Seventeenth Century* (London, 1956), pp. 215–38.

65. Cf. Breward, 'Direction of Conscience', p. 75.

66. Hindle, 'Hierarchy and Community', p. 850.

67. Hindle, 'Power, Poor Relief and Social Relations', p. 86; Emmison (ed.), *Early Essex Town Meetings*, p. 51; North Yorkshire RO, PR/BED 2/1, unfol., resolution of 1 June 1649.

68. Cornwall RO, DD P39/8/1, unfol., resolutions of 7 May 1596, 20 October 1650; Gloucester Public Library, MS 16526, fol. 99.

69. Skipp, *Crisis and Development*, p. 82; North Yorkshire RO, PR/BED 2/1, unfol., formulaic resolutions of the 1630s; Hertfordshire RO, D/P 23/8/1, Braughing vestry minutes 1626–52, unfol.

70. Northamptonshire RO, MISC Photostat 1610.

71. Cornwall RO, DD P39/8/1, unfol., resolutions of 10 June 1598, 20 October 1650; Gloucester Public Library, MS 16526, fol. 99; Suffolk RO, FB77/E2/3, ordinances of 28 March 1608, 17 April 1625; Rushton, 'Poor Law, the Parish and the Community', p. 140.

72. Lancashire RO, QSB/1/70/48; DDC1/1141. See Walter J. King, 'Punishment for Bastardy in Early Seventeenth-Century England', *Albion*, X (1978), 138, nn. 25–6.

73. Steve Hindle, 'The Problem of Pauper Marriage in Seventeenth-Century England', *TRHS*, 6th Series, VIII (1998), 71–89.

74. Anon., *The Vestry*, p. 6.

75. Harrison, 'Manor Courts', p. 45, n. 9.

76. Slack, *Poverty and Policy*, p. 191; John Walter, 'The Social Economy of Dearth in Early Modern England', in John Walter and Roger Schofield (eds),

152   The Politics of the Excluded, *c*.1500–1850

Famine, Disease and the Social Order in Early Modern Society (Cambridge, 1989), pp. 127–8.

77. Hertfordshire RO, D/P 65/3/3, pp. 328, 338; Cornwall RO, DD P39/8/1, unfol., resolutions of 10 June 1598, 20 October 1650; Hindle, 'Hierarchy and Community', p. 851.
78. Wrightson, 'The Politics of the Parish', p. 29.
79. Cf. Dror Wahrman, 'National Society, Communal Culture: An Argument about the Recent Historiography of Eighteenth-Century Britain', *Social History*, XVII (1992), 44–5.
80. Clyde Kluckhohn, 'Covert Culture and Administrative Problems', *American Anthropologist*, XLV (1943), 218.
81. Wrightson, 'The Politics of the Parish', p. 29; Richard Cust and Peter Lake, 'Sir Richard Grosvenor and the Rhetoric of Magistracy', *Bulletin of the Institute of Historical Research*, LIV (1981), 50–1.
82. Fletcher and MacCulloch, *Tudor Rebellions*, p. 117.
83. Smith, '"Modernization" and the Corporate Medieval Village Community', p. 146; Harrison, 'Manor Courts', p. 43.
84. Cf. Alan Macfarlane, *Reconstructing Historical Communities* (Cambridge, 1977), p. 13.
85. Harrison, 'Manor Courts', p. 50; Diarmaid MacCulloch, *Building a Godly Realm: The Establishment of English Protestantism, 1558–1603* (London, 1992), pp. 9–10; MacCulloch, *Suffolk and the Tudors*, 182–85; Jennifer Woodward, *The Theatre of Death: The Ritual Management of Royal Funerals in Renaissance England, 1570–1625* (Woodbridge, 1997), p. 40.
86. Levine and Wrightson, *The Making of an Industrial Society*, p. 345, n. 148.

6

THE UNACKNOWLEDGED REPUBLIC: OFFICEHOLDING IN EARLY MODERN ENGLAND*

Mark Goldie

I

We live in regimes which are, or claim to be, democracies. The defining features of democracy are the universal franchise and the practice of voting. Those who are sceptical of democratic politics as presently conceived have noticed that this tends to reduce political life to the strikingly minimal act of periodically writing 'X' on a ballot paper. Critics argue that citizenship is thereby emptied of content, and citizens made to feel alienated from governance. We occasionally vote, but we do not rule. As John Dunn has remarked, 'One day's rule in four years has very much the air of a placebo – or at least an irregular modern Saturnalia'.[1]

Early modern England was not a democracy. Only a small minority of people could vote in parliamentary elections. Consequently, it is difficult to avoid the presumption that most people were excluded from the political process. Yet once we recognize the limitations of modern democratic politics we can begin to lift the weight of our assumptions about participation in the past. This is particularly so once we grasp that in early modern England the holding of the parliamentary franchise was not regarded as the pre-eminent criterion of citizenship.

The purpose of this essay is not to debate contemporary democratic theory, but to show historically that there is another way of conceiving of political participation, namely through the practice of officeholding. By highlighting officeholding in early modern England, we shift attention away from voting and towards governance; away from the indirect participation by which some people occasionally chose others to represent them in a distant national assembly, and towards the directness whereby large numbers of people undertook the self-management of their local communities. Put in other terms, we shift attention away from what is modern and democratic to what is ancient and republican. For there is a republican tradition in which the active involvement of the citizen rather than the passive exercise of the franchise was the essential feature of a good polity. Such activity took the form of duties incumbent on every householder, and included holding office, and hence ruling others, in however small a role. In this tradition, rotation of office was held to be crucial, so that citizens were sometimes rulers and sometimes ruled. A citizen, wrote Aristotle, 'is one who shares in government'.[2] This 'republican' tradition has little to do with the presence or absence of a monarch. *Res publica* literally means, as Tom Paine pointed out, 'the public thing',[3] and was most often translated as the 'common weal' or 'common-wealth'. Early modern England was neither a democracy nor, in our modern sense, a republic. It was monarchical. Yet it could be said to be an unacknowledged republic, or a monarchical republic.

In opening up the topic of officeholding it is helpful to begin with four premisses. First, the subject comes to life when we draw together the insights of social historians and historians of political thought. Social history and intellectual history touch each other too rarely. Those who painstakingly reconstruct the life of English parish communities have something to tell those who write about the ideals of Renaissance humanism, and vice versa.[4] Accordingly, this essay first synthesizes some of the findings of social historians, and then turns to the history of political thought.

The second premiss is the need to keep in mind a fundamental feature of the early modern English state, namely the lack of a national salaried bureaucracy. In the seventeenth century the royal court typically employed a mere 1200 people. Beyond Whitehall, government was amateur, part-time and unsalaried. Governance was thereby highly dispersed, and was conducted by gentlemen, yeomen and tradesmen in the interstices of their ordinary daily business. The crown's capacity to exert its will depended upon the cooperation of county magistrates and village constables.[5]

The third premiss is the importance of locality. Historical writing too readily focuses upon parliament and privy council. A generation ago historians began to show us that England could be conceived of as a federation of county communities.[6] More recently, attention has shifted

to the parish, the town and the neighbourhood – and for this reason the
accent here will be on the parish more than the county. 'Parish business,
county business, kingdom business' was an eighteenth-century adage.[7]
The importance of locality is underscored by the growing realization
that the level of local taxation was probably at least as high as that of
national taxation.[8] This was above all owing to the demands of the Elizabethan poor law. The salience of the poor law in turn draws attention to
the enormous burden of local administration, and the fact that, for all its
limitations and harshness, governance was directed towards welfare as
well as discipline.

The fourth premiss is the inappositeness of viewing early modern
England as a bipolar society of rulers and ruled. Of course the social
order was hierarchic and marked by massive disparities of wealth, status
and power. Catechisms and homilies inculcated obedience to superiors,
and commentators warned against the 'many-headed multitude', and
the 'rude mechanick' who turned politician. But historians are now
increasingly doubtful that the exercise of power should be construed as
the monopoly of a ruling class, under whom the powerless subsisted
either in deferential awe or truculent disobedience. The tendency of
recent, post-Marxian historiography has been to abandon the interpret-
ive vocabulary of hegemony and social control, in favour of a vocabulary
of agency, reciprocity, mediation, participation and negotiation. Governance was not something done from on high to the passive recipients
of authority, but something actively engaged in by the lesser agents of
government; and every citizen was in some measure a lesser agent of
government.

II

We are not yet ready to consider officeholding. We next need to note –
as the previous remarks imply – that historians have already energetic-
ally argued that the scope for popular participation in early modern
public life was in fact considerable. We can, schematically, identify four
historiographical models of participation, which we may call the judicial,
the dramaturgical, the associational and the psephological. By drawing
attention to officeholding this essay offers a fifth. There is space just
swiftly to characterize those four models, though we shall need to pause
to comment on the psephological argument.

By 'judicial' is meant popular involvement in the processes of criminal
prosecution and the arbitration of disputes. There was no police force

beyond the ability and willingness of a community to exercise its own force, and no prosecution without neighbourly cooperation in the hue and cry, the laying of informations, the seeking of warrants, and the witnessing, deponing and bailing of criminals. 'Every Englishman', wrote Sir Thomas Smith in 1583, 'is a sergeant to take a thief'.[9] Consequently, Cynthia Herrup has written, 'the legal system exemplifies the participatory nature of English government in the seventeenth century'.[10] Such participation was 'political' because the enforcement of law was highly discretionary, and shaped by diverse conceptions of what mattered for good neighbourliness.[11]

By 'dramaturgical', or 'theatrical', is meant modes of activity which are often non-institutional and non-textual, and which operated through symbolic and ritual action. This was the participatory politics of the street: parades, riots, demonstrations, slogans, banners, graffiti, cartoons, bonfires, effigy burnings, emblems, cockades, gestures, jeering, cheering.[12] It was also the politics of conviviality and commensality: feasts, toasts, bell-ringing, mayoral pageants.[13] It was the politics of spectacle at the assize courts and the scaffold, functioning as tableaux, both of the majesty of the law and of the subversive heroism of a martyr's dying protests.[14] These are modes of politics which anthropologically attuned historians have explored, though the conventions of classical drama have been inspirational too. They are modes where the theatrical and judicial often met, signally in the popular enforcement of customary law and common right. In his seminal essay on the 'moral economy of the English crowd', Edward Thompson argued that 'riots' were often not outbursts of unselfconscious violence, but deliberate, orchestrated and disciplined negotiations, which invoked a customary understanding of, for example, the just price for grain.[15]

The 'associational' refers to the sphere of voluntary organizations, lying beyond the statutory and common law institutions of local and central government (though often buttressed by private acts of parliament). This is the participatory politics of clubs and societies, charities and trusts, hospitals and schools, civic improvement schemes, pressure groups and press campaigns. It is a perspective on participation strongly influenced by Jürgen Habermas's concept of 'the public sphere' as a domain of political life – a domain called 'civil society' – that flourishes independently of the formal institutions of the state.[16]

The 'psephological' model needs closer scrutiny in the present context, for it was the contrast between voting and officeholding with which we began. By 'psephological' is meant the study of electoral behaviour, of franchises, contests, turnouts and party loyalties. It is the domain of participation in constituencies. A school of historians have borrowed the techniques developed by political scientists since 1945 to analyse modern parliamentary elections, and have applied them to seventeenth- and eighteenth-century elections. They have used computer analyses to invest-igate the size, preferences and volatility of electorates. Their technique is especially feasible for the period beginning in the 1690s because of the existence of pollbooks, which recorded, in that era before the secret ballot, the votes of individual electors. Although most attention has been devoted to 'the first age of party' between 1678 and 1722,[17] similar approaches have been deployed for the mid- and late eighteenth century and, more tentatively, for the early seventeenth.[18]

The psephological school reached three broad conclusions. First, the early modern electorate was larger than we hitherto supposed. Geoffrey Holmes suggested that by 1715 about 20 per cent of adult males had the vote (some 5 per cent of the population), a figure not again achieved until *after* the Reform Act of 1832.[19] More ambitiously, Derek Hirst proposed 27–40 per cent of adult males (7–10 per cent of the population) by 1640.[20] Secondly, and correspondingly, it was shown that the electorate was socially diverse and not a narrow elite. The impact of inflation upon the ancient criterion for the county franchise – the forty-shilling free-hold – resulted in the enfranchisement of many yeomen.[21] In some towns the franchise encompassed most householders. In eighteenth-century Norwich the voters included cobblers, fishmongers, bricklayers and soapboilers.[22] Thirdly, it was shown that there were high levels of parti-cipation and partisanship in electoral politics. Weighing the 'participatory model' against a 'deference model' of voter behaviour, William Speck argued for the former: deference, bribery and pressure notwithstanding, many voters needed persuading, and 'ultimately what conditioned a party's parliamentary strength were the choices made by thousands of individual voters'. In sum, as Speck remarked, 'the electoral system was more representative in Anne's reign than it had ever been before', and, as J. H. Plumb put it, 'England was far more democratic between 1688 and 1715 than immediately after 1832'.[23]

The psephological school has been challenged both for empirical weaknesses and for anachronistically calibrating early modern election-eering against the template of modern universal franchise democracies. Mark Kishlansky and Jonathan Clark have pointed to evidence for low turnouts in contested elections and low numbers of contests.[24] In 1701 there were only 89 contests in 243 English constituencies. These critics

remark that where there is no contest, there is no voting data for statistical analysis, so that uncontested elections rapidly become invisible to the
psephologists. The critics go on to suggest that the lack of contests was
not a sign of democratic failure, of corrupt or somnolent political closure.
On the contrary, argues Kishlansky for the early Stuart period, the
dominant presumption was in favour of parliamentary *selection* not *election*,
a preference for consensus, not contest. Often the gentry travelled
to their county town to acclaim their chosen MP knowing full well there
would be no poll. An effort is needed to understand what conception of
politics lay behind such an action. 'Parliamentary selection was a process
of affirmation rather than a struggle for power'; it entailed 'the conferral
of honour, the practice of deference, and the confirmation of the social
order'. On this view, a contest was a sign not of democratic maturity but
of local breakdown: contests were fractious and embittering, they were a
'catastrophe' for the community.[25] Oddly, however, Kishlansky abandons
his critique when addressing the post-civil war era, and endorses the
psephological model, for 'it is to the mid-seventeenth century that we
must look to understand the origins of participatory democracy'.[26] By
contrast, Clark's critique extends to the eighteenth century, to the whole
of what he dubs the English 'ancien régime' down to 1832. Low turnout
and low polls meant not 'somnolence or repression' but a different sort
of politics, a politics of deference to the norms of regal, aristocratic and
ecclesiastical governance.[27]

We may agree that the psephological model is prone to anachronism,
yet disagree that deference to dynasty, dukes and divines is the appropriate alternative. In the psephological model, the notion of participation
is confined to the franchise: politics are construed as about balloting. The
notion is also confined to parliamentary elections: politics are construed
as national rather than local, albeit occurring in local constituencies. In
taking a statistical approach, the model is apt to leave unexamined the
cultural texture of political agency – the meanings which agents attached
to their activity in voting or not voting. Yet the critics are mistaken in
assuming that evidence for low participation in parliamentary elections
is evidence for low political participation *tout court*. Such a critique con-
cedes too much to the psephologists' conception of the political.

Instead, we need to reiterate our opening contentions concerning
office and locality. Early modern people participated in the political
process not only by occasionally choosing who would represent them in
parliament, but actually by governing. They held office. By virtue of
that, their agency was not only 'out-of-doors' in the informal spaces of the

streets, taverns and coffee-houses, but was also formal and institutional, in the conduct of judicial, executive and legislative functions in parish, town and county.

III

The structure of English local government was bewilderingly complex. Here it is only necessary to sketch an outline, in order to pinpoint the number and kinds of public offices which people were called upon to undertake. We may distinguish counties, towns and parishes. After 1536 there were forty counties in England and twelve in Wales. By 1689 there were approximately 180 incorporated boroughs in England (19 of which had county status which exempted them from shire jurisdiction), and some 9700 parishes. There were other units too: parishes were grouped into hundreds (in some places called wapentakes or rapes); some parishes were divided into tithings (literally denoting ten households); parish jurisdiction often meshed with that of medieval manors which still exercised jurisdiction over their domains through courts leet; large towns were divided into wards; large counties into ridings or sokes.

Counties had civil and military officers. At the summit was the *custos rotulorum* and lord lieutenant, typically a peer or leading courtier. The linchpin of county government was the justice of the peace, or magistrate. In the seventeenth century a county would have between two and four dozen justices; the numbers rose in the eighteenth. Justices were appointed by the crown, but a prudent government chose the weightiest men of the shire, the leading gentry. The relationship between crown and magistrate was symbiotic. The crown needed the business of government to be transacted; the gentleman needed office as a mark of status and an instrument of social authority. The justice's duties were both administrative and judicial. The justice was required to fix wages, set ale prices, license alehouses, license hawkers, inspect weights and measures, control guns, settle bastardy cases, assess local tax rates, regulate apprenticeships, and make provision for the repair of bridges and highways. The statutory duties placed upon the justices grew inexorably, especially during the Tudor period. The justice was a law officer, issuing warrants and making summary convictions. He was not a trained lawyer, though often he had acquired a grounding by attending the Inns of Court. More serious criminal cases were dealt with by the bench of justices, sitting together at the quarter sessions, a certain number making up a quorum. Justices were also present when major cases were heard twice a year by the crown's itinerant assize judges. Assizes and quarter sessions were occasions for county gatherings, feasts, speeches, and for sermons on the duties of magistrates and citizens. The most senior magistrates were likely also to be deputy lieutenants of the county militia. A gentleman of weight could expect to hold a militia captaincy or colonelcy.

There were other county officers too. The sheriff, appointed for one year, had mainly judicial functions and nominated jurymen. The coroner, elected by the freeholders, had investigative and prosecutorial powers in cases of violent death. The high constables served each hundred. All these were amateur, though they could take fees. Counties had only a small body of stipended officials, such as the justices' clerk, the militia mustermaster, the gaol keeper, the keeper of the house of correction.

The governance of the parish was in the hands of the churchwardens, the overseers of the poor and the constable. There were lesser officers too, a surveyor of the highways, a clerk, sexton, scavenger and beadle. Community matters were deliberated in the vestry, the meeting of the chief inhabitants. In areas where land continued unenclosed there were also often field officers – reeves, haywards and pinders – who regulated cropping and drainage.[28] The parish constable stood in parallel to the county justice, each in their respective domains, the former carrying in microcosm similar burdens to the latter. The constable went to and fro to local justices, taking instructions, receiving warrants. He too regulated alehouses and weights and measures. He apprehended vagrants, supervised the watch, enforced curfews, regulated corn supplies in times of scarcity, maintained instruments of punishment (the stocks, whipping post, cage, pillory, ducking stool), supervised the maintenance of hedges, dykes, ditches and bridges, and the extermination of vermin; he supplied testimonials for servants and apprentices. He found a quota of men to serve in the militia; he maintained muskets, swords, pikes, helmets and breastplates; he saw to the upkeep of the butts; he attended musters. He collected taxes, and distrained for non-payment of taxes and fines. He assisted itinerant royal officials, the postmasters and saltpetre men. The Elizabethan Poor Law instructed him to search once a month for vagrants in need of discipline, and for the sick, aged and impotent in need of succour.[29]

An incorporated borough typically had a mayor and a governing body of aldermen or councillors, together with a chamberlain, recorder, clerk, coroner and bailiff. It also had officers of the nightwatch, and scavengers. At Banbury in Oxfordshire there was a bailiff, justice, town clerk, sergeant at mace, two auditors, two chamberlains, two constables, four tithingmen, two aletasters, two searchers and three toll gatherers.[30] The city of Exeter had a mayor, aldermen, councillors, stewards, receiver, recorder, clerk, serjeants, constables, scavengers, swordbearer, porters, watchmen, and wardens of the poor, the bridges and the shambles.[31] At least until the Civil War, the borough's member of parliament was generally treated as an extension of civic office, for the MP was often the recorder, whose task was to speak for the corporation at Westminster.[32] Where a town was exempt from county jurisdiction, the aldermen exercised the same judicial powers as county magistrates. The structure of parish government found in the countryside also existed in the towns, and in large towns each ward also had a complement of officers. A yet further layer of governance existed in the livery companies, which regulated crafts and trades, and were governed by wardens and assistants. The livery companies were economic, convivial and charitable bodies, but they were scarcely distinct from civic government, for to be a freeman of a livery company made one a citizen, with rights of participation and office.

IV

Our concern here is less with the duties of office than with the significance of undertaking office. Evidence of the extent and meaning of officeholding – at least below the level of the county elite – remains partial.[33] Our knowledge is generally one result, sometimes almost a by-product, of the work of the currently thriving school of historians of rural and urban parish communities who seek to recover the microcosmic structures and rhythms of social and economic life. There is a fine study of the parish constable, but as yet we know only a limited amount about vestrymen, churchwardens and overseers.[34] Even so, we may derive several generalizations from existing case studies. I single out six that serve to underscore the extent and centrality of officeholding, but I follow that with four cautions which should prevent us drawing too optimistic a conclusion about participation.

First and foremost, an astonishingly high proportion of early modern people held office. This can readily be deduced schematically. In the seventeenth century there were approximately 9700 parishes in England and Wales. If each had one constable, two churchwardens and two overseers, then we have a total of around 50,000 parish officers at any one time.[35] Thus, around the year 1700, about one-twentieth of adult males were governing in any year; in principle, that might mean one half were governing in any decade. Rudolf von Gneist estimated that around the year 1800 there were 14,000 parishes and townships annually choosing at least one constable, one surveyor, two churchwardens and two overseers, so that perhaps 100,000 people held office. In addition, he reckoned 10,000 assize and quarter sessions jurors at each sitting, 8000 militia officers and 3800 active JPs.[36]

Case studies indicate levels of involvement in particular localities, especially in London, where each of the City's 117 parishes had a full complement of officials. Valerie Pearl found that about one-tenth of London householders in the mid-seventeenth century held office in any year.[37] Ian Archer observed that 'the City enjoyed a large number of elected officials: as many as one in three householders in a wealthy inner city ward like Cornhill might expect to hold some kind of office in any one year'. The annual Cornhill wardmote elected nine common councilmen, a foreman, four speakers, a pricker, a treasurer, a controller, two scribes, two stewards, two butlers, two porters, four constables, four scavengers and a beadle. This was in a community of 165 households.[38] In Portsoken ward there were four constables for 500 households. In Southwark in around 1620 there were 91 officers for 958 households (and jurors in addition): between 1620 and 1624 about one in four payers of the poor rate held office.[39] In eighteenth-century Colchester borough institutions provided official roles for 280 people, including jurors, so that, allowing for repeat officeholding, about one-quarter of resident burgesses held office. Andrew Murrell, a gardener, held fourteen offices during the 1730s, including steward of the town feast.[40] In York 796 householders served as grand jurymen between 1649 and 1673.[41] It was particularly in cities like York, which had four wards and twenty-seven parishes, that, as Philip Withington has written, 'the intensity of civic governance propelled men into public service'.[42]

During the eighteenth century, new kinds of office flourished in the growing towns. Thousands of trustees and 'commissioners' were created, often by statute, for specified public purposes, for such things as paving, lighting and policing.[43] In 1783 alone Acts of Parliament listed 5000 persons as commissioners for turnpike, gaol, canal or poor relief trusts. The Dorchester Paving Act of 1776 appointed 86 trustees, besides the senior members of the corporation, in a town where 200 householders were rated for poor relief.[44] Doubtless these were often devices for engineering consent for collective projects which impinged on private properties, yet even if active service was minimal those named undertook to place themselves and their interests within the frame of the 'publick'. Trusteeships of hospitals, charities and civic improvement schemes could involve a good deal of unpaid committee work and administration. The St Marylebone Turnpike Trust, founded in 1721 with 122 trustees, held monthly meetings at the Mount Street coffee-house.[45] In some cases, statutory commissions were in part deliberate attempts to challenge existing urban oligarchies and widen participation by, for example, involving dissenters. This was so in the case of the Corporations of the Poor formed in several cities after 1696.

The second conclusion we can draw about officeholding, flowing from the first, is that it proves to have been remarkably socially extensive. In parishes, offices were held by an array of people from minor gentry to cottagers. At Stone in Herefordshire the officers included a brickmaker a blacksmith and a tanner. At Highley in Shropshire they included yeomen and cottagers. In Southwark they were typically bakers, glovers, butchers, soapboilers and cheesemongers.[46] Constables were characteristically yeomen, artisans or shopkeepers. A well documented example is Nehemiah Wallington, a London puritan artisan. He was a turner (a carpenter who worked wood with a lathe); a householder and freeman of the City, living in St Leonard's Eastcheap, a tiny parish of seventy households. Remarkably, he left 2600 pages of personal papers, documenting his spiritual anxieties and political animosities. His father, also a turner, was churchwarden in 1599. Nehemiah may also have been a churchwarden, but the vestry minutes and churchwardens' accounts do not survive. He was definitely a constable in 1638 and 1639, and grand juryman in 1643, 1645, 1649 and 1655. He was elected an elder of both the local and the London provincial presbyterian 'classes' established in 1646, the system set up by parliament to replace episcopal government of the church. Passionate though he was for furthering godly reformation, he noted that such service involved 'charge and expense of time both of profit (in my shop) and pleasures abroad'.[47]

Wallington was unusually articulate, but illiteracy was no barrier. Before the mid-seventeenth century possibly more than half of rural constables were illiterate. In 1642 few constables in Dorset or Somerset could write; in Westmorland none could. One Wiltshire constable asked to be relieved of his post because he had to travel two miles to a scrivener to get warrants read.[48]

Law-abidingness was not a prerequisite of office either. Many constables were in trouble with the law at some time in their lives, typically being fined by manorial courts for not maintaining gates and ditches, or for unlicensed ale-selling. Disposed though many puritan officers were to rigorous schemes of moral reformation, the body of officeholders was too inclusive, and the duty to take up office too dispersed, for office-holding to be confined to an oligarchy of the righteous.

Similarly, religious nonconformity was no bar. Dissenters and Catholics were never statutorily disqualified from local office. The parish remained the elementary unit of society and governance long after the dissolution of the unity of the Church of England, so that, paradoxically, church-wardens were often people who were, in some sense, nonconformists. This need not mean that they abandoned church services for sectarian meetings; more typically it meant partial conformity, either mingling church worship with attendance at illegal conventicles, or demitting from the strict requirements of the Prayer Book or canon law. At Romford in Essex a schoolmaster in trouble with ecclesiastical authority in the 1580s for private catechizing nonetheless became a respected vestryman. At Terling between 1662 and 1688 11 people convicted for nonconformity served as churchwardens, 8 as overseers of the poor and 4 as vestrymen. At Tiverton in the early eighteenth century Martin Dunsford, sergemaker, was, though a dissenter, four times churchwarden, as well as overseer, portreeve and hospital governor.[49]

The social inclusiveness of officeholding was of course relative to jurisdictional spheres. Parish and county elites were dramatically different in their social make-up. There was, however, some osmosis at the boundaries. There are cases of hundredal constables becoming JPs. In the 1650s and again, momentarily, in 1687–8, a good many yeomen and urban tradesmen joined the county bench. In 1680 Sir William Jones complained of upstarts being made justices: he knew of a brewer in Cambridgeshire. Robert Doughty of Hanworth was a JP in Norfolk in the 1660s: his was the only heraldic family in his parish, and he was barely gentleman enough to warrant his county status.[50]

Our third conclusion is that the holding of office was generally a valued marker of social status. The visible evidence survives in many churches, where the roll of churchwardens is displayed. At Over parish church in Cambridgeshire there is a list of every churchwarden, two each year, since 1598. On the whole, village elites did not thrust office upon others as a chore to be avoided. At Lewes in Sussex the 'Fellow-ship of the Twelve' was firmly oligarchical, but the burdensome office of constable rotated among them. In Southwark the highest contributors to the poor rate were most likely to hold office.[51] Deponents in courts would cite even minor office to establish their credentials.[52] Mid-seven-teenth-century grand jurymen, though characteristically no more than yeomen, were styled 'gentlemen' by virtue of the dignity of their office.[53]

Of course office offered material advantages to the holder, in its scope
for adjusting tax assessments, or for handling vagrants and mothers of
bastards so as to lessen parish liabilities, or for patronage: the disposing
of leases, the placing of contracts with traders to supply the workhouse
or repair the church, the allocation of places in almshouses. Office
offered a platform for religious zeal, whether in puritan projects for moral
reformation, or Anglican attempts to purge nonconformists. Overseers
could make doles for the poor dependent upon church attendance; they
might be keen to help the prosecution of nonconformists because the
fines helped defray the costs of maintaining the poor. There were myriad
material motives for exercising local power. Yet undoubtedly the exercise
of local power came with exacting administrative burdens, and the
motives were mixed. Ambrose Barnes, merchant of Newcastle, reflecting
upon his aldermanship, wrote that he could not 'abandon the post without preferring his own inclination before the choice God had made'.[54]
Daniel Defoe remarked that the constableship 'takes up so much of a
man's time that his own affairs are frequently wholly neglected'.[55] To
examine the notebook of Robert Doughty, JP in Norfolk, is to witness
'the sheer amount of ordinary business that occupied [him] almost
daily'.[56] At Exeter, office was 'tedious', it involved 'heavy burdens', yet
it was 'coveted'.[57] Writing of JPs, Norma Landau concluded that 'they
did what they did because they wanted to do it and thought they should
do it'; and 'by assuming the duties of . . . office [they] paid homage to
the concept of voluntary self-government'.[58]

One common practice tended to ensure that lesser offices were not
spurned by superior people. This was the *cursus honorum*, the principle
that greater office ought not to be entered by those who had not first
served in lesser office. The vestry of St Saviour Southwark told a newcomer he could not immediately be admitted a vestryman but should
first 'make trial of other offices'.[59] At Gloucester an aspirant alderman
was expected first to serve twice as both steward or treasurer, and as
sheriff.[60] At Exeter one could not hope to rise to mayor without serving
as steward or bailiff, sheriff and receiver.[61] Parish officeholders generally
held more than one office at different times, graduating from minor to
major. Well over half the constables in Joan Kent's sample were also, at
another (generally later) time, churchwardens. In Little Munden, 22
of 37 constables were also churchwardens, 8 were also overseers; in all,
28 of 37 held another office.[62] In London, it was common for the great
aldermen, however wealthy, to continue also to be vestrymen within
a ward, where they attended to mundane matters of petitions for poor

relief. The greater elite thereby retained some rootedness in lesser spheres.[63] There are signs, too, that progression up the ladder of office was policed with some care. In 1606 at St Botolph Aldgate the vestrymen rejected the candidacy of Humphrey Gonson for constable because his term as scavenger had been marred by bitter quarrelsomeness.[64]

Our fourth conclusion is a broader one. It is that the recovery of parochial officeholding reveals a national regime not only dependent on the good will and competence of county magistracies, but in turn utterly dependent upon the same at parish level. As Paul Langford concluded of the yeomen, artisans and shopkeepers of the parish elites of the eighteenth century, 'this was pre-eminently the class which staffed local offices, and which, notwithstanding the supervisory power of justices, commissioners, and corporations, possessed an unshakeable hold on much of the political infrastructure of the age'.[65] Just as at the county level, perhaps more so, the capacity of central government to exert executive control was compromised and mediated by what was felt to be tolerable in local communities. Historians of the parish have demonstrated the pressure of 'neighbourhood values'. Constables often would not enforce what the law strictly required, for they were guided by the community's moral consensus. The constable was not an executive from outside the community, but a member of it: he was a neighbour as well as a governor.[66] It has been remarked of Somerset before the civil war that the privy council 'had no terrors to match those that the constables' neighbours threatened'.[67] Such pressures were conspicuous during the Restoration when attempts to enforce religious conformity often foundered upon the unwillingness of communities, and in turn constables, to ruin the livelihoods of their neighbours because they happened to worship at illegal conventicles.[68] Equally, it was so when local officers sided with the hungry in times of high bread prices. Edward Thompson recorded a constable at Handborough in Oxfordshire in 1795 who was enlisted by food rioters to set what they regarded as a fair price for grain.[69] Local officers were the agents of their communities as much as of the crown.

The fifth conclusion is that among the important principles at work in officeholding were those of selection by rotation and by lot. It is true that some offices were filled by appointment (justices and sheriffs by the crown) and some by election (generally true of churchwardens and overseers). But many offices fell to people because it was their turn: it fell by automatic rotation among householders. This was the principle known as 'houserow'. Chief Justice Holt stated in 1698 that 'people are to be constables by house-row'; Thomas Gilbert in 1787 said the office of overseer 'generally goes by house-row in rotation through the parish'.[70] Visiting London in 1689, Robert Kirk noted that 'the offices in every ward of London go in order through all the housekeepers': he meant the lesser offices like constable and scavenger.[71] In the parish of Publow in Somerset the office of overseer was filled by houserow, and, by virtue of his ancestral property in the village, it fell to the philosopher John Locke to supply a tithingman twice every nine years.[72] The principle of rotation functioned in two senses: as a means of selection, and as a means for limiting terms of office, for most offices were held for a fixed term, usually one year.

Some offices fell to people by a form of lot. Juries were chosen by sheriffs from lists of eligible freeholders. The process was very far from ensuring random selection: status, experience, locality and political colour all drove jury selection. As well as the 'petty' juries of 12 men who sat in criminal trials, there were also 'grand' juries, of between 17 and 23 men, who sat to hear indictments and to judge whether there was a prima facie case which should go forward to trial. If men of substance tended to be found on grand juries, there were complaints that they avoided service in criminal trials. An Act of 1730 aimed 'to oblige men' to serve and to entrench selection by lot.[73] Two weeks before each quarter session and assize the clerk of the peace instructed the sheriff to summon a panel of freeholders from among whom the grand jury would be selected. In Cheshire, eight grand juries were sworn each year: in the period 1625 to 1659, 609 men from 497 families were called.[74] In Hertfordshire, in the years 1589 to 1618, 246 men were assize grand jurors, at least 906 were quarter sessions grand jurors, and at least 832 were trial jurors.[75] Between 1692 and 1699, 2530 men were sworn jurors in the City of London.[76] In the counties they were chiefly yeomen rather than gentlemen, members of village elites. Much energy was expended on keeping up lists of freeholders eligible for jury service, and an act of 1696 required constables to draw up an annual register.

In the work of the grand jury, as in that of JPs, there was no exact boundary between judicial and administrative business. The grand jury might issue addresses stating matters of common concern. Grand juries were conceived of as a kind of county parliament. Stephen Roberts remarks that 'of all the institutions of local representation, the sessions grand jury was the closest thing to a mouthpiece for the yeomanry of the county. It was nearly a parliament of the middling sort'.[77] The grand juries were especially active as voices of their counties in the wave of petitioning against Charles I's regime just prior to the civil war.[78] In the

Wilkite agitation of the 1760s the Duke of Newcastle strove to curtail the critical addresses published by grand juries.[79] In 1702 Daniel Defoe declared, in his *Original Power of the Collective Body of the People of England*, that if the House of Commons should turn tyrant then grand juries should act in the people's defence.[80] Unelected though they were, grand juries were commonly described as 'the representatives of the people of England'. 'The consent of the whole people [is] given by their representatives the jury'.[81] The phrase the 'consent of the whole people' sounds familiar to us as the language of democracy, but it was here spoken without reference to parliaments or the franchise. Two key principles were recognized here: that the county was a coherent commonwealth within the nation, and that lot rather than election was a proper means for filling offices and representing the community.[82]

The sixth and final conclusion is that an important principle at work in some aspects of officeholding was that of compulsion. The assumption was not the characteristic modern one that people would volunteer – still less 'run' – for office, and do so only if they felt an inclination to profess politics. Politics was not a profession. Rather, governance was the required activity of any, and every, citizen. It was expected that people would take up the burdens of office when their turn came around. It is true that many dodged officeholding, but there were fines for avoidance, and the existence of fines entails an assumption that office was an incumbent duty. Robert Kirk noted that in London 'if any[body] scorn' to take their turn, then they are fined: £10 for the constableship, £3 for the questorship, £2 for the scavengership.[83] The three guineas fine paid by John Minter in 1713 to avoid being overseer at St Marylebone was hefty.[84] The minute books of justices show fines of those failing to appear when chosen for the grand jury. The philosopher John Locke, an absentee freeholder of Somerset, had to secure a certificate instructing the sheriff to release him from a fine for non-appearance when summoned to the grand jury in 1666.[85] In 1701 Humphrey Prideaux noted that though some categories of person were disbarred from being churchwardens, 'all others are eligible, and *must serve*'.[86]

The principle of compulsion is apparent at the level of the duties imposed on every householder. It was, in law at least, compulsory for freemen to attend the annual wardmote meetings in the towns.[87] John Hooker wrote that Exeter freemen 'must come' to the annual meeting to elect officers.[88] Near universal public service was expected in urban policing, especially in times of emergency. By the Statute of Westminster of 1285 every householder must take turns to patrol the neighbourhood.

Keeping the watch was done by rotation among heads of households. Hooker wrote that in Exeter, householders 'by course [in turn] are to watch'.[89] In York householders took it in turns to do duty at the bars (entrances) and posterns of the city.[90] In 1734 it was still necessary for the parishioners of St George Hanover Square, London, to secure a private act of parliament to exempt themselves from householder duty, so that they could hire a waged watchman.[91] An act of 1662 required Londoners to sweep their frontages daily. An act of 1691 required the householders of Westminster to put out lamps from dusk to midnight.[92] When new streets were built in the eighteenth century, householders were responsible for paving and cleaning their segments of the public highway. The propertied were required to supply men and equipment for several days each year for the repair of highways. In 1585 William Lambarde bound a man to appear at quarter sessions for failing to serve on highway repairs.[93] Citizens also had a duty to supply the county militia with its needs. In 1673 Edmund Fitzgerald was instructed to appear before the magistrates at the Lion Inn in Walsingham 'to show cause why he should not deliver . . . two complete suits of arms for sending out two light horses'.[94] Many writers on the militia insisted upon compulsory service. In 1704 John Tutchin called for a revival of the ancient practice by which every freemen should personally serve in the militia, as a matter of 'public service'.[95] A universal duty of charitable giving was implied by the regular practice of churchwardens, sometimes accompanied by chief inhabitants, going from door to door to collect money under royal 'briefs' which established emergency funds, for example to help Huguenot refugees.

Many of these obligations became steadily eroded during the early modern period, and especially during the eighteenth century in the urban setting, with the creation of special rates to provide waged labour. At that period the office of county gaoler steadily became a waged public service. Yet even in the eighteenth century, communities hesitated between the ancient principle of universal citizen service and the modern principle of waged professional service. For a long period a 'rate' remained officially a fine in lieu of compulsory labour. As late as 1756 Westminster insisted on household liability to pave and repair street frontages, to be enforced by presentment of defaulters to a new annoyance jury. Even when St Marylebone created a lamp and highway rate, it continued to require that the unpaid citizens chosen for a term as constable – there were now six of them – should find one of their number to be on duty every night in the watchhouse.[96] In the military sphere, scholars have made much of the eighteenth-century transition from the principle of a universal citizen militia to a modern professional army, and of the passionate debates that surrounded it, but they have made little of the fact that, in the emergence of modernity, much hung upon equivalent questions in the sphere of civil obligations – upon the question of who should sweep the pavements and light the streets. At a late date, the practice of civil governance was a sphere of action that was meant to lie outside the cash nexus. In 1785 Lord Chancellor Mansfield protested against the growing practice of employing 'hireling' overseers of the poor: the office was meant to be done 'without fee or reward'.[97]

The presence of the domain of compulsory service reveals that, in an important sense, officeholding was simply coextensive with being a citizen. The Latin word *officia* translates as 'duties' or 'responsibilities'. In 1584 John Hooker began his recitation of Exeter's particular officers and their duties with 'the office and duty of a freeman', and he detailed what they must do under their general responsibility 'to keep the peace, and defend the liberties of the city'.[98]

V

It would be foolish to take too sanguine a view of the practice of early modern officeholding, and we need now to record four cautions against too roseate a picture of communal participation. Some of these have already been hinted at.

First, while Joan Kent found that 'there were few recorded instances of men openly refusing to serve as constable',[99] it is certain that for some offices and some periods there was a visible reluctance. Some offices were thought too demeaning; some too laborious; some too burdened with expensive obligations. Substantial hospitality was expected from mayors and aldermen.[100] There was a widespread system of substitution – the nomination of deputies – and of fines for refusals. There are cases of bribes being paid to avoid being picked for grand jury service, poorer substitutes being chosen instead.[101] In 1600 the aldermen of St Dunstan-in-the-West in London complained that the queen's service was neglected by the number of people who were fined and dispensed from being constables and scavengers. Ian Archer assessed the force of this complaint. He showed that, of 616 positions between 1603 and 1630, there were 91 cases of fining of demurrers, but that many of those fined in fact served in other offices instead.[102]

Most unpopular of all was the office of county sheriff. It was onerous and expensive, and only had tangible advantage at parliamentary election time, for the sheriff was the returning officer who could determine when, where and for how long the poll would take place. Shrieval appointments were often a device to punish people, the victim choosing between the burden of office and the fine for refusal. In 1587 a draper complained he was chosen sheriff out of 'malice'.[103] In 1714 the Tory Lord Cheyne recommended a Whig in order to save 'a very honest Tory, not to be loaded with that expense'.[104]

The second caution concerns the tendency towards oligarchy and social exclusiveness. The principle of rotation jostled with the presumption that only the socially and economically weighty were qualified for office. There are strong signs of a drift towards oligarchy during the early modern period. Anthony Fletcher concluded that during the seventeenth century 'village society was gradually becoming more polarised', the middling sort increasingly standing apart from the poorer sort, and 'by the 1660s most petty constables, tithingmen and headboroughs... probably came from the middling ranks'.[105] Gwyneth Nair similarly argued for a growing divide. At Highley from the 1620s to the 1640s the house-by-house rota for office persisted, but by the end of the century offices were monopolized by the substantial yeomen. Of course patterns varied from place to place. Little Munden in Hertfordshire tended to the oligarchical in the 1630s and 1640s: just 14 men filled 50 out of 70 terms as constable, churchwarden and overseer; whereas Pattingham was more open: in the same period, 39 men filled 56 terms.[106] Even so, the old principle must have persisted through the eighteenth century in some measure, since in 1796 complaint was made that strict rotation of offices led to incompetence and negligence.[107] Peter Clark argued for 'increasing social polarization' and governmental oligarchy in Gloucester in the decades before 1640.[108] London government in the seventeenth century was more elitist than it had been in the fourteenth, when a constitutional revolution had limited tenures of office and created mechanisms for popular accountability. Grand juries became gentrified in the eighteenth century, their composition very different from petty juries, a disparity which had not existed in the Elizabethan era.[109]

The drift to oligarchy was most explicit in the growth of legislation imposing property qualifications, especially from the late seventeenth century. By an act of 1691 a property qualification was imposed upon parish office for the first time: only persons of £30 per annum, 'if such there be', could serve as surveyors of the highways.[110] By an act of 1693 eligibility for jury service was confined to men with freehold, copyhold or life tenure worth £10 per annum. In 1711 a bill was introduced to enforce a property qualification of £300 income from land for JPs, but failed to become law.[111] By an act of 1756 finely graded property qualifications for each rung in the hierarchy of militia office were stipulated.[112]

Officeholding was exclusive in some categorical senses. In the cities, those who were not freemen of the livery companies were excluded from office. The poorest, those who received alms, were almost invariably excluded. Proverbially, the overseers' regime was often a grim despotism of the pettily powerful over the impoverished and powerless.[113] Even so, historians of poverty now find a relatively high degree of life-cycle mobility whereby people might move into and out of the domain of the poor. If this is so, good conduct in the office of overseer might be a form of insurance for old age, when the former officer might himself become needy. Taken together with the principle of the *cursus honorum*, office might be said to have been exclusive, because age-specific, yet inclusive, because part of the life cycle. Oligarchy was in part age-specific rather than status-specific.[114]

Women were excluded. Where officeholding rotated among properties, and a property was held by a widow, we find gender substitution, the chosen woman hiring a substitute. Thus in Highley in 1628 the churchwarden was 'Francis Dovey for Elizabeth Low, widow'.[115] In 1684 at Little Wilne in Derbyshire Mary Jacques was elected churchwarden, but the justices declared this void and ordered a new election. However, there are recorded instances of women holding office. In 1712 Isabel Eyre at Woodland in Derbyshire said she was out of pocket because she was headborough and overseer.[116] At Thriplow and Fowlmere in Cambridgeshire, women served as overseers in 1774–5 and 1757–62.[117] A woman served as surveyor of highways at Sutton Bonington, Nottinghamshire, in 1750.[118] Women, usually widows, were sometimes employed in stipended public capacities, as gaolers, keepers of houses of correction, hospital matrons and plague searchers. Data collection for the Bills of Mortality, the demographic tables of death in London, was carried out chiefly by women plague searchers. In mid-eighteenth-century Norfolk the keeper of the county gaol and three of the five keepers of the houses of correction were women.[119] In the same period women shareholders attended and voted at stockholder meetings of the South Sea and East India Companies.[120]

The third caution concerns the susceptibility of local office to central control, which mitigated local autonomy. Both through privy council orders and the interventions of assize judges, county and parish officers were sometimes subject to powerful pressures from the centre. This is strikingly so in the relentless inquisitions by Caroline governments, for example in the Book of Orders of 1631.[121] At various periods the office of JP was subject to political and religious purging. Under Elizabeth, Lord Burghley combed the lists of justices in order to weed out papists. From 1680 to 1720 repeated and drastic party purges occurred, for instance of Whigs in the 1680s and Tories after 1714.[122] In the early 1680s London constables were purged by the City magistrates if suspected of Whiggery or sympathy for dissent.[123]

The fourth caution amounts to a truism of social theory. Formal structures of officeholding rarely tell the whole story of the distribution and exercise of power. The mechanics of influence operated through networks of patronage and deference, landlordship and employment, credit and debt, in ways that could readily cut across the institutional fabric of communal self-government. Village officers might gather at the inn to conduct parish business, but it might be that the inn sign – say, the 'Duke of Newcastle's Arms' – is just as revealing.

VI

So far we have stressed officeholding, in the sense of executive and judicial functions, rather than deliberative assemblies. Yet an important office of a citizen was attendance at the parish or ward meeting. Historians' preoccupation with national parliaments occludes the pervasiveness of the practice of deliberation and decision making in the assemblies of the parish republics. The parish meeting or vestry was both a source of policy and an electoral body which chose officers. David Eastwood estimates that at the close of the eighteenth century perhaps 400,000 people attended vestry meetings, most of whom had no parliamentary franchise.[124] Generally the parish held an annual meeting around Easter – though it could be more frequent – comprising all those who paid the poor rate. In London the wardmote or 'inquest' occurred annually, to discuss matters of concern and elect officers.

It was not supposed that citizenship pertained to every adult. The citizen body was defined in the Aristotelian sense as comprising heads of households who were economically independent. Until the late eighteenth century conduct books explicitly paralleled the good conduct of the domestic household economy and the public economy of the parish.[125] Ambrose Barnes, merchant and alderman of Newcastle, thought himself suitable for 'public government' because he was an apt 'governor of his own family'.[126] The householder principle was deeply ingrained, and there seems to have been an almost complete absence of modern aggregative or majoritarian notions entailing the head-counting of *all* adults. When parishioners of St Nicholas Bristol in 1449 spoke of 'the unanimous consent of all the parishioners' they clearly did not intend our sense of *all* the parishioners.[127] Some communities did approximate to a democracy of householders, but of course weightier households tended to matter more. The phrase 'the advice and consent of the major part of the inhabitants' was frequently used, 'major' meaning the weightier part and not the majority.[128] The phrase occurs in an act of 1662 which stipulated that parish surveyors were to be chosen by churchwardens and constables 'with the advice and consent of the major part of the inhabitants'. The parish meeting at Ardeley in Hertfordshire in 1713 called itself a 'convention' of 'the major part of the inhabitants'.[129] At Highley in the 1760s a meeting of the 'the major part' meant about one-fifth of household heads.[130] This is what the ancient Greeks would have *called* democracy, for Athens was a direct democracy, but with a limited citizenry.

Parish constitutions varied with bewildering variety.[131] Some had open vestries comprising all ratepaying householders. Some had select or close vestries, which were narrow oligarchies. Even so, a select vestry in a town might comprise bakers, glovers, butchers and cheesemongers – select, but of the middling sort. Often there was a mixture of the two, a select vestry sometimes summoning the larger citizen body, thus resembling what Aristotle called a 'polity', which balanced aristocratic and democratic elements. In Elizabethan Lewes in Sussex the 'general assembly of the common weal of the town' gathered in the Castle grounds.[132] In St Margaret's Westminster the select vestry met in the chancel of the church while the citizenry met in the nave. At St James Piccadilly in the eighteenth century the vestry comprised three equal estates, of noblemen, gentlemen and tradesmen. At Braintree in Essex the select vestry met monthly, electing a new chairman for each meeting, and voting by placing balls into a box: they also sometimes summoned open meetings of the parish.[133] Early modern English parish history is a saga of struggles between open and select vestries, a struggle which resembles the contests between *governo largo* and *governo stretto*, between popular and aristocratic republics, in Renaissance Italy or eighteenth-century Geneva.[134]

At St Saviour's Southwark in 1608 the parish leaders petitioned for closure, for there is 'great confusion if the whole parish should be electors': it would 'incite the ruder sort to extreme liberty'. At

St Dunstan's Stepney in 1662 a select vestry was imposed since 'by reason of the vast number of inhabitants the public business of the said parish cannot be orderly despatched in general assemblies'.[135] There is a tantalizing question concerning female participation posed by the Chelsea vestry in 1735 which ruled that 'the ladies and gentlewomen, widows and maidens, who pay and stand charged [for the rates] have not a right to vote in the elections'; and at St Pancras in 1788 which decided 'that ladies should not be admitted to vote for parish officers'.[136] That exclusion was specified implies that the question of female participation was raised or that the practice had occurred. It is known that between 1674 and 1694 at Tempsford in Bedfordshire Ann St John attended vestry meetings constantly and sometimes chaired.[137]

There were popular uprisings and reform movements against select vestries, some succeeding and others failing. At St Mary's Westminster in 1667 the community in the nave of the church refused to be content to hear the vestry in the chancel announce to them the choice of churchwardens, and instead elected their own; they lost their case in King's Bench. In St Martin-in-the-Fields in 1741, 200 inhabitants tried to invade the vestry meeting to join in the election of churchwardens; when they were shut out they elected their own; but they also lost their case. In 1742 a rebellion at St Anne's Soho succeeded: the inhabitants invaded the vestry, threw out the vestrymen, and burned the records; thereafter the parish was governed by open vestry. Likewise, in 1738, after two centuries of a close vestry at Great St Mary's in Cambridge, an open meeting resolved that 'government should henceforth be by open meeting and freely elected churchwardens'. In 1798 the citizens of Alnwick in Northumberland overthrew the select vestry and ruled for two years by open meeting, establishing their new constitution in a series of five assemblies held over seven weeks. In the wake of the French Revolution, open vestries sometimes imagined themselves to be miniature revolutionary conventions, with appropriately inflated rhetoric: 'We the said inhabitants so assembled ... do hereby consent, agree, ordain, enact, and declare ...' – thus the parish of St Patrick Exeter in 1804.[138] It is scarcely surprising that the Reverend Hammond Robertson in 1818 denounced the turbulent anarchy of the open vestry system as 'a kind of republic'.[139]

VII

The early modern English polity was paradoxically cross-grained in character. People saw themselves as subjects of an anointed monarch who was armed with awesome prerogative powers, yet also saw themselves as citizens of self-governing communities. 'Citizens were concealed within subjects', Patrick Collinson has written.[140] Collinson's essay, *De Republica Anglorum*, pinpoints the paradox. The growth of the Tudor and Stuart state, of court and royal power, in fact enhanced the role of the locality, because extra burdens of legislation and administration fell upon local elites and officeholders. The machinery for raising national taxes, and above all the ramifications of the poor law, resulted in a more intensively governed nation, but still a largely self-governing one. 'Early modern England consisted of a series of overlapping, superimposed communities which were also semi-autonomous, self-governing political cultures. These may be called, but always in quotes, "republics": village republics; in the counties, gentry republics; and at a transcendant level, the commonwealth of England, which Sir Thomas Smith thought it proper to render in Latin a *Republica Anglorum*'.[141] We have here the claim that early modern England was in some sense a republic, a claim more explicitly made in the title of another of Collinson's essays, 'The Monarchical Republic of Elizabethan England'.[142] Similarly, for a later period, David Eastwood has judged that the 'Hanoverian political system embodied institutions the character of which might best be described as republican, participatory, and communitarian'.[143]

Evidence for the articulation of abstract political principles amid the quotidian practices of local government is inevitably fugitive. But it is there. It was commonplace for incorporated towns and cities to be construed as quasi-republics or 'commonwealths'. In 1677 John Nalson remarked that whereas ancient direct democracy was impossible in large, populous modern states, nonetheless it did remain possible in 'small municipal societies, as with us in corporations in England . . . and several small republics beyond the seas', where 'the laws are the *plebiscita*, the votes of the common people in general'.[144] In the Elizabethan period London's self-government was lauded. A tract of 1584 pointed out that no royal viceroy governed the proudly independent City. Aldermen spoke of 'the commonwealth of the City'.[145] In 1771 the *London Magazine* remarked that 'the civil government of cities is a kind of small independent policy [polity] in itself'.[146] John Hooker said of the mayor of Exeter that he was 'head of the whole common weale', 'the president of the publick state'.[147] The friends of Stuart absolutism took such civic prowess to be altogether threatening. William Cavendish warned Charles II that 'every city is a petty free state against monarchy'.[148] Such prowess could threaten parliament too, if parliament turned tyrant. In 1645 the

Leveller William Ball claimed that although parliament was the nation's 'representative body', its 'essential body' was to be found in 'the counties, cities, and towns corporate'.[149]

As with towns, so with parishes. Eloquent testimony of a parish republic in embryo is provided by an account of a meeting of the principal inhabitants of Swallowfield in Wiltshire on 4 December 1596. They met at a time of dearth and unrest, to establish peace and amity, to provide against hunger and poverty, and to instil moral reform. They took it upon themselves to adopt a form of self-government, because 'the justices are far off'. They agreed to hold regular meetings, adopt a constitution and appoint a registrar. They would trouble the justices as little as possible. They would be 'counsellors of one another'. They would share the public burdens: all 'officers whatsoever concerning her majesty's service and all other officers for the public affairs of the tythings and the inhabitants thereof shall be countenanced and borne out of us all'.[150] There were to be scores of Swallowfields during the chaotic years of the 1640s, when the Clubmen sprang up, spontaneously reinventing local commonwealths in areas that had become the ungoverned terrain of rival armies.[151]

The readiness to contemplate quasi-republican forms extended to national government in the concepts of regency and of national associations designed to meet dynastic emergencies. The 1585 Association, intended to sustain government in the event of the queen's assassination, was mimicked by the Whig Association of 1680, an undertaking to take up the reins of government upon Charles II's sudden demise.[152] The Regency Act of 1706, which aimed to forestall a Jacobite coup, stipulated that upon the death of Queen Anne a regency council would immediately assume rule. In 1688, during the collapse of James II's regime, county associations were formed, and, in the face of utter confusion over who was or was not commissioned as justices, leading men took it upon themselves to conduct county government. The prototype of regency schemes was William Cecil's 'monarchical republic' of 1563, prompted by Queen Elizabeth's falling ill with smallpox. Stephen Alford has shown how a feudal-baronial idea of conciliar government melded with Ciceronian ideals of public service. He explores Cecil's education in humanist public service, above all in Cicero's *Offices*, the book 'central to the understanding Elizabethan governors had of their part in the political scheme of things'.[153] A similar kind of mental world nurtured the aristocratic republicanism that flourished in the circles of the Sidney dynasty, explored by Jonathan Scott and Blair Worden.[154] The English both imagined and enacted acephalous rule.

Another kind of evidence to which we can turn is the idealization of local self-government in English utopian writing. Utopias are imagined communities, yet they are apt to be projections or ideal types of existing social practices. In Thomas More's *Utopia* (1515) each group of thirty households annually elect a syphrogrant, and for every ten syphrogrants there is a tranibor. Except for the (elective) prince, everybody holds office for one year only.[155] In James Harrington's *Oceana* (1656) arithmetical neatness is imposed: there are to be 10,000 parishes, 1000 hundreds, and 50 counties (renamed tribes). The existing array of local officers (overseers, high constables, jurymen and so on) are augmented by further officers, such as censors. Each tribe is to have a council, or phylarch, of 66 persons, chosen by parishes and hundreds.[156]

A less familiar example is *The Fundamental Constitutions of Carolina* (1669), which John Locke had a hand in drafting. It never had much impact on the Earl of Shaftesbury's proprietory colony, but it displays an attempt to transpose to North America a stylized version of English government. Its acknowledgement of monarchy was tenuous: Carolina was to be an aristocratic republic. There was to be a parliament, but it would only meet biennially, and there was no intention that it should be in constant session. Regular government was therefore in the hands of a grand council and a complex scheme of local officers. The assumption was that Carolina, for the time being, would be a province comprising eight counties. The province would have an extent of 3,840,000 acres – around 6000 square miles, the size of East Anglia. Each county would have 480,000 acres – about 750 square miles, the size of Dorset. Each county is divided into 40 units of 12,000 acres each, called 'seigniories', 'baronies', 'precincts' and 'colonies'. At any one time there would be 1320 officeholders, 165 in each county. Or, rather, there would be this many at the level of the 'middling sort' and above, for there were also an unspecified further number of assistants to constables. Each principal office had attached to it a property qualification. It is simplest to tabulate these (see Table 1). There is one further provision worth noticing. 'All inhabitants and freemen of Carolina above seventeen years of age and under sixty shall be bound to bear arms and serve as soldiers whenever the grand council shall find it necessary.'[157]

Locke sketched similar notions in jottings he called 'Atlantis' in 1677–9. Here he suggested restoring the ancient office of tithingman, in the true sense of having ten households under his care. His duties would be to police the morals of the community, to apprehend vagrants, and to identify the poor and sick in need of assistance. He was to visit every

Table 1 *Property qualification for principal offices in*
'The Fundamental Constitutions of Carolina'

	Number	Qualification
County sheriffs	8	500 acres
County justices	32	500 acres
County jurymen	96	200 acres
County grand jurymen	96	300 acres
Precinct stewards	32	300 acres
Precinct justices	128	300 acres
Precinct jurymen	384	50 acres
Precinct registrars	32	300 acres
Seignory registrars	64	50 acres
Barony registrars	64	50 acres
Colony registrars	192	50 acres
Colony constables	192	100 acres

house once a month 'to see what lives they lead'. In his *Essay on the Poor Law* (1697), Locke proposed that the management of the poor be put on a hundredal or town-wide basis and placed in the hands of a committee of guardians of the poor. Each parish would elect its own guardian, the franchise lying with the ratepayers. Strict rotation is specified: guardians are to serve for three years 'and no longer', and one-third of the hundredal committee would stand down each year.[158]

Eighteenth-century utopian writing continued to extrapolate from existing patterns of local officeholding, emphasizing the principle of rotation, and generally also citizen militias. These utopias tended to exhibit a passion for arithmetical exactitude. In David Hume's 'Idea of a Perfect Commonwealth' (1752), England's parishes are tidied into 10,000, each electing officers at an annual meeting in the parish church, and sending a representative to the county, 100 counties having 100 parishes each.[159] In James Burgh's *Account of the Cessares* (1764), the citizens are defined as males over 21, who are married, Protestant and have declared their loyalty to the constitution. Each parish (which is to be four square miles) is to choose six inspectors, two each year, for a three-year term. Each county (comprising 25 parishes) is to choose senators; nobody is to be a senator who has not already been an inspector.[160] In Catherine Macaulay's scheme for Corsica, officeholding is strictly rotative, every civil and military officer resigning after one year and being ineligible for another three.[161] It is particularly in English radical writing between about 1770 and 1800 that we find a rich seam celebrating the republicanism of the small commune. In 1782 David Williams protested against the pointlessness of parliamentary reform: instead he envisaged an England of independent tithings and hundreds.[162] In Godwin's quasi-anarchist *Political Justice* (1793) the national state is abolished and replaced by a harmonious confederation of self-governing parish communities. Intercommunal disputes are to be resolved by juries. Likewise, in Thomas Spence's dream of Spensonia the parish republic was the bedrock of the commonwealth, each with its own militia, school and welfare system; and each allowing women to vote. Every parish would be 'a little polished Athens'. There would be 'a national assembly or congress consisting of delegates from all the parishes'.[163] Josiah Tucker, an enemy of the radicals, made a significant concession when he wrote that 'a free and equal republic is absolutely impracticable in any district of larger extent than a common country parish'.[164]

VIII

Historians of political thought, notably John Pocock, have encouraged us to think that English republicanism was both a late and a minority tradition. In this account, the republicanism nurtured in the Italian Renaissance erupted into English discourse with drastic suddenness as a consequence of the Civil War and the execution of King Charles I. The monarchical consensus of early Stuart England was shattered, and the unthinkable began to be said. The outcome was the principal work of English republican thought, Harrington's *Oceana* and a tradition of theorizing influenced by it. But this view is in danger of confining the idea of republicanism to outright rejection of monarchy, and of supposing that the monarchic idiom precluded the republican.[165]

Recently, however, a number of studies – signally Markku Peltonen's on Elizabethan and Jacobean humanism and Quentin Skinner's on the humanist context of Thomas Hobbes's political thought – make it possible for us to see that, far from being unthinkable, a certain type of republican discourse was ubiquitous in the Tudor and early Stuart era.[166] Literary scholars have likewise shown that commentaries upon classical texts like Lucan's *Pharsalia*, and plays like Ben Jonson's Roman series, created an ambient familiarity with republican ideas well before the Civil War.[167] To be sure, this was not an anti-monarchic republicanism: it set out an ideal of a monarchical republic. From an early moment in the sixteenth century, the humanist discourse of the Italian Renaissance was not wholly channelled, upon arrival in England, into conduct books for courtiers contemplating the service of princes. Rather, humanist writers insisted upon the duty of civic participation as the key to the public good. Liberty and the common good depended upon people governing themselves, and upon inculcating a spirit of public service. As Richard Hurd remarked in 1754, 'in the more absolute monarchies of Europe, all are courtiers. In our freer monarchy all should be citizens.'[168]

A tract of 1576 showed how the common good depends upon people being willing to 'bestow . . . pains' on public service, and to engage in 'civil actions'.[169] A handbook for magistrates of 1659 pronounced that a justice should be 'an able man, *vir virtutis*, a man able in body and mind to do the commonwealth service'. The author explained that the 'best of polities' are 'corporations, guilds, and fraternities', about which we may learn not only from the Greeks and Romans, but also 'from our own practice'.[170] In 1575 and 1584 John Hooker, addressing the governors of Exeter, described the city as a 'civitas', 'this our commonwealth and city'; he cited the republican humanist Patrizi and praised government by wise senators who put the well-being of the commonwealth above their private profit.[171] In 1600 Thomas Wilson insisted on the freedom from royal interference of English cities, for, 'every city was, as it were, a commonwealth amongst themselves'.[172] In 1576 the town clerk of Tewkesbury published a tract which surveyed the wisdom of the ancients, Cicero and Seneca among others, by way of establishing how peoples should be gathered up into towns and cities which were 'a body politic and civil in themselves'.[173]

These ideals were grounded in intimate familiarity with classical authors and exemplars. The ubiquitous textbook was Cicero's *Offices*, and the ubiquitous icon of public service was Cato. Cicero urged that it was a vice to despise the undertaking of magistracy; in public service people should be 'forgetful of their own advantage', and citizens should 'abandon any hesitation' about engaging in public life.[174] A treatise of 1579 spoke of the importance of 'the true knowledge of duties, than the which nothing is more commendable in youth, nothing more profitable in a commonwealth, and nothing more acceptable unto God, which thing Cicero, the flower of eloquent philosophers, showed in his book on duties'.[175] Hooker opened his account of the duties of the officers of Exeter by quoting Cicero: 'nothing doth more nourish love, and preserve common society, than good will performed in the offices of humanity'.[176] Robert Sanderson, adviser to the nation's consciences in the mid-seventeenth century, claimed to have read Cicero's book twenty times and to know it by heart.[177] When John Locke drew up a reading list in 1698, under the heading of morality he listed two books, the New Testament and Cicero's *Offices*.[178] As for Cato, when the leathersellers of London in the late sixteenth century appealed to Lord Burghley they addressed him as the 'very Cato of the commonwealth'.[179] In the 1780s Vice-Admiral Parker commanded the ship *Cato*. When the Whig journalists John Trenchard and Thomas Gordon launched one of the most influential essay journals of the eighteenth century, they called it *Cato's Letters*. In Letter 13, 'Cato' says that the English are free because they are governed by their own kind and not by the henchmen of a distant prince: the meanest cobbler could judge of English liberty because he can tell 'whether a dragoon, or a parish officer, comes to him for his taxes'.[180]

Such ideals remain visible in the epitaphs of English parish churches. At Iwerne Courtney in Dorset, Sir Thomas Freke's monument – he died in 1733 – says he was 'a worthy patriot', a county officer for 30 years, serving with 'prudence and justice'. In St Mary's Church, Godmanchester, it is said of Alfred Clark, who died in 1744, that 'he was an active useful upright magistrate in this town above sixty years, a lover of justice and friend to the public', and of Robert Hicks, apothecary and town bailiff, that 'he was at all times anxious to promote the public good'. It is plain that classical ideals of public good mingled with Christian ideals of service. Readers of the King James Bible were familiar with a scriptural conjunction of the two in the affairs of the Greek city of Ephesus, visited by St Paul, where we read of the 'town clerk' who calmed the grievances of the citizens in the assembly.[181]

Students of the impact of Renaissance humanism tend to stress civic, in the sense of urban, ideals, which were underpinned by a Roman and Greek tradition. They take the city-state to be the paradigm of the commonwealth. Yet, as we have seen, there was an equally vigorous idealization of the rural parish republic. The ideological underpinning of the latter had an independent source: the tradition of celebration of the perfections of the Anglo-Saxon constitution.[182] In the work of Elizabethan antiquaries, in the common lawyers' investigations of King Edward the Confessor's laws, in Leveller polemics against the 'Norman yoke', and in the mid- and late eighteenth-century craze for King Alfred's England, there was a persistent effort at recovery of the pristine Saxon origins of juries, moots, hundredal courts, reeves and tithingmen. Scholars have yet to recover what might be called the Saxon republicanism of early modern England.

The office that was most enthusiastically idealized by Saxonists was that of juryman. Juries provided Englishmen with the opportunity to be tried by their peers, and not be convicted and punished by the summary justice of state functionaries. In 1682 Henry Care proposed that jurors should keep their hats on in court as a mark of the dignity of their office.[183] Grand juries were especially susceptible to declamations on the dignity of officeholding, because it was the custom for judges and county leaders to deliver a 'charge to the grand jury'. These charges mainly exhorted vigilance in the execution of the laws, but they also expatiated on the 'dignity' and 'antiquity' of the juryman's office. Jurymen were said to be 'watchmen upon an high tower', keepers of 'the public safety and benefit'.[184]

IX

The old world[185] of the parish republic ended abruptly in the 1830s, principally with the passing of the Poor Law Amendment Act. As Sidney and Beatrice Webb noted, it signalled 'the death of the parish'.[186] It was explicitly a matter of complaint by the Poor Law Commissioners in 1833 that, without reform, 'as things now are each parish is . . . an independent nation . . . [there are] fourteen thousand republics'.[187]

After the 1830s the old world of English local government became the object of ideologically driven historical investigation. The Webbs' classic study of 1906 remains unsurpassed, but they were heirs of the Benthamite Radicals: for them, the old regime was corrupt, oligarchic, venal, unaccountable, incompetent, amateur and chaotic: in its place had to come the salaried officials of the national democratic state.[188] But nineteenth-century foreign observers, among them Alexis de Tocqueville, Hypolite Taine and Rudolf von Gneist, admired aspects of the old regime,[189] while in Joshua Toulmin Smith it found a passionate celebrant. His *Local Self-Government and Centralization* (1851) denounced the iniquity of the modern police state now being imposed, a government by state functionaries, the child of the 'pseudo-liberalism of modern times'. He delivered a paean to local self-government as socially and morally uplifting, as integrative, as bonding rights with duties, as building trust and mutual service. His Tacitean sentimentalism led him to ground the parish vestry in the folkmotes of the Anglo-Saxons. Yet his critique of the reduction of modern man to an ignorant and manipulated 'mere voting machine' was penetrating, for he thought that voting should never be severed from mooting. In citizen assemblies the people form considered judgements, become 'familiar with the discussed merits of any question, impressed with a moral sense of due responsibility, and competent to give their votes'. Toulmin Smith further argued that officeholding, together with mooting, gave thousands of people practical experience in handling problems of social policy. Only by actually governing could people be responsible citizens.[190]

Outside England, no writer was more tersely prophetic about the impending dangers of the politics of the democratic suffrage than the German philosopher Hegel, in his *Philosophy of Right*. Writing in 1821, he observed that popular suffrage, especially in large states, 'leads inevitably to electoral indifference, since the casting of a single vote is of no significance where there is a multitude of electors'. The result would be the opposite of what was intended: it will place power in the hands of the few, the party caucuses. The problem lay in the faulty assumption that political society was composed of 'an agglomeration of atomic individuals', for it was a deep mistake to think of society as 'dispersed into atomic units, collected to perform only a single and temporary act'.[191] English writers had apprehensions of a similar sort. When John Stuart Mill reviewed Tocqueville's *Democracy in America* he reflected on the dangers of there being 'a political act, to be done only once in a few years, for which nothing in the daily habits of the citizen has prepared him'.[192] Elsewhere, Mill suggested a remedy. In his essay *On Representative Government* he emphasized the value of parish office and jury service as the 'school of public spirit'.[193]

NOTES

*Versions of this essay were presented at seminars during 1997–2000 at Cambridge, London, Munich and Sussex. I am particularly grateful to Eckhart Hellmuth for the invitation to Munich, where he sustains a distinguished school of British historical studies. For advice and encouragement I am indebted to Steve Hindle and Tim Harris.

1. John Dunn, *Western Political Thought in the Face of the Future* (Cambridge, 1979), p. 16. Contemporary critics of democracy fall broadly into two schools: theorists of deliberative democracy, who seek ways of embedding voting in informed debate, and theorists of republican democracy, who seek alternative forms of participation besides voting. The argument of this essay runs parallel to the latter school. See Benjamin Barber, *Strong Democracy: Participatory Politics for a New Age* (Berkeley, 1984); Richard Dagger, *Civic Virtues: Rights, Citizenship and Republican Liberalism* (Oxford, 1997); James Fishkin, *Democracy and Deliberation* (New Haven, 1971); Adrian Oldfield, *Citizenship and Community: Civic Republicanism in the Modern World* (London, 1990); Carole Pateman, *Participation and Democratic Theory* (Cambridge, 1970); Philip Pettit, *Republicanism: A Theory of Freedom and Government* (Oxford, 1997).

2. Aristotle, *Politics*, III.13.
3. Thomas Paine, *The Rights of Man, Part II* (1792), in *Political Writings*, ed. Bruce Kuklick (Cambridge, 1989), p. 168.
4. A pre-eminent practitioner of the first sort is Keith Wrightson, and of the second, Quentin Skinner. See Keith Wrightson and David Levine, *Poverty and Piety in an English Village: Terling, 1525–1700* (Oxford, 1979, 1995); Quentin Skinner, *Liberty before Liberalism* (Cambridge, 1998). Particular inspirations for the present essay have been David Eastwood, *Government and Community in the English Provinces, 1700–1870* (London, 1997), and Keith Wrightson, 'The Politics of the Parish in Early Modern England', in Paul Griffiths, Adam Fox and Steve Hindle (eds), *The Experience of Authority in Early Modern England* (London, 1996).
5. It is commonplace to contrast England with France's machinery of absolutism, the large salaried state bureaucracy of local *intendants*. A possible objection to the present essay is that England was administratively a relatively unified and centralized state, in contrast with the entrenched communalisms and provincialisms of much of Continental Europe. See Peter Blickle (ed.), *Resistance, Representation and Community* (Oxford, 1997). The topic raises in turn the question of the relative strengths of national and local identities. Even an historian of English urban prowess suggests that 'nowhere in eighteenth-century England would it be possible to find the intensity of civic feeling which was found in independent city states such as those in Germany': Rosemary Sweet, *The Writing of Urban History in Eighteenth-Century England* (Oxford, 1997), p. 236. For a related objection, see below, n. 185.
6. See especially Alan Everitt, *The Community of Kent and the Great Rebellion, 1640–1660* (Leicester, 1966); and J. S. Morrill, *The Revolt of the Provinces* (London, 1976). For critical surveys see Clive Holmes, 'The County Community in Stuart Historiography', *JBS*, XIX (1980), 54–73; Cynthia Herrup, 'The Counties and the Country', *Social History*, VIII (1983), 169–81.
7. Paul Langford, *Public Life and the Propertied Englishman, 1689–1798* (Oxford, 1991), pp. 256–7.
8. On the burden of the poor rate see Steve Hindle, 'Power, Poor Relief and Social Relations in Holland Fen, *c*.1600–1800', *HJ*, XLI (1998), 67–96; and Valerie Pearl, 'Change and Stability in Seventeenth-Century London', *London Journal*, V (1979), 3–34. On the burden of local militia rates in the early Stuart period, see Thomas Cogswell, *Home Divisions: Aristocracy, the State, and Provincial Conflict* (Manchester, 1998), pp. 181–3.
9. Sir Thomas Smith, *De Republica Anglorum*, ed. Mary Dewar (Cambridge, 1982), p. 107.
10. Cynthia B. Herrup, *The Common Peace: Participation and the Criminal Law in Seventeenth-Century England* (Cambridge, 1987), p. 205. See also Griffiths et al. (eds), *Experience of Authority*.
11. Cynthia B. Herrup, 'Law and Morality in Seventeenth-Century England', *P&P*, CVI (1985), 102–23; Joanna Innes, 'Politics and Morals: The Reformation of Manners Movement in Later Eighteenth-Century England', in E. Hellmuth (ed.), *The Transformation of Political Culture: England and Germany in the Late Eighteenth Century* (Oxford, 1990).

12. For example: Tim Harris, *London Crowds in the Reign of Charles II* (Cambridge, 1987); Paul Monod, *Jacobitism and the English People, 1688–1788* (Cambridge, 1989); Kathleen Wilson, *The Sense of the People: Politics, Culture and Imperialism in England, 1715–1785* (Cambridge, 1998); Nicholas Rogers, *Crowds, Culture and Politics in Georgian Britain* (Oxford, 1998). See also the chapter by Nicholas Rogers in this volume.

13. For example: Peter Borsay, ' "All the Towns's a Stage": Urban Ritual and Ceremony, 1660–1800', in Peter Clark (ed.), *The Transformation of English Provincial Towns, 1600–1800* (London, 1984); Newton Key, 'The Political Culture and Political Rhetoric of County Feasts and Fast Sermons, 1654–1714', *JBS*, XXXIII (1994), 223–56; David Cressy, *Bonfires and Bells: National Memory and the Protestant Calendar in Elizabethan and Stuart England* (London, 1979).

14. Douglas Hay et al., *Albion's Fatal Tree: Crime and Society in Eighteenth-Century England* (London, 1975); Thomas W. Lacqueur, 'Crowds, Carnival and the State in English Executions, 1604–1868', in A. L. Beier, David Cannadine and James M. Rosenheim (eds), *The First Modern Society* (Cambridge, 1989); J. A. Sharpe, ' "Last Dying Speeches": Religion, Ideology and Public Execution in Seventeenth-Century England', *P&P*, CVII (1985), 144–67.

15. E. P. Thompson, 'The Moral Economy of the English Crowd in the Eighteenth Century', in his *Customs in Common* (London, 1991), pp. 185–258. See also E. P. Thompson, 'Custom, Law and Common Right', in ibid., pp. 96–184; Bob Bushaway, *By Rite: Custom, Ceremony and Community in England, 1700–1880* (London, 1982); J. M. Neeson, *Commoners: Common Right, Enclosure and Social Change in England, 1700–1820* (Cambridge, 1993); Andy Wood, 'The Place of Custom in Plebian Political Culture: England, 1550–1800', *Social History*, XXII (1997), 46–60.

16. See especially Hellmuth (ed.), *The Transformation of Political Culture*; and Langford, *Public Life*. A recent contribution is Peter Clark, *British Clubs and Societies, 1580–1800* (Oxford, 2000).

17. Geoffrey Holmes, *The Electorate and the National Will in the First Age of Party* (Lancaster, 1976), repr. in his *Politics, Religion and Society in England, 1679–1742* (London, 1986); W. A. Speck, *Tory and Whig: The Struggle in the Constituencies, 1701–1715* (London, 1970).

18. Nicholas Rogers, *Whigs and Cities: Popular Politics in the Age of Walpole and Pitt* (Oxford, 1989); J. A. Phillips, *Electoral Behaviour in Unreformed England: Plumpers, Splitters and Straights* (Princeton, 1982); F. O'Gorman, *Voters, Patrons and Parties: The Unreformed Electoral System in Hanoverian England, 1734–1832* (Oxford, 1989); Derek Hirst, *The Representative of the People? Voters and Voting in England under the Early Stuarts* (Cambridge, 1975).

19. Holmes, *Politics, Religion and Society*, p. 14.

20. Hirst, *Representative of the People?*, pp. 104–5.

21. More recently, historians have noticed that enfranchisement also came about by landlords converting copyhold property into freehold: Richard Hoyle, 'Tenure and the Land Market in Early Modern England', *EcHR*, XLIII (1990), 1–20.

22. Speck, *Tory and Whig*, pp. 119–20.

23. Ibid., pp. 17, 78; J. H. Plumb, 'The Growth of the Electorate in England from 1600 to 1715', *P&P*, XLV (1969), 116.
24. J. C. D. Clark, *English Society, 1688–1832* (Cambridge, 1985), ch. 1; Mark Kishlansky, *Parliamentary Selection: Social and Political Choice in Early Modern England* (Cambridge, 1986).
25. Kishlansky, *Parliamentary Selection*, pp. 23, 48, and *passim*. A similar claim could be made for the Hanoverian period. Paul Langford has written, 'The view that it was better to have no representation at all than a form which involved public election was widely held': *Public Life*, pp. 270, and 264ff.
26. Kishlansky, *Parliamentary Selection*, p. 230.
27. Clark, *English Society*, p. 21, and *passim*.
28. Neeson, *Commoners*, ch. 5.
29. 14 Elizabeth c. 5 (1572).
30. J. S. W. Gibson and G. R. C. Brinkworth (eds), *Banbury Corporation Records: Tudor and Stuart* (Banbury, 1977), p. 58.
31. John Vowell alias Hooker, *A Pamphlet of the Offices and Duties of Everie Particular Sworn Officer of the City of Exeter* (London, 1584).
32. Kishlansky, *Parliamentary Selection*, pp. 15, 39.
33. For the county magistracy see J. H. Gleason, *The Justices of the Peace in England, 1558–1640* (Oxford, 1969); Norma Landau, *The Justice of the Peace, 1679–1760* (Berkeley, 1984). Also: Irene Gladwin, *The Sheriff: The Man and his Office* (London, 1974).
34. Joan Kent, *The English Village Constable, 1580–1642* (Oxford, 1986); Keith Wrightson, 'Two Concepts of Order: Justices, Constables and Jurymen in Seventeenth-Century England', in John Brewer and John Styles (eds), *An Ungovernable People: The English and their Law in the Seventeenth and Eighteenth Centuries* (London, 1980); E. Carlson, 'The Origins, Function and Status of the Office of Churchwarden', in Margaret Spufford (ed.), *The World of Rural Dissenters, 1520–1725* (Cambridge, 1995).
35. This counts only the principal offices of the parish.
36. Rudolph von Gneist, *The History of the English Constitution* (London, 1889), II, 358.
37. Valerie Pearl, *London and the Outbreak of the Puritan Revolution* (Oxford, 1961), ch. 2.
38. Ian W. Archer, *The Pursuit of Stability: Social Relations in Elizabethan London* (Cambridge, 1991), p. 64; J. M. Beattie, 'London Juries in the 1690s', in J. S. Cockburn and Thomas A. Green (eds), *Twelve Good Men and True: The Criminal Trial Jury in England, 1200–1600* (Princeton, 1988), p. 249.
39. Jeremy Boulton, *Neighbourhood and Society: A London Suburb in the Seventeenth Century* (Cambridge, 1987), pp. 267–8.
40. Shani D'Cruze, 'The Middling Sort in Eighteenth-Century Colchester', in Jonathan Barry and Christopher Brooks (eds), *The Middling Sort of People: Culture, Society and Politics in England, 1550–1800* (London, 1994), pp. 193, 198.
41. Philip Withington, 'Urban Political Culture in Late Seventeenth-Century England: York, 1649–1688', University of Cambridge PhD thesis (1998), pp. 44, 109.
42. Ibid., p. 98.

43. Langford, *Public Life*, p. 491ff.; Eastwood, *Government and Community*, p. 66.
44. Langford, *Public Life*, pp. 207–8, 239.
45. F. H. W. Sheppard, *Local Government in St Marylebone, 1688–1835* (London, 1958), pp. 56–60.
46. Kent, *English Village Constable*, p. 94; Gwyneth Nair, *Highley: The Development of a Community, 1550–1880* (Oxford, 1988), p. 142; Boulton, *Neighbourhood and Society*, p. 142.
47. Paul S. Seaver, *Wallington's World: A Puritan Artisan in Seventeenth-Century London* (London and Stanford, 1985), pp. 146–7, 150.
48. Anthony Fletcher, *Reform in the Provinces: The Government of Stuart England* (New Haven, 1986), p. 65; Wrightson, 'Two Concepts of Order', p. 28; Kent, *English Village Constable*, p. 130ff.
49. Wrightson, 'Politics of the Parish', p. 28; Wrightson and Levine, *Terling*, p. 168; Sweet, *Writing of Urban History*, p. 175.
50. Fletcher, *Reform in the Provinces*, pp. 32–34; James M. Rosenheim, 'Robert Doughty of Hanworth: A Restoration Magistrate', *Norfolk Archaeology*, XXX–XXXVIII (1983), 296–312.
51. Jeremy Goring, 'The Fellowship of the Twelve in Elizabethan Lewes', *Sussex Archaeological Collections*, CXIX (1981), 157–72; Boulton, *Neighbourhood and Society*, p. 141.
52. Archer, *Pursuit of Stability*, p. 64.
53. John Morrill, *Cheshire, 1630–1660* (London, 1974), pp. 17–18.
54. *Memoirs of the Life of Mr Ambrose Barnes* (Surtees Society, vol. 50, 1867), p. 99.
55. Quoted in Kent, *English Village Constable*, p. 220.
56. Rosenheim, 'Doughty', p. 300.
57. Wallace T. MacCaffrey, *Exeter, 1540–1640* (Cambridge, Mass., 1958), p. 37.
58. Landau, *Justice of the Peace*, pp. 2, 359.
59. Archer, *Pursuit of Stability*, p. 64.
60. Peter Clark, 'The Civic Leaders of Gloucester, 1500–1800', in Peter Clark (ed.), *The Transformation of English Provincial Towns, 1600–1800* (London, 1984), p. 317.
61. McCaffrey, *Exeter*, p. 36.
62. Kent, *English Village Constable*, pp. 140–1.
63. This reached the level of fantasy politics when the new vestry of the parish of St George Hanover Square was constituted in 1725: it contained seven dukes, fourteen earls, two viscounts and seven barons.
64. Archer, *Pursuit of Stability*, p. 68.
65. Langford, *Public Life*, p. 177.
66. Wrightson, 'Two Concepts of Order'; Kent, *English Village Constable*, chs 1, 7.
67. T. H. Barnes, *Somerset, 1625–1640* (Oxford, 1961), p. 230.
68. Mark Goldie, 'The Hilton Gang and the Purge of London in the 1680s', in Howard Nenner (ed.), *Politics and the Political Imagination in Later Stuart Britain* (Woodbridge, Suffolk, 1997).
69. Thompson, *Customs in Common*, p. 229.
70. Sidney and Beatrice Webb, *The Parish and the County* (Vol. 1 of *English Local Government from the Revolution to the Municipal Corporations Act*) (London, 1906), pp. 16–17.
71. Edinburgh University Library, MS Laing III.545, fol. 125r.

72. E. S. De Beer (ed.), *The Correspondence of John Locke*, 8 vols (Oxford, 1976–89), letters 952 and 1204.
73. Douglas Hay, 'The Class Composition of the Palladium of Liberty: Trial Jurors in the Eighteenth Century', in Cockburn and Green (eds), *Twelve Good Men and True*, pp. 317–8.
74. John Morrill, *The Cheshire Grand Jury, 1625–1659* (Leicester, 1976), p. 9.
75. P. G. Lawson, 'Lawless Juries? The Composition and Behaviour of Hertfordshire Juries, 1573–1624', in Cockburn and Green (eds), *Twelve Good Men and True*, p. 144.
76. Beattie, 'London Juries in the 1690s', p. 231.
77. Stephen K. Roberts, 'Juries and the Middling Sort: Recruitment and Performance at Devon Quarter Sessions, 1649–1670', in Cockburn and Green (eds), *Twelve Good Men and True*, p. 184.
78. Everitt, *Community of Kent*, pp. 95–6.
79. J. M. Beattie, *Crime and the Courts in England, 1660–1800* (Oxford, 1986), p. 322.
80. Mark Goldie (ed.), *The Reception of Locke's Politics*, 6 vols (London, 1999), I, 335.
81. Georges Lamoine (ed.), *Charges to the Grand Jury, 1689–1803* (Camden Society, XLIII, 1992), pp. 376, 379.
82. On the history and theory of selection by lot see Bernard Manin, *The Principles of Representative Government* (Cambridge, 1997). The present-day British political pressure group, Charter 88, includes in its council twelve members (six men and six women) drawn by lot from the membership database. The Royal Commission on Reform of the House of Lords which reported in 1999 heard a submission arguing that some members of the House of Lords should be chosen by lot.
83. Edinburgh University Library, MS Laing III.545, fol. 125r.
84. Sheppard, *St Marylebone*, p. 11.
85. Bodleian Library, Oxford, MS Locke, c.25, fol. 10.
86. Humphrey Prideaux, *Directions to Churchwardens* (London, 1701), pp. 15–16. Emphasis added.
87. Archer, *Pursuit of Stability*, p. 83.
88. Hooker, *Offices of Exeter*, sig. Ci.
89. Ibid., sig. Ii.
90. Withington, 'Urban Political Culture', ch. 4.
91. Beattie, *Crime and the Courts*, p. 68.
92. Sheppard, *St Marylebone*, p. 87.
93. Conyers Read (ed.), *William Lambarde and Local Government* (Ithaca, 1962), p. 39.
94. R. M. Dunn (ed.), *Norfolk Lieutenancy Journal, 1660–1676* (Norfolk Record Society, 1977), p. 135.
95. Tutchin, *Observator*, vol. III, no. 71.
96. Sheppard, *St Marylebone*, p. 79ff.
97. Webb and Webb, *The Parish and the County*, p. 128.
98. Hooker, *Offices of Exeter*, sig. Ci.
99. Kent, *English Village Constable*, p. 72.
100. Felicity Heal, *Hospitality in Early Modern England* (Oxford, 1990), pp. 325–7.

101. The evidence for the popularity or unpopularity of jury service is contra-
     dictory: compare the views of Beattie, Cockburn, Lawson and Roberts in
     Cockburn and Green (eds), *Twelve Good Men and True*, pp. 126–9, 158–60,
     247.
102. Archer, *Pursuit of Stability*, p. 93.
103. Ibid., p. 21.
104. Speck, *Tory and Whig*, p. 83.
105. Fletcher, *Reform in the Provinces*, pp. 63–4.
106. Nair, *Highley*, pp. 128–9; Kent, *English Village Constable*, p. 285.
107. Lamoine (ed.), *Charges to the Grand Jury*, p. 556.
108. Peter Clark, ' "The Ramoth-Gilead of the Good": Urban Change and Polit-
     ical Radicalism at Gloucester, 1540–1640', in Jonathan Barry (ed.), *The
     Tudor and Stuart Town: A Reader in Urban History, 1530–1688* (London,
     1990), pp. 254–9. See also Robert Tittler, *Architecture and Power: The Town
     Hall and the English Urban Community, c.1500–1640* (Oxford, 1991), p. 98.
109. Beattie, *Crime and the Courts*, p. 324.
110. Webb and Webb, *The Parish and the County*, p. 170.
111. Fletcher, *Reform in the Provinces*, pp. 119, 36.
112. Langford, *Public Life*, pp. 296–7.
113. A classic indictment of parish officers as the oppressive viziers of 'the parish
     state' occurs in John Clare's poem, *The Parish* (1820), lines 1220–1399.
114. Peter M. Solar, 'Poor Relief and English Economic Development before the
     Industrial Revolution', *EcHR*, XLVIII (1995), 7–12; Jonathan Barry,
     'Introduction', in Jonathan Barry (ed.), *The Tudor and Stuart Town*, p. 25.
     More generally, see Steve Hindle, 'Exhortation and Entitlement: Negoti-
     ating Inequality in English Rural Communities, 1550–1650', in Michael
     Braddick and John Walter (eds), *Order, Hierarchy and Subordination in Early
     Modern England and Ireland* (Cambridge, 2001).
115. Nair, *Highley*, p. 129.
116. J. C. Cox, *Three Centuries of Derbyshire Annals*, 2 vols (London, 1890), II,
     137–8.
117. I owe this information to Shirley Wittering.
118. W. E. Tate, *The Parish Chest* (Cambridge, 1960), p. 34.
119. Joanna Innes, 'Gaolers as Officeholders: the Early Modern Experience'
     (unpublished paper, 1996).
120. Susan Staves, 'Investments, Votes and Bribes: Women as Shareholders in
     the Chartered National Companies', in Hilda L. Smith (ed.), *Women Writers
     and the Early Modern British Political Tradition* (Cambridge, 1998).
121. Steve Hindle, *The State and Social Change in Early Modern England, c.1550–
     1640* (Basingstoke, 2000).
122. Lionel K. G. Glassey, *Politics and the Appointment of the Justices of the Peace,
     1675–1720* (Oxford, 1979); Fletcher, *Reform in the Provinces*, ch. 1.
123. Goldie, 'Hilton Gang', pp. 50–52.
124. Eastwood, *Government and Community*, p. 48.
125. David Eastwood, *Governing Rural England: Tradition and Transformation in
     Local Government, 1780–1840* (Oxford, 1994), p. 15.
126. *Memoirs of Ambrose Barnes*, p. 90.
127. Webb and Webb, *The Parish and the County*, p. 183.

128. There is a parallel here with Marsilius of Padua's usage of 'pars valentior' (weightier part) and 'major pars' (greater part) in his *Defensor Pacis* (1324).
129. Webb and Webb, *The Parish and the County*, p. 29.
130. Nair, *Highley*, pp. 129–31.
131. On the evolution of vestries see the chapter by Steve Hindle in this volume.
132. Goring, 'Fellowship of the Twelve', p. 170.
133. Webb and Webb, *The Parish and the County*, pp. 213, 222–5.
134. J. G. A. Pocock, *The Machiavellian Moment: Florentine Political Thought and the Atlantic Republican Tradition* (Princeton, 1975), p. 117ff; Linda Kirk, 'Genevan Republicanism', in David Wootton (ed.), *Republicanism, Liberty, and Commercial Society, 1649–1776* (Stanford, CA, 1994).
135. Webb and Webb, *The Parish and the County*, pp. 195, 199. See Paul Seaward, 'Gilbert Sheldon, the London Vestries, and the Defence of the Church', in Tim Harris, Paul Seaward and Mark Goldie (eds), *The Politics of Religion in Restoration England* (Oxford, 1990).
136. Webb and Webb, *The Parish and the County*, p. 106.
137. Tate, *Parish Chest*, p. 172.
138. Webb and Webb, *The Parish and the County*, pp. 54, 217, 248–9, 257, 260.
139. Quoted in ibid., p. 92.
140. Patrick Collinson, *De Republica Anglorum: or, History with the Politics Put Back* (Inaugural Lecture, Cambridge, 1990), repr. in his *Elizabethan Essays* (London, 1994), p. 19.
141. Collinson, *Elizabethan Essays*, p. 16.
142. Patrick Collinson, 'The Monarchical Republic of Queen Elizabeth I', *Bulletin of the John Rylands Library*, LXIX (1987), 394–424, repr. in his *Elizabethan Essays*.
143. Eastwood, *Government and Community*, p. 9. For a parallel argument on the monarchical republics of Continental Europe see H. G. Koenigsberger, 'Republicanism, Monarchism and Liberty', in Robert Oresko, G. C. Gibbs and H. M. Scott (eds), *Royal and Republican Sovereignty in Early Modern Europe* (Cambridge, 1997).
144. John Nalson, *The Common Interest of King and People* (London, 1677), pp. 22, 23–4.
145. Archer, *Pursuit of Stability*, pp. 50, 54.
146. Langford, *Public Life*, p. 438.
147. Hooker, *Offices of Exeter*, sig. Ci.
148. Quoted in Conal Condren, *The Language of Politics in Seventeenth-Century England* (Basingstoke, 1994), p. 105.
149. William Ball, *Tractatus De Jure Regnandi & Regni: Or, the Sphere of Government* (1645), p. 13 and *passim*. I owe this reference to Geoff Kemp.
150. Steve Hindle, 'Hierarchy and Community in the Elizabethan Parish: the Swallowfield Articles of 1596', *HJ*, XLII (1999), 848–9.
151. Morrill, *Revolt of the Provinces*, p. 199; Collinson, *Elizabethan Essays*, p. 33.
152. Collinson, 'Monarchical Republic', in *Elizabethan Essays*, p. 48ff; K. H. D. Haley, *The First Earl of Shaftesbury* (Oxford, 1968), *passim*.
153. Stephen Alford, *The Early Elizabethan Polity: William Cecil and the British Succession Crisis, 1558–1569* (Cambridge, 1998), p. 22, and chs 1 and 4.

154. Jonathan Scott, *Algernon Sidney and the English Republic, 1623–1677* (Cambridge, 1988), pt 1; Blair Worden, *The Sound of Virtue: Philip Sidney's Arcadia and Elizabethan Politics* (Yale, 1996).

155. Thomas More, *Utopia*, ed. G. M. Logan and R. M. Adam (Cambridge, 1975), p. 48ff.

156. James Harrington, *The Commonwealth of Oceana*, ed. J. G. A. Pocock (Cambridge, 1992), p. 77ff.

157. John Locke, *Political Essays*, ed. Mark Goldie (Cambridge, 1997), pp. 160–81.

158. Ibid., pp. 182–98, 252–9.

159. David Hume, *Political Essays*, ed. Knud Haakonssen (Cambridge, 1994), pp. 221–33.

160. *Utopias of the British Enlightenment*, ed. G. Claeys (Cambridge, 1994), pp. 71–136.

161. Catherine Macaulay, *Loose Remarks . . . with a Short Sketch of a Democratical Form of Government, in a Letter to Signior Pauli* (1767).

162. David Williams, *Letters on Political Liberty* (London, 1782).

163. G. I. Gillop (ed.), *Pigs' Meat: Selected Writings of Thomas Spence* (Nottingham, 1982), p. 53; *The Political Works of Thomas Spence*, ed. H. T. Dickinson (Newcastle, 1982), *passim*.

164. Josiah Tucker, *A Treatise Concerning Civil Government* (1781), in Goldie (ed.), *Reception of Locke's Politics*, IV, 118.

165. Pocock, *The Machiavellian Moment*.

166. Markku Peltonen, *Classical Humanism and Republicanism in English Political Thought* (Cambridge, 1995); Quentin Skinner, *Reason and Rhetoric in the Philosophy of Hobbes* (Cambridge, 1996); and also his *Liberty before Liberalism*. See also Richard Tuck, *Philosophy and Government, 1572–1651* (Cambridge, 1993); Andrew Fitzmaurice, 'The Civic Solution to the Crisis of English Colonization, 1609–1625', *HJ*, XLII (1999), 25–52.

167. David Norbrook, *Writing the English Republic: Poetry, Rhetoric and Politics, 1627–1660* (Cambridge, 1999); Anne Barton, *Ben Jonson, Dramatist* (Cambridge, 1984); Malcolm Smuts, 'Court-centred Politics and the Uses of Roman Historians, *c*.1590–1630'; and David Norbrook, 'Lucan, Thomas May, and the Creation of a Republican Literary Culture', in Kevin Sharpe and Peter Lake (eds), *Culture and Politics in Early Stuart England* (London, 1994).

168. Richard Hurd, *Dialogues on the Uses of Foreign Travel* (London, 1754), p. 100.

169. Peltonen, *Classical Humanism*, p. 39.

170. William Sheppard, *A New Survey of the Justice of the Peace his Office* (London, 1659), sigs. A5v, A3r.

171. Quoted in MacCaffrey, *Exeter*, p. 275; Peltonen, *Classical Humanism*, pp. 57–8.

172. Quoted in David Harris Sacks, *The Widening Gate: Bristol and the Atlantic Economy, 1450–1700* (Berkeley, 1991), pp. 302–3.

173. Peltonen, *Classical Humanism*, pp. 59–72.

174. Cicero, *On Duties*, ed. W. T. Griffin and E. M. Atkins (Cambridge, 1991), pp. 29, 33. Early modern editions of Cicero's *De Officiis* translated the title either as *Offices* or *Duties*.

175. Peltonen, *Renaissance Humanism*, p. 22.

176. Hooker, *Offices of Exeter*, sig. Ci.

177. Mordecai Feingold, 'The Humanities', in Nicholas Tyacke (ed.), *The History of the University of Oxford*, vol. IV: *Seventeenth-Century Oxford* (Oxford, 1997), p. 323.
178. Locke, *Political Essays*, p. 377.
179. Archer, *Pursuit of Stability*, p. 38.
180. John Trenchard and Thomas Gordon, *Cato's Letters*, ed. Ronald Hamowy (Indianapolis, 1995), p. 103. An objection to this line of argument, and to this essay, is that there was nothing specifically humanist or post-Renaissance about the practices and beliefs described here, for they were deeply embedded in the medieval world. Janet Coleman has insisted on this in unpublished papers; so did Victorian historians of medieval corporate life, notably F. W. Maitland. See especially Susan Reynolds, *Kingdoms and Communities in Western Europe, 900–1300* (Oxford, 1984). The response would be that in the early modern period traditional practice became conceptualized through a new language. On the question of 'how did Cicero get into the vestry?' see Hindle, *State and Social Change*, pp. 27–8.
181. Acts 19:30–40.
182. Though this too had an important Roman source, in Tacitus's *Germania*, which extolled Teutonic self-rule.
183. Henry Care, *English Liberties* (London, 1682), p. 211.
184. Lamoine (ed.), *Charges to the Grand Jury*, pp. 112, 195. See Fletcher, *Reform in the Provinces*, pp. 170–6.
185. A further objection to the argument of this essay is that it offers an exaggerated 'old world' view of pre-modern English governance. One recent historical school has argued that eighteenth-century Britain was governed by a 'fiscal-military state' that exerted exceptional power from the centre. See John Brewer, *The Sinews of Power: War and the English State, 1688–1783* (London, 1989); Lawrence Stone (ed.), *An Imperial State at War: Britain, 1689–1815* (London, 1994); John Brewer and Eckhart Hellmuth (eds), *Rethinking Leviathan: The Eighteenth-Century State in Britain and Germany* (Oxford, 1999); Thomas Ertman, *Birth of the Leviathan: Building States and Regimes in Medieval and Early Modern Europe* (Cambridge, 1997).
186. Webb and Webb, *The Parish and the County*, p. 171.
187. Quoted in Eastwood, *Governing Rural England*, pp. 31, 166. The number of parishes and townships had grown by this time.
188. Sidney and Beatrice Webb, *English Local Government from the Revolution to the Municipal Corporations Act*, 9 vols (London, 1906–29). *The Parish and the County*, cited above, is vol. 1.
189. Alexis de Tocqueville, *Journeys to England and Ireland*, ed. J. P. Mayer (London, 1958), pp. 96–7, 114; Hippolyte Taine, *Notes on England* (London, 1957), ch. 5; Rudolph von Gneist, *Die Selfgovernment . . . in England* (Berlin, 1871).
190. Joshua Toulmin Smith, *Local Self-Government and Centralization* (London, 1851), pp. 198, 200, 232, and *passim*. Better known figures implicitly adopted his stance in their historical writing: Green, Maine, Freeman and Stubbs. See J. W. Burrow, *A Liberal Descent: Victorian Historians and the English Past* (Cambridge, 1981), pt 3; idem., '"The Village Community" and the Uses of History in Late Nineteenth-Century England', in Neal McKendrick (ed.), *Historical Perspectives* (London, 1974).

191. G. W. F. Hegel, *The Philosophy of Right*, trans. with notes by T. M. Knox (Oxford, 1967), paras 311, 273, 308.
192. J. S. Mill, *Essays on Politics and Society*, ed. J. M. Robson (*Works of J. S. Mill*, vol. XVIII, Toronto, 1977), p. 167.
193. J. S. Mill, *On Representative Government* (3rd edn, London, 1865), pp. 87–8. See Eugenio Biagini, 'Liberalism and Direct Democracy: John Stuart Mill and the Model of Ancient Athens', in idem. (ed.), *Citizenship and Community* (Cambridge, 1996); Dale E. Miller, 'John Stuart Mill's Civic Liberalism', *History of Political Thought*, XXI (2000), 88–113.

7

'VENERATING THE HONESTY OF A TINKER': THE KING'S FRIENDS AND THE BATTLE FOR THE ALLEGIANCE OF THE COMMON PEOPLE IN RESTORATION ENGLAND

Tim Harris

When the playwright and propagandist, Elkannah Settle, publicly recanted his Whiggery in 1683, he acknowledged that the Whigs had deliberately sought to stir up the masses against their king, insinuating 'into the Brainless heads of the People' (as he chose to put it) the ridiculous notion that Charles II was 'leaguing with France to bring in the Pope'. The 'multitude' were 'unreasoning', and that explained why they could be persuaded to believe such 'rank Forgery'; the Whigs knew with whom they were dealing, namely 'the Headlong Mobile of England'.[1] In making such remarks, Settle was reiterating commonplaces of the age, in language anticipated to appeal to those who supported the court. During the Exclusion Crisis of 1679–81, the Tory press had repeatedly condemned the rabble-rousing tactics of the Whigs, who had sought to stir up the masses in order to put pressure on the king to agree to exclude the Catholic Duke of York from the succession. How could any appeal to opinion out-of-doors be justified when it was well known, as Roger L'Estrange put it in 1679, that the 'multitude' were 'undiscerning', 'simple' and 'credulous'?[2] Indeed Christopher Hill has argued that it was a widely held opinion amongst the propertied classes of Elizabethan and Stuart England that the masses were incapable of rational thought, and therefore that 'the poorer and meaner people' had 'no interest in the commonweal but the use of breath'; 'no account' was to be 'made of them, but only to be ruled'.[3] As one Elizabethan clergyman put it in a sermon preached *c*.1580, 'that everie prentise should prate of Princes, and everie Cobler seeme a Counsellor' was not 'tollerable in a Christian common-wealth'.[4] The 'Coffee-House Statesmen who think themselves wiser than the Privy-Council', the authors of the Tory periodical, *Heraclitus Ridens*, insisted a century later, in February 1681, were in reality 'only fit to make Senators of Goatham, to hedge in a Cuckow, or drown an Eel'.[5]

Charles II's actions as king, at least towards the end of his reign, however, seem to belie the notion that the dim-sighted mobile counted for nothing. Far from trying to keep his subjects out of politics, in the wake of the Exclusion Crisis he chose to engage in the battle for public opinion, and actively sought to solicit the support of those out-of-doors. His licenser of the press, Roger L'Estrange, conducted a press campaign specifically designed to win support amongst the lower orders, and the king himself even went so far as to encourage royalist crowds and loyal addresses, rewarding those who publicly engaged in collective demonstrations of support for the crown against the policy of Exclusion promoted by the Whigs. In short, the king and his advisers quite deliberately chose to appeal to the masses, even to the point of engaging in activity that might be described as rabble-rousing. Why, we might wonder, did they do this?

In fact, as the opening section of this essay will show, they probably would have preferred not to have done this. Recognizing the shortcomings of the early Stuarts in the sphere of public relations, the instinct of the Restoration regime was to follow what they took to be the Elizabethan model: awe the masses through a few carefully-staged royal spectacles, but otherwise keep the people out of politics and do their best to stifle public political debate. The strategy failed, however, and by the late 1670s the crown was facing a serious crisis as a result of the alienation of public opinion. The court and its supporters therefore changed tack, and decided to appeal to opinion out-of-doors, in order to win back the common people and rally support behind the crown. The main part of this essay will explore both why and how they sought to do this, as well as seek to measure the extent to which they were successful. A final section will offer some more speculative reflections about what our findings tell us about the changing significance of politics out-of-doors and public opinion in seventeenth-century England. One disclaimer is necessary before I proceed. Although this chapter is concerned with how those 'from above' sought to appeal to opinion out-of-doors, it is not my intention to imply that public opinion was manufactured by the elite. Elsewhere, I have been at pains to stress the vitality of the political culture of the masses in Restoration Britain, and warned against taking a top–down approach to popular politics or assuming that the lower orders were incapable of coordinating political activity themselves.[6] The particular focus adopted here is intended to be complementary, by looking at how the elite reacted to the fact that they had a politically aware and self-assertive populace whom they could not afford to ignore. Indeed, it reinforces why we, as historians, need to take opinion out-of-doors seriously, since it reveals just how seriously it was taken by those in power at the time.

I

To assess the significance of developments under Charles II, we need some point of comparison with the ways in which his predecessors had sought to manage opinion out-of-doors. Queen Elizabeth's success in the sphere of public relations has become a commonplace of Tudor historiography. Through a combination of royal entries and processions and the encouragement of anniversary celebrations, we have been told, she was able to promote a strong sense of attachment to the new Protestant regime and portray a powerful image of the majesty and charisma of the late Tudor monarchy. Her magnificent coronation entry of 1559, with accompanying pageantry, or the powerful effect achieved by her formal entry into London following the defeat of the Armada in 1588 (to give the two most frequently cited examples), show that she knew how to woo the masses, uniting her people behind her in a royal cult that appealed to patriotic, xenophobic and broadly based Protestant sentiments. Her regime also encouraged the commemoration of 17 November, the anniversary of her accession, as an alternative to the holy days that came under attack from the Protestant reformers; from the 1570s onwards 'Crownation Day' came to be celebrated throughout much of England with services, the ringing of church bells, parish bonfires and general festivity, thus helping to forge a strong identification amongst the population at large with the Protestant dynast. There was also some commemoration of Elizabeth's birthday (7 September), whilst a few communities even adopted an annual celebration for deliverance from the Armada, although these tended to be overshadowed by 17 November. Moreover, Elizabethan propagandists were skilled at selling their product. The clergy (in their sermons), judges (at the assizes) and loyal balladeers all helped construct a positive image of Gloriana as a loving and caring mother, devoted to the interests of her children and regime, that reminded English Protestants of how lucky they were to have Elizabeth as their sovereign.[7]

Elizabeth's public appearances, Malcolm Smuts has suggested, served a number of functions. On one level, they emphasized the bonds that united subjects and sovereign; their interests were one and the same, and in return for loyalty the ruler would provide justice, charity and protection. By appearing to demonstrate the popularity of the ruler, moreover, royal entries and progresses conferred an additional aura of legitimacy, since according to late medieval and Tudor notions of kingship rulers were supposed to have the unenforced obedience of their people. Elizabeth's accessibility and basic humanity enabled her, in an albeit limited and stylized way, to break through some of the barriers that separated her from the common people; during her coronation entry, for example, she was noted to have stopped her chariot to receive flowers from people in the crowd or to hear the requests of onlookers. Yet on a more fundamental level, the ceremonial structure of royal entries, and the privileged place given to the social and political elite in terms of access or proximity to the royal presence, was designed to provide a forceful reminder to ordinary people of the subordinate position they occupied in a huge and multi-layered hierarchy of power and authority.[8] Elizabeth wanted to make sure her subjects knew their place: the image of splendour and majesty that she projected – albeit with a human face – was designed to inspire a sense of awe: it was intimidatory as much as populist. Moreover, Elizabeth did not relish the prospect of her subjects getting drawn into public political disputation; she might have cultivated public support, but she did not engage in a dialogue with her subjects about government policy, or in that sense seek to appeal to informed public opinion. Indeed, her basic instinct was to suppress public debate. When works critical of the government appeared, the regime responded by ordering the offending works to be publicly burned and by taking legal action against the authors and publishers.[9]

The early Stuarts, we have traditionally been taught, paid much less attention to their public image. Caution is needed here, since there has been a tendency to caricature the failings of James I and Charles I in this respect. James I certainly received a bad press from contemporary observers, who commented upon his unease in appearing before his subjects or engaging in 'those formalities of State, which set a lustre upon Princes in the peoples eyes', leading them to conclude that he 'could not endure to be seen' by 'the commons'. On one occasion, when crowds of royalty-gazers interrupted his recreation, he angrily protested to those around him that if the people wanted to see so much of him he would 'pull down [his] breeches' so they could 'also see [his] arse'.[10] Yet he was not as remiss in his responsibility to appear before his subjects as such comments might lead us to conclude. His long and slow progress south from Scotland in 1603 to take possession of his English throne, marked as it was by 'Banquetting and Feasting' along the way, provided the king with an opportunity to capture the hearts of his new people, who greeted him with such 'obsequious and submissive ... applause' that James himself was prompted to predict: 'This people will spoil a gud King'.[11] James's coronation entry of March 1604 was a grandiose and spectacular affair, and according to one historian he received 'the most splendid welcome accorded to an English sovereign'.[12] Although Elizabeth's demise put an immediate stop to the annual celebration of 17 November, James's accession brought with it the addition of new days to the festive calendar: 24 March (James's accession day), 5 August (the anniversary of James's delivery from the Gowrie plot in Scotland), 19 June (James's birthday), and 25 July (coronation day). In 1606 a fifth day was added by parliament, namely 5 November, to commemorate deliverance from the Gunpowder Plot of the previous autumn.[13] James made a number of entries into his capital during his reign, often to powerful effect. Thus he was greeted by cheering crowds when he publicly attended church in London in late March 1606, following rumours of a successful assassination attempt against him at Woking (Surrey), James 'telling them that he tooke these demonstrations more kindly than yf they had won a battell for him'.[14] Other staged events, such as the installation of Prince Henry as Prince of Wales in 1610, or the marriage of Princess Elizabeth in 1613, could provide the occasion for public celebration of the Stuart dynasty.[15]

Yet it is probably fair to say that courting his public was not something that came naturally to James.[16] Even on his march south, in 1603, he quickly tired of the multitudes that flocked to see him, 'especially in his Hunting (which he did as he went)', and ordered 'an inhibition to be published, to restrain the people from hunting him'.[17] During his coronation entry, he reportedly hurried hastily along the way, without stopping to view the scenes or listen to the speeches at the various pageants, or to address the people.[18] Not only was James more reluctant to appear before his subjects than Elizabeth, but he became more distant as time went on. Thus the latter part of the reign, it has been noted, witnessed a noticeable decline in public ceremony centring on the monarch (though this may have been, in part, due to James's declining health).[19] Moreover, James firmly believed that the people should not be drawn into the *arcana imperii*. When controversy began to develop over the king's foreign policy following the outbreak of the Thirty Years' War on the continent in 1618, he saw no need to explain his actions or seek public approval for them; the people, he felt, should simply trust the king to do what was right.[20]

Charles I, it has been observed, 'was the least theatrical monarch since at least Henry VI' and seemed to want to keep a distance between himself and his subjects.[21] There are perfectly understandable reasons why this should have been the case: with limited financial resources and ruling a plague-ravaged country, for Charles to have indulged in lavish royal ceremonials or to allow the public too easy access to the royal person would surely have proven costly to both the economic and physical health of the Caroline monarchy. Thus on 17 May 1625, shortly after his accession, Charles gave orders that no one was to come within twelve miles of the court, either when he went to greet the arrival of his new French wife at Dover, or when he went on other journeys or progresses during the summer, and no one was 'to follow or resort to the Court with Petitions'. Although he protested that he could not 'but conceive great joy and contentment, when His loving Subjects, out of their loyall and dutifull affections towards him, shall desire to see' him or his Queen, he was 'contented to dispence with those publicke shewes of their zeale, chearefulnes, and alacritie at this time', because he was concerned about the possibility of spreading the plague.[22] When he was crowned in February of the next year, Charles postponed the royal procession from the Tower to Westminster through the streets of London, again for fear of the plague; instead, he chose to travel privately by river, promising to hold the procession at a later date (although in fact he never did).[23] He avoided making any entries into London until 1638, when etiquette demanded that he accompany his mother-in-law, on her arrival from France, as she passed through the city on her way to St James's Palace; he did not make a royal entry on his own behalf until the autumn of 1641, on the very eve of the civil war. His royal progresses, it has been claimed, were less grandiose affairs than those of his immediate predecessors; they have certainly been less well documented, which in itself is telling, though to dismiss them as little more than hunting trips, as one historian has, is perhaps going too far. He also severely limited the extent to which he was prepared to touch for the King's Evil, despite the fact that a belief in the thaumaturgical power of the king was fundamental to the ideology of divine-right monarchy.[24]

It would be wrong to give the impression that the early Stuarts were insensitive to the need to court opinion out-of-doors. The government responded to the increased circulation of illicit news in the 1620s by authorizing, in 1621, the publication of weekly gazettes or corantos to furnish 'the ploughman and the artisan' with official interpretations of the news in order to prevent 'rumors amongst the vulgar'. Pro-government rhymesters rose to the challenge of the anti-court 'pot-poets' in the 1620s and 1630s to put the case for the government in punchy, if typically inelegant, couplets. Both James and Charles published declarations explaining their dealings with their parliaments in the 1620s, whilst the crown certainly recognized the propaganda value of sermons; for example, Charles I authorized the publication of a number of sermons preached at court, praising the absolute authority of the king over his subjects' property, in an attempt to defend the Forced Loan of 1626 (though it can hardly be said that this proved effective in swaying opinion out-of-doors).[25] Some Laudian clerics appear to have been aware of the need to appeal to the people, and even sought to couch their discourse in the language of moderation and consensus, in the hope of mobilizing what scholars are coming to recognize was a potentially broad body of anti-Puritan opinion in support of their position.[26] And the government also seems to have had some sense of the value in trying to orchestrate public demonstrations in support of the royal family. Thus the Privy Council ordered Londoners to light bonfires on 1 April 1623 to mark Prince Charles's safe arrival in Madrid, whence he had gone to continue negotiations for the Spanish match. The Spanish match failed, of course, but in November 1624, following the successful conclusion of a French match, the Privy Council ordered the Lord Mayor of London, the Lieutenant of the Tower and the Middlesex JPs, to publish the news of Charles's betrothal to Henrietta Maria 'by bonefyers, fyerworkes, lightes in the windowes, and ringing of belles . . . and all other the lyke demonstracions of rejoyceing as cann be thought on or put in practice thus on the suddain'.[27]

Yet the efforts made by the early Stuarts were limited: there was no attempt to mimic the type of propaganda machine being developed by Cardinal Richelieu in France on behalf of Louis XIII, and in the 1630s, with the foreign crisis receding and in the absence of parliaments, the crown appears to have retreated from any initiatives begun in the 1620s.

Thus we see a return to a more strenuous effort to stifle public debate. The government imposed an outright ban on corantos in 1632, and Charles used Star Chamber to impose severe penalties – such as mutilations – to try to silence the press.[28] A revealing indication of the extent to which the early Stuarts were falling short in their public relations endeavours is provided by the way in which Protestant calendar festivals, such as 5 and 17 November, were increasingly becoming occasions for expressing criticism of the current regime.[29] It was not until the very eve of the civil war that the king and his supporters made a serious attempt to appeal to opinion out-of-doors, by which time it was too late to avert the crisis that was rapidly overtaking the royal government.[30] More generally, it has been suggested that the neglect of their public persona by the first two Stuarts led to a dramatic weakening of royal charisma, and is part of the explanation of why there was such a decline in the popularity of the monarchy by the eve of the civil war.[31]

This brief summary oversimplifies, and future research will no doubt refine and even modify the picture just presented. What we can say with confidence, however, is that royalists, in retrospect, came to believe that the early Stuarts had been too remote. It was for this reason that the Duke of Newcastle, in his famous *Advice* to Charles II, written on the eve of the Restoration, recommended a return to the Elizabethan style. Even so, Newcastle remained adamant that as king Charles should create distance between himself and his subjects and keep the people out of politics. 'Shew your Selfe Gloryously, to your People; Like a God', Newcastle advised, since then the people would 'pray for you with trembling Feare, and Love, as they did to Queen Elizabeth, whose Government Is the beste presedent for Englandes Governmente, absolutly'; for 'nothing Keepes upp a King', he continued, 'more than seremoney, and order, which makes Distance, and this bringes respecte and Duty'. But one of the biggest mistakes that had been made in the previous two reigns was that the people had been drawn into public political debate though the circulation of 'weekly Corants, Both att home and a broad'. Charles should ensure, therefore, that he kept strict control over the press, and 'forbid Eyther Domesticke or forayne news'.[32]

At his Restoration, Charles II's intent was to follow Newcastle's advice. He would show himself gloriously to his people, in imitation of Queen Elizabeth, but do his utmost to stop political disputation out-of-doors. Thus he tapped into the popular enthusiasm for the return of monarchy in the spring of 1660, by making a triumphant royal entry into London on 29 May, his birthday,[33] and later that year the Convention Parliament directed that Restoration Day should be annually commemorated as a special day of thanksgiving. In the early years of the reign 29 May became the occasion for annual bonfire celebrations in a number of communities throughout the land.[34] Charles II's coronation in the spring of 1661 was an elaborate and meticulously planned three-day celebration, designed to revive the cult of monarchy after over a decade of republican government: there was a royal progress from the Tower to Whitehall on 22 April, the coronation itself on the 23rd, St George's Day, and a fireworks display the day after, whilst according to one contemporary 'the sumptuousness of it' exceeded 'the glory of what hath passed of the like kind in France'.[35] At the same time, the Restoration regime made its views about political activism out-of-doors patently clear by passing an Act against tumultuous petitioning in 1661 and restoring pre-publication censorship with the Licensing Act of 1662. Public disturbances were dealt with severely; when crowds of Londoners rose up against bawdy houses in Easter week of 1668, demanding 'Reformation and Reducement' and an end to religious persecution, the government responded by having the ringleaders indicted for high treason.[36]

As a strategy, however, it failed. It proved impossible to silence the press, clamp down on public political debate, or stop those out-of-doors from expressing their political dissatisfaction with government policy. A number of reasons might be suggested for this. The civil wars and subsequent republican experiments in government had not only helped generate and sustain a heightened level of political awareness amongst broad cross-sections of the population, but had also left a bitter legacy of political and religious tensions.[37] There had, to be sure, been extensive support for the return of monarchy in 1660, as people looked for a return to older constitutional arrangements as the only way to restore political stability; indeed, arguably it was the active intervention in politics by those out-of-doors, in the form of petitions, demonstrations and collective protest, that secured the downfall of the republic over the winter of 1659–60. Yet many welcomed the restoration of monarchy in the hope that it would lead to a return to the rule of law and constitutional propriety, or a relaxation of the tax burdens suffered under republican regimes propped up by a standing army; such people would soon become alienated if the new regime failed to live up to expectations. On the religious front, whilst there was considerable support for a return to the old Church of the bishops and the prayer book, others looked for a more comprehensive settlement in the Church, whilst the separatists hoped for some degree of religious toleration. Two points are thus worth emphasizing here: first, that the Restoration occurred in a climate of mass activism; and, secondly, that it clearly was not going to be possible to satisfy everyone's expectations. The pursuit by the Restoration regime of controversial measures in Church and state which had a direct impact on broad sections of the population made it impossible to prevent the people from becoming deeply concerned about the implications of government policy. The re-establishment of a narrow and intolerant episcopalian Church, accompanied by a savage penal code aimed at those who chose to worship outside it, perhaps did most to perpetuate the old divisions bequeathed by the 1640s and 1650s and generate a sense of disillusionment with (and antagonism towards) the new regime. But Charles II also failed to deliver on the economic and political fronts: the burden of taxation remained high; trade and industry did not pick up in quite the way anticipated (with some occupational groups, most notably the weavers, remaining depressed); whilst the king's own style of government and apparent willingness to vaunt the prerogative over parliamentary statute caused concern about the threat to the rule of law (notably with regard to his Declarations of Indulgence of 1662 and 1672).

It was not only the working out of the implications of the Restoration settlement that created tensions. New issues and concerns that arose in the 1660s and 1670s also exacerbated the political situation: concern about the pro-Catholic and pro-French leanings of the court, and the Catholicism of the heir to the throne; failings in foreign policy; the management techniques developed by the court to try to control parliament; the emergence of a standing army; and the style in which Charles II chose to rule his other kingdoms of Scotland and Ireland, which seemed to presage what he might have in store in England – all raised fears that there was a conspiracy to introduce popery and arbitrary government into England.[38] Such anxieties came to be articulated more and more vociferously as the reign progressed, both in the press and in the street. Despite the Licensing Act, unlicensed tracts did get published, whilst other works of controversy circulated in manuscript form, often being distributed via the coffee-houses that were springing up all over the country at this time.[39] The growing fear of popery and arbitrary government in the 1670s reflected itself in the revival of 5 and 17 November as days of anti-Catholic demonstrations, and the staging of the first pope-burning processions in the capital, to protest against the pro-French leanings of the court and the Catholicism of the heir to the throne.[40]

Censorship controls broke down completely during the Exclusion Crisis, with the lapsing of the Licensing Act in 1679. Whereas in 1677 only about 800 titles were published, and just over 900 the following year, in 1679 this figure rose to 1300, and shot to nearly 1800 in 1680, before stabilizing at 1600 in 1681.[41] Taking into account average print runs, one historian has estimated that between five and ten million pamphlets were in circulation in the years 1679–81.[42] Those opposed to the court – soon to become known as the Whigs – managed to saturate the market with both printed and unpublished materials reflecting their interpretation of political developments in Church and state, whilst they also developed a sophisticated distribution network to ensure that their propaganda reached as broad a geographical and social base as possible. As a result, public opinion initially seemed to swing overwhelmingly behind the Whigs in support of their campaign to exclude the Catholic heir. Not only were the Whigs able to draw huge crowds to their elaborate pope-burning processions staged in London on Elizabeth's Accession Day, but there were also similar, lesser-scale pope-burnings on both 5 and 17 November throughout much of England, demonstrations against the Duke of York and in favour of the Duke of Monmouth (the illegitimate but Protestant son of Charles II), as well as widespread petitioning activity in London and the provinces in support of parlia-ment's stance against the alleged dual threat of popery and arbitrary government.[43] At first, the government attempted a clamp-down. Thus in 1679–80 the king issued a series of proclamations against tumultuous petitions and unlicensed books, whilst an effort was made to strike at opposition publicists through the common law of seditious libel. Such efforts, however, met with limited success.[44]

It is important to appreciate the seriousness of the crisis facing the Restoration regime by c.1679–81. The government was haunted by the prospect of renewed civil war, and genuinely feared that disaffection was sufficiently widespread that the people might rise in rebellion. As early as January 1679 it was being reported that Charles had 'lately read much of the History of '41' and had 'strong apprehentions of like Events and Consequences in the Course of things'.[45] Some radical Whigs did indeed contemplate insurrection in the years following the dissolution of the Oxford Parliament in 1681, and the Duke of Monmouth was, of course, eventually to launch a rebellion in the west country following the acces-sion of James II in 1685.[46] Yet fear of rebellion was not the only reason why the government was concerned about the alienation of public opinion. In the face of considerable public opposition, as Charles II's regime found out to its cost, it could prove difficult to govern the country effect-ively. A series of disastrous general elections between 1679 and 1681 meant that Charles lost control of the House of Commons, with court candidates being least successful in constituencies with more open franchises and large electorates.[47] Faced with hostile parliaments, Charles found it impossible to legislate or raise taxes, or indeed to pursue any constructive policy, beyond trying to stave off the challenge of the Whigs.

Local elections also went against the court, with the result that in some areas dissenters were able to re-establish a power base in the corporations (in contravention of the Corporation Act of 1661, which had provided that all officeholders had to be communicating members of the Church of England), and opposition interests managed to secure control of key municipal offices. In London, most of the dissident aldermen and common councilmen, who formed the core of a powerful civic opposition that emerged in the mid-1670s, were nonconformists, whilst in England's second city, Norwich, nonconformists or nonconformist sympathizers had become so entrenched in office by 1673 that the local bishop could describe it as 'the worst corporation ... [he] had met with'.[48] Judith Hurwich found that in Coventry, a notoriously fanatic town, some 37 per cent of those who held municipal office between 1660 and 1687 were dissenters or possible dissenters and sympathizers, and a staggering 48 per cent of the mayors.[49] Yet even in places not renowned for being major centres of dissent, nonconformists made their presence felt. In Oxford, traditionally regarded as a royalist stronghold, former mayor John Lambe, a Presbyterian who had been excluded in 1662, found his way back onto the council in 1667, and during a further stint as mayor in 1668–9 sought to reintroduce other purged men back into the city's government. Two formerly purged men were mayors of the city during the Exclusion Crisis: Robert Pauling (elected in 1679), and John Bowell (elected the following year). On the day of Pauling's election, the council made a pointed political gesture by admitting the Popish Plot informer, Titus Oates, and his brother, to the freedom of the city, whilst the following year they granted freedom to the Duke of Monmouth and the Whig peer, Lord Lovelace, celebrating their admission with a toast 'to the confusion of all Popish princes'.[50] A riotous mayoral election in the borough of Saltash in Cornwall in the autumn of 1679, at which 'great disturbances' were committed 'by a Rabble of unsworn Inhabitants of the said Burrough, having no Right of Election', resulted in the choice of one Mr Skelton, a nonconformist who had formerly been ejected from the aldermanic bench for not taking the oaths prescribed by the Corporation Act.[51]

The loss of control over local government – not everywhere, by any stretch of the imagination, but nevertheless in some important areas – made it increasingly difficult to use the law as a weapon against the enemies of Church and state, whether those accused of attending illegal conventicles, publishing unlicensed tracts, engaging in anti-government demonstrations or speaking seditious words: sympathetic sheriffs would impanel juries that would refuse to convict, whereas local magistrates would refuse to entertain informations brought against those with whose political views they identified. For example, William Glyde, who served as mayor of Exeter in 1676–7 before going on to represent the city in parliament, sought to build up electoral support amongst the dissenters by allowing 'fifteen or sixteen Nonconformist ministers to resort thither and preach in their seditious conventicles without control', thereby – according to a hostile source – 'poisoning and depraving the people's loyalty and obedience to the government both of Church and State'.[52] At York both magistrates and those impanelled to serve as jurors were notoriously lax in dealing with conventicles; in April 1682 the circuit judge at the local assizes bemoaned the 'misgovernment' of the place and reckoned that no more than two of the aldermen were fit for office.[53] In London, in the late 1670s and through to the early 1680s, the government found it impossible not only to bring indictments against religious nonconformists, but even against those accused of high treason; a hand-picked Whig jury would simply refuse to find the bill true and throw it out. A number of alleged Whig conspirators were thus saved by *ignoramus* juries, most famously, of course, the Earl of Shaftesbury himself.[54] As Secretary of State Sir Leoline Jenkins complained to the Duke of Ormonde in October 1681, the composition of jury panels in London and Middlesex were such 'that the King cannot hope to have justice . . . in his own courts'.[55] Local officials in town and countryside, such as the parish constables, beadles and nightwatchmen – being, as they were, unpaid members of the local community, typically of middling or even lower social status – often sympathized with those who confronted the government either by worshipping in illegal conventicles, or speaking seditious words against those in authority, or by taking to the streets in political demonstrations or riots, and would refuse to make arrests.[56] Even when the sympathies of local magistrates or agents of law enforcement lay with the government, they might decline to initiate a clamp-down on dissident activity if they perceived that public sentiment would be hostile to such an attempt. Thus in December 1682 the Tory Lord Mayor of London found that he dare not enforce an order from the king to suppress nonconformist meetings in the capital, fearing that 'mischiefe and ruine' would follow: you could 'read as much', he protested, 'in the peopells faces'.[57]

II

In the face of such a crisis, and with the government seemingly unable to re-establish effective control over the media, those close to the court and supporters of the crown came to realize it would be necessary to meet the Whig challenge in kind. A counter-propaganda campaign was launched, with the deliberate aim, as L'Estrange put it, of instilling 'Dutfyfull and Honest Principles into the Common People'.[58] Loyalist works poured forth to respond to the arguments from the Whig presses: lengthy treatises and legal-historical tracts, for those who had the literacy skills and requisite background to grapple with complex constitutional and philosophical issues; newspapers, pamphlets, broadsides and almanacs for a broader audience; songs, poems, prints and playing cards for those on the margins of literacy. Although we see a steady stream of loyalist literature from early in the Exclusion Crisis, such material became more numerous and in higher demand as the crisis unfolded, so that by 1681 it is arguable that the initiative in the propaganda war had passed to the Tories. The press was backed up by the pulpit, as high church clerics preached up principles of non-resistance and passive obedience.[59]

The precise role that the government played in directing this activity is difficult to ascertain. Loyalist publicists and clerics often worked on their own initiative. One of the most notorious Tory journalists, Nathaniel Thompson, who published not only highly influential newspapers such as the *True Domestic Intelligence* and the *Loyal Protestant Intelligence* but also collections of loyalist songs and poems, was himself at times in trouble with the government for his publishing activities.[60] Nevertheless, there undoubtedly was direction from the centre. Francis North (later Lord Guilford), Charles's Lord Keeper, gave advice on strategy; in his papers are a series of notes about how to write a pamphlet for 'undeceiving the people about the late popish plott'.[61] Indeed, it was North who authored one of the most effective pieces of royalist propaganda of the Exclusion Crisis, namely Charles's *Declaration of Reasons* of April 1681, explaining why he had dissolved the last two Exclusion Parliaments. The most prolific pro-government publicist was Roger L'Estrange, who operated from his position as government licenser of the press and was rumoured to have been financed in part by a pension from the crown. L'Estrange produced not only one of the most influential periodicals of the period but also a host of important pamphlets and broadsides – one modern scholar has estimated that 64,000 copies of L'Estrange's tracts were in circulation in the two years prior to the launching of his *Observator*. Secretary of State, Sir Leoline Jenkins, and the Lord Lieutenant of Ireland, the Duke of Ormonde, also played a role in organizing the government's propaganda efforts, whilst both Ormonde and L'Estrange established their own clubs to help coordinate their activities.[62] Then there was the official government news-organ, *London Gazette*, which appeared twice a week with a print run of about 15,000 per issue, and which could be used to report the news in a way that was most favourable to the crown.[63] There was also some attempt made by the government to exploit the medium of the pulpit to its own advantage; Charles instructed all the clergy to read his *Declaration* of April 1681 to their congregations,[64] whilst officially appointed days of thanksgiving – such as for the deliverance from the Rye House Plot in 1683 – provided a cue for an outpouring of loyalist sermonizing across the land.[65]

We have come to understand a great deal about the nature of Tory ideology in recent years: how the Tories sought to portray the Whigs and their nonconformists allies as the ones who really posed the threat to the existing establishment in Church and state, and endeavoured to represent themselves as being *against* popery and arbitrary government and *for* the true Protestant religion and the rule of law.[66] What I wish to emphasize here is the extent to which Tory propagandists self-consciously targeted the lower echelons of society. In the preface to the first volume of the collected edition of his *Observator*, L'Estrange explained that what induced him 'to Enter upon This Province' was 'The Needfullness of some Popular Medium for Rectifying of Vulgar Mistakes'.[67] Elsewhere he wrote that his paper 'was Design'd purely for the People', and for that reason it had to be 'Course, and Popular' and also 'Timely, Cheap, and Easy'.[68] To achieve such a goal, much Tory propaganda was couched in a distinctively populist idiom. A favourite device was the dialogue, which L'Estrange, for example, used in his *Observator*, 'as a Method that is more Familiar, and Entertaining'.[69] The dialogue allowed the Whig case to be put first, only to be refuted point by point by the more ingenious and compelling arguments of the spokesman for the other side. Dialogues also mirrored the way people would themselves discuss political issues, capturing in written form an oral exchange of ideas; they were ideal texts for reading aloud, to bridge the gap between literate and oral culture, and would further serve to stimulate political discussion in turn.[70] Another common technique was to simplify the issues at stake, reducing them to extremes by positing a stark dichotomy between one side and the other, so that the struggle could be represented as being between the forces of good and the forces of evil. Thus the Whig leader, the Earl of Shaftesbury, was said to be Satan's 'Viceregent', and his supporters agents of 'the Devil of Hell', whilst Hell was 'a Democratic State' (like Holland), which the Whigs wanted to establish in England.[71] All forms of sin were attributed to those who opposed the crown. The London Whigs were 'Anti-monarchick Hereticks of State, Immoral Atheists, Rich, and Reprobate'.[72] If they were immoral, then they were obviously guilty of violating the sexual norms of this society. Titus Oates, the man who gave the initial informations about the alleged Popish Plot that triggered the Exclusion Crisis, was accused of sodomy (with two London Aldermen);[73] the wife of the famous Whig publicist Henry Care, of bestiality;[74] whilst the Tory press frequently carried sensationalist 'revelations' of the alleged sexual transgressions committed by nonconformist ministers and conventiclers.[75] Moreover, the prose style was designed to resonate with the lower orders: hence the use of simple words, colourful language and frequent allusions to activities or functions that were an everyday part of human existence – from drinking, to health care provision, sexual functions and going to the toilet. For example, in September 1682 Thompson published an 'Elixer' or 'Infallible Cure for the Good Old Cause', which he claimed had been pinned up in a London coffee-house, and which involved, amongst other things, taking 'at least 2 Hogsheads of the Tears of holy Sisters', which should be infused with 'a handful of Nonconformist Ministers' and 'a full bottle of . . . [Whig] Ballad Singers', and all this mixed 'with the simple Extract of 4 pair of brother-like Buttocks, and the species of the Inclination of a Salamanca Doctor' (i.e. Titus Oates).[76]

Yet if the Tories were self-consciously targeting the lower orders, the 'mobile', the 'rabble', how does this fit with the fact that they also condemned the rabble-rousing techniques of the Whigs and insisted that the multitude were 'dim-sighted'? L'Estrange was explicit about his own reasoning. He, too, shared the view that the 'common people' were 'Rude and Illiterate', and in his mind there could be 'Nothing more Dangerous to a State, or more Ridiculous in it Self, then a Pert, a Prag-matical, and a Pretending Multitude'. He recognized that they had a tendency to be 'Headstrong and Intractable' and 'to take Strong Impres-sions of Things'. Nevertheless, he was adamant that they were 'As

Susceptible of Good, as of Bad'.[77] The problem was that 'the Multitude' was 'Easily Impos'd upon by Fopps, and Hypocrites, under the Masque of Saints, and States men': 'the Common People have This of the Sheep in 'em ... if One Leaps a Bridge, the Rest will Follow'.[78] This was what had happened during the Exclusion Crisis. 'The Common People' had been 'Catechis'd into a Sedition' by the faction;[79] they had been 'Poyson'd with False Doctrines, and Positions, upon the Subject of Power, and Duty'.[80] Where this could lead was illustrated by the experience of the 1640s, when an alliance between the faction and the rabble had helped bring about the civil war and led ultimately to the murder of Charles I.[81] 'No State' could 'be Supplanted, but by Turning the People's Hearts, against the Persons, and the Actions of their Superiors'.[82] Yet the common people themselves were not to blame; they were misled by 'Artificial Seducers'. 'It is Seditious Instruments', L'Estrange insisted, 'that make a Seditious People', and therefore 'if the Kings Friends would but take Half the Pains, to set them Right, that his Enemies do, to Mislead them, you would find ... the Common People as well Dispos'd to Preserve the Government, as they are Otherwise, to Embroil it'. It was a question of how they were managed. 'If you put Good Men in the Head of 'em, they shall Troup Right, as well as Wrong ... For they are as Capable of Good Impressions, as of Bad; and as Ductile to Honest Purposes, as they are to Evil'. Such reasoning led him to the remarkable conclusion that the government was partly to blame if the common people went astray: 'when they do Amiss, 'tis not so much the Malevolence of their Nature, as the Looseness of a Political Discipline ... Insomuch, that the Government itself is Answerable in a High Measure for the Distempers of the Multitude'.[83] Hence why he chose to produce his *Observator*: his aim was 'To Beat down All Popular Errors ... To lay the Naked Truth of Things before the Multitude: To put Reasons, and Plain Arguments, for their Allegiance, into their Mouths'.[84]

The fact that L'Estrange found it necessary to devote so much space to justifying his appeal to the people testifies that he recognized it was a controversial strategy. At one point, he has his protagonist, the Trimmer, charge the Observator with being

the First Man certainly (of a Pretender, to either Books, or Family) that ever stood up to Advocate for the Common People, *Eo Nomine*, as they Are the Common People; That is to say, to Advocate for Men that have neither Brains, Letters, Fortune, Interest, Title, no Quality to Recommend them.

The Observator retorts, however, that this is a deliberate misunder-standing: he does not love the common people for their rank; he simply loves truth, wherever he finds it.[85] Yet those who mislead the mobile, L'Estrange is at pains to emphasize, are just as bad as the mobile them-selves. 'By "Mobile" is meant "Popular" in Opposition to "Government" ', and there was both an upper and a lower mobile: 'the Upper Mobile Imposes upon the Lower; and the Common People are the Tools they work with, for the bringing of their Ambitious Ends about'.[86] His 'Reflex-ions upon "People" ', therefore, were not intended 'to be a Charge upon an Entire Body of Men of such or such a Rank, and Quality, as if it were a Poll-Tax'. 'You are to look for My Mobile, among the Corn-Cutters, and Rat-Catchers, at Westminster-Hall Door; But you shall find of 'em in the Hall it self, too; In Palaces, as well as Cottages'. Man is judged, he continued, not by his pedigree or wealth, but by his 'Life', 'Manners' and 'Intrinsick Value', 'according to the Received Estimate, of Good, and Evil'. 'My Mobile is made up, out of the Rubbish, of both Great, and Small; with Veneration to the Honesty even of a Tinker, as well as of a Cavalier'.[87]

This propaganda campaign was accompanied by efforts to promote public displays of support for the king and the Duke of York. Although it was hoped that the ideological counter-offensive against the Whigs would by itself serve to re-arouse loyalist sentiments amongst those out-of-doors, a certain amount of encouragement from the centre can be detected, with the royal brothers themselves playing a key role in promoting, or at least providing the opportunity for, people to demonstrate their loyalty to the regime and the hereditary succession. The first initiative was taken fairly early in the Exclusion Crisis, though it has tended to be missed by English historians because of their narrow focus on the realm of England itself, to the exclusion of the other kingdoms within the Britannic archipelago over which the Stuart dynasty also ruled. In the autumn of 1679 Charles decided to send his brother to Scotland, in essence to get him out of the way while the crisis over the succession unfolded. York chose to travel overland, and the trip became in effect a long royal progress, with the *London Gazette* reporting for its readers every stage of York's journey, documenting the enthusiastic reception he received at the places he visited *en route* – not just from the nobility, local gentry, ecclesiastical dignitaries, town magistrates, militia companies, but also from the crowds of people who would 'throng in to see their Royal Highnesses' or celebrate the Duke of York's visit at specially erected bonfires. The most enthusiastic reception was in Edinburgh itself, where on the night of York's arrival all 'the Streets were filled with Bonfires (which were so great and numerous that the whole Town seemed one fire) . . . and all the people were zealous to demonstrate the joy they had to see [the] Prince . . . among them'.[88] York went back to England early in the New Year, only to return to Scotland the following October (this time going by boat), with again his arrival being greeted with the 'Acclamations of the People, and all other Expressions of Joy imaginable'. However, nothing had been left to chance; Charles II had written to his Scottish Privy Council in advance asking them to ensure that there were suitable 'publick Demonstrations of Joy' when his brother arrived.[89] During his second stay in Scotland, York made two more progresses – one in February, to Stirling, and another in October 1681, to Glasgow, where 'a vast Multitude of all sorts of People' lined the streets, cheering in support – and also played a prominent part in promoting the festivities in the Scottish capital on Restoration Day at the end of May, for his own birthday on 14 October, and for the Queen's birthday on 15 November.[90]

There were further demonstrations on behalf of York when Charles invited him back to England in March 1682. The magistrates of Yarmouth laid on a reception for the duke when he landed on the 10th, whilst there was another formal reception for him at Norwich, where he stayed the night, with 'the Streets being crowded with People and full of Bonfires'.[91] From there York travelled to Newmarket to join up with the king, before eventually returning to London on 8 April, which proved to be the cue for a number of loyalist and anti-Whig bonfire demonstrations in several parts of the capital, typically involving the burning of effigies of Jack Presbyter or leading Whigs.[92] The reaction against the Whigs by this time, even in London, was sufficiently marked that there was genuine support amongst considerable cross-sections of the metropolitan population for the Duke of York. Yet although these demonstrations perhaps did not need to be orchestrated, Charles II himself was determined to see that they would take place, and he wrote to his Tory Lord Mayor of London in advance to make sure that 'his loyall apprentices' would be out in force to 'make a body for his [York's] receptione'.[93] York made another entry into London on 20 April, when he attended the Artillery Company's feast in the City, and on 27 May, when he returned to Whitehall after a brief return visit to Scotland to collect his wife. Again there were bonfire celebrations and anti-Whig demonstrations; and again there was some prompting, this time from the Duke of York's servants and captains of the guards.[94]

In addition to demonstrations in support of the heir to the throne, there was also a rise in public ceremonials centring on the crown. Charles's most significant personal initiative was to increase dramatically the extent to which he was prepared to touch for the King's Evil – prompted (at least in part) by the fact that his illegitimate son, the Duke of Monmouth, had started doing so as part of his own campaign to stake a claim to the throne.[95] Charles had revived the practice at his restoration, and was said to have touched at least 90,000 people during his reign. But the peak came in the aftermath of the Exclusion Crisis: he touched some 8577 between May 1682 and April 1683, and an incredible 3535 in a little over three weeks towards the latter part of 1682.[96] He also made a number of progresses and royal entries. His journey to Oxford to open the Oxford Parliament in March 1681 perhaps qualifies as one; the king and his entourage were met at the county borders by the lord lieutenant and county militia, whence they were escorted into Oxford to be received by the heads of the university and local residents 'with all demonstrations of joy and welcome'.[97] At the end of September 1681, the king, queen and the royal court, whilst resident at Newmarket, made a quick visit to Cambridge, where they were 'joyfully received' by the high sheriff of the county, the heads of the colleges and the town magistrates; to guarantee suitable 'publick demonstrations of joy' the bells of the several city churches rang and the conduits ran with wine.[98] Charles himself brought the Duke of York back to London on 8 April, which ensured that even if people had not been over-enthusiastic to see the return of the Catholic heir, 'all his true Protestant Subjects' would nevertheless have been prompted to express their 'Joy as well as Happiness' at 'His Majesties safe Arrival in good Health'.[99] In late August 1683 the king and queen visited Winchester, where they were building a new royal residence, and again received a splendid reception from the county gentry, the town magistrates and local residents, there being 'bells and bonfires till midnight', according to one newsletter account, and 'candles and lanthorns at every house to keep the streets light'.[100]

A royal presence was not essential for a loyalist display, however. The inhabitants of Dover and Shaftesbury held bonfire celebrations to rejoice at the king and the Duke of York's safe return to London in early April 1682; the towns of Sarum and Oundle held similar displays in May when they heard that York had safely arrived in Scotland after his boat had been shipwrecked.[101] Indeed, in the years following the dissolution of the Oxford Parliament at the end of March 1681 there was a flurry of loyalist activity out-of-doors. Restoration Day, which had passed by rather quietly in the 1670s, was revived in a big way, and became the occasion of anti-Whig and anti-nonconformist demonstrations in many parts of the country – London, Bristol, Derby, Durham, Lynn, Norwich, Portsmouth, Taunton, York and Windsor, to cite the best documented examples.[102] There was even an attempt by Tory groups to reclaim 5 November for their own purposes; in London in 1681, for example, the scholars of St Peter's College, Westminster, staged an elaborate presbyter-burning ritual on that day, and elsewhere in the capital Tory groups sought to disrupt the Whig pope-burnings by seizing their effigies and trying to extinguish their bonfires.[103] In the years 1681 to 1683 hundreds of loyal addresses, some with thousands of signatories, swarmed in from all over the country, to pledge support for York's succession and opposition to the Whigs and nonconformists. Moreover, people from across the social spectrum can be found pledging their support for the Tories in such ways, from local landed and mercantile elites down to more humble types – apprentices, tinners, cooks and watermen.[104]

Tory propagandists were able to tap into deep-seated anti-nonconformist prejudices, widespread popular attachment to the monarchy and the established church, and a desperate fear (amongst significant sections of the population) of a possible revival of civil war. There is thus no doubting the authenticity of popular Toryism; on the whole, the people who signed loyal addresses or celebrated at bonfires did so because they wanted to, whilst there is also plenty of evidence of spontaneous Tory activity in the streets in both London and the provinces.[105] Nevertheless, we can detect a certain amount of encouragement from above, at least from local leaders. The Restoration Day celebrations at Durham in 1682, for instance, were planned weeks in advance by the county gentry and civic officials and were managed by the Bishop of Durham's agent and the Registrar to the Dean and Chapter.[106] In addition, Charles II clearly welcomed such loyal displays and went out of his way to reward some of those who participated in them. Thus the king provided a brace of bucks for a feast for his loyal apprentices in London in August 1681, and again in the following year, the latter occasion being presided over by leading courtiers such as the Duke of Ormonde, the Duke of Albemarle, the Earl (later Marquis) of Halifax and the Earl of Sunderland.[107]

During the Exclusion Crisis, then, we see a self-conscious effort by the royal government and its supporters to engage in the battle for public opinion. They wanted to be able to show – and report back in the press – that there was considerable support amongst the mass of the population for the king, the Duke of York, and the stance they were taking against the Whigs and in defence of the existing establishment in Church and state. Precisely how much responsibility the crown had for formulating such a strategy for dealing with the Whig challenge is not easy to determine. Undoubtedly, we must acknowledge a considerable amount of independent initiative, both from publicists who had little (if any) connection with the court, and well-wishers in the localities who thought it would be an appropriate response to the designs of the Whigs to stage their own bonfires and instigate loyal addresses. It is clear, however, that both Charles II and the Duke of York were willing and active participants, making appropriately-staged public appearances to whip up popular support; the government certainly played a vital role in directing the anti-Whig propaganda campaign; and we can even find the king himself instructing local officials to orchestrate crowd demonstrations or rewarding his followers in the streets.

Charles II and his advisers were fully aware of the risks involved in appealing to public opinion. Inviting people to declare whether they were on your side or not might make some (or even many) determined to make it clear that they were not. The king knew that encouraging the loyal apprentices of London to celebrate his brother's return from Scotland in the spring of 1682 might prompt the Whig apprentices to make a counter-demonstration, and instructed the Lord Mayor to have the trained bands ready, to 'keep the peopell from tumulting'.[108] Charles's fears were well-founded; there were indeed violent clashes between rival crowds on the night of 8 April, the day of York's return to London, as Whig groups sought to extinguish Tory bonfires.[109] When the city of Dublin thought of promoting a loyal address in the spring of 1681, the Lord Lieutenant of Ireland, the Duke of Ormonde, quickly learned that the king did 'not approve of any such address', for although he was 'very glad they are generally so well inclined', he was worried that the collection of signatories might 'make them factious there' and force some of the 'notable knaves amongst them' to come out against the address.[110] When loyal addresses began to come in from Ireland in the following spring, the English government initially thought of getting Ormonde 'to suppresse them in that Kingdom', believing them to be 'of little valew because they are out of the Rode', and being leery of stirring things up in what was after all a somewhat volatile part of the Stuart multiple-kingdom inheritance. Nevertheless, in the end, it decided not to frustrate the initiative, and large numbers did come in from Ireland over the next few years.[111] Similarly, although the court welcomed the loyal addresses that came in from the London Artillery Company and the City Lieutenancy in the early months of 1682 in abhorrence of the Earl of Shaftesbury's alleged 'Association', it advised against trying to instigate such an address in the Common Council, fearing that this would provoke 'the opposite party' into promoting 'a petition for the settling of a Parliament', which might conceivably end up generating more support, and cause other parts of the country to follow suit.[112]

Yet overall, Charles's appeal to public opinion proved highly successful, and enabled him to recover from the crisis he faced at the height of the Exclusion Crisis. It used to be argued that Charles lived his last years in peace because he was able to silence all forms of opposition, by refusing to call parliament after 1681 and conducting a ruthless campaign against his political and religious opponents through the courts.[113] More recently, in recognition of the fact that there was a rise of loyalist activity out-of-doors in the years after the dissolution Oxford Parliament, it has been suggested that the key to Charles's success lay in a dramatic reaction, in the nation at large, against the Whigs, as people rallied behind the crown against the threat of subversion in Church and state. Thus Jonathan Scott has maintained that, with the exception of a few hard-liners, the Whigs of 1679–81 and the Tories of 1681–3 were the same people; they simply changed sides.[114] Both views, in crucial ways, misunderstand what was going on. Although there was a swing opinion, support for the Whigs did not totally evaporate; in fact we can still detect a considerable degree of Whig activism out-of-doors in the years of the Tory Reaction.[115] But the court's appeal to opinion out-of-doors served to deflate the position of the Whigs in a number of significant respects, and made it possible both to stave off the exclusionist challenge and to conduct a rigorous campaign against the perceived enemies of Church and state without driving the masses into rebellion.

Being able to show that there was considerable opposition to the Whigs, for example, enabled the court and its Tory allies to claim that Exclusion was not the wish of the people.[116] Indeed, the early show of support for York in Scotland made it clear, as government spokesmen were at pains to point out, that Exclusion was not a viable solution to the problem of the Catholic succession given the multiple kingdom inheritance over which the Stuarts ruled: for if the English were to pass an Exclusion Bill, this would inevitably lead to war with the Scots, who would never accept it.[117] Moreover, rather than actually winning back the support of erstwhile Whigs (though some people undoubtedly did switch sides), a more important function of pro-government propaganda was to mobilize latent support and encourage people to make public the fact that they had never identified with the Whig position in the first place. As people came to see some actively declaring their loyalism, others would be less afraid of taking a stance; those responsible for law enforcement in the localities would realize that they could perform their duty (for example, in clamping down on religious conventicles) without fear of incurring the wrath of their community; whilst those contemplating rebellion might hold back as they would come to doubt whether the mass of the population really was on their side. It did take a campaign of repression to defeat the exclusionist challenge. The Whigs were removed from local office, whilst the threat of *quo warranto* proceedings compelled many towns to hand over their charters in return for new ones that gave the crown the ability to remodel the composition of corporations in its own interest. Conventicles were shut down and nonconformists hauled before the courts in large numbers. And charges of sedition and treason were brought against leading Whig dissidents and their humbler supporters amongst the rank and file, leading to heavy fines, imprisonment and even execution. Yet the government would not have been able to do all this if they had not been able to find local magistrates, jurors and parish constables willing to take such action (even if it took a purge of local officeholders to ensure that such loyalists were in positions of authority) and felt certain that taking such stern measures would not to provoke further political instability.[118] Confident of the loyalty of the local law-enforcement agencies, the government was finally able to achieve what it had tried but failed to do at the beginning of the Exclusion Crisis, namely clamp down on the expression of dissident opinion out-of-doors. Once the Tories had regained control of the shrievalty in London, from the autumn of 1682, they were able to impanel Tory juries who in turn proved willing to bring indictments against Whig publicists for seditious libel or for printing without authority. By the end of 1682, the Whig periodical press had been effectively silenced.[119] The government was also able to enforce a prohibition against bonfires on 5 and 17 November following disturbances on Gunpowder Treason Day in London in 1682.[120]

The value of the Tory appeal to opinion out-of-doors can be seen, then, in the very success of the Tory Reaction. There is evidence to suggest that people not only acquiesced in the persecution of nonconformists but actively welcomed it, willingly coming forward as informers or in other ways assisting in the suppression of conventicling activity, even 'rejoyceing' to see the meeting houses in their neighbourhood being destroyed.[121] Even the attack on the corporations went more smoothly than might have been imagined; indeed, in many towns, the receipt of the new charter became the occasion for local celebration, with the formal civic ceremony typically accompanied by widespread cheering amongst the townsfolk and followed by street festivities, plenty of alcohol and music, and bonfires at night.[122]

The value of the appeal to public opinion is also reflected in the fact that the Stuart regime managed to prevent itself from becoming vulnerable to the threat of rebellion. The Rye House conspiracy, which was revealed in the late spring of 1683, failed to come to anything because the conspirators could not agree when the time was right to launch their planned insurrection; it was becoming clear, even to them, that by late 1682/early 1683 the right time had passed. Instead, the country celebrated deliverance from the plot with bonfires and loyal addresses; even Taunton, 'lately esteemed one of the most disloyal and factious places in England', saw 'great outward expressions of joy . . . by ringing of bells, beating of drums, bonfires, feasting etc.', prompting the local under-sheriff to conclude 'the populace are undeceived to admiration'.[123] The eventual succession of the Catholic heir in February 1685 went more smoothly than anyone could have predicted. There were loyal addresses from all over the country, public rejoicings at the declaration of the new king, and the general elections of the spring produced a parliament that was overwhelmingly Tory in sympathy, with only 57 Whigs returned to a Commons of 513, and with the Tories even doing extremely well in the more open constituencies.[124] Although the Duke of Monmouth did launch a rebellion in the west country in the summer, the support it attracted proved extremely disappointing, and it was soon put down. Again, the kingdom celebrated its deliverance with bonfires.[125]

III

We have seen, then, that Charles II and his advisers rose to the challenge posed by the Whigs during the Exclusion Crisis by joining the battle for public opinion. They self-consciously sought to appeal to the multitude or the vulgar, developed strategies for communicating their political views and justifying their actions to the broadest possible cross-section of the population, and deliberately sought to promote (both indirectly and directly) mass political activity in support of the crown (in the form of petitions, addresses and demonstrations). Moreover, the strategy served its purposes extremely well. It enabled Charles to stave off the challenge of the Whigs, and guaranteed the relatively smooth succession of his

Catholic brother in 1685. Not only was there no repeat of civil war, as had been genuinely feared during the height of the Exclusion Crisis, but James II succeeded to the throne with considerable public support behind him. From the evidence presented here, it should be clear that those out-of-doors did matter, and that in the later seventeenth century their importance was recognized even by those who ran the kingdom, including the king himself.

Charles II's willingness to appeal to opinion out-of-doors appears in seeming contrast to the approach not only of his father and grandfather, but even of Queen Elizabeth. How do we account for this change over time? A number of general explanations immediately suggest themselves. Perhaps it was a reaction to a growth of popular political consciousness brought about as a result of the upheavals of the mid-seventeenth century, or to the rise of the press, both of which broadened the scope of the political nation and forced those in charge under Charles II to manage those they ruled in different ways. A linear progression is arguably at work: we see 'the rise of mass politics' in the 1640s,[126] and although an attempt was made to put the cap back on the bottle after the Restoration, it inevitably proved impossible to do so. Maybe what we are witnessing in Restoration England, as Steven Pincus has suggested, is the emergence of the public sphere, in the Habermasian sense of a social space for the public discussion and criticism of the state;[127] once it had come into being, those who ruled the country had no option but to engage with it.

Such explanations undoubtedly possess a certain amount of validity. Yet there are difficulties. We have already seen in this book considerable evidence of popular political consciousness in the period before the civil war, and different scholars might well feel (and indeed have felt) justified in talking about a rise in political awareness amongst the masses in the 1620s, the late Elizabethan period or the 1530s. The growth of the press was certainly important in contributing to a better informed political culture, but we should be careful not to exaggerate its significance as an instrument of change. People could become politicized through the press; but they could also become politically informed through sermons, which was a very old medium, or through the circulation of political news and commentary in manuscript or by word of mouth. More directly, it was the impact of government policy (whether religious, fiscal, military or whatever) at the local level that played the most vital role in forcing people to have opinions about the legitimacy of the actions of those who ruled over them.[128] The notion of the rise of the public sphere is equally problematic. The concept has been taken to mean somewhat different things by different scholars, leading to competing suggestions as to when we should locate its rise: for Jürgen Habermas it was the turn of the eighteenth century, for Steven Pincus the Restoration period, for Dagmar Freist on the eve of the civil war.[129] One might suggest that we see heightened public debate about political controversies in earlier periods: the 1620s certainly, at certain times during Elizabeth's reign, and during the 1530s. Instead of invoking the notion of the rise of the public sphere as a one-time phenomenon, historians are surely better advised to try to understand why it was, at certain historical conjunctures, that political controversies came to be fought out in a public arena, what the precise nature of that arena was, what media served to make the debate public, and who, exactly, comprised the public at the time period in question. And whatever one thinks of the validity of the notion of 'the rise of mass politics' as applied to the 1640s, it can certainly not be said that this was the first time we see the masses actively engaged in politics.

There are further reasons to be cautious before drawing too stark a contrast between the strategies employed by Charles II for managing opinion out-of-doors and those of his predecessors. No monarch had ever totally ignored his or her public. Rulers had always found it necessary to make their policies publicly known, and to try to carry their subjects with them in what they were seeking to do. This invariably required a dual-pronged strategy of both policy and police:[130] official pronouncements (whether via royal proclamations, officially sanctioned sermons or other media at the crown's disposal) seeking to explain, rationalize and justify what the government was doing; and the suppression of dissident voices (whether by trying to silence opposition media or prosecuting those suspected of seditious activity). We find the same general strategy being pursued in Charles II's reign as in Henry VIII's reign, as in all the reigns in between. Thus just as Charles II issued an official declaration in 1681 explaining why he had dissolved his last two parliaments, so did James I and Charles I issue official declarations in the 1620s explaining why they had found it necessary to dissolve parliament. Just as authors of seditious literature were dealt with severely by the government in the 1630s (one thinks of Burton, Bastwick and Prynne), so they were in the final years of Charles II's reign (one need only recall the fate of Algernon Sidney). And just as Charles II encouraged demonstrations in support of his heir in the early 1680s, so James I encouraged demonstrations in support of his heir in 1623–4, at the time of the proposed Spanish match and subsequent French marriage.

However, the recognition of certain similarities between the earlier and later periods must not obscure change over time. My own sense of the relevant sources for the seventeenth century leaves me convinced that by the time we get to the 1680s we are in a very different world from that of the 1620s: the whole question of how those in power needed to manage opinion out-of-doors had become much more complicated and necessitated the employment of more sophisticated public relations strategies than had earlier been recognized as either necessary or desirable. Part of this was related to the experience and legacy of the 1640s and 1650s. It was not just that the upheavals of these decades had bequeathed a divided and politically more self-conscious population. It was also that the governmental elite of Restoration England knew how things had worked out in the past, and lived in perpetual fear of the same thing happening again, which they were determined to avoid at all costs. If James I and Charles I did not appreciate the same need to court their public as did Charles II, and preferred to place greater emphasis on policing discontent than in trying to woo opinion, it was because they were not aware of the depths of the crisis that could befall the monarchy if they got things wrong. We also have to recognize the massive expansion in the output of the press (first in the 1640s, and again following the lapsing of the Licensing Act in 1679), the growing sophistication of the media, and the more extensive circulation of political ideas and information as communication networks improved and institutions like the coffee-house that could serve as focal points for the discussion and dissemination of news began to flourish. What we see under Charles II, therefore, is a recognition (from a post-civil war perspective) both that the early Stuart strategy of failing to engage wholeheartedly in the battle for public opinion had proved fatal in the long run, and that such neglect could not possibly be excusable in the changed world of post-civil war England.

The fact that Charles II and his advisers deliberately sought to bring the people into politics did not mean that they embraced a different conception of the place of the people from their predecessors. Just as Elizabeth's magnificent progresses had been designed to remind her subjects of the subordinate position they occupied in a huge and multi-layered hierarchy of power, so the court's efforts to promote loyalist activism under Charles II were designed to encourage people publicly to acknowledge their subordination; to admit that they did not have the right to tell their rulers what to do, challenge the king's prerogative or change the divinely ordained succession; and to make it known that they accepted the existing authoritarian structures in Church and state. In fact, Tory crowds and loyal addressers were protesting against those who dared to challenge the divinely ordained power hierarchy or the king's right to rule. Thus the loyal address from the corporation and inhabitants of Monmouth to James II in February 1685 acknowledged that it was the king's 'Right to Rule and Govern' and 'Subjects' Duty to Obey'.[131] Moreover, although the Tories sought to appeal to the people, their propaganda was designed to teach people their place.[132] L'Estrange was typical when he insisted that 'the Several Members of a Common-Wealth have their Distinct, and Particular Offices, and Functions Assign'd them', and that the common people were made 'for Obedience, not for Government; for Submission, not for Dispute, to Follow, not to Leade'. He even believed that the common people 'would Live, as Contentedly, within the Bounds of their own Sphere, and Bus'ness, as the Earth it Self, in the Place that Providence has assign'd it, if other people would but let 'em alone'.[133] Nevertheless, Charles II's appeal to opinion out-of-doors did involve a certain degree of negotiation with his subjects. He represented himself as being committed to upholding the existing legal establishment in Church and state against those groups that might seek to subvert it, and also as being vehemently opposed to both popery and arbitrary government. In essence, he committed himself to a partisan position – the Tory-Anglican one – which left the monarchy little room for manoeuvre. He could carry the people with him as long as – but only as long as – he continued to respect the rule of law and protect the established Church.

For the last years of his reign, Charles did what Tory-Anglicans expected of him. The degree of negotiation with those out-of-doors that had become necessary in order to rebuild the authority of the crown, however, becomes immediately apparent when we look at what happened under his Catholic successor. James II was well aware of the need to make a public commitment to the existing legal establishment in Church and state, and did so right at the beginning of his reign. Nevertheless, he failed to keep his promise. Not only did he seek to promote the interests of his co-religionists and undermine the monopoly of worship, education and officeholding of the Anglican Church, but he did so in ways that seemed directly subversive of the rule of law. In order to try to sell his policies, he engaged in all the techniques for appealing to public opinion that had worked so well under his brother: a carefully crafted propaganda campaign, royal progresses and the promotion of loyal addresses and demonstrations. But all this was to no avail. Despite the hard sell, as the

drift towards popery and arbitrary government became all too frighten-
ingly apparent, James II's subjects gradually but inexorably deserted
him. They rioted against Catholic meeting houses, refused to cooperate
with the king's plans to promote religious toleration, celebrated the stance
taken by the Seven Bishops against the king's Declaration of Indulgence
and rallied behind the Prince of Orange when he invaded England in
November 1688 in order to rescue English liberties and the Protestant
religion. James II lost his crown not because he did not realize he
needed to engage in the battle for public opinion or because he thought
those out-of-doors did not matter. Rather, he threw away the very
strong position he had found himself in at his accession through the
pursuit of policies which his people – who had been schooled during the
final years of Charles II's reign in the need to be vigilant against both
popery and arbitrary government and to trust in the law as their protection against both – simply would not accept. It was a crisis James brought
upon himself, and it was a crisis that testifies to the significance of public
opinion and politics out-of-doors in the later Stuart period; a significance,
ironically, that was recognized even by James II himself.[134]

NOTES

1. Elkannah Settle, *A Narrative* (London, 1683), sigs B1v–B2.
2. [Roger L'Estrange], *The Freeborn Subject; Or, The Englishman's Birthright*
   (London, 1679), pp. 5, 28, 33. The term 'out-of-doors' is a contemporary
   one. For example, Roger L'Estrange observed how 'the Bus'ness of the Exclusion, and That Controversy, is now out of Doors' . . . 'Witness the Libells that have
   been Lately Posted up, and thrown about the Streets': Roger L'Estrange, *The
   Observator in Dialogue*, 3 vols (London, 1684–87), III, no. 24, 1 April 1685.
3. Christopher Hill, 'The Many-Headed Monster', in his *Change and Continuity
   in Seventeenth-Century England* (revised edn, New Haven, 1991), pp. 181–204
   (quote on p. 186).
4. H[ugh] B[roughton?], *Moriemini: A Verie Profitable Sermon Preached before her
   Maiestie at the Court* (1593), cited in Peter E. McCullough, *Sermons at Court:
   Politics and Religion in Elizabethan and Jacobean Preaching* (Cambridge, 1998),
   p. 80.
5. *Heraclitus Ridens*, no. 1 [1 February 1681]. The periodical was written by a
   club of Tory writers, headed by Edward Rawlins and Thomas Flatman. See
   T. F. M. Newton, 'The Mask of Heraclitus: A Problem in Restoration
   Journalism', *Harvard Studies and Notes in Philology and Literature*, XVI (1934),
   145–60.
6. Most recently in 'Understanding Popular Politics in Restoration Britain',
   in Alan Houston and Steven C. A. Pincus (eds), *A Nation Transformed?*
   (Cambridge University Press, forthcoming).

7. R. Malcolm Smuts, 'Public Ceremony and Royal Charisma: The English Royal Entry in London, 1485–1642', in Lee Beier, David Cannadine and James Rosenheim (eds), *The First Modern Society: Essays in English History in Honour of Lawrence Stone* (Cambridge, 1989), pp. 65–93; David Cressy, *Bonfires and Bells: National Memory and the Protestant Calendar in Elizabethan and Stuart England* (London, 1989), pp. 50–66, 120; David Cressy, 'The Protestant Calendar and the Vocabulary of Celebration in Early Modern England', *JBS*, XXIX (1990), 31–52; Ronald Hutton, *The Rise and Fall of Merry England: The Ritual Year, 1400–1700* (Oxford, 1994), pp. 146–51; Roy Strong, 'The Popular Celebration of the Accession Day of Queen Elizabeth I', *Journal of the Warburg and Courtauld Institutes*, 21 (1958), 86–103; Christopher Haigh, *Elizabeth I* (London, 1988; 2nd edn, 1998), ch. 8.
8. Smuts, 'Public Ceremony', pp. 74–8. Cf. Jenny Wormald, 'James VI and I: Two Kings or One?', *History*, 68 (1983), p. 204.
9. Thomas Cogswell, 'Underground Verse and the Transformation of Early Stuart Political Culture', in Susan Amussen and Mark Kishlansky (eds), *Political Culture and Cultural Politics in Early Modern England* (Manchester, 1995), p. 279.
10. Francis Bamford (ed.), *A Royalist's Notebook. The Commonplace Book of Sir John Oglander Kt. of Nunwell* (London, 1936), pp. 196–7; Arthur Wilson, *The History of Great Britain, Being the Life and Reign of King James the First* (London, 1653), p. 13.
11. Wilson, *History of Great Britain*, p. 3. For the progress, see: John Nichols, *The Progresses, Processions, and Magnificent Festivities of King James I*, 3 vols (London, 1828), I, 53–127.
12. Graham Parry (ed.), *The Golden Age Restor'd: The Culture of the Stuart Court, 1603–42* (Manchester, 1981), pp. 1–21 (quote on p. 21); Nichols, *Progresses*, I, 337–99.
13. Hutton, *Merry England*, pp. 182–3; Cressy, *Bonfires and Bells*, ch. 9.
14. *The Letters of John Chamberlain*, ed. Norman McClure, 2 vols (Philadelphia: American Philosophical Society, 1939), I, 223.
15. Smuts, 'Public Ceremony', p. 87.
16. Cf. McCullough, *Sermons at Court*, pp. 132–7, 143.
17. Wilson, *History of Great Britain*, p. 3.
18. Parry, *Golden Age Restor'd*, p. 21.
19. Smuts, 'Public Ceremony', p. 82.
20. Thomas Cogswell, 'The Politics of Propaganda: Charles I and the People in the 1620s', *JBS*, XXIX (1990), 192.
21. Smuts, 'Public Ceremony', p. 82.
22. *Stuart Royal Proclamations*, ed. James F. Larkin and Paul L. Hughes, 2 vols (Oxford, 1973–83), II, 34–5; Robert Steele, *A Bibliography of Royal Proclamations of the Tudor and Stuart Sovereigns*, 3 vols (New York, 1967), I, no. 1428.
23. *Stuart Royal Proclamations*, II, 82–4; Steele, *Royal Proclamations*, I, no. 1469.
24. Smuts, 'Public Ceremony', pp. 82–93; Judith Richards, ' "His Nowe Majestie" and the English Monarchy: The Kingship of Charles I before 1640', *P&P*, CXIII (1986), 70–96; Michael B. Young, *Charles I* (Basingstoke, 1997), p. 86.
25. Adam Fox, 'Rumour, News and Popular Political Opinion in Elizabethan and Early Stuart England', *HJ*, XL (1997), 611–12; Michael Frearson, 'The

Distribution and Readership of London Corantos in the 1620s', in R. Myers and M. Harris (eds), *Serials and their Readers, 1620–1914* (Winchester, 1993), pp. 1–25; C. John Sommerville, *The News Revolution in England: Cultural Dynamics of Daily Information* (Oxford, 1996), pp. 22–7; Joad Raymond, *The Invention of the Newspaper: English Newsbooks, 1641–1649* (Oxford, 1996), pp. 7–10, 99; Cogswell, 'Underground Verse', pp. 285–7; Cogswell, 'Politics of Propaganda'; Richard Cust, *The Forced Loan and English Politics, 1626–1628* (Oxford, 1987); L. J. Reeve, *Charles I and the Road to Personal Rule* (Cambridge, 1989).

26. Anthony Milton, *Catholic and Reformed: The Roman and Protestant Churches in English Protestant Thought 1600–1640* (Cambridge, 1995), p. 532; Peter Lake, 'The Moderate and Irenic Case for Religious War: Joseph Hall's *Via Media* in Context', in Amussen and Kishlansky (eds), *Political Culture*, p. 57.

27. *Acts of the Privy Council, 1623–1625*, pp. 369–70; *Letters . . . of John Chamberlain*, II, p. 488; Cressy, *Bonfires and Bells*, pp. 84, 96.

28. Raymond, *Invention of the Newspaper*, pp. 10, 97–9; Sommerville, *News Revolution*, p. 27; Joseph Frank, *The Beginnings of the English Newspaper, 1620–1660* (Cambridge, Mass., 1961), pp. 14–15; Elizabeth Skerpan, *The Rhetoric of Politics in the English Revolution, 1642–1660* (Columbia, Mo., 1991), p. 9; Young, *Charles I*, pp. 76–8. For France, see Howard M. Solomon, *Public Welfare, Science, and Propaganda in Seventeenth-Century France: The Innovations of Théophraste Renaudot* (Princeton, 1972).

29. Cressy, *Bonfires and Bells*, pp. 134–8, 152–5; Cressy, 'Protestant Calendar', pp. 43–7; Hutton, *Merry England*, pp. 185–6; John Walter, *Understanding Popular Violence in the English Revolution: The Colchester Plunderers* (Cambridge, 1999), pp. 219–23.

30. We still await a full-scale, scholarly analysis of royalist propaganda during the first civil war. Useful insights can be gleaned from: Joyce Malcolm, *Caesar's Due: Loyalty and King Charles, 1642–1646* (London, 1983); Anthony Fletcher, *The Outbreak of the English Civil War* (London, 1981); Tim Harris, 'Propaganda and Public Opinion in Seventeenth-Century England', in Jeremy Popkin (ed.), *Media and Revolution: Comparative Perspectives* (Lexington, Ky., 1995), pp. 48–73; Dagmar Freist, *Governed by Opinion: Politics, Religion and the Dynamics of Communication in Stuart London, 1637–1645* (London, 1997); Ethan Howard Shagan, 'Constructing Discord: Ideology, Propaganda, and English Responses to the Irish Rebellion of 1641', *JBS*, XXXVI (1997), 1–34; Ethan Howard Shagan, ' "Remonstrating Downwards": Media and Propaganda in the Outbreak of the English Civil War', Brown University Honors Thesis (1994).

31. Smuts, 'Public Ceremony'; Richards, 'His Nowe Majestie'.

32. Thomas P. Slaughter (ed.), *Ideology and Politics on the Eve of Restoration: Newcastle's Advice to Charles II* (Philadelphia, 1984), pp. 45, 56. See also Conal Condren, 'Casuistry to Newcastle: *The Prince* in the World of the Book', in Nicholas Phillipson and Quentin Skinner (eds), *Political Discourse in Early Modern Britain* (Cambridge, 1993), pp. 164–86.

33. John Evelyn, *Diary*, ed. E. S. De Beer, 6 vols (Oxford, 1955), III, 246; Samuel Pepys, *Diary*, ed. R. C. Latham and W. Matthews, 11 vols (London, 1970–83), I, 163; *Mercurius Publicus*, no. 22, 24–31 May 1660; *HMC, 5th Report*,

pp. 167–8, 184, 199; *The Diurnal of Thomas Rugg, 1659–1661*, ed. W. L. Sachse (Camden Society, 3rd series, XCI, 1961), pp. 88–91.

34. *The Statutes of the Realm*, ed. A. Luders, T. E. Tomlins and J. France, 12 vols (London, 1810–28), V, 237; Hutton, *Merry England*, pp. 249–51.

35. *The Rawdon Papers*, ed. Rev. Edward Berwick (London, 1819), p. 201; Pepys, *Diary*, II, 81–8; John Ogilby, *The Entertainment of His Most Excellent Majestie Charles II, in His Passage through the City of London to His Coronation* (London, 1662); Eric Halfpenny, ' "The Citie's Loyalty Display'd": A Literary and Documentary Causerie of Charles II's Coronation "Entertainment" ', *Guildhall Miscellany*, I, no. 10 (September, 1959), 19–35; Gerard Reedy, 'Mystical Politics: The Imagery of Charles II's Coronation', in P. J. Korshin (ed.), *Studies in Change and Revolution: Aspects of English Intellectual History, 1640–1800* (Menston, 1972), pp. 20–42; Paula Backscheider, *Spectacular Politics: Theatrical Power and Mass Culture in Early Modern England* (Baltimore, 1993), ch. 1.

36. Tim Harris, 'The Bawdy House Riots of 1668', *HJ*, XXIX (1986), 537–56.

37. For fuller discussions of the points raised in this and the following paragraph, see: Ronald Hutton, *The Restoration: A Political and Religious History of England and Wales, 1658–1667* (Oxford, 1985); Tim Harris, *Politics under the Later Stuarts: Party Conflict in a Divided Society, 1660–1715* (London, 1993).

38. For the British dimension, see Tim Harris, 'The British Dimension, Religion, and the Shaping of Political Identities during the Reign of Charles II', in Tony Claydon and Ian McBride (eds), *Protestantism and National Identity: Britain and Ireland, c.1650–c.1850* (Cambridge, 1998), pp. 131–56.

39. Steven C. A. Pincus, ' "Coffee Politicians Does Create": Coffeehouses and Restoration Political Culture', *Journal of Modern History*, LXVII (1995), 807–34.

40. *The Burning of the Whore of Babylon, as it was Acted, with Great Applause, in the Poultrey* (London, 1673); *CSPVen, 1673–5*, pp. 174, 178; Evelyn, *Diary*, IV, 26; *The Pope Burnt to Ashes* (London, 1676); *Correspondence of the Family of Hatton, 1601–1704*, ed. Edward Maunde Thompson, 2 vols (Camden Society, NS XXII–XXIII, 1878), I, 119, 157; *CSPD, 1673–5*, pp. 40, 44; *CSPD, 1677–8*, p. 446.

41. Wilmer G. Mason, 'The Annual Output of Wing-Listed Titles, 1649–1684', *The Library*, 5th series, XXIV (1974), 219–20.

42. Mark Knights, *Politics and Opinion in Crisis, 1678–81* (Cambridge, 1994), p. 168.

43. J. R. Jones, *The First Whigs: The Politics of the Exclusion Crisis, 1678–83* (Oxford, 1961); Harris, *London Crowds*, chs 5, 7; Knights, *Politics and Opinion*, chs 6–9.

44. Steele, *Royal Proclamations*, I, nos 3699, 3703, 3715; CLRO, *Common Council Journal*, 49, fols 76, 85, 120; *State Trials*, ed. T. B. Howell, 33 vols (London, 1809–26), VII, cols 926–60, 1111–30; Timothy J. Crist, 'Francis Smith and the Opposition Press in England, 1660–1688', University of Cambridge PhD thesis (1978), ch. 3; Timothy J. Crist, 'Government Control of the Press after the Expiration of the Printing Act in 1679', *Publishing History*, V (1979), 49–77; Phillip Harth, *Pen for a Party: Dryden's Tory Propaganda in its Contexts* (Princeton, 1993), pp. 32–6.

45. Bodl., MS Carte 39, fol. 1. Cf. J. S. Clarke (ed.), *The Life of James II*, 2 vols (London, 1816), I, 515.

46. Richard L. Greaves, *Secrets of the Kingdom: British Radicals from the Popish Plot to the Revolution of 1688–89* (Stanford, 1992); Robin Clifton, *The Last Popular Rebellion: The Western Rising of 1685* (London, 1984).

47. It was not only the enfranchised who influenced the outcome of parliamentary elections; those without the vote could have an impact by turning up in large numbers to voice support for preferred candidates, intimidating those with the franchise into siding with their choice, by scaring away from the poll those who would have voted for the court candidates, or even by giving the court candidates the impression that the fight was not worth continuing and thereby encouraging them to step down before a poll was taken.

48. Gary S. De Krey, 'London Radicals and Revolutionary Politics, 1675–1683', in Tim Harris, Paul Seaward and Mark Goldie (eds), *The Politics of Religion in Restoration England* (Oxford, 1990), p. 137; John T. Evans, *Seventeenth-Century Norwich: Politics, Religion, and Government, 1620–1690* (Oxford, 1979), p. 251.

49. Judith J. Hurwich, '"A Fanatick Town": Political Influence of Dissenters in Coventry, 1660–1720', *Midland History*, IV (1977), 31–3.

50. Anthony Wood, *Life and Times, 1632–1695*, ed. A. Clark, 5 vols (Oxford, 1891–1900), II, 463, 490; *Letters of Humphrey Prideaux, Sometime Dean of Norwich, to John Ellis, Sometime Under-Secretary of State, 1674–1722*, ed. Edward Maunde Thompson (Camden Society, NS XV, 1875), p. 80; *VCH*, *Oxford*, IV, 123.

51. *London Gazette*, no. 1455, 27–30 October 1679.

52. *HMC, Montagu*, p. 174; Basil Duke Henning (ed.), *The House of Commons, 1660–1690*, 3 vols (London, 1983), I, 199, and II, 398–9.

53. West Yorkshire Archives Service, MX/R/18/124, Sir Thomas Fairfax to Sir John Reresby, 16 January 1681/2; ibid., MX/R/20/14, same to the same, 8 April 1682.

54. K. H. D. Haley, *The First Earl of Shaftesbury* (Oxford, 1968), ch. 28.

55. *HMC, Ormonde*, NS VI, 193.

56. See, for example, Harris, *London Crowds*, pp. 20–1, 71–2, 194; Anthony Fletcher, 'The Enforcement of the Conventicle Acts, 1664–1679', in W. J. Sheils (ed.), *Studies in Church History: XXI, Persecution and Toleration* (Oxford, 1984), pp. 235–46.

57. Library of Congress, MS 18,124, VII, fol. 304.

58. L'Estrange, *Observator*, I, 'To the Reader'.

59. Harris, *London Crowds*, ch. 6; Harth, *Pen for a Party*, *passim* (esp. pp. 78–80, 159–61); Knights, *Politics and Opinion*, pp. 166–8.

60. Leona Rostenburg, 'Nathaniel Thompson, Catholic Printer and Publisher of the Restoration', *The Library*, 5th series, X (1955), 186–202; J. B. Williams, 'Nathaniel Thompson and the "Popish Plot"', *The Month*, CXXXVIII (1921), 31–7. More generally, see Harth, *Pen for a Party*, pp. 270–1.

61. BL, Add. MSS 32,518, fols 144–52.

62. Harris, *London Crowds*, p. 132; Knight, *Politics and Opinion*, pp. 164–5, 316–25; Violet Jordan (ed.), *Sir Roger L'Estrange: Selections from the Observator (1681–1687)* (Augustan Reprint Society, no. 141, 1970), intro, p. 1; G. Kitchin, *Sir Roger L'Estrange: A Contribution to the History of the Press in the Seventeenth Century* (London, 1913).

63. Thomas O'Malley, 'Religion and the Newspaper Press, 1660–1685: A Study of the *London Gazette*', in Michael Harris and Alan Lee (eds), *The Press in English Society from the Seventeenth to the Nineteenth Centuries* (London, 1986), pp. 25–46.
64. All Souls Library, Oxford, MS 257, no. 96.
65. Harth, *Pen for a Party*, pp. 224–8.
66. Harris, *London Crowds*, ch. 6; Tim Harris, ' "Lives, Liberties and Estates": Rhetorics of Liberty in the Reign of Charles II', in Harris et al. (eds), *Politics of Religion*, pp. 231–6; Harris, *Politics under the Later Stuarts*, pp. 96–100; Tim Harris, 'Tories and the Rule of Law in the Reign of Charles II', *The Seventeenth Century*, VIII (1993), 9–27.
67. L'Estrange, *Observator*, I, 'To the Reader'.
68. Ibid., I, no. 470, 9 January 1683[/4].
69. Ibid.
70. Freist, *Governed by Opinion*, pp. 248–52.
71. Nathaniel Thompson, *A Collection of Eighty-Six Loyal Poems* (London, 1685), pp. 8, 31, 82, 223.
72. Ibid., pp. 27–9.
73. *Strange and Wonderful News from Southwark* (London, 1684); *The Sodomite; Or, the Venison Doctor, With his Brace of Aldermen-Stages* [London, 1684]. Narcissus Luttrell, *A Brief Historical Relation of the State of Affairs from September, 1678, to April, 1714*, 6 vols (Oxford, 1857), I, 248, states that the charge of sodomy against Oates was shown by the Recorder of London in January 1683 to be false and malicious.
74. *Loyal Protestant Intelligence*, no. 56, 17 September 1681.
75. Ibid., no. 52, 3 September 1681; ibid., no. 130, 18 March 1681[/2]; ibid., no. 210, 21 September 1682. For the politics of sexual slander, see: Ann Hughes, 'Gender and Politics in Leveller Literature', in Amussen and Kishlanksy (eds), *Culture of Politics*, pp. 162–88; David Underdown, *Fire from Heaven: Life in an English Town in the Seventeenth Century* (1992), p. 28; Laura Gowring, *Domestic Dangers: Women, Words and Sex in Early Modern London* (Oxford, 1996); Susan Wiseman, ' "Adam, the Father of All Flesh": Porno-Political Rhetoric and Political Theory in and after the English Civil War', *Prose Studies*, XIV (1991) and in J. Holstun (ed.), *Pamphlet Wars: Prose in the English Revolution* (London, 1992), pp. 134–57.
76. *Loyal Protestant Intelligence*, no. 54, 10 September 1682.
77. L'Estrange, *Observator*, III, no. 206, 4 September 1686.
78. Ibid., III, no. 151, 6 March 1685/6.
79. Ibid., no. 153, 10 March 1685/6.
80. Ibid., no. 206, 4 September 1686.
81. Ibid., no. 153, 10 March 1685/6.
82. Ibid., no. 202, 21 August 1686.
83. Ibid., no. 151, 6 March 1685/6.
84. Ibid., no. 153, 10 March 1685/6.
85. Ibid., no. 207, 8 September 1686.
86. Ibid., no. 203, 25 August 1686.
87. Ibid., no. 206, 4 September 1686.
88. *London Gazette*, nos 1455–1465, 27–30 October 1679 to 1–4 December 1679 (quotes from nos 1461 and 1465).

89. *A Narrative of the Reception of their Royal Highnesses at their Arrival in Edinburgh* [Edinburgh, London and Dublin, 1680]; Robert Wodrow, *History of the Sufferings of the Church of Scotland, From the Restoration to the Revolution*, 2 vols (Edinburgh, 1721–2), II, 153.

90. Wodrow, *Sufferings*, II, 219; *HMC, Dartmouth*, I, 56; *London Gazette*, no. 1623, 6–9 June 1681, no. 1661, 17–20 October 1681; *Historical Selections from the Manuscripts of Sir John Lauder of Fountainhall, One of the Senators of the College of Justice. Volume First, Historical Observations, 1680–1686* (Edinburgh, 1837), pp. 40, 49–51; Luttrell, *Brief Historical Relation*, I, 94, 138; Marguerite Wood and Helen Armet, *Extracts from the Records of the Borough of Edinburgh 1681 to 1689* (Edinburgh: Scottish Record Society, 1954), pp. 15–16; *Loyal Protestant Intelligence*, no. 69, 27 October 1681.

91. *London Gazette*, no. 1703, 13–16 March 1681[/2]; Luttrell, *Brief Historical Relation*, I, 171; *CSPD, 1682*, pp. 119, 124; *True Protestant Mercury*, no. 125, 15–18 March 1681[/2].

92. *Loyal Protestant Intelligence*, no. 140, 11 April 1682; ibid., no. 142, 15 April 1682; *Impartial Protestant Mercury*, no. 101, 7–11 April 1682; L'Estrange, *Observator*, I, no. 122, 12 April 1682; *London Mercury*, no. 2, 10 April 1682; *London Gazette*, no. 1710, 6–10 April 1682; Library of Congress, MS 18,124, VIII, fols 40, 63; Bodl., MS Carte 216, fol. 29; Bodl., MS Carte 232, fol. 99; *HMC, 7th Report*, p. 479.

93. Library of Congress, MS 18,124, VIII, fol. 27.

94. Ibid., fol. 63; *Loyal Protestant Intelligence*, no. 145, 22 April 1682; ibid., no. 161, 30 May 1682; *Impartial Protestant Mercury*, no. 104, 18–21 April 1682; ibid., no. 105, 21–25 April 1682; *True Protestant Mercury*, no. 135, 19–22 April 1682; ibid., and no. 147, 31 May–2 June 1682; *Heraclitus Ridens*, no. 70, 30 May 1682.

95. *Protestant (Domestick) Intelligence*, no. 86, 7 January 1680/1; Clifton, *Last Popular Rebellion*, pp. 127, 136.

96. O'Malley, 'Religion and the Newspaper Press', p. 39; Keith Thomas, *Religion and the Decline of Magic: Studies in Popular Beliefs in Sixteenth- and Seventeeth-Century England* (Harmondsworth, 1973), p. 228; Keith Feiling, *A History of the Tory Party, 1640–1714* (Oxford, 1924), p. 198.

97. Luttrell, *Brief Historical Relation*, I, 70.

98. Ibid., p. 130.

99. *Impartial Protestant Mercury*, no. 101, 7–11 April 1682.

100. *CSPD, July–September 1683*, pp. 352–3. See also Hampshire RO, W/B1/6, fols 153–5.

101. *CSPD, 1682*, p. 165; *Loyal Protestant Intelligence*, no. 143, 18 April 1682; ibid., no. 159, 25 May 1682; *True Protestant Mercury*, no. 142, 13–17 May 1682.

102. *Loyal Protestant Intelligence*, no. 30, 18 June 1681; ibid., no. 162, 1 June 1682; ibid., and no. 165, 8 June 1682; *Domestick Intelligence; Or, News both from City and Country Impartially Related*, no. 108, 1–5 June 1682; L'Estrange, *Observator*, I, no. 151, 8 June 1682; *True Protestant Mercury*, no. 147, 31 May – 2 June 1682; Library of Congress, MS 18,124, VIII, fol. 63; Luttrell, *Brief Historical Relation*, I, 92, 193; *CSPD, January–June 1683*, pp. 286–7; *A Further Account from Severall Letters of the Continuation of the Cruel Persecution*

of the People Called Quakers in Bristol (London, 1682), p. 3; Sir John Reresby, *Memoirs*, ed. Andrew Browning (Glasgow, 1936; 2nd edn, with a new preface and notes by Mary K. Geiter and W. A. Speck, London, 1991), p. 303.

103. Harris, *London Crowds*, pp. 169, 180.
104. Knights, *Politics and Opinion*, pp. 329–45; Harth, *Pen for a Party*, pp. 80–4, 149–53, 213–14.
105. Tim Harris, 'The Parties and the People: the Press, the Crowd and Politics "Out-of-Doors" in Restoration England', in Lionel Glassey (ed.), *The Reigns of Charles II and James VII and II* (Basingstoke, 1997), pp. 143–5; Harris, *London Crowds*, esp. chs 6 and 7; Knights, *Politics and Opinion*, ch. 10.
106. L'Estrange, *Observator*, I, no. 151, 8 June 1682.
107. Library of Congress, MS 18,124, VII, fol. 220; ibid., VIII, fol. 220; *Loyal Protestant Intelligence*, no. 43, 2 August 1681.
108. Library of Congress, MS 18,124, VIII, fol. 27.
109. Harris, *London Crowds*, p. 179.
110. *HMC, Ormonde*, NS VI, 62.
111. Huntington Library, HA 14570, [Earl of Conway] to Sir George Rawdon, Windsor, 6 May 1682; National Library of Ireland, MS 11,960, pp. 85–223.
112. *HMC, Ormonde*, NS VI, 335–6.
113. Slaughter, *Ideology and Politics*, p. xxxiii; J. R. Jones, *Charles II: Royal Politician* (London, 1987), ch. 8.
114. Jonathan Scott, *Algernon Sidney and the Restoration Crisis, 1677–1683* (Cambridge, 1991), pp. 47–8.
115. Harris, 'The Parties and the People', pp. 146–7.
116. John Northleigh, *The Triumph of our Monarchy Over the Plots and Principles of Our Rebels and Republicans* (London, 1685), p. 393; *Loyal Protestant Intelligence*, no. 19, 10 May 1681; *The Misleading of the Common People by False Notions Hitherto, Brought to Light* (London, 1685), pp. 7, 25.
117. Harris, 'British Dimension', pp. 148–9.
118. R. G. Pickavance, 'The English Boroughs and the King's Government: a Study of the Tory Reaction, 1681–85', University of Oxford DPhil thesis (1976); Robert J. Sinner, 'Charles II and Local Government: The *Quo Warranto* Proceedings, 1681–1685', Rutgers University PhD thesis (1976); Paul D. Halliday, *Dismembering the Body Politic: Partisan Politics in England's Towns, 1650–1730* (Cambridge, 1998), ch. 6.
119. Crist, 'Francis Smith', ch. 6; Sutherland, *Restoration Newspaper*, pp. 19–21.
120. PRO, PC2/69, p. 566; *London Gazette*, no. 1772; Steele, *Royal Proclamations*, I, no. 3734; Harris, *London Crowds*, pp. 186–7.
121. *Current Intelligence*, no. 68, 13–17 December 1681; Luttrell, *Brief Historical Relation*, I, 152; Tim Harris, 'Was the Tory Reaction Popular? Attitudes of Londoners towards the Persecution of Dissent, 1681–6', *London Journal*, XIII (1988), 106–20; Mark Goldie, 'The Hilton Gang and the Purge of London in the 1680s', in Howard Nenner (ed.), *Politics and the Political Imagination in Later Stuart Britain: Essays Presented to Lois Green Schwoerer* (Rochester, NY, 1997), pp. 43–73.
122. See, for example: Huntington Library, STT 1514, John Nicholls to Sir Richard Temple, 1 August 1684 (Yarmouth); Huntington Library, HA 3974, John Gery to the Earl of Huntingdon, 29 December 1684 (Leicester);

Library of Congress, MS 18,124, IX, fols 93, 133 (Dover and Colchester); *London Gazette*, no. 2010, 19–23 February 1684/5 (Newcastle upon Tyne); ibid., no. 2015, 9–12 March 1684/5 (Chester); ibid., no. 2017, 16–19 March 1684/5 (Heddon); ibid., no. 2025, 13–16 April 1685 (East Retford); ibid., no. 2029, 27–30 April 1685 (Doncaster); ibid., no. 2060, 13–17 August 1685 (York). This list is far from exhaustive.

123. *CSPD, July–September 1683*, p. 398. For the bonfires, see: Luttrell, *Brief Historical Relation*, I, 279, Library of Congress, MS 18,124, VIII, fol. 385; *CSPD, July–September 1683*, pp. 395; Berkshire RO, R/AC1/1/16/19; Wood, *Life and Times*, III, 72; L'Estrange, *Observator*, I, no. 406, 19 September 1683; Harth, *Pen for a Party*, pp. 213–14.

124. Henning (ed.), *House of Commons*, I, 47, 66; W. A. Speck, *Reluctant Revolutionaries: Englishmen and the Revolution of 1688* (Oxford, 1988), pp. 44–6; Harris, *Politics under the Later Stuarts*, pp. 120–1. The addresses can be traced in the *London Gazette*.

125. West Yorkshire Archive Service, MX/R/41/23; BL Add. MSS, 41,804, fol. 11; Huntington Library, HA 7747, Gervase Jaquis to the Earl of Huntingdon, 11 July 1685; ibid., HA 7749, same to same, 18 July, 1685; ibid., HA 7552, same to same, 28 July 1685.

126. The term comes from Keith Lindley, *Popular Politics and Religion in Civil War London* (Aldershot, 1997), ch. 2.

127. Pincus, 'Coffeehouses', pp. 808, 811.

128. Harris, 'Understanding Popular Politics'.

129. Jürgen Habermas, *The Structural Transformation of the Public Sphere*, trans. Thomas Burger and Frederick Lawrence (Cambridge, Mass., 1989); Freist, *Governed By Opinion*, esp. pp. 19, 21.

130. The phrase is Geoffrey Elton's. See his *Policy and Police: The Enforcement of the Reformation in the Age of Thomas Cromwell* (Cambridge, 1972).

131. *London Gazette*, no. 2012, 26 February–2 March 1684/5.

132. Harris, *London Crowds*, pp. 136–9.

133. L'Estrange, *Observator*, III, no. 206, 4 September 1686.

134. This case is argued at greater length in my forthcoming study, *British Revolutions*, to be published by Penguin.

8

CROWDS AND POLITICAL FESTIVAL IN GEORGIAN ENGLAND

Nicholas Rogers

One of the major problems confronting historians of eighteenth-century politics is how one might reduce the myriad popular interventions of the era to some intelligible order and offer some generalizations about the cumulative presence of the crowd and its relationship to the prevailing power structure. The problem has been compounded by the unwilling-ness of some historians to discuss popular politics prior to 1760, when it becomes possible to annex riot and protest to a more conventional historiography. But it has been also complicated by the pioneering strat-egies for recovering the crowd in history, which tended, at least in the English context, to focus principally upon the most dramatic riots of the period and to derive their meaning from an analysis of the most visible participants and their victims in the records of the courts and state papers. The result was an episodic history of disturbance, diachron-ically arranged, privileging successive political crises and the repressive activities of the authorities. Within this confrontational mode, less atten-tion was paid to the underlying conventions within which popular politics was conducted and to what Sean Wilentz has called 'those dramas of political expression – sometimes contrived, sometimes spontaneous – that reflect and help determine the boundaries of power'.[1]

Within the last two decades this imbalance has been corrected. French historians, in particular, have become increasingly attentive to the ways in which the popular political terrain was shaped and transformed both from above and below. This is especially true of the French revolutionary era when the legitimation of the new regime was pursued in a remarkably self-conscious and explicit manner, to the point of creating a radically new style of politics with its own calendar, ceremonies, space and symbolic

233

modes of expression.[2] The importance of such themes, conventionally consigned to the status of illustrative detail in orthodox political narratives, has been developed in other contexts. Historians have noted the cultural affinities of riot and ceremony in the pre-democratic era, the ways in which festivals provided both a focus and definition of revolt as well as a plausible source of social integration and ruling-class hegemony. They have also become more sensitive to what Charles Tilly has termed the 'repertoires of collective action',[3] the stock of customary practices, traditions and expectations that shaped and sometimes transformed popular interventions and underscored the ambiguous reciprocity between rulers and ruled. It is within this context that I wish to map out the prevailing conventions of street politics within which crowd actions may be situated. What I hope to show is that crowd action was conventionally located within a theatre of politics that was homologous to that of a 'public' summoned to witness punishments or to hear royal edicts within the market-place. Within this framework crowds were seen as rough markers of community sentiment, the pulse of a populace whose passions had to be measured, marshalled, courted and contained. Over the course of the long eighteenth century the structural reciprocity between crowd and authority was disrupted by three interlocking developments. First, the political calendar around which crowd action had centred became more ramified and complex. Second, the leading citizens of market towns and cities became increasingly intolerant of the rough antics of the crowd and more interested in fashioning political festival into a decorous event worthy of their town's social esteem. This involved strategies to immobilize crowds and render them more domesticated and docile. Third, taking their cue from bourgeois radicals, plebeian subjects developed new forms of popular politics that broke with the parodic conventions of crowd action and advanced more democratic notions of citizenship. By 1820, the shift from the demotic politics of the eighteenth century to the democratic politics of the radical mass platform was more or less complete.

I

I shall begin with two prints. In 1714 the *Flying Post* described in some detail a recent satire of Robert Harley, the Tory minister ousted at the Hanoverian succession and widely suspected of conspiring to bring in the rival House of Stuart. The fallen minister's coat of arms included 'an Earl's coronet, filled with French fleur-de-luces, tipt with French gold, the Pretender's head in the middle' and 'three toads in a black field' which 'being in reverse' denoted 'treason in perfection'. His supporters included 'a French Popist priest in his habit, with a warming pan upon his shoulder, and a pen-knife in his left hand, ready to execute what the Popish religion dictates upon Protestants'. On his other side was a Scottish Highlander, 'a pack upon his back, and a letter in his hand, betraying the kingdom's safety'.[4] Nearly 50 years later the *Butiad*, a collection of prints satirizing the king's Scottish favourite, Lord Bute, included one entitled 'The Roasted Exciseman' in which a horned plaid effigy with bags of money dangling from his side was swinging from the gallows while a crowd busied itself with the burning of a huge Jack Boot and several newspapers, fuelling the fire with a barrel of excised cider.[5]

Both prints might be regarded simply as jocular representations of the misfortunes of great ministers. In fact they recalled demonstrations that had actually taken place. Anti-Catholic processions vilifying Tory leaders and featuring effigies of the Pope, devil and Pretender had been staged in several towns in the early eighteenth century. In London the devil resembled Harley in the elaborately orchestrated parade financed by the Kit-Kat Club. At Chichester in 1714, the procession featured a live devil who entertained spectators by offering the Pope and Pretender a pair of clogs or 'wooden shoes', a well-known emblem of French slavery.[6] Nearly 60 years later, Bute and his unpopular excise tax were publicly execrated in London, Guildford and the west country. In Guildford, Bute's effigy was carried through the town backwards on horseback with a cider cask before it and 'treated with great severity by the populace'. At Hereford a plaid effigy of Lord Bute was exposed in the pillory, then launched on a gibbet and finally burnt 'amidst a general Huzza'.[7] At Exeter, on the thanksgiving of the Peace of Paris, inhabitants hung apples covered in crepe before their doors and dressed neighbouring orchards in mourning. Despite the warning of the mayor that he would not tolerate sedition in the streets, a plaid figure with a huge Jack Boot was carried through the town accompanied by thousands of people and hung on the city gates. It was followed by a cider hogshead with a pall over it, on which there were a number of escutcheons bearing the inscription 'From the Excise and the devil, good Lord deliver us'. Later that evening the effigy was burnt at the bonfire.[8] Both the prints and the demonstrations they commemorated underscored the continuing importance of ritual and ceremony in popular vilification.

The derivations of these political rites are not difficult to locate. At the most obvious level they recalled the rituals of public punishment: the whipping at the cart's tail; the judicial terror of the gallows; the grisly executions of traitors whose entrails were ripped from their bodies and consumed in fire. Before punishments became secretive, bureaucratic and panoptic, the state consistently invoked popular support for its judicial decisions. In certain contexts, the public stocks being the most explicit, it explicitly invited popular retribution as an integral part of the punitive process, privileging the assembled crowd as the conscience of the community. It was entirely predictable that these rituals would be adapted to popular demonstrations which sought to underscore community disapproval of political personalities or policies.

But public punishments were only part of the repertoire upon which crowds could draw for their political interventions. The dense fabric of urban ceremonial was also readily exploited. Although the great religious processions that characterized urban life in the medieval era had largely disappeared with the Reformation, the urban renaissance of the eighteenth century enlivened the secular festivals that remained very much part of the town calendar. New prosperity brought a broad revival of urban ceremony: civic inaugurations and perambulations, charity school processions, electoral parades, as well as special events such as the Godiva festival in Coventry and the Whitsun Bower in Lichfield. Predictably, these provided a potential repertoire for collective action.[9] So, too, did the seasonal revels of Christmas, Shrovetide and the annual fairs, when young men swarmed the streets in various disguises, banging pots and pans, begging for alms, scaling cocks, parodying local worthies and reprimanding social deviants.[10] 'Nothing can scarce be more troublesome than the Custom that prentices, journeymen &c have here of going about to beg offerings the Day after Christmas Day of all Trades and Professions', wrote William Arderon of Norwich, not to mention the 'Kitwitches', the cross-dressed men who begged for money from door to door on Plough Monday, 'dancing along with a fiddler'.[11] In his opinion, such misplaced energy could better be spent elsewhere, especially since the plebeian demand for festive perquisites meant that 'Two hundred pounds & upwards' was regularly 'fool'd away' to provide 'the poorest' with 'a pocketful of Money & a bellyfull of Liquor'.

Such 'silly antient' customs, as Arderon called them, often informed more political festivals. Mobs demanded money, beer and victuals on nights of jubilation in much the same way that they might on Plough Monday or Boxing Day. And they sometimes paraded the streets in festive attire to the raucous serenade of fiddles, hurdy-gurdies, pots, pans and marrow cleavers in a manner reminiscent of a springtime carnival or a Christmas mumming. May Day celebrations, too, were appropriated for political purposes. At the thanksgiving for the Peace of Utrecht in May 1713, for example, May Day pageantry was especially evident. At Basingstoke the mayoral procession was preceded by the young maids of the town carrying 'several fine garlands, one of them distinguished by a Crown and all of them set off with Flowers, Ribbons and Little Flags'.[12] At Alton in Hampshire, a maypole was erected 'having PAX for its Motto in Golden Letters, and a Crown Imperial at the Top'.[13] In woollen towns and villages the celebrations took the form of a Bishop Blaize parade, a festival customarily held on 3 February but easily adaptable to other contexts. At Peterborough the master wool-combers

> handsomely clad and adorn'd with a pretty variety of colour'd Wool, Hats Cockaded and Laurel Leaves in them, led up a very great Number of Journeymen in their Holland Shirts and white wands tufted, with Sashes and Scarves of combed Wool. The Person representing Bishop Blaze, the Founder of the Manufacture, was distinguished from all the rest . . . his Cap was made of Wool in Imitation of a Mitre; his Habit of the same, trailing and supported by Two Youths in their Holland Shirts.

The procession was 'so very particular', the correspondent noted, 'that they paraded the Town several times to the great satisfaction of all spectators'.[14]

Political demonstrations thus drew on a rich variety of public rites, legal, civic and seasonal, to transmit their message. Those that commemorated Utrecht were clearly celebratory: they expressed the joys of peace; the prospect of renewed prosperity after an exhausting war; the hopes of renewal. But in other contexts political rituals could be parodic, if not oppositional. Anti-Catholic processions, for example, were frequently droll and derisive. They featured the mock paraphernalia of popery and sometimes even a warming-pan, a signifier which underlined the spurious pedigree of the Stuarts. In the festive convention of misrule, fools performed mock ceremonies and sprinkled holy water on spectators. Few demonstrations were as elaborately orchestrated as these, but even the more spontaneous were often suffused with the folk rites of popular retribution: raucous serenades, rough music, skimmingtons, with participants blacking their faces, turning their coats inside out, or wearing women's clothing. In divided communities such rituals could easily become counter-processionals. At Frome, where the pro-Hanoverian gentlemen, clothiers and weavers staged a triumphant procession on coronation day in 1714, the disaffected paraded a fool whose turnip-tipped stick mimicked the white wands of authority and the dubious regality of the German Elector. Crowds even shouted out 'here's our George, where's yours?'[15] On a more sombre note, the anti-excise protest in Exeter was also tellingly juxtaposed to the official commemoration of the peace treaty of 1763.[16] It was led by a mock champion on an ass, followed by 40 men holding white wands with black-creped apples stuck on top. Staged on the public thanksgiving, it was a clear counterpoint to the official festivities and a pointed critique of the government's foreign and fiscal policies, transgressing official time, official space, competing with the mayoral process to the cathedral and placing a pall on officially-sanctioned merriment.

II

Popular interventions in street politics, then, were often embedded in the ceremonial and festive life of the nation, and the distinction sometimes made between the riotous crowd and that assembled on 'purely ceremonial occasions' becomes harder to make.[17] Disturbances frequently grew out of those occasions and appropriated their rituals. The point is reinforced when one considers another crucial aspect of eighteenth-century street politics, its calendrical regularity. Although some demonstrations were clearly occasioned by momentous events in national politics – a trial, a bill, an electoral and naval victory – many were synchronized to a familiar and predictable set of anniversaries and thanksgivings. The politicization of the calendar was not new. It grew out of the nation's confrontations with the Catholic powers of Europe during the sixteenth century and the internal struggles that so beset the seventeenth. By 1700 state services were held to commemorate the accession of the reigning monarch, the martyrdom of Charles I (30 January), the restoration of monarchy in 1660 (29 May) and the discovery of the Gunpowder Plot and William's landing at Torbay in 1688 (5 November), England's double deliverance from Popery.[18] These occasions were celebrated with bells, sermons, and for those joyous anniversaries at least, festivity and good cheer. They were not the only ones to be so. Until 1730, and in some parishes even later, Queen Elizabeth's accession day (17 November) was celebrated as a symbol of Britain's Protestant destiny.[19] The same was true of William III's birthday (4 November), an anniversary that recalled Britain's libertarian credentials and her rise to first-class European status. Accompanying these was a more varied list of anniversaries celebrating the coronation and birthdays of the royal family.

Officially these anniversaries gave legitimacy to the political order. They aspired to transmit Britain's Protestant and libertarian heritage to the broadest possible audience, to edify people about their rights and responsibilities. By custom and design they also afforded opportunities for ruling-class liberality and display, assuming many of the functions associated with royal progresses and civic processions and echoing the self-conscious paternalism that accompanied patrician homecomings, marriages and birthdays. Local patrons and civic dignitaries regularly contributed to the merriment of political celebrations, donating wine and beer to the public at large and perhaps even a roasted ox to commemorate a special event. There was thus a double articulation to political festival: an effort to recreate and consolidate both political and social loyalties through the transmission of ideology and munificence.

In practice these twin aims proved difficult to effect during the eighteenth century, not least because the craft and corporate solidarities which underpinned the old ceremonial order were perceptibly dissolving. In an age of manufacture in which master–servant relations were in decline, the lower sort retained considerable control over their labour and leisure, disowning the traditional forms of dependency upon which class mutualities had been based. As Defoe recognized in 1724, the independence of the labourer had substantially weakened social deference, producing a refractory workforce tetchily defensive of its customary rights and perquisites;[20] not least of which were the festive doles of public anniversaries. The result was that political festivals became important sites for plebeian licence and self-assertion in which festive largesse was demanded rather than acknowledged, testing the credibility of benefactors rather than sanctifying their generosity. As early as 1706 a London freeman wrote to the Lord Mayor urging him to reconsider the policy of ordering illuminations on public festivals. 'It gives ye Rude Rabble', he averred,

> Liberty to Doe what they list... they Breake windows with stones, fire Gunns with Pease in our Houses to ye Hazard of Peoples life or Limbs because they doe not comply to thare Humours and abusing People in ye Streets yt will not give money to the Bonfire as they call it, which is a very Bad fire and of dangerous consequence all soe mutch swearing, cursing and Blasphemy is occasioned thare by.[21]

Thirty years later the citizens of Cheapside were still complaining of the 'great Riots and Disturbances that frequently happened in that

Neighbourhood occasion'd by making a Bonefire ... on Rejoycing Nights, which caused such number of loose and disorderly persons to assemble together that the Inhabitants ... were in danger of their lives'.[22] Within a generation similar complaints were registered in many provincial towns.

In many respects this behaviour was reminiscent of the traditional rites of misrule, those rituals of inversion, playful, parodic and sometimes menacing, that marked the religious festivals of centuries past and still informed the Shrovetide and May Day revels. But they now took place in a different class context, one that not only afforded the plebs greater cultural space but deepened their political consciousness. This was a development that the ruling classes themselves had helped to engender. Since the 1640s, when John Pym and his allies had first mobilized the London apprentices against the Laudian regime, politicians had become increasingly sensitive to the plebeian presence and attuned their propaganda accordingly. This was very evident in the elaborately staged pope-burning processions of the Shaftesbury Whigs, who sought to mobilize opinion against the Duke of York by invoking the festive rites of popular anti-Catholicism. It was also evident in the anti-Rumpolian revels of their opponents, which recalled the popular protests that had so definitively discredited the Protectorate in its final months of power.[23] As Tim Harris has argued in this volume, the later Stuarts were very aware of the need to create and court a 'public' for their policies.

Two developments in the eighteenth century changed the tempo of street politics. First, the unparalleled frequency of general elections in the years 1694–1716 broadened the geographical range of political contention as well as sustaining popular interest in national politics on a more regular basis. Secondly, the political calendar itself became denser as the dynastic struggle once more absorbed British politics. By the Hanoverian accession, no less than 13 royal and state anniversaries were regularly observed in the parishes of the leading towns and cities, leaving only July, September and December free from commemorative events. The year began with the solemn observance of Charles I's martyrdom, to be followed by three anniversaries celebrating Queen's Anne's birthday, accession and coronation, still observed in some London parishes as late as 1730. May brought George I's birthday and the state-endorsed commemoration of the Restoration; June the unofficial and potentially explosive celebration of the Pretender's birthday. Then there was a brief hiatus until 1 August, the Hanoverian accession, and a further crop of Hanoverian and Protestant-cum-libertarian holidays in October and November.

In this busy calendar Whigs and Tories competed for public space, mobilizing the vocabulary of celebration to their own advantage. Generally speaking, the spring anniversaries privileged the Tories; the autumnal, the Whigs. But every anniversary was potentially susceptible to crossed meanings: to muffled bells, lacklustre bonfires, ambiguous toasts, contentious processions and controversial oaths. The Highgate cobbler who dressed in mourning on George I's birthday (28 May) and donned his finery to celebrate the Restoration knew precisely the message he was transmitting; to emphasize the point he 'insulted several Gentlemen and Ladies', demanded 'money for a bonfire', and even 'Liquor to drink to the Damnation of Whigs and Dissenters'. So, too, did the Shoreditch housekeeper who ridiculed rather than reverenced the same Tory high holiday by placing an owl in an oak-leaved egg-basket over his door together with a crucifix and a pair of wooden shoes.[24] Both understood the script of political commemoration and defamation.

In the decade following the trial of Dr Sacheverell in 1710, the calendar of politics often escalated into a veritable calendar of riot. 'The day begins with a Thanksgiving', mourned Addison, 'and ends with a riot. Instead of the voice of mutual joy and gladness, there is nothing heard in our streets but opprobrious language, ribaldry and contention'.[25] Confronted with a formidable backlash to the trial of the intrepid Sacheverell, Whig clubs took to the streets of London, financing a series of pope-burning processions on the Queen's birthday and taunting their opponents with Jacobite sympathies. Tories replied by celebrating the expiry of Sacheverell's sentence in 1713, sometimes deliberately fuelling Whig fears of a contested succession by playing the Jacobite tune 'Let the King enjoy his own again'.[26] They also upstaged the Whigs in their joyous celebration of the Peace of Utrecht and gave Marlborough a hostile reception upon his return to London.

This exchange set the scene for the turbulent confrontations of the Hanoverian accession. Over 20 riots occurred on George I's coronation, many in response to the overly-zealous festivities of Whig-dominated corporations.[27] By the following spring, in the wake of the trials of the Tory ex-ministers, the country was beset with a second Sacheverellite fury. Throughout the west midlands Tory mobs inflicted a swath of destruction upon dissenting chapels, while in London Burgess's meeting-house in Blackfriars was burnt to the ground. Here, as elsewhere, anniversaries were punctuated with riot and sedition: the burning of Whig effigies; mock-proclamations of the Pretender; Jacobite revels around the bonfire; denunciations of the king and his Whig allies; toasts to Ormonde; and the constant patter of seditious verse and balladry that taunted the government well into the 1720s. James Montagu complained to the grand jury of Dorset that the country buzzed with the 'most daring and insulting Behaviour, both in Words and Actions, perhaps that ever was heard of, towards our Great and Good King'; especially, he averred, 'amongst the ignorant and meanest of the People'.[28]

This theatre of politics, with its oaths, riddles, rhymes and ribald balladry, proved remarkably difficult to control. One reason for this lay in the relative weakness of the civil power, which was heavily reliant upon magisterial support and prosecutory zeal to bring offenders to justice. Despite the purge of the bench after 1714, many local Tory leaders were quite prepared to connive at disorder and sometimes actively incited violence through inflammatory sermons or a visible disrespect for official anniversaries. This was particularly the case in the Tory heartland of the west, where one encounters mayors, aldermen and clergymen publicly abetting anti-Whig protests. Equally important was the local, and often evanescent character of popular protest, one that drew on community support and eluded legal prosecution. Heavy-handed tactics, such as the military occupation of disaffected towns, proved largely counter-productive; in Bridgwater, for example, billeting simply fuelled resentment against the government. So, too, did the local experiments in policing carried out by Whig mughouses in London and Norwich. They precipitated more street confrontations than they suppressed, and because their recriminatory tactics enjoyed unofficial government support, they simply amplified popular scepticism about the Whig rule of law.[29]

Confronted with this sea of sedition, the Whig government fortified its powers to contain popular disturbance. It curbed electoral politics and strengthened magisterial powers against riot, although not as successfully as it might have wished. Conscious that local juries might view Tory sedition leniently, it moved an increasing number of troublesome cases to King's Bench. Among other things, *ex officio* informations broke the resolve of many Tory-Jacobite printers, and even forced some into exile. Yet despite these sanctions, little could be done to eliminate political contention from the calendar, especially when the Hanoverian and Stuart anniversaries of 28/29 May and 10/11 June were so unfortunately juxtaposed. It was only as the dynastic struggle waned that the calendar came to reflect the political dispositions of the Whig order: in the south-east by the mid-1720s, in the more intransigently Tory areas of the country rather later. Before that, the authorities had to tolerate nostalgic Tories bedecking their doors with rue and thyme on George I's birthday and sporting oak leaves on the Restoration; or perhaps toasting the king, even whistling ''Til the King shall enjoy his own again' as the memorable 10th was about to pass to George II's accession (11 June). The Whigs were more tolerant of such indiscretions as their confidence increased, although even after the '45 rebellion, flagrant exhibitions of Jacobitism could still unsettle their equanimity, as the Walsall riot of 1750 so forcefully revealed.[30]

III

The decline of Jacobitism took much of the sedition out of state anniversaries, for after 1750 dynastic and party partisanship were no longer intertwined. It did not eliminate political contention from the official or semi-official calendar. London radicals celebrated the birthday of William III to reaffirm their support for triennial parliaments in an age when electoral contests become increasingly infrequent. They appropriated the victory over the Jacobite clans at Culloden to bait Bute and the Court.[31] Some were so disparaging about officially endorsed Stuart anniversaries that they refused to celebrate them altogether or used the occasion to denigrate the 'King's Friends'.[32] John Wilkes even declared that the British should not observe the 'martyrdom' of Charles I every 30 January, but commemorate the day as a 'festival, as a day of triumph'.[33] In fact, crypto-republicans like Sylas Neville continued to celebrate the day with a calf's-head dinner and toasts to 'The Majesty of the People'.[34] In the 1770s such commemorations were fairly discreet, but by the early nineteenth century they were considered unexceptional, at least when shorn of their republican inflexions. As the *Critical Review* observed of the anniversary of Charles I's execution,

> One regards it as a solemn fast, instituted on the martyrdom of a kingly saint, and repairs to church with due gravity; another regards it as an anniversary of death of a royal traitor, who aspired to govern without law, and celebrates the day by dining off a calf's head, with an orange in his mouth: and drinking to the memory of king William, the Patriots of 1688, and the Principles of the Revolution.[35]

The tone of the *Review* suggests that 30 January no longer had quite the political charge it once possessed, even if it remained a contentious occasion. The same was largely true of other official anniversaries. After the accession of George III, the first genuinely British monarch in the

Hanoverian line, Restoration day survived principally as Oak Apple Day, a depoliticized junket, although ultra-loyalists would continue to reverence the anniversary.[36] Similarly, 4 November, King William's day, lost its significance as a national festival, at least outside of Ireland.[37] In the aftermath of the centenary of 1688 and the rapid advance of democratic politics, 5 November became better known for its youthful revelry and penny guys than for its commemoration of Britain's Protestant and libertarian heritage.[38] Subsequent waves of anti-Catholicism would temporarily revive its old meaning, although radicals would more likely observe the day commemorating the acquital of Thomas Hardy, the Secretary of the London Corresponding Society who was indicted for high treason in 1794.

Royal anniversaries also tended to be celebrated in a fairly perfunctory manner by the late eighteenth century, with the press devoting more time to court fashion than to popular celebration. Nonetheless they, too, could be rejuvenated at opportune moments. Loyalists found them useful in 1792–3 as a buttress against Painite radicalism. Prime anniversaries, such as a 50-year jubilee or a coronation, would inevitably engender a more extensive and carefully choreographed display of royal majesty and employer paternalism, particularly when the language of patriotism was a hotly contested terrain.[39] Such singular events could also include an invitation to local craftsmen to perambulate the town with their respective guilds or companies, or to local villagers to process to town with their 'kings' and 'queens'.[40] But on an annual basis the celebration of royal anniversaries become more formulaic.

What was significant about the political calendar of the late Georgian era was the way in which it became more ramified. Supplementing the official calendar with days of special import was not a novel phenomenon. The Exclusionist Whigs and their Hanoverian successors had done just this with Queen Elizabeth's day in order to promote their Protestant, libertarian pedigree. Yet with the growth of political associations and the increasing autonomy of popular politics, such practices increased. During the 1770s the Wilkites created a new calendar of anniversaries to commemorate their eponymous hero, beginning a trend that would be taken up by the Foxite Whigs and the supporters of Pitt the Younger.[41] By the turn of the century the radicals, too, would have their own anniversaries, celebrating Bastille Day (14 July) before the war with France made it dangerous to do so, and investing 5 November with new meaning by commemorating the acquittal of Thomas Hardy (and subsequently Horne Tooke and John Thelwall) in 1794.[42] After the French Wars the radical calendar quickly expanded to include the birthdays of Thomas

Paine (26 January), Henry Hunt (6 November) and William Cobbett (9 March), as well as Peterloo (16 August).[43] Celebrated at public dinners and open meetings where participants were advised to refrain from mobbish activity, the radical culture represented a significant break from the commemorative politics of the previous century.

Those politics were themselves changing, particularly in terms of the organization of public space. In the early eighteenth century, political anniversaries had been overwhelmingly civic in orientation. Their central feature was the civic procession to the leading church or cathedral, where urban dignitaries would hear a sermon appropriate to the day; to be followed by public toasts at the market-place and a substantial, if sometimes boisterous feast at the town hall for its leading citizens. This basic protocol persisted, but in towns that enjoyed an urban renaissance such activities were embellished in ways that expressed the growing wealth and visibility of the middling classes. Anniversary dinners were increasingly held in large taverns and Assembly Rooms, open to all who could pay the price of a subscription ticket. They were followed by lavish balls for the principal inhabitants and neighbouring gentry. At Liverpool, on the celebration of the Peace of Aix-la-Chapelle in 1749, over 800 ladies and gentlemen thronged the Long Rooms of the General Infirmary at the invitation of the mayor to partake in a ball and 'a plentiful cold Collation set out in a very handsome taste'.[44] Such events were increasingly seen as a testimony to the civility and wealth of the town, a symbol of its social harmony and urbanity.

Balls were not the only indication of the 'civilizing process' that informed urban celebrations. So, too, were firework displays. First staged in London in the seventeenth century, they had spread by the mid-century to the provinces, even to towns as small as Watford, Whitby, Dorking, Holt, Hoddesdon and Daventry, where a rocket unfortunately landed on the thatched roof of the Peacock Inn during the celebrations of the king's birthday and burned it down.[45] None were as spectacular as the fireworks exhibited at Green Park during the peace celebrations of 1749. To a prelude of Handel's Fireworks Music and a deafening cannonade, the Green Park gala featured Catherine wheels, rockets, cascades, fountains, girandoles and tornados. They were fired from a Doric temple bedecked with classical statues and a bas-relief in which the king was represented giving 'PEACE to BRITANNIA' with Liberty, Commerce and Industry in attendance.[46]

Outside the capital, too, spectators could gawk at a fair variety of fireworks on important occasions, adding a pyrotechnic flair to the toasts and libations of the market-place. On accession day, 1749, the Newcastle MP and incumbent mayor, Walter Blackett, put on an elaborate display of fireworks that culminated in devices portraying a 'Crown with GR', to be followed by the fire letters, 'Peace on Earth, Good Will to all Men, God Save King George'.[47] At Canterbury, the festivities accompanying the proclamation of the peace in the same year were rounded off with a firework display that began with 'a Variety of Forms and Colours, from Italian Wheels and Stars'. Then, the *Whitehall Evening Post* reported,

> Britannia and Pallas, supporting a Shield, appeared in a bright yellow Transparency; on each Side, at a little Distance, a Vas[e] in Green, streaming Fire in Imitation of Fountains. The third Scene represented the Obelisk... standing upon the Basis on which the Figures were sitting. On the Top, the Representation of the Sun. And lastly, the Whole was concluded... with a Flight of Twenty-four Sky Rockets, and several Vollies of Reports; which Performance was attended with a Band of Musick playing the whole Time.[48]

Performances like this proved so popular that balls were sometimes deliberately postponed until late in the evening so that the ladies could view the proceedings, albeit from the comparative safety of select stands or balconies.

Firework displays were testimony to the growing investment of time, enterprise and money into political festival.[49] The same was true of transparencies, that is, pictures made with translucent paints on calico, linen or oiled paper and illuminated from behind in the style of stained glass.[50] Increasingly fashionable after 1760 as a form of public art on celebratory occasions, particularly to those who could appreciate their allegories, they demanded a measure of decorous spectatorship that did not square with the boisterous antics of popular festivities. Such decorum was not easily achieved, even with the army or local militia regiments in attendance, as they increasingly were from the Seven Years' War onwards, adding a dash of military pageantry to the proceedings. The upshot was that the commercialization of public festival was also accompanied by calls to curb plebeian exuberance and to render the mob less mobile. 'We permit the Innocent, those whom it is our Duty to protect, to be terrified, insulted, by outrageous Mobs, who seem to have no other Conceptions of Joy than what arise from being wicked and mischievous', complained one London correspondent in 1761. 'As soon as the Tower Guns are fired off... the Populace here consider it as a Signal for every kind of Outrage'.[51] Particularly troublesome was the throwing of squibs and serpents at genteel passers-by and the festive perquisites that the common people demanded of them to drink healths at the local bonfire.[52] It was one thing, middling contemporaries argued, to lay on traditional largesse for the crowd; it was another to have one's own celebrations disrupted by the antics of a festive mob, besmirching a town's reputation for politeness and regularity.

How one handled this predicament varied from place to place, dependent in some measure upon the scale of the festival and the estimated number of participants. Patricians of the old school, especially in smaller towns or villages, remained largely tolerant of the carnivalesque excesses of the crowd. Some were even willing to allow maypoles for the Coronation Day celebrations of 1761, although in villages surrounding the royal forests of Northamptonshire this concession was wilfully abused.[53] Others invoked the traditions of commensality to control festive space. At Fakenham in Norfolk, for example, the principal inhabitants entertained 400 people with roast beef, plum pudding and strong beer on tables erected in the market square before departing to their own dinner and ball.[54]

Such a strategy, of course, proved more difficult in large towns. Here urban dignitaries sometimes gave the labouring classes their moment of theatre by integrating the trades into civic parades or allowing them to close urban processions. More often they hoped that firework spectaculars, free beer and ox-roastings would pacify festive crowds, detract from raucous street revels, or at least restrain their excesses. Such liberality did not satisfy everyone, and from the 1760s onwards there were calls for more sober celebrations and the diversion of festive munificence to more deserving causes; to charity hospitals, for example, or as in Gloucester on the occasion of George III's coronation, to the dowries of young women 'of virtuous Characters'.[55] 'We reproach the Romans with the Barbarity of their public shews', claimed one contributor to the London *Public Advertiser*, 'But is a Rabble let loose to commit the most shocking Violences in the Heart of a City like this an instance of more Refinement?'[56]

The social tensions inherent in urban festival were most sharply articulated in London, and they surfaced most dramatically during the Wilkite agitations of 1768–71. Like Admiral Vernon,[57] the projection of Wilkes as the libertarian hero owed much to the press and to the ramified urban culture with its clubs, societies, convivial dinners and passion for political artefacts that grew apace during the mid-century decades. As the eponym for a political movement that quickly embraced a host of

causes surrounding the liberty of the subject and the accountability of
parliament, Wilkes was an instantly recognizable figure whose mischievous
squint was commemorated in prints, coffee-pots, jugs, spoons, buttons
and 26 different coins and medals.[58] According to John Wesley, no private individual had been so lionized in England in a thousand years.[59]
Taverns were opened in his name, feasts held in his honour, and his
confrontations with authority were waggishly portrayed in prints, joke
books and doggerel. Great play was made on the number 45, which
commemorated Wilkes's initial conflict with the government and became
a metonym of libertarian radicalism and an alternative political order.
Readers were treated to anecdotes concerning the number 45; how a
fiver was offered for the 45th lottery ticket, how a Fleet Street porter
worked only in 45s.[60] And if newspaper accounts are to be believed,
Wilkite dinners were highly organized events, with 45 guests, 45 courses,
45 toasts and so on. Thus a landlord of the Ben Jonson pub at Cow
Cross, London, was reported to have invited his parishioners to a meal
of 45 lbs of beef and 45 cabbages. Forty-five toasts were drunk and the
guests straggled home between four and five in the morning.[61] These
celebrations, and the more disorderly street revels that accompanied
them, usually took place on Wilkite anniversaries; on his birthday, on
his release from the King's Bench prison in 1768, upon the Middlesex
electoral triumphs. As with Vernon, the Wilkite anniversaries briefly
eclipsed the Georgian in conviviality and festive display.

Wilkite anniversaries were celebrated up and down the country during
the early 1770s and extended well beyond the established bastions of
metropolitan and provincial radicalism. They were quite diverse in character, featuring the more traditonal forms of festivity: bells, illuminations,
bonfires, ox-roastings, trade processions, mayings, effigy-burnings, even
a 'JACK BOOT filled with combustibles' which exploded from the gallows
to 'the universal acclamations of the populace'; as well as balls, banquets
and club dinners.[62] As public celebrations of liberty and liberality, they
sought to combine the familiar rites of festivity with aspirations to an
alternative political order which stressed open, accountable, egalitarian
principles. The tensions between the message and the media of Wilkite
politics were never resolved. Although '45 dinners implicitly repudiated
hierarchy in the way they were structured, they were usually socially
discrete events, involving men of the same class or standing. Thus while
merchants, tradesmen, shopkeepers and even lesser folks participated
in Wilkite dinners, they did so within their own social sphere, not as part
of a heterogeneous radical assembly. Indeed, the open-air dinner put on

at Brentford for 45 chimney sweeps, who were arranged around tables on a raised platform, with a president at their head, was really as patronizing as any village spree.[63]

Moreover, Wilkites were not averse to exploiting the full panoply of civic privileges to mobilize political support, whether that meant lavish dinners to which the common people were invited to view the confectionary, or electoral parades to which only freemen were invited.[64] Thus at Dover, on the occasion of John Trevanion's candidature in 1770, great care was taken to ensure that only legitimate voters accompanied his entry to the town, members of the SSBR excepted.[65] Nor did Wilkes's principal supporters have much compunction about organizing their festivals in ways that demarcated the wealthy from the rest. At Ongar, in Essex, for example, the gentlemen of the town celebrated Wilkes's release from King's Bench prison by parading his effigy through the town accompanied by a Britannia holding a blue flag, on which was inscribed 'JOHN WILKES, Esq; No. 45, DEFENDER OF OUR RIGHTS AND PRIVILEGES, AND FOE TO TYRANNY AND OPPRESSION'. The festivities concluded with an effigy-burning of Lord Bute and the distribution of 45 bowls of punch to the populace. The gentlemen themselves retired to private dinners at their houses.[66]

If Wilkite political practice never met its highest egalitarian aspirations, neither was it always able to contain demotic politics within acceptable limits. Wilkite radicals were always sensitive to the criticism that their actions encouraged licentiousness rather than liberty and they constantly implored the public to behave in ways that befitted a free people. At Tadcaster, Wilkes's supporters organized a parade through the streets on his release from King's Bench prison, but resolved that 'swearing, rioting, drunkenness, breaking of windows, squib throwing &c. be discouraged throughout the day and night'.[67] This was easier said than done. Wilkite triumphs frequently precipitated exhibitions of carnivalesque licence which embarrassed radical men of probity and property, ones which the eponymous hero himself did little to discourage. Middle-class radicals wanted illuminations on Wilkite anniversaries to be voluntary, not compulsory. As John Brewer has emphasized, their ideal demonstration expressed self-imposed decorum, not coercive disorder.[68] Consequently radicals distributed 'cards of caution' before Middlesex elections urging supporters to exercise due restraint, and similarly exhorted them to sober conduct on anniversary occasions. Those in authority sometimes went further. When crowds smashed unlit windows following an Opposition dinner at the Mansion House in March 1770, the Wilkite

Lord Mayor, Brass Crosby, offered to pay for the damages incurred by these 'Foes of Freedom'. Anxious to frustrate those who would censure the 'Friends of Liberty' as the 'abettors of Licentiousness', he had two rioters committed to the Wood Street Compter.[69] Counter-productive disorder would not be tolerated.

Even so, such actions did little to deter the London crowd from its frolicksome demonstrations of Liberty. On the release of Crosby and Oliver from the Tower during the celebrated printers' case of 1771, a crowd confronted Bishopsgate householders who refused to illuminate by breaking exactly 45 windows.[70] Clearly the mob had its own definitions of order. Two years earlier the crowd had disrupted a procession of loyalist merchants to St James by breaking the windows of their carriages, showering them with dirt and blocking their route at Temple Bar. Not content with this, Wilkite supporters staged a counter-processional featuring a hearse commemorating the St George's Field massacre and the death of a Wilkite at the Brentford election at the hands of Beauchamp Proctor's bruisers. The hearse made a number of symbolic stops on its way to St James, and its coachman even attempted to drive it through the Palace Gates. When the Lord Steward, Lord Talbot, read the Riot Act, he had his wand broken in his hand and was forced to compete, on unfavourable terms, with the harangues of a Wilkite and a drunken woman. 'They each had their audiences', Mrs Harris wrote to her son, 'but the Wilkism and the obscenity of the woman proved the greatest attraction'.[71]

Middle-class radicals remained ambivalent about such episodes, and more generally, about the street politics they had helped to shape. While they disapproved of the lords-of-misrule antics of the Wilkite crowd – its demands for festive perquisites, its jostling of unsympathetic mayors, justices and parliamentarians, even marking them with the number '45' – they appreciated the crowd's role as the shock troops of Liberty. Crowd action, after all, had helped to create radical space; it had dramatized Wilkes's conflict with authority and reaffirmed its popular appeal. However errant crowd politics sometimes appeared to be, it remained integral to the movement.

IV

During the early phase of radicalism the relationship between the middle-class patriots and the crowd remained largely propitious. Whatever reservations middle-class radicals had about the political propensities of the crowd were held in check by the authoritarian responses of the government and its supporters to popular demonstration, both at Brentford and St George's Fields. In the next decade this alliance came unstuck. The loyalist demonstrations of the American war, with its effigy-burnings of Washington, revealed that popular passions did not necessarily follow the radical writ.[72] But it was the Gordon riots that ultimately highlighted the problematic status of the crowd as a progressive force in British politics and undermined middle-class confidence in invoking its support.[73] Those riots dramatically exposed radical divisions over Catholic concessions. They threatened the existence of the newly formed reform associations and discredited mass petitioning. They precipitated an unparalleled military intervention in street politics and potentially closed down the space for radicalism. They also unleashed social forces that potentially threatened property and order. As magisterial authority wilted before anti-Catholic insurgency, the poor reaped the advantages of their superiority by asserting their rights to festive gratuities with a sardonic confidence. 'O God bless this gentleman', mocked rioters to an apothecary who had been forced to concede half-a-crown, 'he is always generous'. Others dispensed with such civility. 'Damn your eyes and limbs', exclaimed a discharged sailor to a well-to-do cheesemonger in Bishopsgate, 'put a shilling into my hat, or by God I have a party that can destroy your house presently'.[74] Such incidents and the unparallelled destruction that accompanied the Gordon riots made radical leaders think twice about mobilizing the crowd. The shift from sectarian targets to the symbols of wealth and authority, from Catholic chapels to the gaols, the Inns of Court, the Bank, to Downing Street, revealed that the theatre of politics could escalate into the theatre of class conflict.

The impact upon political festival was best expressed in the celebrations of the 1688 jubilee and the king's recovery several months later. Although historians have emphasized the radical, populist dimensions of the centenary of the Glorious Revolution,[75] it is worthwhile stressing its central paradox: the invocation of popular rights within a festive framework that self-consciously kept popular participation to a minimum and emphasized social distance, respectability and decorum. In London there was no publicly subsidized celebration, but rather decorous observances by a cluster of gentlemanly clubs and societies, preceded by sermons in the leading churches and chapels. Outside the metropolis the jubilations were only marginally more expansive.[76] At Leicester, Leeds and other provincial centres, local bigwigs organized balls and dinners for a select crowd of gentlemen and principal inhabitants, offering token largesse to the populace at large. Thus at Ipswich three barrels of beer were given to the populace 'that the poor as well as the rich might commemorate the area to which all parties owe their best privileges – as men and citizens'.[77] What parades did take place were largely civic in character, traversing the familiar routes from town hall to cathedral. There was little attempt to involve the local trades in the festivities in a manner comparable to the 4 July pageants in America the same year, when allegorical floats, banners and standards celebrated the ratification of the constitution and the virtues of a republic of independent artisans and farmers.[78] The Yankee festivities of 1788 exalted the independent producer as the crucial repository of political virtue and economic progress. Their tone was democratic. The English celebrations, by contrast, were largely custodial. Most cherished the memory of the 'great deliverer' William III or the Whig lords as the guardians of historic liberties. The minority that did champion the sovereignty of the 'people' did so in terms that privileged the responsible, orderly and largely middle-class political nation as the bulwark of national freedom.

The jubilee was thus cast within a framework that left little room for the jostling crowd save as the recipients of festive fare and the beneficiaries of the rule of law. The celebrations on the recovery of the king in the spring of 1789 were more exuberant, but efforts were again made to control festive space. Several towns ordered general illuminations to forestall the possibility of plebeian recriminations against unlit houses. In London the artful design and brilliance of the transparencies brought so many carriages to the main avenues that the plebeian presence was effectively marginalized. Only in the out-parishes was the rough serenade of marrow bones and cleavers heard. Festive munificence in large towns also seems to have been well organized, and discriminately distributed: to paupers, debtors, employees and Sunday School children. Beyond the big urban centres, the festivities were predictably more indiscriminately convivial. Lord Heathfield laid on a roasted ox for the inhabitants of Turnham Green, as did other patrons elsewhere, not to mention the liberal distribution of ale.[79] But in other parts of the country, especially East Anglia, smaller celebrations were sometimes closely supervised. At Fakenham 500 poor people, two by two, processed to church with drums and fife playing 'O that Roast Beef of Old England', returning to a bumper supper in the market square. 'To see the labouring poor...thus regaled with good Old English hospitality', the *Norfolk Chronicle* reported, 'raised emotions in the hearts of Britons beyond expression; the regularity and good order that was observed afforded the most ample satisfaction to the numerous spectators'.[80] At East Dereham, the gentlemen of the vestry organized a similar feast, this time for 1300 inhabitants, condescending to serve them personally at the tables. One hundred stone of beef was said to be boiled and roasted for the occasion, but drink was restricted to a quart of ale for the men, a pint for the women, and proportionately less for the children. 'More was not given', it was claimed, 'the better to prevent as far as possible, all scenes of folly, irregularity, riot and drunkenness, too usual on public occasions and in which those who should be their betters, 'tis feared set them such bad examples'.[81]

The attempt to contain public festival within more decorous limits and instil its celebration with a self-conscious paternalism and piety became increasingly evident in the nineteenth century. Partly this was in response to Evangelical concerns about the immorality that unregulated festivals generated; partly it was in response to the radical critique of Britain as a decadent ceremonial order, and, in effect, to forestall the growth of radical politics itself. Certainly, some of the victory celebrations in the final years of the French wars were not without their raucous spontaneity. Rawlinson depicted the Norwich jubilations over the victory at Leipzig as a carnival of misrule, if not degeneracy, with two muscular butchers chopping up the roasted ox and throwing steaks to a ravenous crowd, men and women frolicking around the beer barrels, some insensibly drunk, and a revelrous mob hoisting an effigy of Napoleon in another part of the market square.[82] How far this representation of the celebrations exaggerated the anarchy and degradation remains moot, but we should not discount the possibility that such festive licence was underplayed and marginalized in the newspapers. The oblique references to plebeian revels elsewhere, including a Northampton crowd that was kept 'in a constant uproar for several hours', make this entirely credible.[83]

Efforts to contain the carnivalesque are nonetheless quite visible in the celebrations of the royal jubilee of 1809 and the peace of 1814. Both occasions saw a revivifed theatre of paternalism in action, with the gentry hosting bumper feasts for their neighbouring villagers and tenants, and manufacturers treating their workers. Thus in 1809, Sir John Lethbridge, MP for Somerset, entertained a thousand 'poor persons' to roast beef and plum pudding at his seat at Sandhill Park. Similarly, in the industrial vales of Gloucestershire, clothiers Paul, Wathen and Company entertained 600 workers employed at their mill at Woodchester while at Colchester, timber merchant William Hawkins laid on a fat ox weighing 600 lbs for his workmen. Even smaller fry appear to have done their paternal duty. At Rickmansworth it was said that 'every Gentleman-Farmer and Tradesman, from the highest to the lowest in circumstances, provided a most substantial repast for their servants of all description'.[84]

These festive occasions sought to enhance the authority and stature of their benefactors, whose gifts, it was hoped, would be gratefully received by their subordinates. They were also especially noteworthy for their scale and propriety. Raucous ox-roasts and generous libations of beer and wine were becoming a thing of the past. They survived principally in rural villages like Stock in Berkshire, where General Vyse laid on an ox, 12 hogsheads of beer and 13 gallons of spirits for the occasion, while the local farmers gave their labourers two days' holiday to sleep the revel off.[85] In the larger townships and market towns, public subscriptions were regularly raised to provide the poor with a public dinner at local taverns, or in the open market-place, or sometimes in an adjoining field. These were often very extensive affairs, encompassing large sections of the population, not simply those known to be dependent upon public charity, although old paupers, widows or wounded soldiers were regularly mentioned as worthy recipients of the festive purse. A review of some 37 peace celebrations for 1814, reported in the *Leeds Mercury* and *Northampton Mercury*, and encompassing townships from Kent to Yorkshire, reveals that 82 per cent treated over half of their inhabitants to a public beanfeast and that nearly half (49 per cent) catered to 75 per cent of the local residents.[86] In other words, these festivals strove to be socially inclusive events that extended beyond the normal client bases of their sponsors. Some Northamptonshire villages, Upper and Lower Boddington, Broughton, Gayton, Litchborough and Sulgrave, took in everybody. Even the towns with 2000 inhabitants or more took in half, Halifax (40 per cent) and Luton (38 per cent) excepted.

Early nineteenth-century festivals were not only well attended, they were carefully planned and choreographed in ways that sought to contain festive licence within respectable limits by the careful management of time and space. Unlike many eighteenth-century festivals, which tended to let the crowd loose after the official toasts at the bonfire, those after 1800 ran to a tighter programme, with midday or early afternoon dinners giving way to tea parties for the women and children, and perhaps to competitions such as donkey races or running in sacks, to be followed by processions around the town and a fireworks display at the end of the day.[87] This programme was more family-orientated than previously, not only in the sense that it set aside time for women and children to celebrate the day on their own, but also because its sponsors emphasized the need to allow the 'fair sex' the opportunity to participate fully in the proceedings without fear of harassment or festive mischief.[88] Hence the frequent prohibition of squibs and crackers and the tighter regulation of illuminations.

Above all, festive organizers attempted to keep the crowds relatively immobile and spectatorial. At the public dinners, many of which were open to both sexes rather than to men alone, plebeian celebrants were encouraged to join in the singing of patriotic songs and glees rather than leave the tables prematurely. To forestall the formation of roving mobs, young men were sometimes assigned roles in the various parades around the town; perhaps as the official guards and executioners of a dummied Bonaparte or as the emulators of Britain's allies who had given the French emperor such grief. At Windhill in the West Riding, for example, 'the young men of the village . . . preceded by a number of old veterans on horseback representing a General of Cossacks with attendants', marched through Eccleshill, Bradford and back again, accompanied by a band of music and a humbled 'Bonaparte'.[89] At Newport Pagnell the victory parade headed by the constable and beadle was more elaborate, if less taxing.[90] It included:

> six polish lacers, three deep – two trumpeters in full dress on horse-back, bearing banners – a herald at arms carrying a banner, bearing medalions of the Allied Sovereigns, mounted – two youths decorated with white satin hats, plumes &c. bearing Peace and Unity – Marshal del de Campo, bearing the union colours – General Count Platoff – the Emperor Alexander in full robes, wearing an Imperial Crown, Order of the Garter &c. &c. mounted on a white charger, caparisoned, and led by two colonels of Cossacks – four Cossacks on each side, mounted in full uniform – next a military band playing the dead march – then a cart containing Bonaparte, priest and executioner, &c. – and behind him the Devil, followed by upwards of 100 foot guards.

In the 1814 peace celebrations young women were also given a visible role as the standard bearers of peace, plenty and renewal, carrying peace-garlands or processing two by two dressed in white. Sometimes whole factories were accorded local recognition by being invited to process around town. At Leeds, Benjamin Gott's workers were the central attraction, parading 'the streets with a fleece and other emblems of their manufacture'.[91] These events would normally be followed by a visit to the transparencies displayed throughout the streets or by a fireworks display. The latter could be an elaborate scenario, with pyrotechnic representations of Mount Vesuvius or, as was the case of the jubilations at the Soho works, with balloons discharging fireworks during the course of their ascent.[92] Some 50,000 spectators are said to have watched this spectacular from Matthew Boulton's park.

Early nineteenth-century festivals also added a philanthropic motif. Their organizers publicly sponsored dispensaries, schools, Sunday School outings, and perhaps provided needy families with shirts, shifts, blankets and shoes.[93] Hundreds of pounds were raised for these projects, which sought to accent the respectability, order and domestic rectitude of the occasion as well as differentiate the poor from their public benefactors, whether they be local squires, manufacturers or a more amorphous middle-class grouping.[94]

Indeed, the manner in which the festive dinners were arranged, with the principal inhabitants condescending to wait on the tables of the poor before partaking of their own more elegant repasts, and the food that was consumed – turtle, turbot and game rather than roast beef, champagne and wine rather than porter – served to emphasize the gradations of rank and prestige on which a harmonious social order was thought to rest. As far as possible, nineteenth-century sponsors sought to erase the social liminality that festivals invited and to curb the carnivalesque freedoms of the crowd. Through a tighter arrangement of time and space, through consumption itself, they sought to emphasize the importance of hierarchy to the maintenance of social harmony and order.

How far this strategy was successful is, of course, moot. The reports of celebrations in the newspapers usually disclosed only the public transcript of the event. They rarely tell us much about how the poor viewed such festivals beyond getting a good meal and perhaps meat for three days the following week. Occasionally we can discover some dissonant voices on the margins. Diaries sometimes reveal that the celebrations were a good deal more raucous and disorderly than their sponsors would have wished.[95] Home Office papers offer glimpses of resentment at loyalist hoopla at a time of high prices and wartime hardships. In 1809 the rector of St John's Clerkenwell received a letter deeply critical of the jubilee. It demanded that 'ye Middle Class of society . . . shou'd not be insulted by being asked to rejoice at Blessings which do not exist'.[96] But one can only begin to guess at what the jubilee might have meant at a place like Kettering, where the decline of the local woollen industry had forced many men into the army and, no doubt, to the horrors of the Walcheren expedition or the Peninsular war.[97] Some must have agreed with Cobbett that the jubilee was a 'sop to keep the poor and hungry from making clamorous complaints'.[98] Certainly, it was more revelatory of the public transcript of ruling-class paternalism than of any genuine lower-class sentiment, and it must have been disconcerting to many patricians to discover that their efforts to inculcate deference and loyalty to the political order during the French wars did little to mitigate the spread of democratic politics and the rise of new associations in its immediate aftermath.

Even the grander occasions of festive jollity and cheer could turn ugly. At the coronation celebrations of George IV, for example, amid mounting discontent, the crowd at Newcastle upon Tyne spurned the civic ox-roast and turned the event against its sponsors.[99] At Sandhill a sailor grabbed the crown from the fountain and 'crowned' himself. At the Old Flesh Market the butchers were pelted with the very meat they had carved for the people. The spit was subsequently demolished, and the roasted beast (or what was left of it) paraded through the town. Atop the crane which had raised the ox to the spit, another sailor pinned 'the Queen that Jack loves' (a play upon William Hone's *The House that Jack built*) to loud cheers. A similar demolition of the ox-roast occurred at the Spital, and from the greasy symbols of civic bounty, the populace turned its attention to the symbols of royal order, stoning the royal mail coaches and then the local yeomanry. In this farcical and drunken appropriation of festive space, the crowd was telling the Newcastle corporation of merchants and coalowners it could keep its paternalism and royal dandy. At a coronation where the king had excluded his popular consort, it was determined to have the last word. Before the wine fountain one celebrant even dropped his breeches and reputedly washed 'his posteriors' before 'a great number of well-dressed ladies'.[100] Such profanity led the radical *Tyne Mercury* to observe that 'ox roastings, beer swillings, and the like, both in this town and other places, have proceeded from a miscalculation of the spirit of the age'. It was time to break with the time-honoured traditions of festive largesse for a 'better-regulated bounty';[101] an argument that had been gaining credibility for almost 50 years.

V

By the coronation of George IV the controversy over festive licence had been subsumed in a larger struggle over public space. The critical impetus came from 'below' rather than 'above', specifically from the emergence of a radical platform in the aftermath of the Napoleonic wars. The development of organized mass meetings for political reform, organized through an infrastructure of union societies and radical clubs, signalled a significant departure from the conventional pattern of festive politics. Traditionalists within the political elite found this development especially troubling because it multiplied the sites of political contention and eroded the customary bases of street politics through which political order and gentry leadership had been sustained, however imperfectly. Orderly mass meetings underscored the self-activism and growing political consciousness of an emergent working class in the capital and the industrial midlands and the north. As one radical newspaper remarked in 1818, at a time when handbills stressed the polarization of British society into those who earned the 'fruits of their labour' and those who lived 'luxuriously on the labour of others':

> Every public political meeting is calculated to produce benefit, either immediately or ultimately. When men [*sic*] assemble to the amount of thirty or forty thousand, they are then capable of forming some idea of their strength as a *body*, whereas by remaining shut up in houses and workshops, each individual remains ignorant that such a unity of feeling exists among his countrymen.[102]

That collective unity was shown in the determination of working men and women to organize mass marches on London, as in the case of the Blanketeers in 1817, when 'ticket men' from the union societies were to join the original delegation from Manchester in a mounting display of industrial strength.[103] It was also manifested in the call for weekly subscriptions to a 'Universal Union Fund of the Non-Represented People of the United Kingdom' for 'General Patriotic Purposes'. And in the decision by members of the radical platform to elect their own 'legislatory attorney' at Birmingham in 1819. To this act of civil disobedience others were mooted, such as voting for MPs at the regular hustings, even though such votes would inevitably be disqualified.[104] Such strategies of constitutional defiance, which carried with them the threat that all allegiance to constituted government would be withdrawn if radical grievances were not addressed, entailed a clear rupture from the customary conventions of crowd politics. However blasphemous and insurrectionary, those conventions had always been implicitly grounded upon an on-going dialogue between rulers and ruled in which the legitimacy of the existing system was begrudgingly admitted. Such assumptions no longer held, much to the dismay of magistrates who found they could no longer dismiss popular demonstrations as 'mobbish' intrusions on political space.[105] The response to this challenge was not only an inflated and tightly-controlled festive paternalism, but a determined effort to close down the new theatres of popular politics by new laws against seditious or unlawful assembly.[106] In the struggle over public space that generated Peterloo and the Six Acts of 1819, the centrality of old-style festive politics as a barometer of public sentiment was displaced.

That familiar idiom of politics did not, of course, disappear immediately. The controversy over Queen Caroline's return to Britain in 1820 revealed that effigy-burnings, politically inspired skimmingtons, and physical attacks upon Caroline's aristocratic opponents were still part of the popular repertoire of political contention. Given the restrictions on public assembly, it was entirely predictable that the melodrama of the Queen's trial and its aftermath would be fought on familiar festive sites and often to a predictable chronology.

Yet the demonstrations on behalf of Caroline in London and Lancashire were noteworthy for their discipline rather than their disorder and for the development of a radical calendar of commemoration that would blossom under Chartism.[107] In Lancashire, in particular, working-class committees called for and organized the illuminations in honour of Caroline's trial, much to the consternation of the authorities. Rather than invade official space, working-class radicals had begun to develop their own and to distance themselves from the popular interventions of the past. If magistrates were anxious to curb the 'fooleries of riotous exultation'[108] that sometimes characterized public anniversaries, so, too, were radicals. In the era of the mass platform, the irreverent crowd was viewed by radicals as an impediment to political emancipation, a force that might transgress the political order but seldom subvert it. Indeed, by 1820 it was conservatives rather than their opponents who were most anxious to sustain the traditions of festive politics, calculating that the benefits derived from a theatre of paternalism would outweigh any public humiliations they might encounter. Those festivals would live on, but their significance as a weather-vane of demotic politics would diminish. Victorian jubilees would have little of the political punch of the Georgian. New sites of popular political contention, themselves the product of the Georgian era, had eroded their importance within a ramified public sphere.

NOTES

1. Sean Wilentz (ed.), *Rites of Power: Symbolism, Ritual and Politics since the Middle Ages* (Philadelphia, 1985), p. 3.
2. See Mono Ozouf, *Festivals and the French Revolution*, trans. Alan Sheridan (Cambridge, Mass., 1988); Lynn Hunt, *Politics, Culture, and Class in the French Revolution* (Berkeley and Los Angeles, 1984).
3. Charles Tilly, 'Introduction', in Louise A. Tilly and Charles Tilly (eds), *Class Conflict and Collective Action* (Beverly Hills, 1981), pp. 19–23. Tilly has explored this idea in the British context in *Popular Contention in Great Britain, 1758–1834* (Cambridge, Mass., 1995).
4. *Flying Post*, 10 August 1714, cited by Thomas Wright, *Caricature History of the Georges* (London, 1868), p. 70.
5. *The Butiad: Being a Supplement to the British Antidote to Caledonian Poison* (London, 1763).
6. Jonathan Swift, *Journal to Stella*, ed. Temple Scott (London, 1897), p. 283; *Flying Post*, October 30/November 2, 1714.
7. *Northampton Mercury*, 18 April 1763. I owe this reference to Jeanette Neeson.
8. *London Evening Post*, 14/16 April, 12/14 May 1763; *Felix Farley's Bristol Journal*, 14 May 1763.
9. Peter Borsay, ' "All the Town's a Stage": Urban Ritual and Ceremony, 1660–1800', in Peter Clark (ed.), *The Transformation of English Provincial Towns* (London, 1984), pp. 228–58.
10. See Bob Bushaway, *By Rite: Custom, Ceremony and Community in England, 1700–1880* (London, 1982), pp. 167–206. For such celebrations in London, see Nicholas Rogers, *Whigs and Cities: Popular Politics in the Age of Walpole and Pitt* (Oxford, 1989), pp. 354–5.
11. BL, Add. MSS 27,966, fol. 242v.
12. *Post-Boy*, 14/16 May 1713.
13. *Post-Boy*, 19/21 May 1713.
14. *Post-Boy*, 30 May/2 June 1713.
15. *Flying Post*, 30 October–2 November 1714.
16. For the most detailed report, see *Felix Farley's Bristol Journal*, 14 May 1763.
17. George Rudé, *The Crowd in History: A Study of Popular Disturbances in France and England, 1730–1848* (New York, 1964), p. 4.
18. For the long-term development of the calendar, see David Cressy, 'The Protestant Calendar and the Vocabulary of Celebration in Early Modern England', *JBS*, XXIX (1990), 31–52; David Cressy, *Bonfires and Bells: National Memory and the Protestant Calendar in Elizabethan and Stuart England* (London, 1989).
19. For evidence of the celebration of Queen Elizabeth's day in the 1750s, see Bristol RO, All Saints parish, Churchwardens' accounts.
20. Daniel Defoe, *The Great Law of Subordination Consider'd* (London, 1724), *passim*.
21. Bodl., MS Rawlinson D 862, fol. 83.
22. CLRO, Repertories of the Court of Aldermen, CXLII (1738), 568–70. For earlier complaints, see Reps. CXIII (1709), 356 and CXVII (1713), 205–7.

23. K. H. D. Haley, *The First Earl of Shaftesbury* (Oxford, 1968), pp. 557–8, 572–3, 681, 694–5; John Miller, *Popery and Politics in England, 1660–1688* (Cambridge, 1973), pp. 183–7; Tim Harris, *London Crowds in the Reign of Charles II* (Cambridge, 1987), pp. 98–108, 156–88.

24. *Flying Post*, 14–16 July 1715; *The Shift Shifted, or Robin's Last Shift*, 28 July 1716.

25. *The Freeholder*, 11 June 1716.

26. *Flying Post*, 31 March/2 April, 7/9 April 1713.

27. On these and subsequent disturbances, see Nicholas Rogers, 'Popular Protest in Early Hanoverian London', *P&P*, LXXIX (1978), 70–100, and 'Riot and Popular Jacobitism in Early Hanoverian England', in Eveline Cruickshanks (ed.), *Ideology and Conspiracy: Aspects of Jacobitism, 1689–1759* (Edinburgh, 1982), pp. 70–88. See also Paul Kléber Monod, *Jacobitism and the English People, 1688–1788* (Cambridge, 1989), pp. 173–94.

28. *Weekly Journal, or British Gazetteer*, 18 June 1720.

29. See Rogers, 'Popular Protest in Early Hanoverian London', pp. 78–83; Rogers, *Whigs and Cities*, pp. 313–16.

30. On this episode, see Rogers, 'Riot and Popular Jacobitism', p. 83; Nicholas Rogers, *Crowds, Culture, and Politics in Georgian Britain* (Oxford, 1998), pp. 48–50; Monod, *Jacobitism*, pp. 205–9.

31. Rogers, *Whigs and Cities*, p. 373; Linda Colley, 'Radical Patriotism in Eighteenth-Century England', in Raphael Samuel (ed.), *Patriotism: The Making and Unmaking of British National Identity*, 3 vols (London, 1989), I, 171.

32. See the poem on Restoration Day in the *Public Advertiser*, 29 May 1777.

33. John Wilkes, *The Speeches of John Wilkes*, 2 vols (London, 1777), I, 4. I thank John Sainsbury of Brock University for this reference.

34. *The Diary of Sylas Neville, 1767–88*, ed. Basil Cozens-Hardy (London, 1950), pp. 90–1. See also pp. 149, 197.

35. *Critical Review*, 4th series, V (1814), 540.

36. For the celebration of 30 January and 29 May in loyalist Lancashire, see Robert Glen, *Urban Workers in the Early Industrial Revolution* (Beckenham, 1983), pp. 57, 63–4. See also its revival in Worcester in 1821, cited in the *Courier*, 4 May 1821.

37. On the changing significance of 4 November in Ireland, see Jacqueline R. Hill, 'National Festivals, the State and "Protestant Ascendancy" in Ireland, 1790–1829', *Irish Historical Studies*, XXIV, no. 93 (May, 1984), 30–51. For the celebration of 4 November in mid-Georgian Dublin, see *Dublin Mercury*, 3–6, 6–8 November 1770.

38. *The Autobiography of Francis Place*, ed. Mary Thale (Cambridge, 1972), pp. 65–8.

39. Linda Colley, 'The Apotheosis of George III: Loyalty, Royalty and the British Nation, 1760–1820', *P&P*, CII (1984), 94–129.

40. See accounts of the coronation festivities of 1761 in *Northampton Mercury*, 14, 28 September 1761.

41. For Foxite anniversaries, principally commemorating his birthday and his first election as MP for Westminster, see L. G. Mitchell, *Charles James Fox* (Oxford, 1992), p. 262; N. B. Penny, 'The Whig Cult of Fox in Early Nineteenth-Century Sculpture', *P&P*, LXX (1976), 94; *Derby Mercury*, 16 October

1800. For Pittites' celebrations in Lancashire, see James A. Epstein, 'Radical Dining, Toasting, and Symbolic Expression in Early Nineteenth Century Lancashire: Rituals of Solidarity', *Albion*, XX (1988), 277, reproduced in *Radical Expression. Political Language, Ritual and Symbol in England, 1790–1850* (New York, 1994), p. 153.

42. *Selections from the Papers of the London Corresponding Society, 1792–1799*, ed. Mary Thale (Cambridge, 1983), pp. xvii, 313, 318, 412, 441, 451. See also *Courier*, 8 November 1809.

43. See Epstein, 'Radical Dining', pp. 271–91; Epstein, *Radical Expression*, pp. 147–66.

44. *Whitehall Evening Post*, 14–16 March 1749. On the growing polarity between polite and plebeian culture and the way this was played out in urban ritual, see Borsay, 'All the Town's a Stage', pp. 246–53.

45. *Newcastle Courant*, 19 November 1757; *Whitehall Evening Post*, 11–14 February, 2–4 March, 29 April–2 May, 1749; *London Evening Post*, 21–24 January 1749. On fireworks in the seventeenth century, see Cressy, *Bonfires and Bells*, ch. 3; Lois Schwoerer, 'The Glorious Revolution as Spectacle: A New Perspective', in Stephen B. Baxter (ed.), *England's Rise to Greatness* (Berkeley and Los Angeles, 1983), p. 117.

46. *Whitehall Evening Post*, 19–21 January, 7–9 February, 22–25 April, 1749. Not all of the fireworks were exhibited because the left wing of the temple caught fire. See *London Evening Post*, 27–29 April 1749; Martin C. Battestin with Ruthe R. Battestin, *Henry Fielding: A Life* (London and New York, 1989), pp. 466–7.

47. *Whitehall Evening Post*, 15–17 June 1749.

48. *Whitehall Evening Post*, 14–16 February 1749.

49. Those organized for accession day, 1749, at Newcastle upon Tyne, for example, took four months to organize. See *Whitehall Evening Post*, 15–17 June 1749. For evidence of their financing by subscription, see the account of the celebrations at Hackney in the *Whitehall Evening Post*, 7–9 February 1749.

50. On transparencies, see Richard D. Altick, *The Shows of London* (Cambridge, Mass., 1978), pp. 95, 119.

51. *Public Advertiser*, 22 September 1761.

52. See the complaints in the *Whitehall Evening Post*, 13–16 July 1761, and the *Public Ledger*, 22 September 1761. See also the precept issued by the mayor of Northampton for the occasion of the coronation, *Northampton Mercury*, 21 September 1761.

53. A maypole was erected at Odiham in Hampshire on Coronation day, 1761, 'for the Amusement of the young people'. See *Public Advertiser*, 26 September 1761. For the Northamptonshire incident I thank my colleague, Jeanette Neeson.

54. *Whitehall Evening Post*, 26–29 September 1761; *General Evening Post*, 24–26 September 1761.

55. *Northampton Mercury*, 21 September 1761.

56. *Public Advertiser*, 22 September 1761.

57. See Kathleen Wilson, 'Empire, Trade and Popular Politics in Mid-Hanoverian Britain. The Case of Admiral Vernon', *P&P*, CXXI (1988), 74–109.

58. John Brewer, *Party Ideology and Popular Politics at the Accession of George III* (Cambridge, 1976), p. 185.
59. John Wesley, *Thoughts Upon Liberty* (London, 1772), p. 7.
60. *Northampton Mercury*, 30 May, 11 July 1768. For a full discussion of the significance of the number 45, see John Brewer, 'The Number 45: A Wilkite Political Symbol', in Baxter (ed.), *England's Rise to Greatness*, pp. 349–80.
61. *Northampton Mercury*, 27 June 1768.
62. Brewer, *Party Ideology*, pp. 178–9; Brewer, 'The Number 45', pp. 352–7.
63. *Middlesex Journal*, 19–21 April 1770.
64. *Middlesex Journal*, 14–17 April 1770, 21/23 April 1772.
65. *Middlesex Journal*, 6–9 January 1770. The SSBR (Society of the Supporters of the Bill of Rights) was the reform society first formed to pay Wilkes's electoral debts.
66. *Middlesex Journal*, 5–8 May 1770.
67. *Leeds Mercury*, 24 April 1770.
68. Brewer, 'The Number 45', p. 369.
69. *Middlesex Journal*, 22–4 March 1770.
70. *Sussex Weekly Advertiser*, 13 May 1771
71. Cited by George Rudé, *Wilkes and Liberty* (Oxford, 1962), pp. 64–5. See also *Sussex Weekly Advertiser*, 27 March 1769.
72. See, for example, those at Leeds and Wakefield mentioned in the *Public Advertiser*, 10 January 1777.
73. See Nicholas Rogers, 'Crowd and People in the Gordon Riots', in Ekhart Hellmuth (ed.), *The Transformation of Political Culture: England and Germany in the late Eighteenth Century* (Oxford, 1990), pp. 39–56; Rogers, *Crowds, Culture, and Politics*, pp. 170–2.
74. *The Proceedings of the King's Commission of the Peace, Oyer and Terminer and Gaol Delivery for the City of Lonson, Dec. 1779–Oct. 1780* (London, 1780), p. 452; *Morning Chronicle*, 30 June 1780.
75. Kathleen Wilson, 'Inventing Revolution: 1688 and Eighteenth-Century Popular Politics', *JBS*, XXVIII (1989), 349–86.
76. See Rogers, *Crowds, Culture, and Politics*, ch. 8.
77. *Ipswich Journal*, 8 November 1788.
78. For an English report of this festival, see *Gentleman's Magazine*, LXIV (1788), 748, 826–8, 923–4, 1018–9.
79. See *The Times*, 25 April, 2 May 1789.
80. *Norfolk Chronicle*, 4 April 1789.
81. *Norfolk Chronicle*, 18 April 1789.
82. *Catalogue of Political and Personal Studies in the British Museum*, ed. F. G. Stephens and M. D. George, 11 vols (London, 1870–1954), IX, no. 13487, *The Norwich Bull Feast, or Glory and Gluttony* (1813).
83. *Northampton Mercury*, 6 November 1813. See also *Courier*, 6 November 1813.
84. *Courier*, 30, 31 October 1809.
85. *Leeds Mercury*, 21 October 1809.
86. These figures are derived from dividing the number of reported diners/participants by the population figures for 1811. The latter can be found in the parochial returns, *British Parliamentary Papers* (1812), xi, *passim*.

87. For donkey races etc., see the account of the celebrations in Harrold, Bedfordshire, in the *Northampton Mercury*, 16 July 1814.
88. See accounts for Pontefract and Northampton in the *Leeds Mercury*, 18 June 1814, and the *Northampton Mercury*, 18 June 1814.
89. *Leeds Mercury*, 30 April 1814.
90. *Northampton Mercury*, 18 June 1814.
91. *Leeds Mercury*, 23 April 1813.
92. *Courier*, 23 June 1814; *British Press*, 6 November 1809.
93. See *Leeds Mercury*, 21, 29 October 1809, 23, 30 April 1814; *British Press*, 6 November 1809; *Northampton Mercury*, 18 June 1814.
94. For an explicit reference to middle-class sponsorship, see the account of the peace celebrations at Slaithwaite, near Huddersfield, in the *Leeds Mercury*, 23 April 1814.
95. Joseph Rogerson, a fulling miller, described the peace festivities in Bramley in 1814 in the following terms: 'Bells Ringing Guns Firing and Tom Paines Quaking for very fear of the terrible day of the Louis's . . . like as if all was mad'. Cited by Clive Emsley, *British Society and the French Wars, 1793–1815* (London, 1979), p. 167.
96. PRO, HO 42/98/193–4.
97. On Kettering, see Sir Frederick Eden, *The State of the Poor*, 2 vols (London, 1797), II, 530. On conditions in the army, see Godfrey Davies, *Wellington and His Army* (Oxford, 1954), ch. 4.
98. *Cobbett's Weekly Political Register*, 30 September 1809, p. 476, 10 November 1809, p. 746.
99. Robert Colls, *The Collier's Rant* (London, 1977), pp. 67–72.
100. *The Times*, 24 July 1821.
101. *Tyne Mercury*, 24 July 1821, cited by Colls, *Collier's Rant*, p. 71.
102. PRO, HO 42/189/405; *Sherwin's Weekly Political Register*, 25 July, 1818.
103. On the organization of the march, see Public Record Office (PRO), HO 42/161/17.
104. PRO, HO 42/188/155–66. A crowd of some 20,000, including women and children, were reported to have been at the Birmingham meeting that elected Sir Charles Wolseley as a 'legislatory attorney' of the politically excluded in July 1819. See PRO, HO 42/189/22–3.
105. On magisterial concern over orderly radical demonstration, see PRO, HO 42/161/12, HO 40/15/170–1, and E. P. Thompson, *The Making of the English Working Class* (Harmondsworth, 1968), pp. 747–8.
106. Michael Lobban, 'From Seditious Libel to Unlawful Assembly: Peterloo and the Changing Face of Political Crime *c*.1770–1820', *Oxford Journal of Legal Studies*, X (1990), 307–52.
107. See Rogers, *Crowds, Culture, and Politics*, pp. 248–73.
108. *Leeds Mercury*, 7, 21, 29 October 1809.

9

DOMESTICITY IS IN THE STREETS: ELIZA FENNING, PUBLIC OPINION AND THE POLITICS OF PRIVATE LIFE

Patty Seleski

Eliza Fenning was not the first servant in the annals of English legal history to be convicted of attempting to murder the family for which she worked. Nor was she the last. But certainly Eliza Fenning, who in consequence of her alleged crime merits her own entry in the *Dictionary of National Biography*, was among the most famous servants ever convicted of such an offence. Murdering or even attempting to murder one's master or mistress was an act of 'petty treason', and although it was not an everyday occurrence, it was both common enough and important enough to warrant the state's attention.[1] And pay attention the state did. The government acted decisively in the Fenning case, rejecting all pleas for mercy and ignoring the apparent weakness of the circumstantial evidence brought against the accused. In July 1815, Eliza Fenning died on the gallows for the attempted poisoning of her master and mistress.

Eliza Fenning did not go quietly to her death. Nor did she go alone; a huge crowd gathered to watch her die. Emotions ran so high following her execution that authorities feared violence would erupt against her accusers. And rightly so. Angry mobs threatened riot at her former master's house for days, deterred only by a constant police presence. In another part of the metropolis, thousands of Londoners turned out for her funeral procession. The public support given to Eliza Fenning was impressive. Nor was it confined to the streets. From the moment of her arrest until well after her execution, the newspapers eagerly covered the case, reporting every rumour and filling their pages with letters debating her guilt or innocence. Her cause was taken up by reformers and radicals, men who spearheaded the pardon campaign and who churned out pamphlets and propaganda designed to create sympathy for her in the hope both of saving her life and of striking a blow against 'old corruption'. Moreover, Fenning was remembered for decades after her death. More than 40 years after her execution a report in *The Times* that she had secretly confessed her guilt just prior to her hanging set off another long and heated, but still inconclusive, debate about her responsibility for the crime. Honoured in street ballads and on the stage, as well as in passionate legal arguments about capital punishment, Eliza Fenning became a celebrity.[2]

In an age when hanging was quite common – a recent estimate suggests that between 1750 and 1830 some 7000 of the 35,000 people in England and Wales condemned to death actually were executed – what accounts for the furore over the death of this one woman?[3] Surely Eliza Fenning was not the only one among those 7000 condemned prisoners who went to her death insisting on her innocence or who was convicted on shaky or false evidence? Why did the fate of a woman who was neither wealthy nor influential, indeed who was a mere domestic servant, transfix the attention of the public to such an extent and for such a long time? Why did Elizabeth Fenning's plight and not that of some other poor accused criminal become a *cause célèbre*?

Recently, V. A. C. Gatrell has suggested that what he terms the 'beatification' of Eliza Fenning and the public response to her was related to the cause of political reform. This is not an entirely novel idea. In 1909, Horace Bleackley contended much the same thing when he declared that 'the case of Eliza Fenning was used by the opponents of the Government for political purposes, and the unhappy woman obtained much sympathy because she was hanged for a crime less than murder'.[4] Ann Hone sees the involvement of radicals and reformers in the Fenning agitation as symptomatic of the disunity existing among London radicals in the period 1812–16. She suggests that efforts on behalf of Fenning were an attempt on the part of some radicals to influence a wider and more mainstream reform-minded audience by focusing less on formal politics and more on philanthropic causes such as, in the Fenning case, legal reform.[5] Although Gatrell's focus is primarily the history of legal reform around the capital code, he nevertheless sees '*l'affaire* Fenning' as energizing radical indignation about the nature of justice and, implicitly, with sustaining radicalism in a difficult period. Like others before him, Gatrell cites the severity of Fenning's sentence as a key factor in the public response to Eliza Fenning, especially given the flawed, ambiguous and circumstantial nature of the evidence against her. Unlike previous commentators, however, Gatrell recognizes the role that the press played in creating and mobilizing something called 'public opinion' around the Fenning case. Gatrell does not take the existence of a receptive audience or a concerned, humanitarian public for granted. Nor does he assume the reality of such a thing; rather, he details the role the press played in shaping the case and in packaging Eliza Fenning simultaneously as a sympathetic, defenceless victim and as an icon of injustice. He shows how the London press, led by radical publicists such as William Hone and the Hunts, attempted to orchestrate responses to the case which would tap the sentiments of the middling classes. He argues that middle-class sympathizers were less troubled by the death penalty's appropriateness as a form of punishment than they were outraged by the arbitrary and casual behaviour of the government in a capital case. Gatrell argues that reforming elements in the press exploited existing anxiety about injustice in their treatment of the story by constructing a narrative about the nature of the state which was intended to heighten middle-class discontent with their own political disenfranchisement.

By linking the fate of a poor servant girl with hopes for political reform, Gatrell hopes to account for much of the ruckus surrounding the Fenning case. In doing so, he places a great deal of emphasis on the relationship between the press and the reading public and on the power of texts to mediate between private, individual responses and projections of wider political purpose. Thus Gatrell argues that although Fenning was not spared the gallows because of the agitation on her behalf, nevertheless the pro-Fenning campaign was successful because it mobilized a critique of both the law and the government in one narrative – around the fate of a wrongly condemned woman – that made the basic tenets of radicalism accessible (and palatable) to the middle classes. In this way, Gatrell argues, the Fenning case helped to feed a growing sense of public outrage about arbitrary state power after 1815.[6]

This essay considers the power of texts in the Fenning case. In response to Gatrell's persuasive reading of the case, I argue that the Fenning case's notoriety had as much to do with real doubts and contesting interpretations as it did with any widespread assumption of Fenning's innocence or any general outrage at her execution.[7] While conceding the power of the pro-Fenning narrative, this essay argues that we must nevertheless pay close attention to the competing narratives that constructed Eliza Fenning as a public cause. Not only was there an anti-Fenning version of events offered to the public, but the pro-Fenning camp itself offered alternative understandings of Eliza Fenning and her situation that reflected the philosophical and strategic divisions within London radicalism. In essence, each narrative projected a different political purpose. An examination of these texts demonstrates that the very people whom the radical press wished to mobilize around Fenning – the respectable middle classes – had other, equally important, issues at stake in the Fenning case precisely because the story involved the private sphere. As we will see, in many respects Eliza Fenning was a very bad choice around whom to orchestrate a critique against the existing order, if the purpose of that critique was to spread the cause of radicalism. In fact, for much of its intended audience, the pro-Fenning narratives ultimately failed to mediate successfully between the domestic reality in which the story was embedded and any larger projection of political purpose. In the end, Fenning's position as a domestic servant undermined the very narratives offered in her defence by reminding the public that the distance between reform and revolution was perilously short.

I

The lingering mystery about the identity of the perpetrator who attempted to kill the Turner family is not the only mystery hovering over the Fenning case, nor is it one that can be solved here. While a good deal is known about both the Turners and Eliza Fenning, much less can be said with any certainty about what happened in the Turners' home at no. 68 Chancery Lane on 21 March 1815. With the exception of the voluminous but almost entirely partisan press coverage and the other printed commentaries that still exist, there is little extant documentation about the case itself: for example, the appeal file does not survive in the papers of the Home Office and the official Old Bailey trial record is extremely short and unrevealing. It is therefore difficult to sort out something approximating the facts of the case from among the various interested representations that survive. Nevertheless, a brief outline of events might read as follows.[8]

Eliza Fenning was born on the West Indian island of Dominica in 1793. Her father, William Fenning, had been a labourer in Suffolk but at 17 enlisted into the army, afterwards serving the king for 24 years. During that time he was stationed in Ireland, at Cork and Dublin, as well as in the West Indies. In 1787 while stationed at Cork, he met and married

Mary Swayne. Much would later be made of this 'Irish connection', but by most reputable accounts, his wife was the daughter of respectable Protestant people: her father was a slater and her grandfather had worked as a London silversmith. William Fenning obtained his discharge from the king's service in 1802 at the age of 38, moved to London and went to work for his brother who was a potato dealer in Holborn. He stayed in the neighbourhood and in the potato trade, serving three other traders over the years. His wife worked locally too, and was employed at least five years for an upholsterer in High Holborn. The Fennings had ten children together, but by 1815 Eliza was their only surviving child.[9]

Eliza learned to read and write at the Gate Street Charity School in Lincoln's Inn Fields, where she went until she was 12. At the age of 14, she entered domestic service as a servant of all work. Between 1807 and 1815 she worked for nine families. In January 1815, at the age of 22, she became a cook in the household of Mr Orlibar Turner in Chancery Lane.[10] Orlibar, and his son, Robert, were both respectable law stationers. As would be pointed out subsequently by many commentators, their profession connected them as friends and acquaintances of much of London's legal establishment. Though the house in Chancery Lane was home to the family business, it was not the senior Mr Turner's primary residence. He stayed only occasionally in Chancery Lane and lived with his wife at a house in Lambeth. Robert Turner, however, and his wife, Charlotte, lived and worked in Chancery Lane full time with two women servants, of which Fenning was one, and two male apprentices. Charlotte Turner was apparently not the 'real' mistress at Chancery Lane, even though she acted in the capacity of mistress and ran the household on a day-to-day basis: the senior Mrs Turner, not Charlotte, hired the household's servants, including Fenning. This may have been because of Charlotte's inexperience. At 23 she was only slightly older than Fenning and had been married to Robert only for about eight months. At the time of the attempted murder, she was seven months pregnant with her first child.[11]

Trouble began soon after Eliza Fenning entered the Turner household. One night about three weeks after Fenning arrived, her mistress observed her entering the male apprentices' room only partially clothed. The next morning Charlotte Turner reprimanded Fenning, threatening her with dismissal. After denying her culpability, Fenning rather impertinently threw the threat back in Mrs Turner's face and gave her notice. The senior Mrs Turner's timely intervention smoothed the whole affair over and Fenning continued in her place. The incident was virtually forgotten until about a month later on 21 March, when the entire household, including Fenning, became violently ill while eating dinner. A cursory investigation by an intimate of the Turners concluded that someone had laced the dumplings Fenning had prepared with arsenic. At this point, Fenning's earlier disagreement with Charlotte Turner began to suggest a motive. Furthermore, when it was revealed not only that Fenning had requested specifically that she be allowed to make dumplings for the family, but also that she could read and that she had access the family's cache of rat poison, suspicion centred exclusively on her. She was arrested and charged with the attempted murder of the Turner family. At the April sessions of the Old Bailey she was convicted of the crime at a trial lasting only a few hours. The jury brought in their verdict after only a few minutes' deliberation. The judge sentenced Eliza Fenning to hang, which she did on 26 July 1815.

The interval between conviction and execution saw a flurry of activity on Fenning's behalf. Petitions urging mercy were addressed to Lord Sidmouth, the Home Secretary, Lord Eldon, the Lord Chancellor, and even the Prince Regent himself. Even Orlibar Turner expressed his willingness to sign a plea for mercy until the Court Recorder, Sir John Silvester, intervened and ordered him not to do so. The press took up the case. There were daily discussions of the justness of the verdict. Pamphlet after pamphlet was published, the majority insisting on Fenning's innocence, with the rest equally determined to vindicate the court's judgement. The day before the execution, Lord Eldon met twice with Silvester to review the case. In the end, the Lord Chancellor decided against intervening and Fenning's execution went forward.

On the day of the execution, a crowd reportedly larger than at any execution in recent memory gathered to watch her die. Fenning conducted herself with dignity, maintaining her innocence to the very end. After her death, her body was given immediately to her parents rather than being given to the surgeons for dissection. Watkins and Hone reported that:

The public sympathized so generally in the fate of the deceased, that an eminent surgeon, whose anatomical theatre is largely supplied with subjects for his pupils' dissection, in order to avoid an outrage upon popular feeling, gave especial orders to the persons who usually supply him with bodies, that the corpse of Eliza Fenning, however desirable to possess, should on no account be brought to him.[12]

In the days following her death, her body was on public view at her parents' home. Press accounts had visitors flocking there to see it, despite numerous reports of police harassment against them. On the morning of her burial, an estimated 10,000 people took part in the procession that accompanied her body, attended by six virgins dressed in white, to its final resting place in the churchyard of St George the Martyr, Bloomsbury.[13]

By all accounts, the crowd who attended the funeral behaved remarkably well. The only apparent incident occurred when a servant in livery insulted the memory of the deceased: the women in the crowd reportedly turned on him and roughed him up.[14] It was an altogether different story in Chancery Lane, where a crowd estimated at over 500 congregated outside the Turners' house, threatening either to pull it down or to burn it. The assembly stayed until well past midnight. Many in the crowd remained for days afterwards, controlled only by the police who stood guard in the street. Two men – an apprentice pastry cook and an out-of-work waiter – were arrested and charged with incitement to riot.[15]

We can presume that at some point the crowd outside the Turners' home dispersed for good and that its members went back to their everyday lives. Likewise, it is likely that the Turners resumed something like a normal existence once their own notoriety dimmed. Eliza Fenning's parents were said to have collected over £40 in unsolicited donations from the visitors who came to view their daughter's body. What they did with it is unknown, as is what happened to them. Once their daughter was buried, they too disappeared from the public's notice and from the official record.

II

Aside from the short account of Fenning's trial published in the *Old Bailey Sessions Papers*, our knowledge of both the accusers and the accused in this case is dependent primarily on contemporary accounts of events published in newspapers, pamphlets and books. We know both more and less about her supporters and about her critics than about the principals in the case. Although it was reported that gentlemen of 'great respectability' interested themselves in her cause, beyond a few visible and outspoken advocates we do not know who signed the various clemency petitions that circulated around London or how many people in fact did so.[16] Neither can we say with any certainty who attended her execution, who walked with her funeral procession, or who gathered outside the

Turners' house and threatened to burn it down. Nor is it at all clear why the people who participated in these events did so. What motivated them? Why did those who interested themselves in the Fenning case care about the fate of this obscure servant?

Whether or not most, many or merely some Londoners rallied on behalf of Fenning or were outraged at her execution is both unknown and unknowable, since there is little or no specific evidence still extant about the extent or the depth of support for her. That this is the case does not mean that such support did not exist. What it does suggest is that we must distinguish carefully between the campaign to mobilize something called 'public opinion' around Eliza Fenning as an object of sympathy and the complicated responses both to Eliza Fenning and to that campaign by those people who made up 'the public'.

The battle to save Eliza Fenning took place primarily in print. Fenning's supporters in the press and in the publishing world invoked 'public opinion' to lend authority to their cause, at the same time that they hoped to manufacture such opinion. Although the concept of public opinion had been used throughout the eighteenth century, its heyday was in the 1810s and it reached its peak in 1820 during the Queen Caroline affair. Public opinion was a construct, and any appeal to its authority was imaginary in so far as it represented some real or organized commonality of opinion in society. In the 1810s the use of 'public opinion' was at some basic level oppositional, invoked primarily by those who sought to legitimize political claims originating outside the established order. More often than not, to assert 'public opinion' was an act designed as an appeal to reason (as opposed to tradition) and to a shared identity as a participant in a culture of sensibility.[17] To the extent that individual members of the reading public recognized themselves in, and identified with, an assertion of 'public opinion', that opinion might itself be called into being. Thus those in the reforming and radical press, who claimed to speak with the authority of public opinion, also found themselves engaged in trying to actualize that opinion among their readers as a way of building real support for political reform.

Almost by definition, then, it was more likely that pro-Fenning supporters arguing on behalf of enlightened public opinion would outnumber those who supported the government both in the press and in other printed discussions of the Fenning case. This was indeed the case. If Eliza Fenning could have been saved by the amount of ink expended on her behalf, she would not have been executed. With few exceptions, all the books published about the case were pro-Fenning. Many of these books went through multiple editions: Fairburn's *The Case of Eliza Fenning* went through eight editions in 1815 alone. There was even a play, 'The Maid and the Magpie', performed in September 1815 at the Theatre Royal in Covent Garden, which supported the pro-Fenning argument and which was still in print well into 1817.[18] Newspapers, however, were more divided on the question of Fenning's guilt. The loyalist *Observer* believed Fenning attempted to kill the Turners and it strongly supported the justice meted out to her. So too did the government-subsidized *Morning Post*. On the other side, both the radical-leaning *Examiner* and the *Traveller* remained staunch allies of 'justice', proclaiming Fenning's innocence both before and after her execution. Some papers, such as *The Times* and the *Morning Chronicle*, chose sides less obviously, though they printed and reprinted whatever information or rumours were circulating at the moment.

Fenning's chief support in the press and the publishing world came from those associated with reforming and radical causes. Despite just having been released from prison for printing attacks on the Prince Regent when the Fenning episode occurred, Leigh and John Hunt threw the *Examiner* behind her. Another of Fenning's most ardent champions, William Hone, also had radical affiliations. A member of the London Corresponding Society at the age of 14, Hone had been active both in London's radical circles and in publishing since the early years of the nineteenth century. In 1815, aged 35, he embraced Fenning's cause with enthusiasm and eagerly enlisted the pages of his *Traveller* newspaper in her defence. With John Watkins, Hone was responsible also for the most thorough account of the Fenning case, *The Important Results of an Elaborate Investigation into the Mysterious Case of Elizabeth Fenning* (London, 1815). Other prominent and not so prominent radicals also got involved, including John Fairburn and George Cruikshank. Philanthropic reformers, such as Basil Montagu, founder of the Society for Diffusion of Knowledge upon the Punishment of Death, important Quakers, such as the banker Corbyn Lloyd, and a large number of Methodist clergy, also interested themselves in Fenning's cause.

These defenders had more than enough cause to doubt Fenning's guilt. After all, the evidence against her was almost entirely circumstantial. The Turner family took ill at supper. Fenning had cooked the meal and was reportedly alone in the kitchen during its preparation. She admitted having access to the room in which Mr Turner kept an envelope of rat poison unlocked in a desk drawer, and, because she knew how to read, she could not deny that she also would have known what was in the labelled envelope. She supposedly had a motive – hatred of the family – because Charlotte Turner had reprimanded her and threatened to discharge her. In fact, the prosecution offered little but circumstantial evidence. Furthermore, the conduct of the prosecution aroused suspicion on the part of Fenning's defenders. Most members of the court were long-time acquaintances of Mr Orlibar Turner, including both the chief solicitor and the only medical expert called to testify before the court. Further, the Recorder, Sir John Silvester, refused to allow Fenning's defenders to present any exculpatory evidence at her trial. Silvester intervened personally to prevent Mr Orlibar Turner from adding his name to a clemency petition and he actively suppressed new evidence both that pointed to the possibility that someone else had attempted to kill the family and that cast grave doubt on the truthfulness of the witnesses against Fenning.[19]

Despite the radical credentials of Fenning's most vigorous supporters, and in spite of the apparent travesty that masqueraded as her trial, when 'public opinion' was heard in the Fenning case, it spoke on behalf of, and to, London's respectable middling classes and not to its organized radical movement or to its labouring classes. The Hunts' *Examiner*, for example, was a 'highbrow' weekly, known more for its coverage of *belles-lettres* than politics per se. In 1812, its circulation was estimated to have been around 8000, though doubtless its readership was rather higher, since copies were frequently shared and libraries also purchased their share of copies. One historian of the magazine concludes that due to its high price and 'the intellectual demands it made on its readers . . . it is probably safe to assume that typical *Examiner* subscribers were town-dwelling members of the middling sort'.[20] William Hone, whose radical pedigree was even more pronounced than that of the Hunts, set forth his theory of the case in the above-mentioned *Important Results of an Elaborate Investigation*, a book which, at over 200 pages in length and priced at 6s. 6d., was clearly aimed at a well-to-do and respectable reading public most likely dominated by the same 'town-dwelling members of the middling sort' who read the *Examiner*, and not at the vast majority of metropolitan radicals.[21] Not all accounts of Fenning's trial and execution, of course, were either so expensive or had such limited circulation. The case, after all, was widely reported in the popular press too, and no doubt large numbers of London's humbler residents both knew about it and were familiar with its details. However, to the extent that reformers sought to use the Fenning case to shape attitudes towards the government and to project plans for reform, it was the middle classes that they sought to influence and to mobilize. Thus, it was narratives contained in these reformers' accounts of the Fenning case that command our attention and tell us the most about efforts to spread the cause of reform.

III

Fenning's radical defenders understood that any success they might have in mobilizing respectable public opinion on Fenning's behalf depended on being able to connect readers' individual lives and concerns with her predicament. This was not an easy task, considering the nature of her crime and considering how very different Fenning – being both a servant and a woman – was from the vast majority of male middle-class readers whom reformers wished to influence. It was, however, made easier by three things. First, Fenning's supporters initially had the tense and uncertain nature of the times on their side. Secondly, the prejudicial and vindictive conduct of the prosecution in general (and of Sir John Silvester in particular) made it easier to play down her alleged crime, giving her defenders a principle larger than Fenning herself to defend. Finally, but of paramount importance in closing the distance between Fenning and their readers, Fenning's defenders chose to cast Fenning's story in a literary genre – melodrama – that turned gender difference to their advantage.

In March 1815, indeed the day before Fenning made her alleged attempt on the lives of the Turners, Napoleon entered Paris, having escaped from his imprisonment on Elba, and thereby rekindled fears of renewed war. By July, while Fenning awaited execution in her cell at Newgate, the final victory over Napoleon's armies at Waterloo seemed to signal a larger political victory for the forces of reaction all over Europe. For those who had agitated for decades on behalf of constitutional reform, Wellington's victory seemed certain to cement the hold of the existing order on power. Indeed, the signs of conservative victory were already apparent before Waterloo. Worries about the international situation were compounded by serious domestic difficulties. The coming of peace, first in 1814 and finally in 1815, after decades of war, brought with it the problems connected with demobilization and with conversion from a war economy. Social unrest caused by post-war privation and economic dislocation was growing; fear of the masses was widespread. The vestrymen of St George Bloomsbury were worried enough by reports of riot elsewhere in the metropolis that they seriously considered supporting repressive government proposals to seat magistrates permanently and to swear in special constables to keep the peace.[22] Again March 1815 proved an important month as the House of Lords finally passed the Corn Law Bill. The government's introduction of this legislation in 1814 had provoked near universal protest, especially among the urban middle classes. In Westminster alone, more than 42,000 residents signed a petition against the proposed measure. In Eliza Fenning's own parish of St George Bloomsbury the vestrymen joined in the protest, sending their own petition to the government. In it, they declared that the proposed corn law would be 'partial and oppressive upon the inhabitants of these parishes and of other populous districts by securing the Landed Interest an undue advantage over the manufacturing, commercial and trading part of the community'.[23] Despite the massive popular opposition, the government pushed ahead with the bill, and the Lords approved it on 24 March. As if this defeat were not reminder enough of their political impotence, the middle classes also saw their campaign for the repeal of the property tax prove unsuccessful.[24]

Fenning's defenders attempted to link her treatment by the law with apprehension about the reactionary politics of the government. The prejudicial and vindictive conduct of the prosecution in general, and Silvester in particular, made that task easier. Fenning's defenders drew on the language of what James Epstein has called 'popular constitutionalism', the notion that Englishmen had a set of historic rights dating from the Magna Carta, which included things like a fair trial by jury and equality before law.[25] The latter was the question posed by the Fenning case. As Watkins and Hone argued in the 'Preface' to their book on the case, Eliza Fenning's fate touched issues of 'the national interest and the national honour', and whether their readers believed that 'human life be worth protection, or laws are to be considered as the equal right of the poor and the rich'. Thus their purpose was 'to draw the fixed attention of every individual to the administration of those laws in which he has an interest' and to ring 'an alarm to the present, no less than a warning to future generations, not to trust presumptive evidence, and to put little confidence in the reasonings of fallible Magistrates, who have grown old in the ministration of death'. In the end, it was their hope that 'every individual in the community, from the highest to the lowest, will be impressed with a sense of the dangers to which he would be exposed, if suspicious circumstances alone are combined into a charge that shall affect his character or his life'.[26] Knapp and Baldwin considered the case of 'vital importance to every individual' and thought it 'a subject so momentous, and which comes home to the bosom of every man'.[27]

Gatrell argues that, in addition to the relevance Fenning's case had to these concerns about the arbitrariness and legitimacy of government power, Fenning also succeeded in capturing the public's attention because she was a woman. Fenning's defenders, he suggests, drew on the 'high-flown tropes of popular melodrama'. As scholars have noted, melodrama was increasingly the narrative mode of choice during this period. In part, this was because of its flexibility. Melodrama provided for a way of moralizing about the trials of private life, but its simple binaries – good and evil, rich and poor, high and low – could be adapted easily to dramatize public and political life as well. Melodramatic narratives assisted political and social agitation in this period because they challenged the entire continuum of power relationships. In this, the role of gender was especially relevant. By siding with the powerless against the powerful, melodrama easily claimed women's experience as a metaphor for other struggles. Thus a 'narrative of injustice' like Eliza Fenning's provided audiences with multiple opportunities and multiple access points to interpret the moral struggle embedded in the story.[28]

The Fenning case easily – and brilliantly – adapted itself to the conventions of melodrama. That Fenning's defenders constructed her as a wronged woman hardly needs restating. But it is worth remembering that melodrama's appeal lay precisely in its simultaneous accessibility to everyday experience and its adaptability to a larger canvas beyond that of daily life. Wider political questions about the nature of the state, beyond even those raised about the legitimacy of the legal system, hovered over the case, suggested by a wealth of stylistic details. What inference should readers draw from the fact that Fenning's defenders claimed her master was a madman, who was incapable either of controlling himself or of taking care of his family?[29] How should they read reports that identified the sole critic present at Fenning's funeral as a liveried servant? It is surely possible that such uncorroborated details were included to implicate the existing order – a government nominally headed by a mad king and an aristocracy propped up by the sycophancy of their dependants – in the injustice being perpetrated against Eliza Fenning.[30]

Further, melodrama invited the participation of its audience. Thus, the figure of Eliza Fenning – poor, comely, pious, seemingly friendless and insistent on her innocence – encouraged the public to protect her from both the law and those in power. In the weeks after her arrest, and continuing well after her death, the attacks on Fenning and her character were relentless and Fenning's defenders were called upon to contradict a never-ending series of accusations against her. More will be said about the Turners and their relationship with their servant maid, but Watkins and Hone charged that they 'encouraged, by their silence, the circulation of the aspersions upon her, when living, and entertained them after she had been executed'.[31] The *Observer* attributed her savagery to her Irishness, falsely charging her parents with being Catholics. It further reported that she had been expelled when she was only 12 from the Gate Street Charity School for 'lying and lewd talk' that endangered the morals of the other children at the school. In the months after Fenning's death, John Marshall, the Turners' intimate friend and the medical expert who testified at Fenning's trial, claimed that the constables had examined Fenning's belongings and found 'an infamous book, with a register on one of the pages, that explained various methods of procuring abortion'.[32] The range of rumours and charges against Eliza Fenning's character was vast, but perhaps the most damaging and infamous charge was the one that she had twice before attempted to murder a family with whom she lived.[33]

Fenning's supporters challenged 'public opinion' to come to her defence. If it would not do so, then she would have no other protection. Her parents certainly could not help her. Her father 'had no money to procure proper legal advice and assistance with; and his poverty was an effectual bar to obtaining it without'.[34] The public from whom the newspapers and periodicals sought help was a male public, a public that would act to protect an innocent and friendless woman who had been wronged, and who had been hounded by a villainous state personified in Sir John Silvester. Furthermore, Silvester's widespread public reputation for lasciviousness, especially towards the women who came before him in his official capacity, gave the male public's desire to protect Eliza Fenning chivalrous motivations that only added to the political reasons to embrace her cause. Indeed, an appeal to manly chivalry based on a personal investment in Fenning's fate only enhanced the larger political issues. In the same way, Fenning's apparent abandonment while in prison by Edward, her reputed fiancé, provided her male defenders with yet another opportunity to create an emotional connection with her as a wronged and friendless woman who needed their protection.[35] Her father could not protect her, and her lover apparently refused to; to whom else besides manly 'public opinion' could she turn?

In 1820 public opinion would again be asked to rise up to support a woman against oppression and invest its emotional energy in another domestic melodrama. The woman, of course, was Queen Caroline. Not surprisingly, Caroline found much of her support among the same journalists and publishers who also supported Fenning. William Hone, for example, that most vigorous defender of Eliza Fenning, also jumped enthusiastically to the cause of the beleaguered queen. In words which echoed his defence of Fenning, he defined the principle at stake in the Queen Caroline affair as follows: 'the question is not merely whether the Queen shall have her rights, but whether the rights of any individual in the Kingdom shall be free from violation'.[36] Hunt's *Examiner* also entered the lists on the side of the Queen. In rhetoric seemingly borrowed from the Fenning case, the *Examiner* rejected criticism directed at Caroline for appealing to the people and demanded: 'to whom else could she appeal? had not the higher, and as they were called, the more illustrious classes of society, entirely deserted her?'[37]

Comparing the Queen Caroline affair with the agitation surrounding Eliza Fenning's trial and execution is not entirely accurate, but it is nevertheless apt. In both cases, radicals sought to dramatize the abuse of state power by exposing its power to oppress the weak. In each case, there were real political issues involved, but gendering the 'victim' as female raised the stakes even higher because it demanded a response from those respectable men of the middling classes who defined their own manliness in part as protectors of women.[38] The use of melodrama and its conventions by radicals invited what might be seen as a political response – championing Caroline of Brunswick or Eliza Fenning over the state – by disguising radical politics as gender politics.

IV

The Fenning episode and the Queen Caroline affair are comparable not only in their use of melodrama as a political tool, however. As historians of the Queen Caroline affair have demonstrated, melodrama, although perhaps the predominant genre through which the affair was both represented and understood, was not the only genre called into play by supporters of Caroline. Anna Clark argues that satire provided an alternative genre through which to understand Caroline and that, depending upon the audience, representing the Queen as a victim was less powerful politically than representing her as a belligerent wife, and that satire and melodrama emphasized different aspects of radical politics. In the Queen Caroline affair, the multiplicity of messages helped to create, however briefly, a pro-Caroline coalition across class and gender divides.[39]

Although representations of Eliza Fenning as victim dominated the contemporary discussion of the case as they did in the Queen Caroline affair, another Eliza Fenning was also available to readers of the popular press. This Eliza Fenning was not a vulnerable maiden who had been wronged both by her employers and by the state; rather, she was independent and aggressive in her own defence. Whereas Gatrell rightly emphasizes those texts that support his notion of Fenning as a victim whose plight drew public opinion towards her, the texts he cites also contain evidence of a more radical Eliza Fenning, one who cannot be so easily interpreted as anyone's victim. If Eliza Fenning presented as melodramatic heroine supported popular constitutionalist understandings of the state, the other Eliza Fenning evoked the politics of Thomas Paine and an English 'jacobinism' that was resurgent after Waterloo.[40]

In many respects the strongest proponent of representing Eliza Fenning as a more powerful figure was Fenning herself. In her *Own Narrative*, her self-representation eschews the victim's role and emphasizes her competence, independence and virtual equality with her employers. Of the incident that allegedly triggered her dislike of Charlotte Turner and supplied her motive for attempted murder, she reports:

> she [Charlotte Turner] said if I could not behave better I should not suit her: I answered if she did not approve of my conduct when *my mistress* returned I was willing to leave, at which she was so enraged that she sent for her husband.[41]

Indeed, Eliza Fenning had little apparent respect for Charlotte Turner and found it easy to disobey her mistress. After all, Fenning had spent seven years in service and knew her job well; only a year older than Eliza Fenning, Charlotte Turner had only been a mistress for eight months and the task of running a house was new to her. In her narrative, Fenning chafes under Turner's direction. At one point she declares: 'Mrs. Turner told me not to leave the kitchen, but I did not pay any attention to her in that respect, knowing I must leave it to do the remaining part of my work'.[42] Commenting on Mrs Turner's testimony that Fenning's dumplings looked suspicious, Fenning mocked her mistress's knowledge of cookery: 'it surprises me to think she pretends more to know more about them [dumplings] than myself'.[43]

Fenning's self-representation as a self-confident, almost defiant, employee may have been closer to the 'real' Eliza Fenning than the vulnerable figure offered up by Hone and the Hunts.[44] Yet, though Hone was a central figure in constructing Fenning as an object of pity needing the protection of public opinion, Hone's definitive work on the case nearly sabotaged those very efforts. In their report on the Fenning case, Hone and Watkins set out to refute all evidence of Fenning's guilt and all the attacks on her character. To do this, they included all the negative evidence so that they could rebut each charge, item by item. On the positive side, this meant including references from Eliza Fenning's former employers, almost all of which attested to her industriousness, good conduct and excellent character.[45]

But there were also dissenting voices. Although Hone was keen to show that Fenning was the perfect servant and that she was more concerned about her employers than herself, the move almost backfired. Mr Cornish, the baker, resented the way in which Fenning looked after her employers' concerns, complaining that she was too imperious: 'I knew my own business without being told it by a girl like her'.[46] One set of former employers, Mr and Mrs Hardy, who kept a grocer's shop in Portugal Street, Lincoln's Inn Fields, had nothing good to say about their former servant. Indeed, they claimed she had attempted to kill them while in their service. They had no actual evidence to offer in support of this claim; their 'proof' consisted of complaints about her independence. Mr Hardy claimed 'she was a hoity-toity, wild, giddy, unsettled sort of girl; curious and inquisitive, and minding what did not concern her'. Further, 'she was never easy but when she was reading, and was everlastingly inquisitive and prying'. Finally, he complained:

> she was a sly, quick, clever, artful girl, as sharp as a needle, and was of that inquisitive deep turn, that his MIND (!) always misgave him whilst she lived there; and then there was the BOOKS as she used to read, he did not like it – and she was a girl that he did not like, for he never know'd NO GOOD come of SERVANTS READING.[47]

Represented 'as rather shrewd and intelligent for one in her rank of life', and not as a victim, this Eliza Fenning invited the Turners to visit her in her cell before her execution. Rather than asking their forgiveness, as most people expected she would do, this Eliza Fenning denounced the Turners' prosecution of her to their faces. Charlotte Turner reportedly 'was surprised and shocked at the impudence of her conduct, and said she hoped to have witnessed a very different deportment in her truly awful situation'.[48]

Gatrell argues that Eliza Fenning the victim, wronged by her employers and a casual sacrifice to arbitrary state power, was an eloquent testimonial to radical claims of popular constitutionalism whose case helped sustain the radical cause by mobilizing a compelling and emotional critique of the government. But what kind of political statement did an Eliza Fenning who rejected her employers' superiority and who defended herself make? Fenning rejected both her role as subordinate and the mastery of her employers. When Hone mocked the Hardys, ridiculing their suspicion of a servant who not only read books but also owned them, and discounting their dislike of her behaviour ('It would be a waste of time and patience to make a single remark upon the likings or dislikings of such a man as Mr. Hardy'), he too undercut the principle of hierarchy and damaged the notion that servants' subordination to their masters was a natural, and necessary, state of affairs.[49] The rejection of deference echoed Paine and the traditions of popular radicalism. Although employing the idiom of popular constitutionalism embedded in the story's melodrama made Fenning more palatable to public opinion, neither Fenning nor Hone could escape overtones of Paineite thinking and each rejected the idea that birth determined worth or that station need be hereditary.

John Sibly, the shorthand writer who reported the case for the *Old Bailey Sessions Papers*, demonstrated contemporaries' understanding of these distinct traditions within reformist and radical politics when he contrasted the two crowds who observed Fenning's execution and funeral. Sibly described two distinct tableaux, each animated by different political idioms. Outside the Turners' house, a 'mob' threatened 'acts of outrage' that only the 'interference of the civil power' prevented. At the house of Fenning's father in Eagle Street, Eliza's body lay in virtual state and 'respectable' visitors flocked to see it, bringing with them flowers and ribbons. They also undertook to comfort and support Fenning's ageing parents. Sibly declared that 'the compassion excited by the melancholy spectacle naturally produced new converts to the opinions of the innocence of the deceased'.[50] Even though Sibly thought Fenning guilty, he understood the motivations of the respectable crowd who offered their pity and protection to Fenning's parents. In many respects he could, and did, identify with them. The crowd who threatened riot in Chancery Lane, however, was another matter, because it wanted a different sort of justice for Eliza Fenning.

V

In 1800 Hannah More published *The History of Mr. Fantom, the New-Fashioned Philosopher, and His Man William*. This tract told the story of how, by adopting his master's Paineite philosophic system built on ideas of equality and disdain for religion, William the footman came to ruin. Practising what he overheard his master preach while waiting on him at table, William not only set himself on a path that ended in his execution, but he also shattered the good order and peace of his master's house. Only when he sees his former servant preparing for his execution does Fantom understand the advice both his wife and his friend, Mr Trueman, have given him all along: households cannot be governed properly if servants do not accept the rule of their masters and the dependence of their situations. Any disruption of this natural order is extremely dangerous to all concerned and likely to end in social chaos.[51]

Lynn Hunt has argued that when the French revolutionaries overturned paternalism as the model of politics and embraced fraternalism, they challenged the model of family government as well. The Fenning case focused on the opposite dynamic: if the basis on which families were governed were overturned, then the political system itself might be at risk.[52] It may be, as Gatrell suggests, that the case of Eliza Fenning helped to sustain radicalism in the post-war years and made the basic tenets of radical beliefs palatable to a wider and more respectable public. If so, it is equally true that for conservatives and loyalists Fenning's case confirmed what they understood to be the inevitable dangers of reform.

Certainly the insubordination of servants had been a topic of discussion and the cause of extensive anxiety throughout the eighteenth century. Servants – how to hire them, how to keep them, how to make sure they took their employers' concerns seriously – occupied a good deal of a family's time and they were never far from the minds of masters and mistresses. That a respectable house could not function without them, and therefore that employers were more dependent on servants than vice versa, only increased employers' anxieties.[53] Indeed, some commentators on the Fenning case attempted to explain the rush to judge Eliza Fenning within the familiar parameters of the so-called 'servant problem':

She [Eliza Fenning] had been reproved by her mistress, was sulky, and said she should never like her again – there would be something ludicrous in this allegation on any other subject, proving as it does the important fact, that there was the same species of hostility between kitchen and parlour in the house of Mr. Turner, as in that of almost every other person in the Metropolis.[54]

Yet the fact that employers' complaints about servants and their insubordination were perennial ones does not explain the particular viciousness with which Tory papers such as the *Observer* went after Eliza Fenning nor the almost visceral response that her alleged crime provoked from segments of the public. Again the Queen Caroline affair is instructive, for despite the mass agitation on the Queen's behalf, respectable discomfort about the implications of embracing Caroline fuelled a loyalist counter-offensive.[55] Vigorous counter-arguments emerged from the Fenning case too, as Fenning's opponents sought to cut through the melodrama that shrouded the case and to point out the dangers both of 'canonizing' Eliza Fenning or of looking elsewhere in the Turner household for suspects.

The *Observer* drew attention to the very aspects of Fenning's character that Hone and others praised – her independence and her cleverness – as incontrovertible evidence of her guilt, for independence or intelligence were much less sought-after qualities in a servant than loyalty and obedience.[56] The paper cited her 'flippant and unbecoming' manner; it further suggested that although servants normally changed places quite frequently as a way of maintaining some independence over their work lives, Fenning's frequent job changes were evidence that she was 'spiteful and malicious'. 'Truth', the *Observer* declared, 'was a practice with which she seemed at war, and there was not a place in which she was employed . . . that she did not leave behind the character of a confirmed liar'. As regards her habit of reading and her widely acknowledged intelligence, the *Observer* complained that although 'she exhibited an uncommon strength of mind and a degree of talent', these qualities were misplaced and dangerous because they were talents 'far above her situation in life'.[57] To add to its assault on Fenning's character, the paper also attempted to link her (through her mother's Irish ancestry) to Catholic insurrection against English rule and to suggest that the fact she was engaged to be married was evidence of her immorality.[58] The *Observer* seemed content to conclude that being unsuited to a life of service, as Fenning may well have been, was tantamount to being a murderess. Certainly, they could point to no other evidence, besides the circumstantial evidence used by the prosecutors, to prove her guilt.

But there were other suspects. The *Independent Whig* wished that closer attention had been paid to Mrs Turner as a suspect. After all, they observed, 'if Mrs Turner had observed a sullenness in Fenning, or a falling off of her respect to herself, surely it would have been her duty to repeat the warning she had given her'.[59] If Mrs Turner knew Fenning's character was so bad, why had she hired her at all? The paper even suggested that Mrs Turner had had access to the dumplings while Eliza Fenning ran an errand. The *Independent Whig* was less interested, however, in accusing Mrs Turner with actually committing the crime than with exposing her family to danger through her lax supervision of the household: 'it is palpable that any malignant individual might have embraced this opportunity of infusing the poison into the dough'.[60] Fenning suggested that Mrs Turner might have done the deed in a league with one of the male apprentices, who, she hinted, might have been Mrs Turner's paramour. Hone thought the rumour that Robert Turner was unhappily married and mentally unstable enough to pose a danger to his family sufficient reason to consider him a possible suspect.[61]

It is almost impossible from the available evidence to determine whether any of these alternative theories of the crime were likely. Alternative theories, however, were incompatible with good order. It was inconceivable that the family's patriarch should seek to harm those under his care. Equally impossible to countenance was the idea that Charlotte Turner was either an incompetent mistress or an adulteress. To believe any of those things would be to attack the very premise on which middle-class respectability depended. It was also hit at the very heart of the patriarchal state as 'domesticated' by George III that had proven so stable and resilient despite the military onslaught of revolutionary and imperial France.[62] Yet this was precisely what Fenning's supporters asked for when they asked 'public opinion' to protect Eliza Fenning. An attack on the stability of the family, especially in the charged atmosphere of 1815 when Napoleon's final defeat (and thereby the final defeat of the French Revolution) was still in doubt, was unthinkable. In the absence of any direct evidence that pointed to a specific individual, to seize on any suspect other than Eliza Fenning as the murderer was literally unimaginable.

VI

This essay has argued that the reading public understood that more than the life of Eliza Fenning was at stake as it watched her trial and execution in the spring and summer of 1815. As Hone and Fenning's other supporters insisted, there were powerful reasons for the respectable middle classes to rally in support of her cause. Not only could support of Eliza Fenning be constructed as a vote against the arbitrary exercise of government power, but it could also be constructed as a sign of manliness. Through their adoption as melodrama as the dominant genre of the story's narrative, and by asking readers to participate in the narrative as protectors of Eliza Fenning, radicals hoped to make reform an essential marker of respectability. It was a bold move, designed to make reform and reform politics seem a natural ingredient of middle-class virtue. My reading of the Fenning case suggests that, in contrast to Gatrell, there was no automatic way of mobilizing the many who had no effective political voice, no unified or unifiable 'us' to pit against a corrupt oligarchic 'them' – even in a case as sympathetically packaged as Fenning's was. 'Public opinion' was an elusive, and largely imagined, entity, and – despite the best efforts of radicals – it was not yet capable of endorsing the naturalness of reform politics if that meant recognizing the equality of servants or weakening the domestic politics around which the middle classes constructed their family life. A public that could not yet reform its private life was hardly ready to participate in meaningful political reform.

NOTES

1. See J. M. Beattie, *Crime and the Courts in England, 1660–1800* (Princeton, NJ, 1986), pp. 100–1. Petty treason was an 'aggravated degree of murder defined by the Treason Act of 1351 as the killing of a master by his servant, of a husband by his wife, or an ecclesiastical superior by a man in orders'. Frank McLynn offers several eighteenth-century examples of employer-murdering servants in his *Crime and Punishment in Eighteenth-Century England* (New York, 1991), pp. 118–21.

2. The most complete modern discussion of the Fenning case and both its legal and cultural aftermath can be found in V. A. C. Gatrell, *The Hanging Tree: Execution and the English People, 1770–1868* (New York, 1994), pp. 339–40, 353–70. An earlier and more popular account of the case's 'history', which provides references to the many discussions of the Fenning case in nineteenth- and early twentieth-century periodicals, is found in William Roughead, *Malice Domestic* (Edinburgh, 1928), pp. 85–117.

3. Gatrell, *Hanging Tree*, p. 7. The period during which Fenning died was especially active, according to Gatrell: nearly twice as many people were executed in London in the years 1801–30 than were hanged from 1701 to 1750.

4. Quoted in Roughead, *Malice Domestic*, p. 99.

5. J. Ann Hone, *For the Cause of Truth: Radicalism in London, 1796–1821* (Oxford, 1982), pp. 220–3, 237–69.

6. 'The fuss about Fenning was part of a louder anger in these years.' Gatrell can justifiably point past Fenning's death to the impact her exection had throughout the nineteenth century as Fenning's 'ghost' repeatedly haunted debates about capital punishment and the fallibility of the law. Gatrell, *Hanging Tree*, pp. 367–70.

7. It is worth noting here that many people thought Fenning guilty. For example, Fenning's entry in the *DNB* assumes her guilt: 'The case shows how a consistent declaration of innocence on the part of a criminal tends to produce a general belief in it.' Roughead's account of the case shows that throughout the nineteenth century, any discussion of Fenning's innocence was met by equally vehement arguments by those who believed her guilty and who thought her sentence justified. Roughead, *Malice Domestic*, pp. 85–117.

8. Despite the intense interest that surrounded the Fenning case at the time, modern historians have had little to say about it. The exception, of course, is Gatrell. Except as otherwise noted, my retelling of the story here is based largely on his account. Gatrell, *Hanging Tree*, pp. 353–70.

9. John Watkins and William Hone, *The Important Results of an Elaborate Investigation into the Mysterious Case of Elizabeth Fenning* (London, 1815), pp. 1–4.

10. *Observer*, 30 July 1815; *Examiner*, 20 August 1815.

11. Fenning would later insist that Orlibar Turner and his wife, not Robert and Charlotte Turner, were her real master and mistress. Elizabeth Fenning, *Elizabeth Fenning's Own Narrative* (London, 1815), p. 4; *Morning Post*, 31 March 1815; Anon., *The Genuine Trial and Affecting Case of Eliza Fenning* (London, 1815), p. 3.

12. Watkins and Hone, *Important Results*, p. 98. Such popular sentiment against the dissection of executed prisoners was by no means unusual. See Peter Linebaugh, 'The Tyburn Riot Against the Surgeons', in Douglas Hay et al. (eds), *Albion's Fatal Tree: Crime and Society in Eighteenth-Century England* (New York, 1987), pp. 65–118.

13. Watkins and Hone, *Important Results*, pp. 96–8; *Morning Chronicle*, 1 August 1815. Gatrell calls the funeral a 'pageant of the greatest ambition'. The 'virginal' pallbearers were standard accompaniment when a young unmarried woman was executed. Gatrell, *Hanging Tree*, pp. 88–9. The estimated crowd of 10,000 apparently did not include the large police escort detailed to prevent the possibility of violence.

14. Gatrell, *Hanging Tree*.

15. *Morning Chronicle*, 28 July 1815.

16. Andrew Knapp and William Baldwin, *The New Newgate Calendar* (London, 1809–1819), v, 133.

17. Drohr Wahrman, '"Middle-Class" Domesticity Goes Public: Gender, Class, and Politics from Queen Caroline to Queen Victoria', *JBS*, XXXII (1993), 404–6; Sarah Maza, *Private Lives and Public Affairs: The Cause Célèbres of Pre-revolutionary France* (Los Angeles, 1993), pp. 120–1; Gatrell, *Hanging Tree*, pp. 325–6.

18. Gatrell, *Hanging Tree*, pp. 358, 365–6. The most famous and widely circulated anti-Fenning publication was John Marshall, *Five Cases of Recovery from the Effects of Arsenic; With the Methods so Successfully Employed for Testing the White Metallic Oxides . . . to which are Annexed Many Corroborating Facts . . . Relating to the Guilt of Eliza Fenning* (London 1815); John Fairburn, *The Case of Eliza Fenning* (London, 1815).

19. Watkins and Hone, *Important Results*, pp. 121–5, 151–4. For example, there were unconfirmed reports of Robert Turner's mental instability. Four or five

months before the attempted poisoning, Robert Turner reportedly visited a friend's house in a hysterical and violent state. He was said to have begged his friend to 'get me secured or confined, for, if I am at liberty, I shall do some mischief; I shall destroy myself and my wife: I must and shall do it, unless all means of destruction are removed out of my way; therefore do, my good friend, have me put under some restraint: something from above tells me I must do it, and unless I am prevented, I certainly shall do it'. Robert Turner's father reportedly expressed concern after this incident and worried that his son should be 'at large'. Silvester refused to allow this evidence before the court. Watkins and Hone, *Important Results*, pp. 84–5. For more on Silvester and his conduct in the case, see Gatrell, *Hanging Tree*, pp. 359–60.

20. Philip Harling, 'Leigh Hunt's *Examiner* and the Language of Patriotism', *EHR*, CXI (1996), 1160.

21. Gatrell, *Hanging Tree*, p. 366.

22. Holborn Local History Library Archive, P/GG/M/3/13 March 1815. A request to consider this proposal came to the Joint Vestry of St George and St Giles early in March 1815, the very month in which Eliza Fenning's 'petty treason' occurred.

23. Holborn Local History Library Archive, P/GG/M/3/4 March 1815.

24. Hone, *For the Cause of Truth*, pp. 221–2.

25. James Epstein, *Radical Expression: Political Language, Ritual, and Symbol in England, 1790–1850* (New York, 1994), pp. 5–11.

26. Watkins and Hone, *Important Results*, pp. xi–xiii.

27. Knapp and Baldwin, *New Newgate Calendar*, V, pp. 131–2.

28. Gatrell, *Hanging Tree*, pp. 339, 354. On melodrama see Martha Vicinus, '"Helpless and Unfriended": Nineteenth-Century Domestic Melodrama', *New Literary History*, XIII (1981), 127–43; Maza, *Private Lives*, pp. 66–7; Anna Clark, 'The Politics of Seduction in English Popular Culture, 1784–1848', in Jean Radford (ed.), *The Progress of Romance: The Politics of Popular Fiction* (New York, 1986), pp. 47–70.

29. See n. 19 above.

30. Since liveried servants wore clothes purchased by their masters which marked them, not as individuals, but as their masters' men, they were powerful symbols of the corruption of hierarchical systems. See Sarah Maza, *Servants and Masters in Eighteenth-Century France: The Uses of Loyalty* (Princeton, 1983), pp. 289, 305–6. Daniel Defoe reminded livery servants that while 'liberty is the birthright of an Englishman', service meant becoming someone else's man and subordinating that birthright: 'the very name footman intimates, that they are bred at the foot of their Master; their business is to clean his shoes, and to always be ready at his foot, that is to say, for the most servile employment: their post is to go or ride behind, and they ought not to come into the Master's presence, but with hat in hand, bare-headed, and with all the tokens of an entire submission'. Daniel Defoe, *The Great Law of Subordination Considered* (London, 1724), pp. 29–30, 191.

31. This despite reports that both Orlibar and Robert Turner were at one point willing to sign a clemency petition. Orlibar Turner was reported to have said, 'If there is anything which I can do for her, I will go to the top of the ladder to do it'. Watkins and Hone, *Important Results*, pp. 77, 132.

32. *Observer*, 30 July 1815, 24 September 1815.
33. Watkins and Hone, *Important Results*, pp. 136–51.
34. Ibid., p. 121.
35. On the subject of manly chivalry and its motivations, see Leonore Davidoff and Catherine Hall, *Family Fortunes: Men and Women of the English Middle Class, 1780–1850* (Chicago, 1987), pp. 151–2; Anna Clark, 'Queen Caroline and the Sexual Politics of Popular Culture in London, 1820', *Representations*, XXXI (1990), 53–4. The perfidy of the unidentified Edward is documented in letters reportedly written by Eliza Fenning from her cell and reprinted in Watkins and Hone. All evidence is that Fenning was literate and Gatrell considers the letters likely to be genuine, albeit quite probably 'pumped up for public effect by her Methodist friends'. Hone admitted that, at the very least, they were edited and corrected. Gatrell, *Hanging Tree*, p. 362. In one letter, Fenning writes to the mysterious Edward that 'Was you in my place, I never should have slighted you'; in another, she explains the situation more fully, 'I think I have a just right to speak, when you promised me that you would come and see me, and then to disappoint me when there was no excuse; for you well know that my life is at stake, and one would suppose that a person that respected another, should feel happy in seeing them as often as time could permit them. I should feel sorry for you to get anger [*sic*] at coming at any other time than your Sunday; but I feel very much hurt at your being out, an could not spare one single hour with me.' Watkins and Hone, *Important Results*, p. 7. The Fenning letters appear as an appendix to the volume, hence the new pagination.
36. William Hone, *The Queen's Matrimonial Ladder* (London, 1820). See also Hone's *The Queen's Treatment of the Queen* (London, 1820). Hone's use of the language of melodrama and his appeal to manly chivalry in Queen Caroline's cause is discussed in Anna Clark, *The Struggle for the Breeches: Gender and the Making of the British Working Class* (Berkeley and Los Angeles, 1995), pp. 165, 170.
37. Quoted in Wahrman, 'Middle-Class Domesticity', p. 404.
38. Davidoff and Hall, *Family Fortunes*, pp. 150–5.
39. Clark, 'Queen Caroline and the Sexual Politics of Popular Culture', pp. 47–68.
40. Epstein, *Radical Expression*, pp. 5–9.
41. Fenning, *Own Narrative*, p. 4.
42. Ibid., p. 7.
43. Ibid., p. 8.
44. Fenning's self-representation was not entirely defiant. As Gatrell shows, Fenning was also careful to show herself as a committed Methodist. Indeed, she received much energetic Methodist support. Her letters from prison reflect what Gatrell terms her 'tutored piety' and the influence of the Methodist ministers who attended her after her conviction. However, Gatrell acknowledges that her prison letters were probably edited and concludes that 'their piety and finer tropes and those of her petition were doubtless pumped up for public effect by her Methodist friends': Gatrell, *Hanging Tree*, pp. 361–2.
45. Watkins and Hone, *Important Results*, pp. 129–31. For example, Mrs Mary Stokes in whose service Fenning lived twice, wrote the following reference:

'Elizabeth Fenning lived with me a servant, ten months in 1812, which time she conducted herself as a sober, industrious young woman; nor did I ever see anything in her conduct to suppose her capable of committing the act for which she now stands condemned.'

46. Ibid., p. 129.
47. Ibid., pp. 137–42. Capitals in original.
48. Fenning, *Own Narrative*, p. 37; Watkins and Hone, *Important Results*, pp. 152–3.
49. Watkins and Hone, *Important Results*, p. 144.
50. John Sibly, *The Trial of Eliza Fenning, for Poisoning Mr. Turner and his Family at the Sessions House in the Old Bailey* (London, 1815), pp. 18–19.
51. Hannah More, *The History of Mr. Fantom, the New-Fashioned Philosopher, and His Man William* (London, 1800).
52. Epstein, *Radical Expression*, pp. 5–9; Lynn Hunt, *The Family Romance of the French Revolution* (Berekely and Los Angeles, 1992), pp. 1–5.
53. Patty Seleski, 'Women, Work and Cultural Change in Eighteenth- and Early Nineteenth-Century London', in Tim Harris (ed.), *Popular Culture in England, c.1500–1850* (Basingstoke, 1995), pp. 143–67; Anthony Fletcher, *Gender, Sex and Subordination in England, 1500–1800* (New Haven, 1995), pp. 204–21; Amanda Vickery, *The Gentleman's Daughter: Women's Lives in Georgian England* (New Haven, 1998), pp. 141–60.
54. *The Statesman*, 7 August 1815.
55. See Jonathan Fulcher, 'The Loyalist Response to the Queen Caroline Agitations', *JBS*, XXXIV (1995), 481–502.
56. Fletcher, *Gender, Sex and Subordination*, p. 215.
57. *Observer*, 30 July 1815.
58. Ibid.
59. *Independent Whig*, 13 August 1815.
60. Ibid.
61. Watkins and Hone, *Important Results*, pp. 84–5, 153.
62. Linda Colley, 'The Apotheosis of George III: Loyalty, Royalty and the British Nation, 1760–1820', *P&P*, CII (1984), 104.

INDEX